Consciousness and Politics:
From Analysis to Meditation in the Late Work of Eric Voegelin

Other Works of Interest from St. Augustine's Press

Joseph Pearce, *Beauteous Truth: Faith, Reason, Literature and Culture*

Montgomery Erfourth, *A Guide to Eric Voegelin's Political Reality*

Henrik Syse, *Natural Law, Religion, & Rights*

Ellis Sandoz, *Give Me Liberty*

Thomas Heilke and John von Heyking, eds., *Hunting and Weaving*

Richard Bishirjian, *The Conservative Rebellion*

Charles R. Embry and Glenn Hughes, eds., *Timelessness of Proust*

Klaus Vondung, *Paths to Salvation*

Ralph C. Hancock, *Calvin and the Foundations of Modern Politics*

Servais Pinckaers, O.P., Morality: *The Catholic View*

Rémi Brague, *On the God of the Christians (and on one or two others)*

Richard Peddicord, O.P., *The Sacred Monster of Thomism: An Introduction to the Life and Legacy of Garrigou-Lagrange, O.P.*

Josef Pieper and Heinz Raskop, *What Catholics Believe*

Josef Pieper, *Happiness and Contemplation*

Peter Geach, *God and the Soul*

Gabriel Marcel, *Man against Mass Society*

Dietrich von Hildebrand, *The Heart*

Robert Hugh Benson, *Lord of the World*

Peter Kreeft, *The Philosophy of Jesus*

Peter Kreeft, *Jesus-Shock*

Philippe Bénéton, *The Kingdom Suffereth Violence: The Machiavelli / Erasmus / More Correspondence*

H.S. Gerdil, *The Anti-Emile: Reflections on the Theory and Practice of Education against the Principles of Rousseau*

Consciousness and Politics

From Analysis to Meditation in the Late Work of Eric Voegelin

Barry Cooper

St. Augustine's Press
South Bend, Indiana

Manufactured in the United States of America.

1 2 3 4 5 6 24 23 22 21 20 19 18

Library of Congress Cataloging in Publication Data
Cooper, Barry, 1943-
Consciousness and politics: from analysis to meditation in the late work of Eric Voegelin / Barry Cooper.
Includes index.
ISBN 978-1-58731-159-8 (hardback: alk. paper)
1. Voegelin, Eric, 1901–1985. 2. Philosophy. 3. History – Philosophy. 4. Political science – Philosophy. 5. Consciousness. I. Title.
B3354.V884C67 2015
320.092 – dc23 2015005656

¥ The paper used in this publication meets the minimum requirements of the American National Standard for Information Sciences - Permanence of Paper for Printed Materials, ANSI Z39.48-1984.

St. Augustine's Press
www.staugustine.net

This book is dedicated to two philosophical hunters
Ellis Sandoz, eminent scholar,
And
Terry Lauder, eminent non-scholar

Anxiety is the response to the mystery of existence out of nothing. The search for order is the response to anxiety.

—Eric Voegelin

Table of Contents

Preface

After completing a book like this, it may be useful to look back to its beginning. What did I think I was doing when I started work on it?

The simplest answer is that I was trying to discharge an obligation I made when I finished *Eric Voegelin and the Foundations of Modern Political Science* that on a future occasion I would discuss the later work of Eric Voegelin.[1] Since then other projects intervened, but I always thought I would get back to this one.

A second problem that has concerned me over the years was the relation of Voegelin's political science, or of his political philosophy, to Christianity, or more precisely, to the Gospel. Having grown up in a (relatively) high Anglican religious environment, I had long been puzzled by the vehemence of his Christian (mostly Roman Catholic) critics, either in print or by way of even stronger verbal assaults, many of which they shared with me.

It seems to me that the several issues involved need to be distinguished. First, as Leo Strauss once observed, Voegelin "approaches political philosophy and history from the point of view of non-Roman Catholic Christianity, but being extremely critical of the Reformation."[2] Indeed, Voegelin would occasionally joke about being a "pre-Reformation Christian" or a "pre-Nicene Christian" (see CW, 6:307–8; 30:825). In other words, Voegelin kept his distance from institutional Christianity.[3] He certainly distinguished clearly between "the truth of transcendence, as it is experienced in faith" and "the institutional embodiments and symbolizations in the historical churches" (CW, 30:47).

A second issue related to Voegelin's connection with Christianity was that, as Glen Hughes observed, "with his description of human consciousness as divine-human encounter, Voegelin has moved perhaps as far as it is

1 *Eric Voegelin and the Foundations of Modern Political Science* (Columbia: University of Missouri Press, 1999), xi, 435.

2 Strauss to Kenneth W. Thompson, Rockefeller [Foundation] Archive Center, RF 1.2/2005/531/4539.

3 See Manfred Henningsen, "The Emerging Universalism of Eric Voegelin," *Political Science Reviewer* 27 (1998): 101–2.

possible to move from the twentieth-century intellectual mainstream," an observation that seems to me to be entirely accurate.[4] As Voegelin wrote to Strauss about the divine-human encounter, "revealed truth exists only insofar as it is received by humans and is communicable" (CW, 30:76). This also seems to me to be obviously true. So why was Voegelin's position in such matters construed as anti-Christian or even anti-Catholic? Clearly something more was involved. Accordingly, compared to the uncomprehending things said by those whom one might call professional political scientists, including not a few scholars claiming familiarity with Western political philosophy, the remarks by these self-described Christians were perplexing. I wanted to figure out why they said what they did.

A third purpose of this book grew from my failure to receive funding from the Social Sciences and Humanities Research Council of Canada for a project to follow up on Voegelin's interest in his later life with the pre-imperial symbolism of the Upper Paleolithic and Neolithic. The SSHRCC is the main source of scholarly funding in Canada. It has become highly competitive in recent years and, although in the past I had had no trouble securing support for my projects, in 2010 my application was unsuccessful. The reason I was given was that I had insufficiently developed the methodology I would be using.

Leo Strauss once said that the methodology of political philosophy was "content analysis." Voegelin had quoted William Rappard in a letter to a bureaucrat that "cooperation in science consists in one man writing a book, and another man reading it" and that "'memory and comparison' are still the methods of social science as they were when Aristotle laid down the rule" (CW, 30:203, 201). Voegelin also remarked that "methodology" was often used as "a device to kill off philosophical and historical knowledge in order to leave the field open to the pluralism of emotional ideologies" (CW, 30:839). I had explained to the adjudication committee that in political philosophy the criteria of relevance depended on the arguments developed in a philosophical anthropology, which by and large meant avoiding positivism and various kinds of reductionism. In support of what seemed to be to be self-evident observations, I even cited Thomas Nagel's wonderful article "What is it like to be a Bat?"[5]

4 Hughes, *Mystery and Myth in the Philosophy of Eric Voegelin* (Columbia: University of Missouri Press, 1993), 33.

5 *The Philosophical Review* 83 (1974): 435–50. Tilo Schabert discussed my "methodology" in "Eric Voegelin's Workshop: A Study in Confirmation of Barry Cooper's Genetic Paradigm," in Thomas Heilke and John von Heyking, eds. *Hunting and Weaving: Empiricism and Political Philosophy* (South Bend: St. Augustine's Press, 2013), 232–51.

The principle was straightforward. As David Walsh said, "Just as we cannot understand money in terms of the physical analysis of paper, so we cannot understand consciousness in terms of anything but itself." That applied to European Paleolithic consciousness as well as to twenty-first-century Canadian consciousness. When I realized that the adjudication committee was filled with conventional positivists and had likely never heard of philosophical anthropology or of Thomas Nagel, I decided that I had to write about Voegelin's philosophy of consciousness as a kind of methodological prelude to any study of the Stone Age materials. This is the third reason for this book, which was begun in 2010 and which I expected to have finished in time for the 2012 SSHRCC competition. In the event, I did receive a research grant in 2012 and have begun the work on Stone-Age symbolism.

*

"The order of history emerges from the history of order." So began the Preface to the first volume of *Order and History* (CW, 14:19). What was meant by "the history of order" was relatively straightforward. What the "order of history" might be and how it "emerges" from the history of order turned out to be more complicated. By the time of *Anamnesis* (1966), the two by then analytically distinct reformulations of the problem, namely philosophy of history and philosophy of consciousness, were also understood to constitute a "meditative unit" or unity, *Einheit* (CW, 6:41). The constituent elements of this unit, therefore, had to be distinguished as well as unified.

The substantive question this book deals with concerns how Voegelin moved from conventional textual analysis to the production of meditative essays in his later writings. Moulakis noted one peculiarity of Voegelin's textual interpretations: he "worked through avalanches of materials and kept reformulating his theoretical position," often discarding what appeared to him in error in the light of later empirical evidence "or as a result of closer analysis and more acute insight. . . . He did not feel compelled to go back to the beginning on each occasion" (CW, 15:6). This procedure explained why Voegelin was occasionally accused of being arbitrary and dogmatic—and was accused of dogmatism in spite of his own careful discussion of dogma as a serious and fundamental theoretical mistake. Of course, "after almost half a century we detect shortcomings and doubtful, even erroneous interpretations," not just in the early volumes of *Order and History* but perhaps elsewhere as well.[6]

6 Klaus Vondung, "Rereading Eric Voegelin's *Order and History*," *International Journal of the Classical Tradition* 11 (2004): 83.

Occasionally in this study I have drawn attention to how Voegelin's scholarship and that upon which he relied had grown inadequate with new discoveries and new insights, though that is not my chief purpose.

This project requires that one keep in mind the context and changing meaning of the linguistic symbols Voegelin used, rather like the changing meanings of the same word in a Platonic dialogue. Stefan Rossbach noted that Voegelin's terminology "expanded" in his later work while not quite replacing the terminology of his earlier writings.[7] William P. Thompson suggested that "movement" was "something of a Voegelinian *Ursymbol*."[8] I certainly agree with Hollweck and Caringella (and discuss the problem in chapter six) that Voegelin was not "a book author in the commonly used sense" (CW, 28:xv). He was much busier discovering new problems than solving them.

These characteristics of Voegelin's work meant that overlapping formulations and repetitions were unavoidable since Voegelin often reconsidered problems dealt with in earlier contexts. That said, I have tried to keep repetition to a minimum. Likewise, although I cover the same material as others have done, as Michael P. Morrissey said, "it is a long and arduous task to reach up to the mind of Voegelin the philosopher."[9] One more ladder cannot hurt. In addition, people find different meanings of considerable significance in Voegelin's words because, as James Babin put it, "Voegelin reflects on the effort of a lifetime," especially in his later work. Accordingly, "no final resolution rewards this effort. The question has no sense of having moved beyond the condition he earlier described and so of finishing or even being on the way to finishing the story." The interpretation of Voegelin

7 Rossbach, "Gnosis in Eric Voegelin's Philosophy," *First Principles: ISI Web Journal*, 1 January, 2008. Available at: *http://www.firstprinciplesjouirnal.com* (10/19/2014).

8 Thompson, "'The Gospel Movement': Pulls and Counterpulls in Voegelin's Interpretation of Christ and Christianity," in Glen Hughes, Stephen A. McKnight, Geoffrey L. Price, eds., *Politics, Order and History: Essays on the Work of Eric Voegelin* (Sheffield: Sheffield Academic Press, 2001), 444.

9 Morrissey, "Voegelin, Religious Experience and Immortality," in Glenn Hughes, ed., *The Politics of the Soul* (Lanham: Rowman and Littlefield, 1994), 11. Useful introductions to Voegelin's philosophy of consciousness are Anibal A. Bueno, "Consciousness, Time, and Transcendence in Eric Voegelin's Philosophy," in *The Philosophy of Order: Essays on History, Consciousness and Politics for Eric Voegelin on his Eightieth Birthday*, ed. Peter J. Opitz and Gregor Sebba (Stuttgart: Klett-Cotta, 1981), 91–109 or Steven R. McCarl, "Eric Voegelin's Theory of Consciousness," *The American Political Science Review* 86 (1992): 106–11. Other sources are cited throughout this study.

presented in this study, as is true of all acts or events of consciousness, "is at once active and receptive. It must form its expression even as it lets itself be formed. It holds reality as a 'presence' in consciousness only in so far as it achieves a reflective distance from it in 'the adequate Tale.'"[10]

Gerhardt Niemeyer noted that "Voegelin gave us a new Plato and a new Aristotle, through his probing exegesis of the texts, probing for underlying experiences."[11] Such an approach by Voegelin was bound to be controversial, but as Voegelin said to his friend Gregor Sebba in 1933, he returned to the original experiences and the analytic and symbolic vocabulary used to express those experiences because "the water is clearest at the source."[12] This was one reason why Voegelin's philosophical language often borrowed from Plato and Aristotle. As he explained to Eugene Webb, modern terms such as values, epistemology, ontology and so forth

> must be eliminated again from philosophical discourse if one wants to get any nearer to the real problems. I am not so sure that not even the word "consciousness" (as far as I know introduced by Locke) will not have to undergo a serious re-analysis, in order to bring its meaning again closer to the intended meaning of 'participatory knowledge,' and to distinguish the 'participatory knowledge' from the 'intentionality' of consciousness which objectifies the partners in the event of consciousness into 'subject' and 'object.' (HI, 41:5)

As we shall see in considerable detail, the distinction between participatory knowledge and the intentionality of consciousness was both fundamental for Voegelin's political science and subject to extensive, almost continuous, revision.

Given these problems, which are present at the outset, my focus has been on Voegelin's self-understanding, not whether by some other criterion he got things right. I assume, in other words, that some insight can be gained by tracing Voegelin's argument and his changes in emphasis, indeed, his

10 Babin, "Voegelin and the Study of Literature: Restoring Sense to Senseless Sounds," in Hughes *et al.*, eds., *Politics, Order and History*, 578, 582.

11 Niemeyer, "God and Man, World and Society: The Last Work of Eric Voegelin," *Review of Politics* 51 (1989): 112.

12 Sebba, "Prelude and Variations on the Theme of Eric Voegelin," *The Collected Essays of Gregor Sebba: Truth, History, and the Imagination*, ed. H. Sebba, A.A. Bueno, and H. Boers (Baton Rouge: LSU Press, 1991): 209 n. 10.

changes in focus, over the last thirty years of his life. With this objective in mind the highly critical observation that "the struggles that Voegelin discovers in Plato are his own struggles," an observation with which I agree, loses its sting.[13]

There were continuities as well, which for biographical reasons if no others, should come as no surprise. The meditative essays and the fifth volume of *Order and History* continued the task that Voegelin found in Plato, a searching, a quest, a *zetesis*, to understand reality. In practice this often meant the discovery of new problems, not solutions of any kind. Ellis Sandoz called volume five, *In Search of Order*, "a persuasive analysis of meditative analysis" that "constituted the core of the renewed science of human affairs Voegelin struggles to establish and to elucidate in his work of a lifetime." Moreover, as with his earliest work, this new mode of inquiry was consistent with commonsense. "The intricacies of the meditation before us all dissolve into the reflective understanding of ordinary intelligence and common experience" (CW, 15:2). Sandoz's observation, it seems to me, provided an additional reason to clarify the steps by which Voegelin arrived at his final, meditative formulations.

A word of explanation about the title. Voegelin was best known during the 1950s and 1960s for his textual analyses and exegeses of well-known texts in the history of western political philosophy, but also for his discussions of obscure political tracts and religious oddities. He had considerable difficulties, some of them (but not all) a result of his growing theoretical or philosophical acumen, getting the *History of Political Ideas* published. He reconsidered the project after his research trip to Europe in 1950, but even then his approach to "the materials" was chiefly one of textual analysis.

Largely as a result of his gradual discovery of the importance of the equivalence of experiences and symbolization and of his formulation of the concept of historiogenesis, Voegelin undertook to reconstitute the meaning of an author's words in the widest possible context, which entailed the practice of what we conventionally call meditation. Much of what Voegelin understood by way of reorientation can be traced in the correspondence, which was exceedingly frank, even though not explicitly intended for publication. These documents were especially valuable when Voegelin was explaining himself to philosophically competent and friendly correspondents. His

13 Zdravko Planinc, "The Significance of Plato's *Timaeus* and *Critias* in Eric Voegelin's Philosophy," in Hughes *et al.*, eds, *Politics Order and History*, 373.

response to the criticism of hostile ignoramuses revealed aspects of his personality. They were also highly amusing.

*

Thanks, both personal and financial are also in order. First I must again thank my wife, Denise Guichon, for her loving support and analytical acumen as well as her forbearance in dealing with a husband who was often either physically or intellectually absent. My son Brendan missed several hunting and fishing trips because of this book. Daughter Meghan was able to ride along and assist on some of the research trips for the next book, so she was less deprived. Thank you all. I am grateful for all that I have enjoyed doing this work.

The Eric Voegelin Society, which has met annually since 1985 in conjunction with the American Political Science Association, has provided many occasions to discuss Voegelin's work over the years. It has also brought together three academic generations of scholars from across North America, Europe, South America, and Asia, many of whom have become my good friends. Among Voegelin's associates and students, living and dead, I have benefitted from discussions with Paul Caringella, Jürgen Gebhardt, Manfred Henningsen, Thomas Hollweck, Thani Moulakis, Gerhard Niemeyer, Peter Opitz, Ellis Sandoz, Peter von Sivers, Tilo Schabert, Klaus Vondung, and Eugene Webb. Among my contemporaries I have especially benefitted from conversations with Tom Darby, Steve Ealy, Tom Flanagan, Michael Franz, Tim Fuller, Thierry Gontier, Chip Hughes, Wolfgang Leidhold, Tom McPartland, Martin Palous, Bill Petropoulos, Brendan Purcell, Jim Rhodes, Henrik Syse, David Walsh, Gilbert Weiss, and Jim Wiser. Students, who will be sure to continue work on "the problems," as Voegelin would say, are always a great help in clarifying one's own thinking. My thanks to: Amanda Achtman, Richard Avramenko, Jodi Bruhn, Thomas Heilke, John von Heyking, Steve McGuire, Zdravko Planinc, Mathias Reidl, Sarah Shea, Trevor Shelly, HaJo Sigwart, and SaraBeth Vosburg.

On the financial side of the leger, particularly during the period when the SSHRCC source went dry, I would like to thank a Calgary businessman who wished to remain anonymous, Joe Donner and the Donner Canadian Foundation, the Earhart Foundation and the Alexander von Humboldt Stiftung. I would also like to thank the SSRRCC for its support over the past two years.

*

Abbreviations used in the text are: (1) CW, which refers, as has now almost become customary, to the *Collected Works of Eric Voegelin*, available from the University of Missouri Press in thirty-four volumes, by volume and page; and (2) HI, which refers to the Voegelin collection at the Hoover Institution, Stanford, by box and file. Voegelin was inconsistent in his capitalization. I have consistently capitalized terms such as Gnosticism and Ground of Being.

Calgary

Christmas, 2014

CHAPTER ONE
METHOD: FROM POLITICAL IDEAS TO THE HISTORICITY OF TRUTH

The transformation of the eight-volume *History of Political Ideas* into the more systematic argument of *The New Science of Politics* (1952) and the first three volumes of *Order and History* (1956–57) was not simply of philological or biographical interest. These changes also documented the development of Voegelin's philosophical anthropology and, especially as found in his later work, the changes indicated a new direction in his thought toward the meditative exegesis of his philosophical consciousness of reality. In *Eric Voegelin and the Foundations of Modern Political Science* I noted that the change between the early volumes of *Order and History* and the later ones could be characterized as a shift from a focus on philosophy of history to a focus on philosophy of consciousness.[1] Because Voegelin was concerned with problems of consciousness in his earliest writings one might argue that the shift was one of emphasis within a single research program. However, it seems to me that the shift was a major change in direction if not a decisive break in continuity. The preliminary evidence can be found in the changes made to the *History* over the years.[2]

1. Publication History

The publication history of the *History of Political Ideas* is straightforward though the reasons for the well-documented changes are sometimes obscure.

1 Cooper, *Eric Voegelin and The Foundations of Modern Political Science* (Columbia: University of Missouri Press, 1999), 433.

2 Central to this account is the guidance of the editors' introductions to the separate volumes of the *History* in CW 19–26 as well as the introductions to the *Selected Correspondence*, CW, 29–30. Equally important because of his critical analysis of several of these introductions is Arpad Szakolczai, *Reflexive Historical Sociology* (Florence: Routledge, 1999) and Szakolczai, "Stages of the Quest: Reconstructing the Outline Structure of Eric Voegelin's *History of Political Ideas*," *Occasional Papers: XXV* (Munich: Eric-Voegelin-Archiv, 2001).

In February 1939 Voegelin agreed to write a college text-book under the general editorship of Fritz Morstein-Marx for McGraw-Hill. The contract "came at the best possible moment for Voegelin. It was a major asset in his difficult fight to get himself established in a new country."[3] The original version of *The History of Political Ideas* was to be around two hundred pages long and delivered to the publisher in the fall of 1940 (HI, 24:32). The complex publication history has prompted some commentators reasonably enough to question whether Voegelin ever intended to write such a text. For example, at the same time as he began to work on the *History* (1939–40) Voegelin began to learn Hebrew. "This was clearly not something *any* [conventional] textbook on the history of political ideas could possibly require."[4] It is certainly possible that Voegelin began the project in good faith but, as he proceeded to complete it, the direction and size of the enterprise changed as he worked on it so that, eventually, it grew too large for McGraw-Hill's requirements. And later, when he had secured Macmillan as a publisher, the problem of size recurred, along with the internal direction of the *History*.

In the spring of 1941, Morstein-Marx inquired about the status of the manuscript (HI, 24:24). Voegelin replied on 6 May, and included a table of contents that, he said, was ready for publication. Most of it was self-explanatory, but Voegelin added "a few remarks" that "may prove helpful" to his editor and presumably to the publisher (CW, 29:265). Specifically, Voegelin noted that he had divided the subject-matter into an "upper stratum of ideas" and an "undercurrent" of "movements." In the section titled "The People of God," discussed in the following chapter, Voegelin called them two "planes." This section surveyed "undercurrent" movements that existed from the tenth century to the present and accordingly dealt with the problem of medieval and modern revolutions. Such an approach, Voegelin said, "makes it possible to isolate the rational systems of ideas and treat them very succinctly without burdening their presentation with extensive explanations of the [historical] situation." Even then, however, Voegelin had a concern: "my only real sorrow is that you will find my unorthodox treatment too much at variance with the expectations of readers who [still] live in the time when Queen Victoria was young and beautiful." A glance at the chapter headings of Sabine's *History of Political Theory* (or even of Strauss and Cropsey's *History of Political Philosophy*) reveals a stately march of great men from Plato to the

3 Szakolczai, *Reflexive Historical Sociology*, 40.

4 Szakolczai, "Stages of the Quest," 17.

twentieth century, which was and arguably remains the conventional treatment. Such tables of contents also indicate the source of Voegelin's misgivings.

Later that summer Morstein-Marx expressed his concern about the delay and the size the book was likely to be (Voegelin had provided page counts and estimates for the several chapters and Morstein-Marx was capable of adding up the numbers). A few days later Voegelin provided an explanation (CW, 29:278–80). The "technical problem" was that the existing texts on the history of political thought ignored at least a generation of scholarship so that, if Voegelin were simply to summarize the recent monographic literature and add nothing original, the result would be "a revolution in the field." But that approach was not possible since the book would then "be discarded as simply crazy." Hence he must supply "argumentative support," which had caused delay and caused the manuscript to grow. He made some additional deprecatory remarks about "the college-fauna" and concluded: "I cannot write outrageous nonsense on essential questions and ruin my reputation in order to comply with the pictures of the world of the text-book tribe; and I cannot be as brief as I could be in a treatise for educated readers because the book is supposed to be in competition with the text-book literature." Morstein-Marx appealed again (twice) in August 1941 for Voegelin to send him the manuscript but for two and a half years nothing was sent.

In April 1944 Voegelin wrote Morstein-Marx that the *History* had reached the point "where conversations concerning publication can be started" (CW, 29:402–3). The manuscript was now over fourteen hundred pages and was designed to be "the standard treatise on the subject for a couple of decades." If McGraw-Hill were no longer interested, Voegelin asked Morstein-Marx and his former mentor at Harvard, W. Y. Elliott, to help him place it with Macmillan.[5] By September 1944 Voegelin had secured a contract with Macmillan, which agreed to publish the manuscript in three volumes of four hundred, five hundred, and six hundred pages. Elliott said in response to Voegelin's request that while he was happy to support Voegelin's publication and was impressed by the size of his book, "I now have mixed feelings about three-volume editions of anything. My scholarly inclinations are entirely in favor, but my day-to-day contact with the paper shortage in the civilian economy somewhat curbs my enthusiasm" (HI, 11:2). Elliot at the time was working in the Office of Civilian Requirements of the War

5 Harvard University Archives, W.Y. Elliott Papers, HUG4360.8. Voegelin to Elliott, 9 June 1944.

Production Board in Washington. Apparently only the first two volumes were sent for the publisher's inspection, but that proved to be sufficient (CW, 29:414). As Hollweck and Sandoz said, "the second phase of the 'History' had begun" (CW, 19:5). If the initial growth in the size of the modest manuscript McGraw-Hill expected is counted as a "phase," the Macmillan version would be phase three.

By early 1946, Voegelin had delivered a presumably revised manuscript of the first two volumes to the publisher, who then sent it to Francis W. Coker at Yale for review. Coker's report was favorable but Voegelin took exception to one observation Coker made about Voegelin's "fondness" for finding mystical implications in political texts.[6]

> Of course, I do not deny that this fondness is quite visible throughout the work. But I would plead that it is more than a mere fondness. The principles of interpretation which I use were developed after the breakdown of an attempt to write a systematic theory of politics (around 1930) [i.e., Voegelin's *Herrschaftslehre* or *Theory of Governance*, CW, 32:224–413]. I had finished the "Theory of Law" and the "Theory of Power." Then I found that I could not handle the problem of political ideas in a satisfactory manner because meanwhile (that is: between 1900 and 1930), there had come into full swing the new monographic literature on the religious implications of political ideas. And I simply did not know enough about history of religion and about theology to tackle the problems on the level of scientific standards that had been established by this new literature. If I may do a little self-criticism, I would say, that even today my performance will still lie open to severe criticisms on the part of such authorities as Dempf, Przywara, Étienne de Greeff, H. U. von Balthasar, etc. (May I draw your attention by the way, to Balthasar's 3 volumes of *Apokalypse der deutschen Seele*; a masterpiece of analysis of ideas.) May I repeat that I do not wish to reject a criticism of yours. But since you have gone to so much pains [*sic*] over the MS, I thought I owed to you an explanation of the reasons that induced my attention to the religious problems. (CW, 29:465)

6 Coker wrote to Voegelin (18 April 1946) that "the detailed analysis and criticism is the joint work of my colleague Cecil H. Driver and myself" (HI, 24:8).

In February 1948 a second reviewer's report had been returned to Macmillan (CW, 29:711–20). It also examined only the first two volumes. This review was anonymous.[7] There is no explanation in the correspondence with Macmillan for the twenty-month period between reviews. This report, though indeed favorable, was also filled with criticism of Voegelin's use of the English language: it did not contain "current American ways of talking." Moreover the reviewer was clearly hostile to Voegelin's "point of view." Much of the criticism was simply a reflection of the ignorance of the reviewer, particularly regarding the monographic literature that Voegelin had earlier referred to in his correspondence with Morstein-Marx. The reviewer expressed his ignorance by questioning whether "English or American scholars" would be likely to assign the book in political theory courses. He particularly objected, as did Coker and Driver, to Voegelin's "mystical attitude" towards Plato, remarking that Freud was a better source of a "reputedly scientific account to the ways myths are generated by the unconscious and projected into human relationships."

The reviewer was nevertheless impressed by Voegelin's scholarship and raised one significant question that merits detailed attention.

> POINT OF VIEW. The author uses the expression "political ideas" in a special and quasi-technical sense that depends upon his own conceptions of the subject, and of politics and history generally. This special sense pervades the book and is briefly but not very clearly stated in the Introduction. To state it fully and with precision, might require a lengthy exposition since it amounts to something like a philosophy of history.
>
> The author's purpose is to write a history of "evocative ideas" or "myths" that in his conception provide a kind of cement to hold a political and social structure together, and that underlie its constitutional, legal, and governmental institutions. Such evocative ideas are not theories since they cannot be subjected to confirmation or refutation by fact. Yet they are inevitable, in the sense that no social group can exist without some such ideas. . . . They are misconceived when they are imagined to be "theories" (because they cannot be scientifically confirmed), and this misconception,

7 Cleanth Brooks reported to Voegelin, 16 February 1948 that Cecil Driver had again reviewed the *History* for Macmillan "and pronounced it a remarkable book, a great book" (HI, 8:46).

> together with the parallel misconception that human beings can live without myths, is regarded as the fundamental error of the eighteenth and nineteenth centuries. A theoretical system of political philosophy is conceived to be the culmination of a period in which the myth has been formed or "evoked," and systematization usually foreshadows the decline of the evocative idea.

The reviewer was not clear about the "status" of these evocative ideas and myths apart from their being "mystical" in some unspecified way.

The reviewer was also critical of the distinction between an evocative *idea* and a *theory* and of Voegelin's emphasis on the former, which "tends to minimize the rational or factual content of the subject-matter" and thus tends to be "subjective." Where Voegelin did deal with the place of social and economic factors in forming political ideas, the reviewer expressed his approval—though he noted that, for Voegelin, these factors were "ancillary" rather than central. Unfortunately, Voegelin's "point of view"

> results in an unusual allocation of space. The account of Plato fills a considerable part of the first volume, while Aristotle receives one short chapter. The reason of course is that the author regards Aristotle as "contemplative" or a theorist, while he regards Plato, in intention at least, as a "founder" or the creator of a new evocative idea. For the same reason the account of Plato is largely taken up with an imaginative interpretation of the Platonic myths, to the neglect of the logical or scientific purposes that most historians of philosophy attribute to him.

Voegelin replied to his editor, Charles Anderson, with a set of "observations" almost as long as the original report (CW, 29:551–57). With regard to style, Voegelin replied that the report contained no examples of what the reviewer considered unidiomatic, but mere voiced a "general complaint." In the manuscript sent to Coker, Voegelin admitted that he "shuddered" at his use of English when he re-read what he had written six years earlier (CW, 29:464). The 1948 version was presumably an improvement since it had passed the scrutiny of Robert Heilman and Cleanth Brooks.[8] Voegelin added that these readers were "by general

8 See Heilman to Voegelin, 10 November 1947, in Robert B. Heilman and Eric Voegelin, *A Friendship in Letters: 1944–1984*, ed. Charles R. Embry (Columbia: University of Missouri Press, 2004), 37–39.

agreement . . . counted among the best critics in English literature. . . . Now: whom shall I believe? And whom are you going to believe?"

The reviewer may, Voegelin said, be justified in noting that Voegelin used words "in unfamiliar senses." Voegelin was reminded of "several learned gentlemen" at the University of Vienna, "fine scholars in their special fields, who considered books written in philosophical language as un-German. Perhaps this is a similar case."[9] Voegelin suggested sending the objectionable treatment of Plato, for example, to scholars of unquestioned philosophical competence such as John Wild at Harvard or Richard Niebuhr at Yale to elicit their comments. Likewise the objections to inserting Greek and Latin terms (along with English translations) was necessary because "English philosophical language (which was formed in the eighteenth century) conveys entirely different meanings" than were intended by the original Greek- and Latin-speaking authors.[10]

As for his reliance on questionable "Continental" scholars rather than, presumably, good solid English and American ones, Voegelin said: "this is true in the sense that a good deal of the work on Antiquity and the Middle Ages has been done by French, German, and Italian scholars. I happen to have read these scholars: what's wrong?" The report also correctly said that Voegelin developed his "own conceptualization of the subject" that was "largely unfamiliar" to Anglo-American professors such as the reviewer. Why, Voegelin asked, would "I devote ten years of my life to the elaboration of a treatise if I have nothing to say but what somebody else would say anyway?" And why bother to write a book "if the reader can find only things in it which are familiar to him already?" In short, "political science has become somewhat an intellectual backwater; it is high time somebody makes the profession familiar with what's going on in the world."

As for Voegelin's "point of view":

> *IV. Point of View*
>
> The Report gives on the whole a correct account. I also agree with the Report that the theory of ideas and of the myth is

9 Ludwig von Mises, incidentally, made a similar observation: "many professors" at the University of Vienna, he said, "could not even be called educated men" (*Notes and Recollections* [South Holland, Il.: Libertarian Press, 1978], 95).

10 See also Voegelin's comments to William Havard on "the English conception of man" and the language, derived from Locke, used to describe what the English took to be human being (Voegelin to Havard, 23 November 1947 [HI, 16:23]). If Driver was the second reviewer, this objection would be entirely appropriate because Driver was in fact British.

> nowhere stated succinctly and formally. The proper place—as the Report suggests correctly—would be the Introduction. The Report, however, also states the reason why such a formal exposition was not given: the reason of space. The Report says: "To state fully and with precision, might require a lengthy exposition since it amounts to something like a philosophy of history." This is quite true. A serious exposition of this problem would be practically a new book. And even if compressed, one could give this account hardly in less than a hundred pages. . . . I could write, of course, a new Introduction; and I am quite willing to do it of you consider it desirable—but you will have to consider the problem of space.

Voegelin did write a holograph version of an Introduction where he explained in detail the purpose of "ideas" as "evocations" and their relationship to theory, but it was not included in the manuscript sent either to Coker or to the second reviewer. It is discussed in the following section.

The rest of the publication history can be recounted briefly. As late as the spring of 1949, the project seemed to be on track with Macmillan, though now it had expanded to four volumes.[11] Regular correspondence in the late 1940s seems to have been replaced with occasional meetings when Voegelin was in New York or, on one occasion, when his editor was in Baton Rouge. In the summer of 1950 Voegelin received a Guggenheim Fellowship and travelled to Europe to discuss "the problems" with several major thinkers, including von Balthasar, Hans Barth, Karl Jaspers, Karl Barth, Edgar Salin, and many of his old friends in Vienna. As Hollweck observed, he found "a flourishing intellectual life that had survived the human catastrophe of the Nazi rule over Europe" (CW, 30:3). During the fall of 1950 Voegelin necessarily put the *History* aside to compose his Walgreen Lectures given at the University of Chicago in January 1951. By April the lectures were in the hands of the University of Chicago Press, which meant additional revisions, proofing, and so on.[12] This interruption of his work on

11 CW, 29:626. Between 1945 and 1948 there is considerable cordial correspondence between Voegelin and Henry B. McCurdy, his editor at Macmillan (HI, 24:8).

12 In the summer of 1952 Voegelin wrote Eduard d'Armes of the Rockefeller Foundation that he was "engaged in a major project of historical and theoretical studies. The first volume of the theoretical studies will come out in September 1952, by the Chicago University Press, under the title 'The New Science of Politics.' The 'History of Political Ideas,' in four volumes, to be published by Macmillan is in

the *History* proved decisive in his reorganizing the entire project, as we argue in the following chapter.

Correspondence with Macmillan resumed in the fall of 1953, when Voegelin announced he had a new title, *Order and Symbols*, for a manuscript that now was closing in on forty-five hundred pages. Voegelin explained to Charles Anderson that he thought it could be published in three volumes:

> Volume I: *Myth, History, and Philosophy*. From the Beginnings to c. 300 B.C.
>
> Volume II: *Empire and Christianity*. From c. 300 B.C. to c. A.D. 1500.
>
> Volume III: *The Gnostic Age*. From c. A.D. 1500 to the present. . . .
>
> In explanation of the title and subdivisions: The older title (History of Political Ideas) is inadequate, because the liberal ideology on which it was based is by now exploded in critical science. "Order and Symbols" is the theoretically correct description, for the subject-matter is the development of the experiences of order and their adequate symbolization. Hence, the subdivisions also have their systematic significance. The first volume deals with the three great symbolic forms developed in antiquity, that is, with Myth, History, and Philosophy; it closes with Aristotle. The second volume begins with Alexander, and deals with the respective orders of Empire and Christianity, down to the time of their crisis in the Reformation. The third volume is a systematic unit, insofar as it deals with the development of Modern Gnosis and its crisis in our time. The sequence of subject-matter, thus, is no longer a simple string of authors and ideas in time. (CW, 30:181)

All were substantially complete though each had a few "gaps and needs revision in detail." He was currently filling in the gaps on the first volume and anticipated it would be complete by the end of February 1954. The

process of revision. Two volumes could be finished for the printer, unless new disturbances intervene, by the fall. The other two volumes in about two years" (HI, 6:19).

second volume would be ready a year later and the third by the fall of 1955. Voegelin was enthusiastic about this work.

> With regard to style: It has substantially improved. Recent sections I have submitted to critical revision by Herman Finer in Chicago. He found practically nothing to amend. The only defects were too generous use of the semicolon; and a slip here and there in the sequence of tenses. That is the sort of thing I expect to iron out during January and February for Volume I. When you receive the MS., I don't think you will have an editorial job on hand, worth mentioning. Footnotes and bibliographies have been kept to a minimum. The book is a readable story, with practically no critical apparatus at all. This should be done through judicious references to the most recent literature and the bibliographies given therein.
>
> Finally, let me say, that the delay, embarrassing in some respects, was all to the good. The whole work is now really up-to-date and will be a standard work for at least a generation. This is due largely to the fact that I could incorporate in the final form the new literature that has come out since World War II. (CW, 30:182)

In June, 1954 Voegelin again wrote to Macmillan and reiterated that the manuscript of *Order and Symbols* was coming along well. Apparently all three volumes were by then in the hands of Macmillan (HI, 24:8), but Henry McCurdy had become manager and executive editor of the College Department and Henry C. Cloudman had replaced Anderson. McCurdy observed that the current version of the *History* bore little resemblance to what Macmillan had contracted for a decade earlier (HI, 24:8). Voegelin replied more or less along the lines he used when answering a similar comment by Morstein-Marx in 1941: Science had moved on and as a consequence the manuscript had grown though its "nature" or "intention" had remained the same. Moreover, Voegelin had also "learned a few things in the course of the work, as you may see from my *New Science of Politics*, which has come out in the meanwhile." Consequently, he explained, "what you get as the result of the labor [i.e., of Voegelin's labor] is a standard treatise on the subject that runs no danger of finding a rival in less than a generation" (CW, 30:222–23).

Apparently Voegelin met with McCurdy in New York in August 1954 to discuss the future of the manuscript. In September McCurdy informed

Voegelin that they had reassigned *Order and Symbols* from the College Department to the Trade Department. Since a trade book, even a big one such as Voegelin's, was supposed to make money for the publisher fairly quickly rather than on the basis of sales to college students "over a generation," this was a clear signal that Macmillan had lost interest. McCurdy confirmed the decision on 11 October 1954 (HI, 24:8) and Voegelin tried over the winter of 1954–55 to find another publisher in New York (HI, 8:22; 28:9; 28:5). In February 1955 he made a final pitch to Macmillan to publish a smaller three-volume study, starting with the Greeks and ending with the mid-twentieth century. This version, Voegelin said, could bear the traditional title of a *History of Political Ideas* (CW, 30:244–45). This, too, Macmillan declined to publish.

Voegelin had an offer dating from 1944 from Louisiana State University Press to publish the *History* (HI, 23:27), but, as he explained to Morstein-Marx, although LSU had an excellent production team, "their sales-organization is non-existent; to give the book to them might be a funeral" (CW, 29:403). In the spring of 1955, after a few more changes in the title, LSU Press agreed to publish the manuscript as *Order and History* (CW, 30:247).

2. Evocation and Theory

The reasons for the delay are complex. Sandoz and Hollweck argued that more than Voegelin's adherence to "the monumental tradition of German scholarship," was involved, though it is doubtless true that Voegelin felt himself duty-bound "to produce an original work that would be a standard in the sense of providing a theoretically thorough examination of its field, integrating the most advanced state of valid scholarship pertinent to the field" (CW, 19:49). Thus "monumentalism" undoubtedly did play a part.

Second, as Walsh observed, "Viewed as a history of political ideas, these volumes are at best idiosyncratic if not downright wayward. . . . Voegelin's approach as the project went on was to follow the threads of problems rather than the conventional presentation of thinkers." That is, he did not discuss figures and their writings because they were conventionally understood to be important. Nor was he interested in providing an overview of "the history of political thought," or the "tradition," whatever that might be.[13] Thus, "the

13 John G. Gunnell, "The Myth of the Tradition," *American Political Science Review* 72 (1978): 122–34, criticized Leo Strauss for his use of "the tradition," as a rhetorical device. He included Voegelin as well, referring to *The New Science of Politics*

impossibility of ever fitting his project within the textbook genre was ultimately what forced its abandonment" (CW, 26:1–2). Walsh suggested that Voegelin was interested instead in engaging with texts "in a common search for truth," from the inside, so to speak.

In the summer of 1948 Voegelin explained to the Rockefeller Foundation and to the Guggenheim Foundation the nature of his "serious treatise," which "is not a text-book." It would have "independent value as a standard treatise." For Voegelin personally "the work on it had primarily the purpose of acquiring a thorough understanding of the theoretical problems of a philosophy of politics." Now that it was completed, Voegelin proposed to undertake "the systematic exposition of a philosophy of politics and history." It is for that reason that he wished to spend his sabbatical, with the help of a Guggenheim, in Europe. As he explained in the original proposal submitted to Rockefeller (which was not acted upon because the individual who decided who would receive grants was in Europe and would remain there for the next several months), the purpose of the *History* "was not the elaboration of the general categories that can be applied in the interpretation of political phenomena throughout history. The materials digested were historical; the intention was systematic" (CW, 29:573). By "systematic" Voegelin meant philosophical, which is to say, he was developing an argument based on a philosophical anthropology and, eventually, on a philosophy of history, a large project akin to the *Herrschaftslehre* of two decades earlier (CW, 19:16). Moreover, this "systematic" work would be part of "a new science of politics and history that has arisen on an international scale" since the end of the First World War. Voegelin likely was referring to Max Weber, Karl Jaspers, Henri Bergson and Edmund Husserl.

Later that year (1948) Voegelin provided a report to the Social Science Research Council explaining how he had used their research grant along with an account of the progress and delays of the *History*.

> The delays, very considerable ones, have been due to the fact that the architecture of the whole work did emerge only on occasion of the actual analysis of the materials. Frequent reconstruction proved necessary. The worst happened two years ago when, as the result of the analysis of Vico and Schelling, it was

(1952) and *Science Politics and Gnosticism* (1959). In fact Voegelin had abandoned a concern with "tradition" sometime during the 1930s and focused instead on the problem of "sentiments" and then on "experiences."

> necessary to rewrite the whole first volume and to double its size. This alone had cost me one whole year. No such surprises are to be expected for the future because, by now, the whole analysis and theoretical construction is completed. The revision which I am undertaking now, is more or less routine work; and I expect to have it completed before the end of the present academic year. (CW, 29:584–85)

Beyond reports to granting agencies and publishers, as Sandoz and Hollweck observed, "the real story of the 'History' emerges from Voegelin's correspondence with friends and colleagues" (CW, 19:14), especially with Alfred Schütz. In early 1943, for instance, Voegelin wrote that his *History* was "not a 'history of ideas' ['*Dogmengeschichte*,' or history of doctrine] but an attempt to present the respective theoretical positions as determined by 'sentiments.'" Accordingly, the thinker's explicit theories and doctrines were understood as reflecting his "attitude toward the world." That attitude in turn was conditioned by the spiritual personality of the thinker, his social milieu and its "tradition of sentiments," and immediate occasions that elicit from him a particular concrete response.

> An example for the first factor: The ontological assumptions of Thomas of Aquinas are determined by his personality to the extent that the experience [*Erlebnis*] of a fundamental harmony between the world and man gives rise to the thesis that the order of reality and the order of reason are identical. An example of the second factor: The weight of the tradition of the polis leads Aristotle to define man as a *zoon politikon*, and thus leads to the thesis that, in the territorial ethnic state, it is impossible of the human being to realize the fullness of existence. An example of the third factor: Dante's idea of a future *monarchia temporalis* was occasioned by the dissolution of the medieval empire following the *Interregnum*. (CW, 29:352; cf. 29:335)

Schütz had some reservations about Voegelin's emphasis on "sentiments," which became a recurring theme in their epistolary conversation.[14]

14 See *A Friendship that Lasted a Lifetime: The Correspondence between Alfred Schütz and Eric Voegelin*, trans. William Petropulos, ed. Gerhard Wagner and Gilbert Weiss (Columbia: University of Missouri Press, 2011), 44–45; 79; 83.

Voegelin began his explicit discussions of "sentiments" in the early 1940s, though it was doubtless based on his analysis of race "ideas" and "authoritarianism" that he made during the 1930s.[15] The "process of history," he told Schütz, did not proceed in terms of problems but in terms of sentiments. Accordingly, "there is no history of problems." Sentiments, in contrast, are "pre-theoretical" experiences that nevertheless may also be expressed theoretically. Voegelin here drew attention to the similarity of his use of "sentiment" to the use of the term "individual essence" in the context of the "historicity of an epoch" as developed by their mutual friend, Fritz Kaufmann in a recent article.[16] One may simplify Voegelin's argument with the observation that, in the political context, sentiments are taken-for-granted attitudes about right and wrong, the meaning and purpose of a regime and similar conventions that sustain commitments to it as an acceptable and legitimate undertaking.

Voegelin's use of the term "idea" was more systematic. There was, however, some controversy surrounding what Voegelin meant by the term at this time and how it may have changed over the years. According to a statement in his *Autobiographical Reflections* (1973) Voegelin simply "gave up" on "ideas" as objects of a history and turned to the "experience of reality—personal, social, historical, cosmic—as the reality to be explored historically" (CW, 34:105–6). But if that were so, why did Voegelin insist to Macmillan that his treatise was still a history of political ideas? Was he simply being disingenuous in the hope of publishing a large book with a commercial publisher? Granted, as he said in the *Autobiographical Reflections*, the period between 1945 and 1950 was one of "indecision, of not paralysis, in handling the problems that I saw but could not intellectually penetrate to my satisfaction" (CW, 34:91), we still need to know what the term "idea" meant for him.

Peter von Sivers has provided the most elaborate account that relies (it seems to me) on some of Voegelin's subsequent formulations. According to him, Voegelin's use of the term "idea" in the *History* was connected to his use of the terms "sentiment" and "evocation." Evocations, he said were

15 See Cooper, *Beginning the Quest: Law and Politics in the Early Work of Eric Voegelin* (Columbia: University of Missouri Press, 2009).

16 Kaufmann, "The Phenomenological Approach to History," *Philosophy and Phenomenological Research* 2 (1941): 167. Kaufmann's argument was presented in the specialized and technical vocabulary of classical 1940s phenomenology that was also used by Schütz.

"live" ideas, and ideas were "dead" evocations, where vitality was determined by the suitability or appropriateness of attitudes and sentiments towards political institutions, arrangement, or "evocations." Sentiments and attitudes were central because in the actual, concrete situation they did or did not sustain the commitments of persons to existing institutions and evocations. Moreover, because sentiments and attitudes could change over the years more quickly than institutions could change, particularly if their operational procedures were written in texts or enacted in rituals, the texts or rituals could be used to "conjure up false sentiments" that no longer expressed or evoked the original meaning of an institution.

In his later work, Voegelin would use the metaphors of opacity and transparency to describe the change from the original and appropriate connection between sentiment and evocation to a later evocation conjured by "false" sentiments. On the former instance, Voegelin said, the evocation was "transparent" for (or to) the sentiment; in the latter it was "opaque." By von Sivers' argument, "Voegelin calls 'evocation' mixed up with false sentiments 'ideas'" (CW, 20:5). Or, to be more historically precise, Voegelin came to use the term "ideas" in this way after he clarified the relationship of sentiments and evocations.

A first step in that clarification was to consider how change in the relationship of attitude or sentiment and evocation came about. When sentiments and attitudes were appropriate to the evocation or institution, Voegelin would speak of the latter being transparent for the former. That is, the institution would faithfully or properly express the sentiments that were expressed in and through it. Either element of this pair could, however, become disconnected, either by the application of no longer appropriate evocations, which von Sivers called ideas, to actual and existing configurations of sentiments, or by applying genuine existing evocations to earlier periods where the appropriate existing sentiments were absent. For example, it is relatively common to apply Aristotle's account of just and unjust regimes to the practice of contemporary states or ideological empires, notwithstanding the atrophy of sentiments that made the context of the polis "alive." Likewise one can take contemporary ideas of church and state and apply them to medieval times or to ancient Egypt with the result that they would suggest false sentiments that never existed during those earlier periods.

Von Sivers' interpretation clarified an important problem that later became thematic, namely the historicity of truth, which we discuss in the following section. Other accounts of Voegelin's changing use of the term ideas were less elaborate and followed more closely Voegelin's text. Hollweck and

Sandoz for example observed first, that although Voegelin used the term "idea" throughout the 1940s and into the 1950s, by the mid-1950s ideas "had moved from the center to the periphery of the theoretical inquiry" (CW, 19:17). According to Gebhardt, Voegelin "exaggerates somewhat" in emphasizing the change from political ideas to experiences of reality.[17] In his introduction to the first volume of Voegelin's *Selected Correspondence*, Gebhardt said that his statement in the *Autobiographical Reflections* "is not quite true, because a closer inspection of his earlier writings will always reveal that the fundamental experiences of human existence were the pivot of his hermeneutical study of the historico-political world" (CW, 29:63). As evidence for modifying Voegelin's later self-appraisal of his having abandoned ideas for experiences, Hollweck, Sandoz and Gebhardt all pointed to Voegelin's "Introduction" to an early version of the *History*, to which we now turn.[18]

The establishment of a government, this "Introduction" began, is "an essay in world creation," which Voegelin would later call an evocation. From a chaotic soup of "conflicting human desires [or sentiments and attitudes] rises a little world of order, a cosmic analogy, a cosmion, leading a precarious life under the pressure of destructive forces" and compelled to maintain itself by violence against internal law-breakers and against external threats. The use of violence to preserve political order was to be sharply distinguished from the purpose of political order, which "is the creation of a shelter [or evocation] in which man may give to his life a semblance of meaning." The purpose of "what are commonly called political ideas" was "to rationalize the shelter-function of the cosmion, the little world of order." The details of these ideas varied a great deal; the general structure however remained constant and consisted of three constituent elements: "[1] the ideas concerning the constitution of the cosmos; [2] the ideas concerning the internal order; [3] the ideas concerning the status of the cosmion in the simultaneous world and in history."

A major implication of the "shelter-function" of the cosmion was that it reflected a desire

17 Jürgen Gebhardt, "The Vocation of a Scholar" in Stephen A. McKnight and Geoffrey L. Price, eds., *International and Interdisciplinary Perspectives of Eric Voegelin* (Columbia: University of Missouri Press, 1997), 24.

18 Quotations are from CW, 19:225–37. See also HI, 25:23; CW, 29:243–45. The original, dating from the fall of 1939 (see HI, 21:33), exists only in holograph. Paul Caringella made a copy available to me; Voegelin's handwriting is not easily deciphered, and I have no emendations to suggest for the version Hollweck, Gebhardt and Caringella published in CW, 19.

> to give to the questionable achievements of an individual life an added meaning by weaving it into the texture of group achievement. Interpreted in these terms, the political cosmion provides a structure of meaning into which the single human being can fit the results of the biologically and spiritually [productive, procreative] energies of his personal life, thereby [relieving] his life from the [disordering aspects] of existence that always spring up when the possibility of the utter senselessness of a life ending in annihilation is envisaged.

The problems of establishing a finite cosmos of meaning came into focus when they were compared to alternative ways of responding to the fragmentary, temporary, and even "senseless character" of human existence. There have always been people who have held that the perishability of human life meant that it could only be a preparation for a life of meaning "beyond" life on earth. Such a belief could lead to a range of "apolitical attitudes" to organize one's personal life—from monasticism to an over-achieving work ethic. It is worth noting first that Max Weber's *Protestant Ethic and the Spirit of Capitalism* argued that the source of "inner-worldly asceticism" was medieval monasticism, and second that Voegelin's use of the term "intramundane" was simply a Latinate cognate term to Weber's "*innerweltlich*." Voegelin's initial point was that the coexistence of both political and apolitical attitudes expressed the incompleteness of the cosmion and thus the incompleteness of human life, both of which existed in contrast to the completeness of the divine cosmos.

That is, the cosmion was to be understood as an analogue to the divine cosmos and so, to a degree, was speculative, mythic, or imaginary. One central feature of political ideas, by this formulation, was to provide a provisionally acceptable solution to the contrast between a finite particular cosmion and an absolute and unitary meaning at which it aimed. Whatever the configuration of ideas may be, any "attempt to create an absolute cosmos out of the finite forces of human desire and will, . . . may be called magic." Once the "shelter-function" of the cosmion was understood in this way, it became clear that the purpose of political ideas, as Voegelin used the term in 1939, was only to a limited extent descriptive. Its "primary function is not a cognitive but a formative one," not a descriptive term but a creative and evocative term. Here Voegelin quoted Schelling: it is not the nation that produces the myth but the myth that produces the nation. This evocative power of linguistic symbols was a "primitive magic" that enabled humans to transform the chaotic and amorphous field of human forces, emotions, and anxieties into an "ordered unit."

Since by this argument the primary function of language was to shape sentiments to constitute political reality, another problem arose when language was used to describe the result theoretically. This remained a continuing problem for political science because it has always been possible to use language terms that refer to nothing real, which is to say to something imaginary, even though we presume that, in using a term, it actually referred to something real. And the problem was particularly vexing because there was "no clear division between evocative and descriptive language in political thought." Thus one must enquire into a number of different elements:

> The primary purpose of the political idea is to evoke a political unit, the cosmion of order, into existence; once this purpose is achieved, the cosmion is a real social and political force in history; and then a series of descriptive processes sets in, trying to describe the magic unit as something not magically but empirically real.

As a result, we are faced with a wealth of political theories that all tried to describe the magic unit as empirically or objectively real, from mechanical forces to organisms, from contracts to a collective soul. All these "theories," which were intended to be descriptive, were still evocative "magic adventures."

Voegelin developed further his sense of a political idea in a letter to Schütz in 1945.

> Ideas, especially political ideas, are not theoretical propositions concerning reality but part of reality themselves. I discussed the reality-character of ideas in the introduction to volume one under the term of "Evocation." Let me give you a few concrete examples that have gained mass relevancy. 1) If the Germans talk long enough about being "encircled," in the end the encircling will become a reality. 2) If the Western democracies talk about German aggression long enough, in the end the Germans really will turn aggressive. . . . Or, applied to phenomenalism: If one insists long enough that the only knowledge of reality we have is that which can be known through the categories of natural science, then the reality of moral substance does indeed disappear. (CW, 29:439; cf. CW, 10:27ff)

Voegelin's developing understanding of ideas as evocative magic adventures confirmed the remarks of Macmillan's second reviewer as well as Voegelin's statement that an Introduction that described his use of the term "idea" would be desirable.

In fact, as Gebhardt pointed out (CW, 25:12), Voegelin introduced the notion of political idea as a state-creating component of the reality of the state, that is an evocation, that originated in fundamental human experiences, which he earlier called sentiments, namely those of the person and of the community, as early as 1933 in *Race and State* (CW, 2:4–5; see also von Sivers, CW, 20:6 n. 13). Thus the idea of the community, which actually undertook the "shelter-function," lived in the individual members who happened to be sheltered by the institutions of an actual community. They directly experienced the spiritual world constituting the community. "Objectively" the community was the realization of the idea; "subjectively" the idea was generated in the minds of the individuals who sustained the idea and so constituted the community. The idea, thus, was the "real substance that appears as the one [community] in the many" individuals (CW, 2:117). As Voegelin wrote to Schütz later in 1945, he thought that this use of the term "cosmion" was "especially appropriate for the political realm of meaning because here it is an empirical fact that, in the actual constitutions [of order], meaning is bestowed by analogy to cosmic order. The political cosmion is a cosmic analogy."[19]

In short, once the political community had been magically evoked, it existed as a real, empirical, political, and historical force. As noted above, Voegelin called these new developments—the "theories" of ethnicity, a social contract, a collective soul and so on—"ancillary political ideas" because their purpose was to re-create the cosmion by continuous or "live" evocations. And, of course, these ancillary political ideas could be doubted—perhaps, indeed, more easily than the original magical evocation. When the magic was no longer effective, new problems emerged, from skepticism to "realism" that saw through the magic and introduced immanent explanations for political action: tradition, heredity, lust for power, *etc*. "Disenchantment," the Weberian term for such realism, then produced a spirit of revolt and introduced yet another meaning to the term "political idea." When the original

19 *Friendship that Lasted a Lifetime*, 104; CW, 29:447. For an account of the origin and use of the term "cosmion" by Voegelin and Schütz, see Ilja Srubar, *Kosmion: Die Genese der pragmatischen Lebensweltheorie von Alfred Schütz und ihr anthropologischer Hintergrund* (Frankfurt: Suhrkamp, 1988).

evocative power of an idea had been shattered by disenchanting analysis, the result may be an ideology or a utopian dream. These (Mannheimian) options had always been present because "there are always men who wish to overcome the misery of the finite imperfection of the political cosmion by the invention of an order of intrinsic value that would settle definitively the struggle of the evocative forces." Such dreams invariably eliminated one or another aspect of human nature. Indeed, some persons dreamed of abolishing the political order entirely.

> A thinker who interprets man may detest the phenomenon of political order and wish to eradicate it, but he cannot ignore it. He has to take into account the experience of life and death, of the anxiety of existence, and of the desire and force to create out of the perishable existence a cosmic analogy. The problem of politics has to be considered in the larger setting of an interpretation of human nature.

We have been returned, that is, to the question of philosophical anthropology.[20]

On the basis of the foregoing argument regarding evocative ideas, Voegelin proposed a strict meaning to the term "political theory," namely "the product of a detached contemplation of political reality." Because all humans beings, including aspiring political theorists, were part of a political cosmion and participated in its evocation, all that most theorists could accomplish was a degree of detachment beyond the daily struggles that preoccupied and engulfed their fellow citizens. Moreover, as he wrote to Hermann Broch in 1945 in response to a memorandum Broch sent him about protecting the dignity of man, "there are times in history where you can do nothing but sit back and wait until the plague had reached the end of its stench, and meanwhile try to keep alive and do your own work to the best of your lights" (CW, 29:425; cf. HI, 8:42). Whether during war or peace, however, the distinction between political theory and political idea was determined by the different attitudes or sentiments behind them, namely contemplation and evocation, not the different kinds of words they used. By seeking to explain what the political cosmion was, namely a magical entity, and what it attempted to do, namely provide an absolute shelter of meaning, the consequences of political theory may be, to the inhabitants of the

20 See Cooper, *Eric Voegelin and the Foundations of Modern Political Science*, ch. 5.

cosmion, indistinguishable from deliberate acts of disenchantment or deliberate and subversive new evocations.

Accordingly, every theorist must deal with resistance from the political forces of the cosmion because for them the detached contemplation and analysis of the meaning of the cosmion were taboo. As a further consequence, therefore, political theory tended to be an individual rather than an institutional endeavor. No political order has ever tolerated an "intellectual enterprise that questions the value of its cosmic analogy." And those who did explore "this delicate subject-matter" were typically reluctant to hand over the results of their enquiry to the general public. Voegelin's position in this respect, Gebhardt observed, "comes close to Leo Strauss's understanding of philosophy as an esoteric enterprise" (CW, 29:53; cf. CW 29:243; CW, 25:19).

The concluding few pages of the 1939 "Introduction" consisted of Voegelin's reflections on the relationship between the history of political ideas and the history of political theories. As Gebhardt said, "the confrontation of the two forces—contemplation and evocation—remained a vexing problem in Voegelin's overall hermeneutical scheme of a historical sequence of types of evocation" (CW, 29:54). To consider the history of political ideas as creating the history of political theories, as with Hegel or Marx, was as misleading as to consider the history of political theories as the accumulation of evermore systematic knowledge of political ideas. Even so, it was not entirely a waste of time to construct a history of political theory around the great personalities of the "tradition," from Plato and Aristotle to Machiavelli, Hobbes, Marx, etc. Nor was it entirely misleading to divide the history of Western political ideas into the well-established institutional periods of early empire, polis, Christian empire, national state, etc. That is, even though there may be no continuity of theoretical contemplation, there are long periods of history characterized by the same or the same kind of evocation, within which one can find outstanding theoretical efforts to systematize the evocations of the period. Indeed, much (but not all) of the content of the *History* could be approximated as a dialectic of political ideas and political theories.[21]

A history of political ideas written by a political theorist would by this argument consist of an account of a gradual growth of theory from an evocative situation leading to the abandonment of the theoretical position under

21 This was approximately Voegelin's position in "Political Theory and the Pattern of General History," a paper given at the APSA in 1944. See CW, 10:157ff.

the pressure of a new evocation. This process of evocation, theoretical analysis or "penetration" and subsequent dissolution furnished "the rough general structure of the history." Applying the approach to the selection of materials to be included in the *History* did not mean beginning with the Greeks. Granted, the Greeks may have created the first major theoretical account of politics, but they did so on the basis of pre-existing and pre-theoretical evocations. Moreover, their achievements were hardly decisive for subsequent imperial evocations of the Ancient Near East—as with Alexander, for example. Moreover, regarding the pre-polis empires of the Ancient Near East,

> a good point could even be made for starting with an analysis of more primitive stages of human society, because their traces can be found in the later history. There are certainly the reflections of a *gynaiocratic* stage of development to be found in Plato's idea of a community of women, in the role of Diotima, in certain remarks of Saint Paul, in the [Carpocratian and similar Gnostic accounts] as reported by Clemens Alexandrinus, as still in certain formulas expressing the equality of women in the *Codex Iustinianus*. Primitive ideas of the totemistic period reach into the structure of the Greek polis, of the Christian communities' and the Mithras communities' ideas of Roman soldiers. But considering the space at my disposition I thought it better to confine myself to an occasional remark concerning those problems, and in general not to go further back than the early Asiatic empires.

Voegelin deviated from the conventional approach because he sought to describe the connection between one evocative situation—the Greek, for example—with another—the imperial Near Eastern, for example. Obviously, if the materials were known, it would be possible to describe even earlier evocations, the "more primitive stages of human society." The later developments were better known: from the Diadochic empires to the Roman and Sassanian, the effects of the Germanic tribes on dividing the Roman Empire again into East and West, the evocations of the Byzantine and Islamic empires in the East and the Carolingian in the West, the renewed contacts by way of the Crusades and the recovery of eastern learning in the West, a period made more complex because of the new evocations of nations and states starting in the fifteenth century and the current ambiguity of the persistence of nation-states during a period we now conventionally characterize in terms of globalization. Voegelin's point here reiterated the observation made above, that a proper history of political ideas consisted in an analysis of the relationship of sentiments and evocations and how they changed historically. To recall the earlier example, the political science of Aristotle, which was animated by the sentiments of polis-life, could not simply be applied to a nation state or to the medieval *Sacrum Imperium*.

Voegelin made several subsequent statements that reaffirmed one or another aspect of the 1939 "Introduction." We already noted the panel discussion at the annual meeting of the American Political Science Association (CW, 10:157ff). Likewise in *The New Science of Politics* (1952) Voegelin spent some time distinguishing the "language symbols" that constituted the meaning of political life in the cosmion and identical words that constituted the vocabulary of political theory (CW, 5:109ff.).[22] That is, the distinction between the language symbols as evocative ideas and language symbols as constituents of theory or of science remained an important one. Once again there were slightly differing interpretations of the significance of this distinction.

Hollweck and Sandoz's commentary on Voegelin's "Introduction" to the History began by noting that the question Voegelin posed was "whether political societies represent a truth that legitimizes their existence or whether the political is ultimately little more than an imaginative construct that has no ontological foundation" (CW, 19:18). They drew a parallel with the "Introduction" to *Order and History*: "God and man, world and society form a primordial community of being" (CW, 14:39), but also emphasized the difference that, in the earlier text "the cosmic community has not yet become a partnership." Instead, in the "Introduction" of 1939, "the whole burden of making sense of his life rests on man" (CW, 19:18). In one sense this was surely correct. One may believe that the gods or God created the political cosmion and to that extent there was a partnership between human beings and divine being. On the other hand, whatever divine being had to do with the political cosmion, divine being was also evoked by the human believer, which was the aspect of the process Voegelin emphasized in the 1939 "Introduction."

Hollweck and Sandoz's second point also seemed incontestable: "the ideas that constitute a substantial part of the political cosmion and give meaning and institutionalized shelter to the individual life do so at a very high price: the price of the truth of human existence" (CW, 19:19). Living

22 See also Cooper, *Foundations*, ch. 9.

within a meaningful but finite cosmion, humans have been apt to think they were operating within the absoluteness of the cosmos. The apolitism of monastic contemplation, for example, reminded all human beings that it was merely an analogue to the absolute cosmos. The forgetfulness of humans in this respect was expressed in their belief in "magic."

Third, the theorist contemplating the "magic web of ideas and institutions" could not, at least by intention, be taken in by it. Contemplative theorists did not believe in magic. This was what put them at odds with their societies and occasionally put them in opposition to, or in conflict with, their societies. The paradigmatic cases were Socrates and Jeremiah.

Fourth, politics had to be understood within the context of human nature, which is to say, in light of a philosophical anthropology. Accordingly, the disjunction and possible conflict between political idea and political theory could not be resolved either in theory or in practice, which was itself evidence of "the existential uncertainly that again and again calls for the imaginative evocations that are meant to assuage our anxieties and give us a tentative foothold in reality" (CW, 19:22–23).

Fifth, this pattern of contemplative theory and evocative idea, and of their interaction, must be understood as a fundamental reality, "as a structure of consciousness," to use a later formulation (CW, 19:24). The ideas constituted evocations of the "fundamental human substance" and theory constituted an account of it that, at least in principle, included a philosophical anthropology.

Sixth, although it remained true that evocative political ideas helped constitute political reality, there was more to political reality than that which was articulated or articulated itself as ideas. This was why, instead of using the phrase "history of ideas" it was more accurate, as Voegelin noted in his "Autobiographical Statement at Age Eighty-two" to speak of a history of experiences (CW, 33:442). The specific event that apparently caused Voegelin to reconsider his argument regarding ideas and theories was, based on his reading of Schelling's philosophy of myth, the realization that an Egyptian coronation ritual or the ceremonial reading of the *Enuma Elish* was not the evocation of an idea and even less a theory (CW, 34:90). To provide a provisionally adequate account of what such events actually were required an understanding of the range of human experience, the forms it took, and the modes of human consciousness that were expressed in such symbolic complexes and were described by terms such as myth and revelation. That was the subject-matter of philosophy of consciousness.

In this section on "Evocation and Theory" we have argued that Voegelin's analytical language changed during the decade after 1940. By the later 1940s he no longer distinguished between ideas and sentiments as he did in the 1939 "Introduction." The process of what in *The New Science of Politics* he would call "critical clarification" was under way during this period, with the result that certain inconsistencies—in the use of the term "idea," for example—remained. The initial argument regarding sentiments and evocations was partly retained in the distinction between ideas and theories. That is, the clarification of the relationship of sentiments, evocations, ideas, cosmion, and then of experiences and symbolization, began around 1943 and continued for about a decade. And at the same time, as was indicated, Voegelin began, or rather continued, his reflections of philosophy of consciousness, to which we now turn.

3. Remembrance

Voegelin's retrospective accounts of his later perspective in the *Autobiographical Reflections* and the "Autobiographical Statement" may easily suggest a simple change in his "point of view," to use the language of the 1948 report to Macmillan. It would be more accurate to describe the process of clarification as rhythmic or intermittent, with the discovery of new problems taking, in some instances, several years to be resolved, then reflectively digested, and finally integrated with preceding formulations in such a way that Voegelin could undertake additional analyses. In particular, the relationship between the theorist and the ideas he contemplated and for which he provided a philosophically acceptable account remained unclear. Beginning in the fall of 1940 in an exchange of letters with Schütz that continued over the next few years and was devoted to a discussion of Edmund Husserl and phenomenology, Voegelin developed a provisionally satisfactory account of the problem, but it took several years more to work out the implications so far as the *History* and the sequence of what he came to call evocative ideas was concerned.

In the fall of 1939, Voegelin asked Schütz to send the "Introduction" to their mutual friend, Max Mintz, for his comments. Mintz replied the following March and sharpened the issue of the attitude of the theorist or the political scientist to the sentiments and evocations and ideas he studied. Mintz observed that Voegelin was writing a history of political ideas that included political theory, which is to say the *History* was to be "systematic." Why, Mintz then asked, did Voegelin not discuss the motives of those theorists who concealed their results from the public? "Or do you mean to say that the historian [of political ideas] has to be a theorist as well—at least to the extent that he shares this prudent discretion" of hiding the results of his theory from the public? (HI, 21:33). Mintz, as Gebhardt, had noticed an "esoteric" element to Voegelin's work.

Voegelin replied a couple of weeks later noting, first, that he had changed his mind a number of times on

> the question of "history and theory": at the moment I tend more to the view that the two, at least as far as political theory is concerned, cannot be separated. A systematic depiction of theory today—not in other periods—must reflect on the history of ideas in order to show that certain problems, and which ones, are tied to historical phases. And vice versa: I don't think a history can be good unless it is presented against the background of a system. The Introduction is *not* itself history, but it suggests, if only very roughly, a few points concerning the background of the system. As to the questionable comment, that it is wiser to keep quiet about certain things, this touches on the existential problem of theory that Aristotle raised when he stated that theory is the theorist's conduct of life [*Lebenspraxis*]. Theory is not just a statement about objects but a way of life [*Lebenshaltung*] in regard to them; radical contemplation implies the refusal to let oneself get involved with the objects because the value of getting involved is doubtful. On the other hand, the withdrawal from political reality is also an action taken in relationship to that reality, especially when the results of one's contemplation are published and transmitted to others. This raises rather curious questions: Isn't an attitude of radical contemplation self-contradictory? Perhaps it is immoral because it destroys the magic of the idea, which is the soul of praxis. And as long as life is lived, [the soul of which] is praxis, it is only possible within the magic of an idea. The practice of contemplation is strictly individual, solitary, and cannot construct a social order; therefore should it not, as Plato maintained, be kept secret, at least as far as its most disturbing results are concerned? But then again, it must be cultivated, because otherwise every idea that emerges at some point in history would have to remain sacrosanct and could not be criticized. But this, again, would be immoral, because it would

> make moral development toward higher forms of social order impossible. That would be the result: that "progress" with a *good* conscience would only be possible if a thinker were clever enough to criticize and to destroy, and at the same time stupid enough to believe that he himself had found the solution to the problems through his new magic? For Plato, the answer is that it is forbidden to record the wise men's secrets in writing.
>
> Please excuse the length of this explanation; it has troubled me for many years, and I don't know what to do about it. (CW, 29:244–45)

For the next couple of years the problem remained unaddressed in Voegelin's correspondence. The problem of the relationship of the theorist to political ideas, however, continued to "trouble" him, as the letter to Mintz clearly indicated. The reason was clear enough and can be stated with precision. Political ideas, as Voegelin used the term in the early 1940s, were not descriptions of political reality but had the purpose of creating a meaningful image of a group as a political unit capable of enacting political history. Or: political symbols, as Voegelin later would refer to such phenomena, helped constitute political reality by providing the political community with a meaningful image of itself (cf. CW, 10:27–28). As Voegelin wrote to Schütz in September 1945, the purpose of an idea was to evoke reality, not describe it (CW, 29:439). Moreover, as noted above, this evocative power of ideas was described as "magical" inasmuch as it brought political order into existence as a cosmion that was in turn defended by human beings who find it to be meaningful.

The theorist who reflects on this process, however, was in a precarious position, as the letter to Mintz so clearly indicated. On the one hand, the theorist was a human being and so was bound to the magical evocation of a particular cosmion, which is to say the theorist was a member of a particular political order. But as a theorist contemplating the evocative forces at play in politics, the cosmion was not magic and was not an absolute source of meaning. Hence the problem of disenchantment and the inevitable conflict between the theorist and persons whose sentiments ensure that the cosmion remained a meaningful evocation. The dramatic examples of Socrates and Jeremiah could be recast in terms of a theoretical as well as an existential questions: what was the position of the theorist with respect to the historical process? To answer that question the theorists had to reflect on his or her own motives because: (1) the theorist, willy-nilly, was a member of, and participant in, some political community; and (2) by seeking to understand the process of evocation, the theorist would be seen by the community as critical of it, subversive, and so on; but (3) the theorist was incapable of evoking another cosmion under pain of abandoning the vocation of theorist.

Voegelin had worked through this problem *de facto* during the 1930s but had not reflected on its significance as a general problem of theoretical consciousness or philosophical existence.[23] Now he was conscious of what he had done and, more important, was aware to the need to clarify further the characteristics of a contemplative life. The occasion arose in the fall of 1943 in an exchange between Voegelin and Schütz regarding the significance of Husserl's 1936 lecture on the *Crisis of the European Sciences and Transcendental Phenomenology*.[24] Voegelin's remarks on Husserl ranged far beyond the immediate problem of reflection on his own motivations as a theorist.

Voegelin and Schütz had long disagreed about Husserl (CW, 29:291). In 1940, for example, Voegelin wrote to Schütz that his friend's account of Husserl's working habits struck Voegelin as being distinctly odd.

> I shudder at the thought of the forty thousand pages that have not yet been published. As an intellectual phenomenon, Husserl appears more and more strange to me all the time. The idea of sitting down every day for three hours and recording a process of thought *in continuo* in shorthand, with all the unavoidable repetitions and irrelevancies which that entails, borders on the pathological. I get the impression of a type of agoraphobia: As he wanders through intellectual space, in the middle of adventure, everything must be immediately transcribed into words and these must be reworked. And then there is the odd interpretation of the compulsion to write everything down as "conscientiousness."[25]

We have already quoted from Voegelin's letter to Schütz of 16 January 1943 where he drew attention to "the spiritual personality of the thinker" as an important factor in conditioning the sentiments that were expressed in

23 Or so I argued in *Beginning the Quest*.

24 Trans. David Carr (Evanston: Northwestern University Press, 1970).

25 *A Friendship*, 21.

the political ideas of, in this instance, St. Thomas Aquinas.[26] This theme reappeared in the course of a long letter to Schütz dated 17 September 1943.[27]

Voegelin began by noting that Husserl's style had improved in the *Crisis* lectures and stated that it was a significant epistemological achievement. But, he added, epistemology was a prelude to philosophy and Voegelin found no reason to expect anything more from the forty thousand unpublished pages. Moreover, he indicated why, on the basis of the *Crisis* lecture "nothing more in a philosophically fundamental sense is to be expected." The reason, very simply, was that Husserl's conception of history was "Victorian." All that counted in the history of humanity was ancient Greek philosophy followed by modern European philosophy, starting in the Italian Renaissance. The European Middle Ages were no more than "a superfluous interlude" and the Indians and Chinese "are slightly ridiculous curiosities found on the periphery of the flat earth, at the center of which we find not Western man, but humanity per se." Such "demonic historiography," Voegelin said, ensured first that Husserl's position was irrefutably absolute, and second that he was then in a position to misappropriate the historical material in support of his own philosophy. As a consequence, the Husserlian "transcendental philosopher" becomes a "functionary of mankind."

Husserl was led to these unfortunate results because he was, despite his claims, not a radical philosopher in the sense that he had no clear notion of the roots of his own thinking. He lacked, Voegelin said, an attitude of "philosophic existence," preferring instead to adopt both an Averroistic notion of a collective soul, confined moreover to the Europeans who knew how to philosophize in Husserl's manner (the Indians and the Chinese and other non-phenomenological philosophers being mere "anthropological types"), and a notion that human progress ended with his phenomenological philosophy. In this respect Husserl was far less systematic in his thinking than was Kant who was at least astonished or puzzled (*befremden*) by the implications of a final realm of phenomenal truth: "Husserl's radicalism has a messianic component in which the final establishment, with its apodicticity in the

26 *A Friendship*, 26; CW, 29:352.

27 Subsequent quotations are from this document. See *Friendship*, 30–43; CW, 29:363–79. See also Cooper, *Foundations*, 178–84. Other translations are available in Peter Emberley and Barry Cooper, eds. and trans., *Faith and Political Philosophy: The Correspondence between Leo Strauss and Eric Voegelin, 1934–1964* (University Park: Penn State University Press, 1993) 19–34 and CW, 6:45–61. The German original is in *Anamnesis* (Munich: Piper, 1966), 21–36.

realm of the social and historical, turns into the establishment of an apocalyptic philosophical sect."

The proper task of a "history of the Spirit" (*Geist*), Voegelin added,

> is to penetrate each historical-spiritual position to the point at which it rests in itself, i.e., in which it is rooted in the author's own experience of transcendence. Only when [spiritual or] intellectual history [*Geistesgeschichte*] is carried out with this methodological goal can it attain its philosophical goal of understanding the spirit in its historicity, or, to put it another way, to be able to understand the historical expression [*Ausformungen*] of the spirit as variations on the theme of experiences of transcendence. Such variations follow one another, not arbitrarily, but empirically and factually.

The variations on experiences of transcendence, Voegelin argued, were not a disconnected series but expressed "sequences" or "configurations" of order. The purpose of such a "historical meditation" was not to interpret "the thinker's precious position" as the culmination of history, but "to penetrate the other thinker's spiritual-historical form [*Gestalt*] to the point of transcendence and, in such a penetration, to train and clarify one's own expression of experiences of transcendence." The empirical result would be a philosophy of history and the condition for it was for the theorist to understand the "personal testimonies" or "self-testimonies" of the thinkers themselves by means of the meditative exegesis of the surviving texts.

As an example of what not to do, Voegelin criticized Husserl's misinterpretation of Descartes on the grounds that it ignored the experiential context of Descartes' meditations, namely the experience of transcendence.

> I don't know whether Husserl was insensitive to experiences of transcendence, whether he drew back from them in fear, or whether there is a biographical matter involved—that he had distanced himself from Jewish religiosity but did not wish to take up Christian religiosity. In any case, in order to ground his position he took recourse to the immanence of a historical problematic and very carefully barred the way to the problematic of philosophic transcendence—the decisive problems of philosophy.

Voegelin's next step was to undertake his own "radical reflection" or "radical meditation" on the decisive problems of philosophical transcendence that Husserl refused to take. The literary product was his *anamneses* or "Anamnetic Experiments" of 1943 and the essay "On the Theory of Consciousness."[28] Part One of *Anamnesis* is called "Remembrance" and consists of four chapters, "In Memoriam Alfred Schütz," the letter to Schütz on Husserl just discussed, and the two other chapters just noted. Together they form a "meditative unit," not least of all because the last three were written between September and November, 1943. The "experiments" were written in the hopes of uncovering "the experiences that, in my case, motivate the philosophizing consciousness," and consisted in twenty recollections of Voegelin's experiences prior to the age of ten (CW, 6:84–98).[29] The theory of consciousness was written afterwards.

The "experiments" were, no doubt, charming vignettes and reveal, as Walsh observed, a "somewhat precocious, inquisitive, self-important, and imaginatively sensitive young boy" (CW, 6:6). In 1946, Voegelin was asked by the editor of the *Sewanee Review*, J. E. Palmer, if he might contribute to that journal. Voegelin turned down a couple of suggestions and indicated that perhaps Palmer would be interested in his essay on "Nietzsche and Pascal" or a reworked essay on "the cycle theory of history" that he had presented to the Southern Political Science Association (CW, 25:251; 33:41). "If," he went on,

> you would rather have something on the literary side, I have also lying around an MS entitled *Anamnesis*. It is an intellectual autobiography of my first ten years. The crazy thing originated in a correspondence with a friend on the question of whether the

28 Both texts are in *Anamnesis*, CW, 6:62–98. References are to this text, sometimes slightly altered in light of the original (1966) *Anamnesis*. See also Cooper, *Foundations*, 187–207.

29 The holograph of the "Anamnetic Experiments" is titled "Materials on the Genesis of Consciousness of Time" (HI, 72:14; 111:281; 117:2). There are very few changes between the holograph and the printed version apart from the insertion of number 13, "The Comet," and the renumbering of the recollections that followed. In *Anamnesis*, as Voegelin explained to Dante Germino (7 February 1971), the "experiments" were followed by a "selection" of materials taken from chapters of the *History* among other sources, "in order to bring out the high-points of anamnetic reconstruction of a theory of consciousness, which happens to be the centerpiece to political science" (HI, 14:14).

> Cartesian type of meditation is a legitimate approach to a philosophy of the mind. I denied the legitimacy on the ground that the life of the spirit and intellect is historical in the strict sense, and that the determinants of mature philosophical speculation have to be sought in the mythical formation of the mind in experiences of early youth. In order to prove my point, I made anamnetic experiments on myself and collected twenty-odd such early experiences which determined my later metaphysical attitudes. The thing is of objective importance; the autobiographical element is of little relevance. (CW, 29:480)

The only problem was that, because "the myths of childhood are fragile" Voegelin wrote his descriptions in the only language of which he was then a master, namely German, so they would have to be translated. In the event, Palmer declined to publish them (HI, 36:8).

Voegelin, however, thought they were important, and not simply important enough to be published but, as Gebhardt noted, he "attached such great importance to his anamnetic experiments that he gave a facsimile of the holograph to each member of his Munich staff when he departed for America" (CW, 29:56). The document may be summarized as consisting of recollections of the "excitements" that agitated his consciousness when he experienced several different kinds of transcendence of consciousness: into the body, the world, the community, history, space, time, wishful spaces, wishful times, the Ground of Being, and a mysterious Beyond.[30] The "Theory of Consciousness" was written as a four-part reflective analysis of the results of the recollections.

Voegelin's motive in conducting the experiments and analyzing the results, was to clarify the attitude of the theorist with respect to the materials,

30 For a brief analysis see Cooper, *Foundations*, 196ff. Eugene Webb, *Eric Voegelin: Philosopher of History* (Seattle: University of Washington Press, 1981), 35ff, said they dealt with "wonder, awe, fear, perplexity and longing." Voegelin's friend, Gregor Sebba, provided him with a Jungian account of Number 7, the "Cloud Castle," which Voegelin said did not have a clear meaning (HI, 35:7). See also Thomas W. Heilke, "Anamnetic Tales: The Place of Narrative in Eric Voegelin's Account of Consciousness," *Review of Politics* 58 (1996): 761–92; Lewis P. Simpson, "Voegelin and the Story of the Clerks," in Ellis Sandoz, ed., *Eric Voegelin's Significance for the Modern Mind* (Baton Rouge: LSU Press, 1991), 108–9. See also Charles R. Embry, *The Philosopher and the Story-Teller: Eric Voegelin and Twentieth-Century Literature* (Columbia: University of Missouri Press, 2008), 37.

namely the evocation of the cosmion by way of political ideas. The "Theory of Consciousness" initially arose, Voegelin said, because of his discontent with the "problem area" he had discussed with Schütz, namely time-consciousness. Time-consciousness of intramundane human existence, Voegelin argued, was a modern replacement for meditation that had existed from a time before Christian categories dissolved; it amounted to a "laicist residue of the Christian assurance of existence in meditation with its spiritual climax of the *intentio animi* [tension/intension of the soul/mind] toward God" (CW, 6:62). Most of the philosophical accounts of time-consciousness focused on the body as the sensorium and condition of consciousness. But this approach typically turned into a reductionist conclusion that the body was the cause or determinant of consciousness rather than that consciousness was "anchored" in the body, as had been argued by contemporary philosophical anthropologists upon whom Voegelin relied such as Portmann and Scheler.

Such a reductionism was obviously incompatible with the results of the "experiments" that dealt with the phenomena of sleep, dreams and other subconscious psychic processes. Moreover, "in experience, consciousness and its structures, whatever they may be, is a given antecedent." Thus it was not consciousness of time that was generated by the "flow" of time but the experience of flow that was generated by a consciousness that did not flow. Accordingly, speculation about the stream of consciousness could be a substitute for meditation because it led consciousness towards transcendence—either into the body or into the Ground of Being, but in both cases the transcendence was not a datum of consciousness.[31]

The starting point for describing the structure of consciousness, he said, was the phenomenon of attention and the focusing of attention. Moreover, "the consistent practice of concentration results in an increased capacity of concentration." And this centre of energy that could be concentrated or dispersed could not be observed from without. "Rather, it has the character of an inner 'illumination,' i.e., it is not blind but can be experienced in its inner

31 Voegelin here drew attention that he had been interested in the problem of time-consciousness since the 1920s, See CW, 1:23–63. The term "Ground of Being" is used here as an "ontological hypothesis without which the actually experienced ontic nexus [*ontische Zusammenhang*] in human existence remains incomprehensible" (CW, 6:80).We discuss this passage in more detail below in this chapter. Clarification of the term and formulation of a more precise description of the reality to which it referred was a major problem that Voegelin pursued in his later work. We discuss the several steps in its clarification in subsequent chapters.

dimensions of past and future," as distinct from the external past and future of dates and times.

> In the illuminative dimensions of past and future, one becomes aware not of empty spaces but of structures of a finite process between birth and death. The experience of consciousness is the experience of a process—the only process we know "from within." Because of this characteristic quality, the process of consciousness becomes the model of the process as such, the only experiential model to serve as the orientation point of the conceptual apparatus through which we must also grasp the process that transcends consciousness. The conflict between the finiteness of the model of experience and the "infinite" character of other processes results in a number of fundamental problems. (CW, 6:69)

A second and, for political science more interesting, "problem area" concerned the formation of myths.

> Since processes transcending consciousness are not internally experienceable and since for purposes of characterizing their structure we have no other symbols available than those developed during other finite experiences, conflicts of expression occur. These conflicts are, if not the only, still the most important root of the formation of myths. A mythical symbol is a finite symbol intended to provide "transparence" for a transfinite process: for example, a myth of creation, which renders transparent the problem of the beginning of a transfinite process of the world; an immaculate conception, which mediates the experience of a transfinite spiritual beginning; an anthropomorphic image of God, which finitizes an experience of transcendence; speculation about the preexistence or postexistence of the soul, which provide a finite formula for the beyond of birth and death; the fall and original sin, which illuminate the mystery of finite existence through procreation and death; and so on.[32]

32 CW, 6:70. In his later work, Voegelin provided more precise descriptions of myth that were nevertheless compatible with this one. See, for example, CW, 11:233; 33:189. The problem is discussed below in chapter four.

There is, Voegelin noticed, a "tendency" to spiritualize the physical mythical symbols, from polytheistic myths with several "physical" gods to monotheism and within a monotheistic myth there was a further tendency to conceptualize a deity without physical attributes. Plato, in particular, used creation myths as an instrument of philosophy in order to express the experience of transcendence. Possibly, Voegelin said, he did so "because he felt that the myth is a more precise instrument than speculation for communicating the spiritual excitation of the experience of transcendence. Besides, speculation is not an instrument that everyone can handle safely." Moreover, with Plato, we find an additional problem: he used two myths to render the experience of limit, one in the *Republic* and a "superior" one in the *Laws* (645a ff.). The myth of metals in the soul in the *Republic* (415a ff.) was "pragmatic" in the sense that it was useful "as an external expedient to hold together a human community." Accordingly, it was "emotionally well-nigh indifferent." In contrast, the myth of the metal threads by which the gods guide men like puppets more adequately symbolized "the nodal point of determinants that we call, respectively, the 'I' and 'world-transcendent being.'" The emotional intensity of the myth in the *Laws* "evoked the 'shudder' of transcendence, the 'numinous' in the sense of Rudolf Otto" (CW, 6:71).

The problem of "conscious" or "philosophical" myths and the problem that brought Plato to revise the myths from the *Republic* to the *Laws* "seems to throw some light on *Geistesgeschichte*," intellectual/spiritual history. Both myths dealt with the other as human and thus equal to us even though we can have no "inner experience" of the other. For Voegelin, the transcendence of other human beings, just as the transcendence of nature, was not a problem of Husserlian "constitution" by perceptual consciousness, but a given that finds expression in myth.

> Historically we know of only two original myths of equality: the myth of equality of children by virtue of their origin in the same mother's womb, and the myth of equality of children created in the spiritual mold of the same father. All other ideas of equality are demonstrably historical derivatives of one or the other of these two myths. Only *within* the framework of these myths can one stake out the epistemological problems of knowing the Thou. (CW, 6:72)

The basic function of myth, Voegelin said, was "to render transcendence finite" [*die Transzendenz zu finitisieren*], which was attested historically "mostly in the appearance of finite mystically unified human communities that present human being as such in their own image." Conflicting myths may be expressions of conflicts between communities, the extreme form of which was the denial of full humanity to members of a rival community. And within any single community there may be pressure to standardize the variant of transcendence that the respective myth was able to encompass. "The problem is of major spiritual-historical [*geistesgeschichtlich*] importance, since human consciousness, occurring in a multitude of successive and simultaneous exemplars, shows a wide range of variations of experiences of transcendence and their articulation, which is what we call the history of spirit [*Geschichte des Geistes*]." Not everyone in a given community would respond positively to the prevailing myth—particularly in monotheistic communities some of whose members "feel a need for orgiastic cults" (CW, 6:74). Such cults provided access to experiences of transcendence, chiefly by way of the body.

In the polis community of Plato and Aristotle, the polytheistic myths were acceptable both to the philosophers, who used them instrumentally, and to the political "gentleman" (*kalos k'agthos*). But beneath these two social strata were "mystery cults and orgiastic cults of which we know but little." Likewise in the monotheistic Israelite myth of the "chosen people" there were "idolaters," that is, members of the community who needed the orgiastic cults to express their experience of transcendence. And so too today, under the dissolving effects of western rationalism and its myth,

> for ever-increasing masses of people, the sensual myths of the Christian tradition are in the process of dissolving, while spiritualized expressions of the experience of transcendence in intellectual mysticism and philosophical speculation are accessible only to a small minority. The inevitable result is the phenomenon of "forlornness" [*Verlorenheit*] in a world that has no more fixed points in the myth. People, of course, do not cease to have experiences of transcendence, but these experiences remain in the psychic strata of shudder and anxiety [*Angst*]; they cannot productively contribute to the creation of an order of symbols through which the transfinite process, which cannot be experienced internally, can be made comprehensible in the transparency of the myth. In the social dynamics of our time, the most important symptoms are the "movements" that in part have obvious orgiastic character, and "great wars." The wars are

> symptomatic not only insofar as they must be endured. Actions that might prevent these wars have become impossible because of a paralysis of the will to order, which can be active only where its meaning is secured in the community myth. (CW, 6:74)

The first two fundamental problem areas that Voegelin discussed in clarifying his own theoretical attitude were: (1) the inadequacies of conventional phenomenological philosophical investigations of consciousness, starting with time-consciousness, and (2) the problem of the myths.[33] The third section dealt with "process theology." By this term Voegelin indicated a symbolic system that attempted to express the relationship of consciousness to the world, which transcended consciousness, and the relationship of consciousness to the Ground of Being, which transcended the world. Voegelin allowed as he "was inclined to believe" that process theology and its enlargement, "a metaphysics that interprets the system of transcendence of the world as the immanent process of a divine substance, is the only meaningful systematic philosophy." In this context Voegelin referred explicitly to Schelling and his (Leibnitzian) questions: Why is there something? Why not nothing?[34]

Voegelin's reason for introducing Schelling's "attempt to interpret the world order that transcends consciousness" rested on two "experiential complexes," one of which was discussed in his letter to Schütz dealing with Husserl's *Crisis*, namely that in the experiential complex of meditation, consciousness was not ultimately directed towards the contents of the objective world but toward the non-objective Ground of Being. The second, discussed in this essay on the theory of consciousness, was that it was given in the human experience that consciousness was not confined to cognition. "Rather it is founded on animal, vegetative and inorganic being." Such a structure

> seems to be the ontic premise for man's ability to transcend himself toward the world, for in none of its directions of transcending does consciousness find a level of being that is not also one on which it itself is based. Speaking ontologically, consciousness

33 These two divisions were indicated clearly in the German edition; the division between the first and second parts is not evident in the English version. Compare *Anamnesis* (German), 45 with CW, 6:69.

34 We discuss "process theology" in more detail below in chapter eight.

> finds in the Order of Being of the world no level that it does not also experience as its own foundation.

In this foundational experience [*Fundamenterfahrung*] of consciousness, human being was present to itself as a microcosm. We do not know of what this "foundation [*Fundierung*] *really* consists" because all our experience is of differentiated levels of being so that

> the nature of their connections is inexperienceable, whether this nexus be the foundation of the vegetative in the inorganic, of the animal in the vegetative, or of human consciousness in the animal body. There is no doubt, however, *that* this base exists. Even though each level of being is clearly distinguishable with its own structure, there must be something common that makes their continuum in human existence possible. The base- [or foundational-] experience [*Fundamenterfahrung*] is further reinforced through the experience that we are dealing here not with a static complex but with intimate interrelationships in a process. (CW, 6:75–76)

The process of aging, for example, included both body and consciousness and we could "date" the succession of inner illuminations of consciousness by symbols of external time—as Voegelin did with his anamnetic experiments of October 25 –November 7, 1943.

The considerations that led Voegelin to discuss process theology and Schelling were based on the two aforementioned experiential complexes. To summarize the results: if the levels of being that constituted human existence—inorganic, vegetative, animal—were based on each other, if there were parallel processes in play, if human existence were part of the spatiotemporal and causal world, and, if consciousness could reflect on the world, then there must be, from the perspective of ontology, "substantive identity among the levels of being" and this substance could be interpreted only in terms of a process that unfolded to attain "its illumination phase in human consciousness." Accordingly: "the meditative complex of experiences in which the reality of the Ground of Being reveals itself then makes it necessary to ground the world-immanent process of being in a process within the Ground of Being." That is, consciousness was a process that occurred alongside other processes in the world; it is distinguished by the descriptor of being illuminated from within or, as Voegelin often said in his later work, by being "luminous," but is connected to these other "non-luminous" worldly processes as well. The process of consciousness, in the context of this philosophical anthropology, was the starting point for any philosophy of consciousness. On the basis of Voegelin's reflections to this point, one could provisionally conclude that "process consciousness" did "not have the form of the 'I,' but does nevertheless have both a center of energy with directional attentiveness and it is illuminated," or experienced, from within.

Voegelin then discussed in the fourth section the "illumination dimension" of past and future. In analyzing the first area of fundamental problems, namely that consciousness did not have the form of the "I," Voegelin argued that the past and future dimensions of consciousness were not "something like empty slates on which data can be entered" (CW, 6:68). When I remember something it is not because it "lies in the past" but rather I have a past because "I can make present a process of consciousness that is completed." Likewise, I do not project into the future; rather, I have a future because I can project. "Past and future," Voegelin said, "are the present illuminative dimensions of the process in which the energy center is engaged" (CW, 6:78). That is, past and future can be made present by directing attention to them. This is not, however, a kind of "solipsism of the moment" because human consciousness is not "pure" consciousness but is embodied and thus not separate from the spatio-temporal world. Granted, we can experience our consciousness only from within, and that "within" is neither spatial nor temporal; however, we must accept as an ontological hypothesis the substantive unity of human existence in order to grasp that the foundation [*Fundierung*] of consciousness is in the body and in matter even though that foundation cannot be experienced directly or conceptually grasped. Instead, we can experience indirectly and by interpretation grasp a human consciousness as consciousness-in-the-body and in-the-world. In this way, images, memories, and projects become incorporated into the "experiential nexus" [*Erfahrungzusammenhang*] of the history of the body and the external history of the world. By implication, the being of external nature without reference to consciousness is a "nothing." It only "turns into a process with time dimensions as its facts become historical dates for consciousness." There was, therefore, an intimate connection between the dating of consciousness and the external dates for that consciousness. "Reference to the natural processes provides consciousness with the evidence [*Korpus*] of its own process; the relation to the illuminated dimensions of past and future in consciousness provides natural being with the order of time; the intersection of these relations is the 'presence' of consciousness" (CW, 6:79).

Before drawing conclusions from his analysis, Voegelin situated his theory of consciousness in the familiar context of Kant's distinction of phenomena and noumena. He agreed with Kant that the experience of consciousness was not phenomenal but added that the noumena of reason

> are not the noumena of being as a whole. That being which is the Ground of all experienceable concrete being is an ontological hypothesis without which the actually experienced ontic nexus in human existence remains incomprehensible. But it is never a datum in human experience; rather, it is always strictly transcendent, which can be approached only through meditation. It cannot be drawn from the beyond of finiteness into finiteness itself. We remain, with our human finite-being, always within being. At one place, namely in consciousness, this being reaches the level of illumination. However, the illumination remains at this particular level; it illuminates neither the basic being of nature nor the Ground of Being. (CW, 6:80)

The imagery of illumination and of the luminosity or luminousness of consciousness have already been introduced a number of times by Voegelin. He did so to provide a contrast with Husserl's understanding of consciousness as constituting objects of which it is perceptually aware. We will have occasion to discuss the implications of luminosity below.[35]

On the basis of this argument Voegelin then formulated several "general principles for a philosophy of consciousness." First and most important: there was no absolute beginning or starting-point for a philosophy of consciousness because all such philosophizing was also an event in the philosopher's consciousness, and thus in the life history of the individual, the community, of humanity, and of the cosmos. That is, consciousness was embodied in a human being with a specific biography whose experience—as Voegelin indicated in his "experiments"—was present in memory. Thus no philosopher could ever turn consciousness into an object to be grasped. Rather, his reflection was "an orientation within consciousness with which he can push to its limits but never cross them." Moreover, since the philosopher, as everyone else, lived within the context of his own history, within

35 For an extensive and insightful treatment of the problem see David Walsh, *The Modern Philosophical Revolution: The Luminosity of Consciousness* (Cambridge: Cambridge University Press, 2008).

the history of human existence in the community and within the world, "systematic reflection on consciousness is a late event in the biography of a philosopher" (CW, 6:81). In other words, philosophical reflection or the activity of the theorist clarified his or her own prereflective experiences in such a way as to lead the theorist to ask about his own consciousness and about the communal, historical, physical and cosmic reality of which it was a part. This "asking" was in fact a meditative activity that engendered an awareness of the beginning, originary, or foundational experiences of consciousness, called by Voegelin the Ground of Being, as well as the experience of a transcendent beyond or Divine Being. But in neither instance was the beginning nor the beyond constituted by or in consciousness. It took Voegelin many years to develop the conceptual language sufficiently precise to describe the structure of a non-constituting consciousness. He was, however, fully aware of the problem by 1943.[36]

In light of the foregoing argument, Voegelin then reconsidered Husserl's effort to formulate a philosophy of pure constitutive consciousness that somehow had just such an absolute beginning: why, Voegelin asked, would Husserl have thought that it was necessary to establish a new foundation [*Neugründung*] of the world from consciousness and within consciousness? That is: what was Husserl's motive, a motive he assiduously avoided ever considering?

> The answer seems to be obvious to me: the desire to create a *tabula rasa* and begin anew is felt when the symbolical language, in which the ontic contexts are expressed, has become doubtful, or—historically speaking—when a civilization and its symbols have fallen into a crisis. In such a situation, an attempt to begin anew is not only legitimate in the sense that an old symbolism can no longer be authentically used when its communicative value had diminished, but it is also the indispensable requirement for the development of a new symbolism, adequate to the new situation. Protesting against such a new beginning in

36 See the accounts by Michael P. Morrissey, *Consciousness and Transcendence: The Theology of Eric Voegelin* (Notre Dame: University of Notre Dame Press, 1994), Glenn Hughes, *Mystery and Myth in the Philosophy of Eric Voegelin* (Columbia: University of Missouri Press, 1993), and Eugene Webb, *Philosophers of Consciousness* (Seattle: University of Washington Press, 1988), Ch. 3, for helpful discussions of these problems. In subsequent chapters we discuss Voegelin's later analyses, reflections, and formulations of the fundamental experiences of consciousness.

> the name of tradition is nothing more than a symptom of spiritual sterility. (CW 6:81–82)

That said, it remained a separate question whether Husserl's response to the crisis "is worse than the tradition against which it critically reacts." If we compare, for example, the reaction of Plato to the crisis of the polis and his creation of "a new spiritual world based on the fundamental experiences of *thanatos*, *eros*, and *dike*" with that of Husserl, it must be said "that not much can be noted of a new spiritual creation and the development of a new spiritual symbolism." Husserl's phenomenology certainly clarified "the structures of consciousness in which the objective order of the world is modestly constituted," as Voegelin had noted in his letter to Schütz, but the cost was to abandon philosophy "as the creation of an order of symbols through which man's position in the world is understood" (CW, 6:83). In contrast, Voegelin's anamnetic experiments were intended, as he wrote to Palmer, to clarify the early experiences that determined his later theoretical attitude.

Given the genesis of this "meditative unity" as reflections on the problem of the motivation and attitude of the theorists with respect to the historical evocations and political ideas, it necessarily had a bearing on the evolution of the *History of Political Ideas*. The first consideration, as Walsh said, was that the "existential and historical dimensions are inseparable" (CW, 6:2). This was so because the interpretation by the philosopher-theorist of the text of one of his or her predecessors was as much an event in reality as the original experience that led to the original evocation and political idea expressed in the original text. Accordingly, Voegelin's on-going argument regarding philosophy of consciousness was not just a presupposition for the empirical and historical studies of previous texts but was an essential constituent of those studies. The "experiments" and the analysis of them provided Voegelin with greater awareness of the motivational experience that eventually led to his understanding of his own philosophizing as an event within reality.

In other words, what joined philosophy of consciousness so understood to empirical analysis, and what made the entire section on "Remembrance" a "meditative unity," was the existential connection of meditative exegesis of consciousness undertaken in the "experiments" with the problems of historical evocation discussed in section two of this chapter. By undertaking the meditative exegesis of his own consciousness or, rather, by initiating the process, Voegelin gradually came to understand his own position as a theorist or philosopher with respect to the history of political ideas. Although the language changed with Voegelin's deepening insight into the problem of theorist-and-his-relationship-to-political-ideas, to use the formulation of the 1940s, his philosophy of consciousness necessarily remained a historical undertaking. This was true first because human being could never be exhausted in any particular historical evocation or institutional realization, and second, because philosophical reflection itself was "the creation of an order of symbols through which man's position in the world is understood" (CW, 6:83). That position and human understanding of it changed historically. Hence the changes in evocations, institutions, ideas, sentiments, and so on. The problem of what Gebhardt called "esotericism," which first came to light in Voegelin's correspondence with Mintz discussed above in this section, was resolved insofar as the philosopher was able to achieve a new orientation within reality by means of the creation of a new complex of symbols that expressed that orientation. These insights led Voegelin to conclude that writing a history of political ideas necessarily became a critical reflective analysis of the analyst's position with respect to them, which entailed the elaboration of a new and more difficult understanding of truth. This new understanding is discussed in the following section.

4. Historicity of Truth

Until Voegelin had to deal with the modern period, his argument, summary and interpretation developed along what he called a "double-tracked intellectual and spiritual history of Western civilization." The upper track or "plane" focused on the great institutions of church and empire and later on the national state; in his 1944 *APSR* article Voegelin called this concern with institutions "political history" (CW, 10:157ff). On the "lower" plane there was the "millennial drama of sentiments and ideas that are in revolt against the superstructure of civilization" (CW, 22:132), the orgiastic cults, movements, and wars noted above. As Voegelin worked through the "materials" leading to the modern world, it became increasingly difficult to integrate and link these two kinds of "ideas" into a single narrative. The problem was that the "lower plane" of sentiments began to dominate the "upper plane" of political institutions when sectarian movements that had been suppressed as heterodox or heretical during the medieval period transformed themselves into politico-religious creeds that captured the popular imagination and eventually informed the public institutions. As Walsh observed, all the volumes of the *History* struggled with the problem of "the disintegration of the precarious medieval Christian synthesis and the emergent spiritual crisis of the modern world," at the center of which was totalitarian domination (CW, 26:4).

Voegelin grew aware of the theoretical problem only gradually. In 1945 he wrote to Schütz that the disjunction between these two "planes" led to some serious difficulties in organizing the content of the *History*:

> Up to 1700 I was able, in the main, to proceed chronologically, taking, in turn, one thinker after another. But this becomes impossible in the 18th century because the secular political problematic, with which political theorists in the more restricted sense of the term are concerned, continually intersects with the development of the post-Christian intramundane eschatology. But the history of eschatology can only be treated in broad overviews such as, for example, the leap from Bruno to Schelling or, in the survey of the problem of nature, from Poggio to Tycho Brahe. If I were to neglect writing such summarizing passages, the history of political ideas would dissolve into a general European history of ideas. Thus in the part of "Revolution" I must somehow find a way to bring together the concrete chronology of Vico, Montesquieu, Hume, Rousseau, Kant, etc., with chapters on eschatology and history that span centuries. (CW, 29:438)

Voegelin added that the general problem was that the issues that had attained "*mass* relevancy" were by no means "the *objectively* relevant ones," by which he meant the issues that mattered in reality and in political science. Specifically, what mattered in reality was found "in Hegel and Schelling, Kierkegaard, Bakunin, Marx and Nietzsche, and *not* Darwinism, economic liberalism, and similar phenomena that dominate the public scene." If one were to focus only on what had mass relevancy, it would be "the equivalent of, say, in a history of ideas of Greece in the 4th century, putting Plato in a corner and bringing into the center a dozen questionable rhetoricians who had won mass approval" (CW, 29:439). In short, the framework Voegelin developed in the 1939 "Introduction" that related theory to evocation was no longer adequate because the experiences and ideas evoked not order but disorder and unintelligible fantasies.

In order to deal with the modern period and in light of the insights gained by his "theory of consciousness," regarding the attitude of the theorist to his subject-matter, Voegelin had to change his approach from one where the Aristotelian theorist could argue that "ideas" did, in fact, evoke a "fundamental human substance" to one where "ideas" did not evoke anything but appearances, phenomena, and more specifically images of an intramundane eschatology that, in terms of political science, were nonsense—notwithstanding the claims made by those who subscribed to the intramundane eschatology that it was "science" or "theory." Voegelin sensed the problem before he formulated a way of dealing with it. In October 1945 for example, Voegelin wrote to his publisher at Macmillan that "the work is more than a mere history of theories; it has become a comprehensive, systematic critique of politics and modern civilization, of general interest" (CW, 29:450). It took some time for the implications to become clear to Voegelin and even longer for him to find an adequate way of expressing his insight.

One of the earliest expressions of this new approach to "the materials" produced after about 1700 was the long study "The People of God," the final version of which Voegelin completed in the spring of 1948 (CW, 22:131–214; CW, 29:566–67). Here Voegelin argued that there was continuity between the sentiments or experiences of medieval heresies and modern mass movements. This was the earliest formulation of what we can call the "Gnosticism thesis," discussed in the following chapter.[37]

The implication of the "Gnosticism thesis" compelled Voegelin to reconsider the interpretative strategy he had hitherto employed. Specifically, he concluded that modern Gnosticism had reversed, or occluded the insights of antiquity and the Middle Ages. As he said explicitly in *The New Science of Politics*, the growth of Gnosticism in modern Western society indicated a "civilizational cycle of world-historic proportions," the ascending branch of which lay in the pre-Christian civilizations of antiquity. The descending branch was modern Gnostic civilization (CW, 5:221–22). These insights did not appear overnight.

In Volume VII of the *History*, there is a preliminary formulation of the problem of a "civilizational cycle" presented under the heading of an "Intermission" between Locke and Schelling. Gebhardt noted that Voegelin's "moderate language," which was typical of a textbook treatment of such figures, changed in his discussion of Locke. Locke became the "bête noire of modern political thought" because he eliminated "the spiritual personality of man from the public realm" leaving only a "caricature of bourgeois

37 In his *Autobiographical Reflections*, CW, 34:92, Voegelin said he first became aware of the importance of Gnosticism in 1937.

society" (CW, 25:22, 25). In a 1953 draft letter to Strauss, which apparently was never sent, Voegelin provided a critical analysis of Locke leading to the conclusion that he was "one of the first very great cases of spiritual pathology." Locke was not a philosopher at all but the author of "a brutal ideological construction to support the ideological position of the English upper class, to which Locke belonged through his social relations. The construction is consistent, insofar as *concupiscentia* is maintained from the beginning as the driving motive; it is inconsistent, insofar as the introduction of a vocabulary of natural right forces a repeated redefinition of the concept of nature."[38] More informed Voegelin's attitude to Locke's "ideas" than Locke's evasiveness and inconsistency. He was, as Voegelin later wrote of Marx, an "intellectual swindler."

In the "Intermission" Locke marked the end of the first cycle of modern political thought that began with the evocation of a post-medieval political order, which was initiated by Grotius. For Voegelin, an important aspect of Grotius's theory of what we now call international law was that it excluded religious groups as units capable of waging war. "Only the nonreligious power units shall have public status." By the end of the seventeenth century, Locke's theory of toleration removed the church from the domestic public scene as well, which thereby banished whatever remnants of "the spiritual personality of man" remained (CW, 25:151). It was, Voegelin said, a mark of Locke's "severe spiritual disturbance" and "pneumatopathology" that he considered anticivilizational destruction to be the growth of "Civilization, written large, based on Nature and Reason" (CW, 25:152–53). The continuation of Locke's "revolutionary caricature" and its being overlooked by generations of students of his thought was to Voegelin further evidence of the spread of a "deep spiritual disorder." Locke's predecessor, Hobbes, whom Voegelin called a "psychological realist," had already exposed the experiential source of Locke's disorder: the passion for power after power that ceaseth only in death.

> Under the veneer of sectarian religiousness appear the "madness" of self-inflation and the intolerance of conscience; under the veneer of Reason and Nature appear in Grotius the exploitation of commercial opportunities at the expense of less developed nations and in Locke, in his neat slip, the desire for property expansion untrammeled by social obligations. Spinoza,

38 *Faith and Political Philosophy*, 92–97; in his reply, Strauss did not disagree.

> the mystic, struggles valiantly for the Life of Reason but cannot do more than prove that the Life of Reason is incompatible with the [Lockean] reasonable life to the point of mutual exclusion. (CW, 25:154)

There was an order to Locke's bourgeois caricature, but it was devoid of spirit. The second cycle of modernity, therefore, was focused on the recovery or "reassertion" of spirit. Here Voegelin detected three distinct developments. The first was found in Vico's *New Science*, which was motivated by the experience of Western decline and decadence. Nietzsche and Weber marked the later phases of those who recognized the evidence of decay, described it, and attempted to restore in their own person "the consciousness of the standards of a spiritual civilization." In the context of Lockean toleration they were, of course, publicly ineffectual though they did achieve "a science of politics—a personal effort and scientific achievement that, on the whole, has gone to waste in terms of public effect" (CW, 25:155).

A second group was both diagnosticians of the decline and disorder as well as spiritual activists. As derivative of the Lockean bourgeois settlement, their efforts at revolutionizing decadent Western civilization disrupted it even further. The third group comprised the acolytes of Progress and Reason who both shared in Locke's spiritual disorder and celebrated it. These secondary thinkers were publicly successful but of no further importance to political science. The importance of Voegelin's *History* for political science was therefore its focal concern with the practitioners of the New Science. The publicly successful but secondary thinkers—the Darwinists, economic liberals and so on—were simply not very interesting.

In response to his discovery of these two cycles, Voegelin developed the concept, the historicity of truth, which first appeared in print in Voegelin's analysis of Aristotle (CW, 16:418–19).The problem came up indirectly in a letter from Voegelin to Strauss early in March 1949 in response to Strauss's article, "Political Philosophy and History."[39] Voegelin said he thought that he and Strauss "are in very much greater agreement in the direction of our work that I first supposed" and summarized his own version of the problem: "To restore the experiences that have led to the creation of certain concepts and symbols; or: Symbols have become opaque; they must be made luminous again by penetrating to the experiences they express"

39 *Journal of the History of Ideas* 10 (1949): 30–50.

(CW, 29:608–9). The problem came up again later in the year in letters between Voegelin and Schütz.[40] In a 1950 letter to Strauss, Voegelin provided further clarification in response to Strauss's objection to his use of the term "existential." Voegelin wrote:

> Why and in what sense I use the term "existential" in the text of the article[41] should be explained. Terminologically, the case is easy: I know no better expression; if I find one, I would gladly be prepared to use it; and if you could give me ideas I would be very grateful. It has to do with the problem itself. . . . The truth of ontology (including in particular philosophical anthropology) is not a datum that can be recognized by anyone at any time. Ontological knowledge emerges in the process of history and biographically in the process of the individual person's life under certain conditions of education, social context, personal inclination, and psychic conditioning. *Episteme* is not just a function of knowledge, it is also in the Aristotelian sense, a dianoetic *arête*. For this *non*cognitive aspect of *episteme* I use the term "existential."
>
> In a history of ideas I must use the term quite often. A history of ideas should not be a doxographic report, or a "history of dogmas" in the classical sense, but rather a history of existential transformations in which the "truth" comes to sight, is obscured, is lost, and is again recovered. A history of political ideas, in particular, should investigate the processes in which "truth" becomes socially effective or is hindered in such effectiveness. You see, it does not have to do with a negation or relativization of ontology, but rather with the correlation between knowledge in the cognitive and existential sense; this correlation is for me the theme of "history."[42]

40 *Friendship*, 125–26; 132; CW, 29:662.

41 "The Philosophy of Existence: Plato's *Gorgias*," *The Review of Politics* 11 (1949): 477–98. This article was incorporated into the chapter on the *Gorgias* in *Order and History*, CW, 16:78–99.

42 *Faith and Political Philosophy*, 64; corrected in light of the German edition, *Glauben und Wissen: Der Breifweschel zwischen Eric Voegelin und Leo Strauss von 1934 bis 1964*, ed. Peter Opitz with the assistance of Emmanuel Patard (Munich: Fink, 2010), 69. See also Patard, "Supplement and Corrections to 'The Strauss-Voegelin Correspondence,'" *The Political Science Reviewer* 39 (2010): 291.

As Gebhardt observed, historicity of truth "blended the theory of politics with philosophy of history" and so compelled a revision of the theory of evocation and sentiments[43] (CW, 25:9). In addition, as the observation Voegelin made to Strauss regarding the emergence of the truth of ontology "biographically in the process of an individual person's life" it also required, as was argued in the previous section, an explicit philosophy of consciousness.

The process by which Voegelin's analysis of the history of political ideas led him to the concept of the historicity of truth can be indicated with brevity. Initially the "New Order" of the nation state could be understood in light of the theory of evocation. The atrophy of the institutions of Church and Empire left European human beings "unsheltered" by a political cosmion, which in turn led to a "rediscovery of man."

> This man is a fragment, reduced to his co-called natural elements, including the faculty of reasoning. The main line of thought, drawn by the outstanding political philosophers—Hobbes, Locke, Hume, Montesquieu, Rousseau, Kant, Hegel, Marx—is concerned with the rediscovery of man, with the arduous task of adding to his stature the elements that he has lost in the transition from the Middle Ages to the seventeenth century. Political theory must give him back his passions, his conscience, his sentiments, his relation to God, his status in history. The movement culminated, in the late nineteenth and early twentieth centuries, in philosophical anthropology becoming the center of political thought. (CW, 25:51)

A further set of problems was to describe the new social substance of the nation in the absence of a suitable vocabulary and in light of widely different historical experiences in the different European countries as well as the persistence of ideas of humanity, derived from Christianity, that could not be absorbed into the national mystical bodies. Later, nineteenth- and twentieth-century international mass movements also conflicted with the national evocations and they too had to be understood.

43 CW, 25:9. See also Thomas Hollweck, "Truth and Relativity: On the Historical Emergence of Truth," in *The Philosophy of Order: Essays on History, Consciousness and Politics for Eric Voegelin on his Eightieth Birthday*, ed. Peter J. Opitz and Gregor Sebba (Stuttgart: Klett-Cotta, 1981), 125–36.

In this respect, Schelling had a direct influence on the modification of Voegelin's philosophical anthropology especially as Voegelin revised the arguments of the 1939 "Introduction" to the *History*.[44] Schelling did not restore traditional Christian metaphysics so much as establish "a new level of consciousness in Western intellectual history in general and in the history of political thought in particular" (CW, 25:236). With some trepidation,[45] Voegelin argued that, after Schelling, anthropology was the systematic key to political analysis. "Nothing must enter into the content of speculation that cannot be found in human nature, in its depth as well as in its heights, in the limitation of its existence as well as in its openness to transcendent reality" (CW, 25:210). Voegelin concluded that Schelling "gained a clear consciousness of the foundations on which speculation must rest." In a sense, Voegelin's analysis of Schelling confirmed his own anamnetic experiments (CW, 25:29).

Just as Voegelin discovered in his anamnetic experiments, the philosopher "does not begin with a tabula rasa but finds himself existing historically in a realm of knowledge that is coextensive (in mythology, revelation, rational philosophical speculation and empirical historical sciences including those of nature) with the universe itself to its origins." Indeed, mythology and revelation provided the key to understanding the historical dimension of the universe.

> Pagan polytheism, Hebrew monotheism, and Christianity are stages of a theogonic process in which divine revelation and human creation of symbols interpenetrate each other. Myth and revelation are the vessels of divine self-affirmation in the world through man; they are part of the history of the universe just as much as of the history of living forms. And this process has not yet come to an end but is continuing through the souls of man as its medium and manifesting itself in the creation of new religious symbols—such as the *Potenzelehre* of Schelling. (CW, 25:211)

Voegelin's conclusion was that, after Schelling, history has a "double meaning." First it was the actual course of events, both natural and human,

44 For details, see Jerry Day, *Voegelin, Schelling and the Philosophy of Historical Existence* (Columbia: University of Missouri Press, 2003).

45 *A Friendship*, 94.

in the universe; and it was historical in a second sense when it was understood by human beings as a meaningful unfolding of the universe.

> This internalization of the course of events, this immersion of the external process into a movement of the soul, is possible because the internalizing soul is itself part of the stream. When the soul gives meaning to the stream, it discovers the stream and its meaning in itself. In this sense the soul is knowledge, and history is a science of the soul. (CW, 25:211)

The "knowledge" of the soul was not that of objects known by a subject but a knowledge made intelligible through recollection, an anamnesis by means of which the meaning of the external process was recovered from the human unconscious.

Voegelin noted that Schelling did not restore traditional Christian metaphysics but created new religious symbols such as *Potenz*, potency.[46] At the same time, because Schelling was living within the Christian era, his "philosophy of existence" was neither that of a prophet nor of a sectarian but of a philosopher with "a new level of critical consciousness within Christian history" (CW, 25:227). He was, Voegelin said, "a realist who expressed in his dialectic the existential fact that he, as an individual, is beyond the churches because the meaning of the churches has become actualized in history to the point where it has become part of the past of his soul" (CW, 25:237). Schelling therefore "marks the end of a period, not a beginning; he marks the end in the same sense in which Plato, or Saint Augustine, or Saint Thomas marks the end of an age." And at the same time, because Schelling also expressed "a new level of consciousness and critique" his work became "the point of orientation for those [such as Voegelin] who wish to gain a solid foothold in the surrounding myth of decadent traditions, conflicting eschatologies, phenomenal speculation and obsessions, ideologies and creeds, blind hatreds, and orgiastic destructions" (CW, 25:241–42).

In his introduction to Volume Seven of the *History*, Gebhardt suggested not only that Voegelin's analysis of Schelling confirmed, as was indicated, his anamnetic experiments but that, following Schelling, Voegelin's "anamnetic reflection reaches into the unconscious psychic depth of human nature that unfolds its potentiality historically in order to bring into consciousness

46 See Day, *Voegelin, Schelling*, 97ff; Cooper, *Foundations*, 401ff. Voegelin's later appraisal of Schelling was more critical. See CW, 5:189.

the fundamental experiences at the root of the historical unfolding of human nature" (CW, 25:31). Or, as Voegelin wrote to Heilman in 1956:

> History is the unfolding of the human Psyche; historiography is the reconstruction of the unfolding through the psyche of the historian. The basis of historical interpretation is the identity of substance (the psyche) in the object and the subject of interpretation; and its purpose is participation in the great dialogue that goes through centuries among men about their nature and destiny. And participation is impossible without growth in stature (within the personal limitations) toward the rank of the best; and that growth is impossible unless one recognizes authority and surrenders to it.

So as there could be no misunderstanding, Voegelin distinguished sharply between the historicity of truth and historicism or historical relativism. The motives of the historical relativist, he said to Heilman,

> are distinctly shady and shabby; in my field of political science I speak of these arguments as the humility racket. In the first place, the argument is methodologically ludicrous. For one cannot discern historical determinants in a mind or its work, unless one can distinguish between the mind and the determinants. If one really could not distinguish, there would be no historical works but only oddities, not recognizable as human on our own terms, beyond comprehension. But we all can distinguish quite well. . . . The argument is so ludicrous indeed that it would not be worth any attention, unless historical relativism were a social force for quite different reasons.
>
> In determining these other reasons, one may well follow the Roman question: *cui bono*? Who profits by the assumption that works of the mind are so thoroughly determined by historical circumstance that the pursuit of truth about the nature of man is not recognizable in them? The answer is obvious: the spiteful mediocrity which hates excellence. The argument of historical relativism is the defense of the little man against the recognition of greatness. If Plato is encased in the circumstances of the 4th c. B.C. and Mr. Jones in the circumstances of the 20th c. A.D. the community of the psyche is interrupted; no confrontation

> from man to man is possible; the discomfort of discovering and admitting one's own smallness before the great is averted; and above all, the obligations arising through confrontation with greatness have disappeared. All men are on the same level of circumstanced equality. Behind the personal viciousness that puts social strength into historical relativism, there lies the much larger issue of the revolt against God and the escape into Gnosticism. For "the measure of man is God," and the life of the psyche is the life in truth. By interrupting communication with those who live in truth, the life in truth itself is avoided. Historical relativism is the radical attack on the communication of truth through the dialogue in history. (CW, 30:294ff)

Gebhardt concluded his introduction to this pivotal volume in the *History* with the observation that the studies assembled there "tell the story of the ultimate failure of modern thinkers to evoke a political cosmion befitting the true humanity of human beings" (CW, 25:33). In the 1939 "General Introduction" to the *History* discussed above (CW, 19:225–37), the theorist, detached from the evocative ideas, analyzed the magical creativity in operation. This original position proved to be mistaken because, on the bases of his own anamnetic experiments, of his theory of consciousness, and of his analysis of Schelling, Voegelin discovered that "the contemplative personality was the source of the imaginative evocation of the ordering idea" and depended on political institutions to represent his spiritual experiences in public (CW, 25:33; cf. CW, 21:70–71). With the advent of modernity, however, the "spiritual realist," which is to say, those personalities capable of experiencing spiritual reality who are "conservators of the spirit" along with "philosophers who live in their tradition," were increasingly isolated from "mass trends toward a field of secular and despiritualized particular powers and movement." As a result, "the actually existing communities and movements of social relevance have broken away so far from the Western spiritual order and remnants of its tradition that the voice of the spirit can no longer reach them on their blind course" (CW, 25:193–94).

This problem was not entirely new—Voegelin mentioned St. Thomas, Dante, Bodin and Spinoza as predecessors. The characteristic social and political position of such individuals—and one might add Machiavelli, Schelling and Nietzsche—was one of isolation. And yet, they provided "a modern understanding of human existence, which ran counter to the prevalent modern ideas of human life from which the spirit had evaporated in favor of despiritualized happiness and despiritualized brutality." Despiritualized happiness was precisely the objective of the Lockean bourgeois settlement that Strauss famously described as "the joyless quest for joy."[47] "Despiritualized brutality" characterized the second group of revolutionary activists discussed in Voegelin's "Intermission."

*

By way of conclusion we would simply endorse Gebhardt's insight: "we can discern in Voegelin's *History* two meanings of modernity: the socially dominant modernity of sociospiritual disintegration and the modernity of spiritual realism that prepares for a modernity after modernity. The true heroes of the story told in this volume are the secular spiritual realists representing a spiritually authentic modernity" (CW, 25:34). They were, moreover, the originators of philosophical anthropology that was so central to Voegelin's work from beginning to end. Whether these spiritual realists were also secular, at least in the ordinary sense of the term, remains to be seen.

47 Strauss, *Natural Right and History* (Chicago: University of Chicago Press, 1953), 251.

CHAPTER TWO

GENEALOGY OF THE "GNOSTICISM THESIS"

Voegelin's Walgreen Lectures, published as *The New Science of Politics*, is probably his best-known book, at least in the sense that it has been in print in English since 1952. By 2000, translations were available in German, French, Italian, Spanish, Portuguese, and Polish.[1] The most striking feature of the book, as we discuss in section 3 of this chapter, is what we call the "Gnosticism thesis." The argument was initially developed a decade earlier in the chapter "People of God," which was part of the *History of Political Ideas*. The earliest version of this chapter was completed by May 1941 and was sent to Fritz Morstein-Marx along with the information that Waldemar Gurian, editor of the *Review of Politics* might publish it (CW, 29:265). A second version was finished during the summer of 1941 in response to Max Mintz's criticism that Voegelin needed to supply references and tone down his polemical language (HI, 25:23; CW, 29:287). Friedrich Engel-Janosi received a copy of the chapter in January 1942 (CW, 29:316) and in December Voegelin sent a copy to Leo Strauss in Strauss's capacity as an editor of *Social Research* for consideration for publication. In the event, it was rejected for the "technical reason" that *Social Research* did not publish chapters from forthcoming books.[2] As Szakolczai observed, had it been published "it would have ranked with and preceded" the works of Hannah Arendt, Norman Cohn, Karl Löwith and J. R. Talmon "as a classic on the origins of totalitarian movements and ideologies."[3] A final version was finished in 1949. Apart from *The New Science of Politics*, the

1 Geoffrey L. Price, *Eric Voegelin: International Bibliography, 1921–2000* (Munich: Fink, 2000), 21–22. The University of Chicago Press contracted for a Japanese translation but none was produced (HI, 38:21). A Chinese translation is reportedly underway.

2 CW, 29:340–41; *Faith and Political Philosophy: The Correspondence between Leo Strauss and Eric Voegelin, 1934–1964*, ed. and trans. Peter Emberley and Barry Cooper (University Park: Penn State University Press, 1993), 9–15.

3 Arpad Szakolczai, *Reflexive Historical Sociology* (London: Taylor and Francis, 2000), 157.

"Gnosticism thesis" was further refined in his later writings, notably in "Gnostic Politics" (1952) and in his inaugural lecture (*Antrittvorlesung*) at Munich in 1958 published under the title *Science Politics and Gnosticism*.[4] These and other later writings on the subject are discussed in chapter five. In chapter three of *The New Science of Politics* Voegelin identified Gnosticism with "the nature of modernity." In that context, the *History of Political Ideas* may be seen as a lengthy prooemium, the purpose of which was to clarify "the factors that led to the rise of modernity."[5]

1. The People of God

In chapter one, we quoted David Walsh's observation that Voegelin's entire *History* was a struggle with the problem of the disintegration of the balanced medieval Christian synthesis and the genesis of the spiritual crisis that helps constitute the modern world (CW, 21:7; 26:4). Part III of the *History* was called *Sacrum Imperium*, a term Voegelin used from 1941 on to describe the spiritual-temporal order of the medieval period.[6] The papal and imperial authorities together constituted a cooperative cosmion, a common order that was presupposed by the subsequent disintegration into separate churches and states. Following the "extinction" of the *sacrum imperium*, Western humanity still understood itself as a spiritual and civilizational unit—as arguably it does today. Once the old institutions of

4 Voegelin, and nearly everyone else, was inconsistent in the use of the term Gnosticism or Gnosis. The original version of his inaugural lecture, for example, was *Wissenschaft, Politik und Gnosis*; the English, *Science Politics and Gnosticism*. The use of capital letters was also inconsistent. We consistently capitalize and discuss the Gnosis/Gnosticism question below. Eugene Webb, *Eric Voegelin: Philosopher of History* (Seattle: University of Washington Press, 1981), 200–1 proposed a different scheme, to use the term "Gnostic" to refer only to the ancient religious movement, and "gnosticism" to refer to "all movements based on claims to *gnosis* of any sort."

5 Szakolczai, "Eric Voegelin's History of Political Ideas," *European Journal of Social Theory* 4 (2001): 352.

6 The term was taken from the treatise of Alois Dempf, *Sacrum Imperium: Geschichts- und Staatsphilosophie des Mittelalters und der politischien Renaissance* (Munich and Vienna: Oldenbourg, 1929). Voegelin told Dempf that his book was a "prerequisite" for his own treatment of the Middle Ages, "so much so that without it I would hardly have been able to complete my volume in an adequate way, and most certainly not in its present form" (CW, 29:646). In other letters Voegelin offered a more critical appraisal of Dempf's book: CW 29:565–66, for example. Even so, Voegelin certainly made extensive use of this source.

papacy and empire lost their representative purpose, the need to find a more adequate expression of the existentially real civilizational substance grew intense. Beginning in the sixteenth century, Europeans developed political ideas that determined the shape of the institutions and organizations—international law, for example, or the laws of war—that exist into the present day (see CW, 23:108ff).

Volume Four of the *History of Political Ideas* bears the title *Renaissance and Reformation*, which was supplied by the editors.[7] So far as the Renaissance is concerned, the expected names of Machiavelli (1469–1527), Erasmus (1466–1536), and More (1478–1535) figured prominently in Voegelin's analysis and Luther (1483–1546) and Calvin (1509–1564) were equally obvious figures to discuss with respect to the Reformation. Between the analyses of the dominant personalities of the century-long change was the chapter "The People of God," which we examine in this section.

The historical role of "The People of God" in the development of the modern world was complex. In Volume Five, on *Religion and the Rise of Modernity*, Voegelin discussed "The Problem of Modernity" as it appeared toward the end of the sixteenth century (CW, 23:134–38). There Voegelin detected a change in the sentiments and ideas that he described as a change in "atmosphere" rather than a systematic new understanding of human being and the world. One of the components of this "modern" complex of sentiments was precisely the public expression of the free sectarian spirituality that Voegelin analyzed in "The People of God." As we shall see, that particular element was medieval. However, when anti-ecclesiastical sectarian spirituality became sufficiently effective as to create a schism in the Church (see CW, 22:220ff), when the results were consolidated as a plurality of churches, each claiming to embody the truth of Christian faith, and finally, when Europeans came to reflect on the new institutional arrangements, then one could speak of a self-conscious modernity.

The relationship of institutional change to the pattern of sentiments and ideas was, therefore, extremely intricate. For example, the discovery of a plurality of civilizations, starting with the recovery of classical learning also shattered the taken-for-granted security of the medieval cosmion. The plurality of churches and of religious wars led to a series of new sentiments and attitudes, from a mystical spirituality that transcended dogmatic differences

7 For a critical discussion of the organization of the *History*, see Arpad Szakolczai, "Stages of a Quest: Reconstructing the Outline Structure of Eric Voegelin's *History of Political Ideas*," *Occasional Papers XXV* (Munich: Eric-Voegelin-Archiv, 2001).

among churches, to tolerance, skepticism, indifference and agnosticism—to present the available options in terms of declining spiritual insight. The medieval idea of a closed cosmos with a providential straight line of history that began with the creation of the world and ended with its apocalyptic destruction was replaced with a "universe that owes its meaning to the fact that it has been evoked by the mind of man" (CW, 23:136). This "new awareness," Voegelin said, was what he meant by "modern."[8] In short, the change from medieval to modern was for Voegelin never simply a matter of institutional change but included a response to the fact of institutional change in light of new sentiments and ideas that, in turn, were conditioned and shaped by these same external institutional changes.

Obviously the European state looked like the temporal successor to the medieval empire, but in fact matters were not so simple. Machiavelli, who first applied the word state to political affairs also sought to create a "new spiritual substance" through the *virtù* of a new national savior-prince, but he was entirely aware that in the end not *virtù* but *fortuna* must triumph because even the most virtuous prince must die—and often at a most inopportune time (see *The Prince*, ch. 7). That is, even so modern and "secular" thinker as Machiavelli managed to endow his new savior-prince with spiritual significance. Neither Machiavelli nor anyone else, Voegelin said, "foresaw the massive forces that would bring about the spiritual reorientation of the Western world" when "the typically recurrent" outbursts of the "spiritual movements of the people" created the new cosmion associated initially with the reform of the medieval one (CW, 21:131).

As noted in the previous chapter, Voegelin analyzed the process of renovation by distinguishing "two planes" of Western civilization, the "upper" plane of public institutions and the "lower" plane of popular sentiments that in an earlier period he had identified with various orgiastic cults and that from the eleventh century on had been "in revolt against the institutional superstructure of our civilization" (CW, 22:132). More than the "apolitism" of a philosopher living in a polis was involved, not least of all because moderation ranked high among philosophical virtues but often was conspicuously absent from the zeal of reformers. One reason was that, in the Christian cosmion, the person was immediately related to God and the

8 Later in his analysis Voegelin characterized Bodin's political philosophy as exemplifying "Mediterranean modernity," as distinct from the trans-Alpine modernity more closely associated with the growth of natural science. See CW, 23:134–38; 181–84.

institution of the Church was already a compromise with the "world" (CW, 22:140ff). That is, compromise, and thus moderation, was a problem.

The reason, Voegelin argued, was because for Christian sectarians, that is, for Christians who expressed the spiritual sentiments outside the Church,[9] any ecclesiastical organization entailed a compromise with the immediate experience of the divine. Moreover, the civilizational longevity and civilizing success of the Church exacerbated the problem inasmuch as *any* civilizational order was hierarchically organized in terms of the things of the world and this kind of institutional hierarchy could readily be interpreted as being in conflict with the equality of all humans in the mystical body of Christ. Historically, that is, the Church had to adapt the strict teachings of the Sermon on the Mount (1) to the flaws and weaknesses of human beings, (2) to the necessities of government among flawed human beings, and (3) to the existing cultures of pre-and non-Christian social reality. None of this was acceptable to the sectarian reformers.

Consider, for example, the problem of the reception of the sacraments, particularly baptism and the Eucharist, according to the account accepted by the Church. On the one hand, receiving the sacrament did not guarantee salvation, which was known only to God; on the other, the validity of the sacraments did not depend on the personality or worthiness of the person whose office it was to administer them. That is, the Church was preeminently a sacramental organization that mediated divine grace to individual persons. The purpose of the sacraments administered by the Church was to incorporate the recipients into the mystical body of Christ. Accordingly, through the celebration of the sacraments, particularly the Eucharist, the Incarnation was continued as a historical and civilizational reality. At the same time, the existence of the historical reality of the sacramental Church as an institution meant that it had to accept governmental power. Doing so enabled the Church to endure in the face of political hostility and indifference. Likewise, the compromise with existing cultures enabled the Christian community to integrate the law of nature, particularly in its Stoic form, with the Old Law given by God to the Israelites and to integrate both these spiritual complexes into the law of the heart that had been revealed through the Logos that had become flesh.

9 Voegelin borrowed the distinction between Church and sect from Ernst Troeltsch and Max Weber. Voegelin's discussion of Christianity was modified in his later analysis, which focused more on Christian experience and symbolization than on institutions, politics, and doctrine. See chapter six below.

By making such compromises, the Church was able to civilize the "world." That is, it was able to accept existing social, economic, and political institutions and add to them such Christian virtues as human beings might accept. Those who were more spiritually gifted might more closely enact the vicarious sacrifice of Christ, but all—layman and priest, warrior and peasant, educated and uneducated, king and subject—were members of the Christian community. As a consequence, there was to be no eschatological revolution to establish the realm of Christ today or tomorrow. Until the seventeenth century, one or another aspect of the compromise of the Church was attacked by sectarians. By and large, therefore, the sectarians rejected the mediation of the Church in light of the immediacy of spiritual experience, and with it the radical equality of all individuals.

The direction of the change was evident from the beginning. Granted that the spiritualism of the Sermon on the Mount was an accepted and ongoing standard that could be invoked "against the institution that is supposed to represent it," and granted as well that all Christians would accept the spiritual direction of the Sermon, it was always possible to argue that Christianity ought properly to be understood as an uncompromising realization of the message of the Gospel. Under this interpretation, intense personal spiritual experience would outweigh the mediation of the sacraments. "We must," Voegelin concluded, "recognize church and sect as equally authentic manifestations of Christianity" (CW, 22:142). Accordingly, if the conduct of Church incumbents were seen as a gross violation of expected spiritual standards, an appeal could always be made to the Sermon on the Mount as a model that, at least in principle, was accepted by Church incumbents as binding (CW, 22:134; CW, 19:160–62). The result, depending on circumstances, could be a reformation of the Church as an institution if the new spiritual movements, which considered themselves to be the embodiments of the original spirituality, could be "digested" by the institution; or, on other occasions, the movement might be indigestible and would have to be suppressed. Moreover, since anti-institutional political movements, whatever their animating sentiments, were movements of political opposition, they could easily enough afford ruling groups an excuse not to address legitimate grievances that all hierarchies, including ecclesiastical ones, are bound to engender, which in turn might lead to more violent political outbreaks in the future that might well be entirely independent of the original sentiments in favor of spiritual reform.

Voegelin discerned around 1300 a significant change in the ability of the Sacred Empire to absorb reformist movements. Before that time, the new mendicant orders absorbed the sentiments and discontent of popular religious movements just as Thomas and Albert adapted the intellectual movements of Arabic Aristotelians. By the fourteenth century, however, the new mystical movements were marginalized by Church authorities as heresies and such political reform movements as the Hussites were suppressed by means of a domestic crusade. Meanwhile the institution of the Church itself was divided in schism. That is, between 1300 and about 1500 the strategy of absorption was replaced by one of suppression. After 1500, suppression was no longer possible and the spiritual movements tended to blend with the incipient nationalism of the new state organizations. After 1700, however, the spiritual movements showed a marked tendency towards internationalism, thus undermining the national component of the institution of the state. Unlike the earlier internationalism of the Catholic and Protestant spiritual movements, which were a kind of afterglow to Christian universalism, the new international movements were anti-Christian (see also CW, 23:108ff).

Concerning the origin and history of the spiritual movements that erupted in the Great Reformation, Voegelin indicated that "we have not yet perceptively advanced beyond the account given by Edward Gibbon" in his (1776) *Decline and Fall of the Roman Empire* (ch.54). There were two major problems: first, the spiritual movements tended to exist chiefly in the souls of individuals and their followers who typically lacked the literary and organizational culture to produce a coherent body of doctrine. Second, there were few sources available and even they had not been sufficiently studied.[10] Following the eschatological terrorism exemplified in 2001 attack by al Qaeda on the United States, a renewed interest in the Islamic variant of the problem has arisen.[11] The direction of the struggle between the Church and the sectarian movements was in essence a reversal of the process by which the Church overcame its initial eschatological expectations of a quick return of the Messiah and transformed itself into an apocalyptic and sacramental organization as outlined above (see also CW, 1:166ff). Given the integration

10 Matters have improved since Voegelin wrote. See for example, Norman Cohn, *The Pursuit of the Millennium* (Oxford: Oxford University Press, 1970); Herbert Grundmann, *Religious Movements of the Middle Ages: The Historical Links between Heresy, the Mendicant Orders, and the Women's Religious Movement in the Twelfth and Thirteenth Century, with the Historical Foundations of German Mysticism* (Notre Dame: University of Notre Dame Press, 1995).

11 I discussed some of these issues in *New Political Religions, or an Analysis of Modern Terrorism*, (Columbia: University of Missouri Press, 2004).

of spiritual and temporal power in the institutions of the *sacrum imperium*, it was often impossible to separate the element of spiritual reform from the element of political rebellion and civilizational destruction (CW, 22:144).

Historically the earlier movements emphasized the element of spiritual reform; later the element of destruction predominated. But in either case the emphasis was on an eschatological but also an intramundane transformation. Voegelin provided a brief description of the typical elements of a "floating mass" of symbols available to a specific religious personality who then might draw upon them to express his experience of grievance and redemption (CW, 22:154). For example, the notion that the imperfections of human life—sin— could be overcome was a common theme shared by sectarian and non-sectarian Christians. The interpretation often made by the sectarians on how to overcome sin was at odds both with commonsense and with the sacramental doctrines of the Church. The most important commonsensical indication that a person was without sin was that the person, in fact, did not sin. For the sectarian the relationship was reversed: because the sectarian had somehow been restored to sinlessness, any activity, and especially acts that otherwise and commonsensically would seem to be criminal, must be understood as manifestations of "the divine energy that is operating within him."[12]

Voegelin described the attitude of the sectarians as one of "activist mysticism," a term that he continued to use in his later work. An activist mystic was distinct from a genuine mystic insofar as the genuine mystic "dissolves the sensuous image and tries to penetrate to the experience that has produced the symbol; but he preserves distinction and distance between experience and symbol" (CW 22:166). For example, the symbol of perfection or sinlessness, as in the example just noted, was

> rooted in the experience of an imperfection that can be overcome only through grace in death. That is the point at which the genuine mystic stops in his speculation; and that is the point from which the activist mystic carries on. The "activist" accepts the dematerialization of the symbol like the genuine mystic; but then he goes one fateful step further: he abolishes the distance between the symbol and the experience and mistakes the symbol

12 CW, 22:156. See also the amusing remarks by R. C. Zaehner on the mystical properties of LSD or gin and tonic in *Drugs, Mysticism and Make-Believe* (London: Collins, 1972), 48.

for the experience that can be realized existentially in the life of man in society. (CW, 22:166–67)

The danger posed by activist mystics, Voegelin observed, "makes the philosopher wonder whether there is not solid merit even in the most naïve forms of fundamentalism." Someone convinced that "a glorious free lunch and a brothel" awaits him in the beyond "will at least not write letters to his congressman demanding such bliss here and now" (CW, 22:167). The transformation of a mystical symbol into a plan of action clearly was at odds with the sacramental teachings of the Church. More to the point for political science, the confusion of the two invariably meant that *the* political problem, for the sectarian, was to bridge the gap between present imperfection and future perfection by means of human action. One way or another, sectarians typically argued, the transition would involve a redistribution of earthly goods, positions, and advantages, and especially the transfer of the position of the ruling class to the membership of the sectarian movement. In short, what was typically sought was not a pragmatic adjustment of social grievances but an imaginary change in the human condition, not to say human nature.

In reality, however, faith in a transfigured world through divine grace after death cannot be transposed into historical events. When activist mystics were serious about creating a new world there would not occur the succession of the world of light from the world of darkness "but the coexistence of two ordinary worlds in a world war" (CW, 22:174). Such wars, moreover, were world wars not because they were conducted in a global theatre of military operations but "because the mysticism of sectarian exclusiveness endows the parties with the will to universal destruction" (CW, 22:172). This transitional period of catastrophic political action, Voegelin said, was marked by "eschatological violence" (CW, 22:174). That is, the violence undertaken by the activist mystics was understood by them as an operation by the divine spirit so that ordinary or commonsensical moral judgments did not apply. As a consequence, the activist mystics necessarily were engaged in political acts of annihilation that, to commonsense observers, looked like atrocities. Moreover for the activist mystics there were no sanctions in law because what looked to be senseless killings were, to them, redeemed as a divine plan to deliver the world from evil.[13] But because human beings were, in reality, incapable of transforming the human condition, the recalcitrance of the world to change

13 In his later work Voegelin discussed the dreams of activist mystics as indulgences in a second reality. See below, chapter five.

its nature simply became an excuse to redouble the eschatological violence to ensure the impossible become possible. This was, obviously, a magical operation and a recipe for endless and escalating violence.

In terms of commonsensical historiography and a history of ideas in the conventional sense, Voegelin drew attention to the fact that there was hardly any awareness of the existence of continuity in sentiments between the twelfth and sixteenth centuries or of an understanding of positivism, Marxism and Hitlerism as activist eschatological speculations that existed in some kind of continuity with the activist mysticism of the thirteenth century. And likewise, Hegelian and Marxian dialectics were not "a new historicism or a new realism but . . . a renewed ascendancy of Gnostic speculation" (CW, 22:178). Indeed, the contemporary struggle between the aforementioned ideological movements and Christianity was "not . . . a struggle between 'modern' ideas and Christianity but . . . a renewal of the old struggle between Christianity and Gnosis" (CW, 22:179). As Voegelin wrote to Engel-Janosi when he sent him a revised version of the chapter, he had undertaken an "effort to identify the unchanging elements that the modern age has in common with the Middle Ages" (CW, 29:567).

As a conventional problem in genealogy, the answer Voegelin gave was relatively straightforward: the Gnosticism of the Free Spirit of the sixteenth century had changed by the eighteenth century into the Gnosticism of Enlightened Reason, not into "respectable" sects such as Quakers and Baptists. "When we look for the successors of the medieval *perfecti* who are godded with Christ and from whom the logos flows like the living waters, we have to look in the direction of Locke, in whom reason was incarnate so perfectly that his personal mind became the criterion for the truth of revelation" (CW, 22:194). Voegelin developed this argument at length in the later volumes of the *History* (CW, 26:236ff) and in *The New Science of Politics*. Even in the discussion of the Renaissance and Reformation, he expanded his discussion of subsequent political sectarianism to include President Woodrow Wilson's "appealing formula" used to characterize the Great War as a "war to end war" or President Franklin Roosevelt's "senseless" demand for unconditional surrender. Wilson's slogan clearly expressed an eschatological enthusiasm; Roosevelt's policy made no sense "because in the historical continuity of statecraft, conditions of new order must prevail on the day after the conditions of the old order have broken down."[14]

14 CW, 22:176. "Unconditional surrender" was first introduced by Abraham Lincoln where arguably, in the context of civil war, it made sense.

Pointing to a "family resemblance" between medieval sectarians and modern ideologues was not, on its surface, a particularly compelling argument. Whatever the continuity between National Socialists and Bolsheviks (to say nothing of liberal American presidents) and the activist mystics of the Middle Ages, it was not one of direct influence. Besides, Voegelin certainly did not mean to suggest, for example, that Lenin or Hitler had assiduously studied medieval sectarians in order to put their ideas into practice. So what, then, did he mean by "continuity in sentiments"?

Bernard Yack gave one answer by arguing that discontent with the things of the world could certainly lead to similar, even common action but that response said nothing about the motivation of the actors or the historical continuity provided by a tradition.[15] However, as Thomas A. Heilke has pointed out, "Voegelin was well aware of the problems that Yack raises in this regard."[16] Early in "The People of God" Voegelin reflected on the difficulty of drawing a "genealogical line" from the Paulicians or Bogomils to Deists and Unitarian groups to the Utilitarian and Socialist clubs of the Enlightenment. Because of the aforementioned absence of coherent argument and doctrine, it was very difficult "to establish whether one can speak of a 'history' of the movements in a more rigorous sense at all." They were, however, "clearly related with each other through the centuries by the general structures of their sentiments and attitudes." Accordingly, whether there was an "actual historical influence" or whether the "experiences that supply the drive of the movements spring up anew every time, without close determination by preceding similar movements, is largely an open question" (CW, 22:139). It was also not a particularly interesting question because it was a question of historical fact and historical contingency. Voegelin, however, was concerned with *meaning* or as he said, "the general structure of . . . sentiments and attitudes." Thus it was a matter of relative indifference whether one found the attitudes of medieval activist mystics present in modern ideological actors or found ideological motives in the actions of medieval activist mystics: both aimed to alter the structure of reality chiefly through eschatological violence.[17]

15 Yack, *The Longing for Total Revolution: Philosophic Sources of Social Discontent from Rousseau to Marx and Nietzsche* (Princeton: Princeton University Press, 1986), 10–18.

16 Heilke, *Eric Voegelin: In Quest of Reality* (Lanham: Rowman and Littleford, 1999), 111.

17 See the insightful remarks of Hans Jonas on the hermeneutical parallels and biographical-scholarly significance of his studying with Heidegger and his work on an-

These historical events and actions were not merely analogous. They were expressions, under distinct historical circumstances, of a complex of sentiments and attitudes that remained constant. In the language of the argument developed in the previous chapter, one might say that, just as there existed a historicity of truth, so too did there exist a historicity of untruth, of pneumopathological experiences expressed in different historical circumstances that nevertheless carried the same or an equivalent meaning. This did not mean, as has sometimes been argued, that Voegelin took the side of the Church and expressed some kind of moral preference that the sectarians ought to have been crushed. To begin with, as he had many times reiterated over the whole course of his writings, the task of the political scientist is not to advance moralizing opinions. Second, the Church was as much a part of the historically problematic reality as the sectarians.[18] If, as he argued in *The New Science of Politics*, Gnosticism was the essence of modernity, the actualization in history of that essence would have been evident in the disintegration of the medieval balance.

In the *History of Political Ideas* Voegelin formulated the process as follows:

> The deepest sentiment that causes the postmedieval spiritual tensions of the West, we might say: the bearers of Western civilization do not want to be a senseless appendix to the history of antiquity. On the contrary, they want to understand their civilizational existence as meaningful. If the church is not able to see the hand of God in the history of mankind, men will not remain peaceable and satisfied but will go out in search of gods who take some interest in their civilizational efforts. The church has abandoned its spiritual leadership insofar as it has left postmedieval man without guidance in his endeavors to find meaning in a complex civilization that differs from the ancient

cient Gnosis, initially published as "Gnosticism and Modern Nihilism," *Social Research* 19 (1952): 430–52, then as an Epilogue to the second edition of *The Gnostic Religion: The Message of the Alien God and the Beginnings of Christianity* (Boston: Beacon Press, 1963), 320–40, and then in *The Phenomenon of Life: Toward a Philosophical Biology* (Chicago: University of Chicago Press, 1982), 211–34. See also Gregor Sebba, "History, Modernity and Gnosticism," in *The Philosophy of Order: Essays on History, Consciousness and Politics for Eric Voegelin on his Eightieth Birthday*, ed. Peter J. Opitz and Gregor Sebba (Stuttgart: Klett-Cotta, 1981), 190ff.

18 See for example, Voegelin's remarks on Aegidius Romanus, CW, 21:46–53.

> civilization that was absorbed and penetrated by the early church. In the face of this abandonment of the *magisterium* it is futile for Christian thinkers to accuse modern man who will not submit to the authority of the church of *superbia*. There is always enough *superbia* in man to make the accusation plausible, but the complaint dodges the real issue: that man in search of authority cannot find it in the church, through no fault of his own. From dissatisfaction at being engaged in a civilizational process without meaning stem the attempts as a reconstruction of meaning through the evocation of a new "sacred history" that began with Voltaire. (CW, 24:56–57)

As Heilke pointed out, Voegelin was not promoting some sort of univocal secularization thesis where intramundane content could be shoveled into now emptied religious forms.[19] Rather, as Voegelin put it in a 1946 paper delivered to the American Political Science Association: "History does not wait for those who do not catch on; to the failures of the Church correspond the secular movements that try to solve the problems of the moment, as best they can, without guidance from the Church and even in opposition to it."[20] The consequence of the reduction of the Church from a public representative of the authority of the spirit to a private organization was "dangerous because the life of the spirit is an essential part of human existence." As a result, a new spiritual force would "pour into the vacuum and give sacramental sanction to the existence of the community." That is, the initial schismatic religious movements were succeeded by other schismatic religious movements, not by secular ideologies. This theme was resumed in *The New Science of Politics*.

2. The Breakthrough of 1950

In chapter one we quoted a number of letters where Voegelin expressed his confidence that the *History of Political Ideas* would begin to appear in print during 1950. During the fall of 1949 Voegelin was completing the revised version of "The People of God," including a long section on Hieronymus Bosch (CW, 22:194–202), and he had begun to revise his understanding of myth. These intellectual developments, Szakolczai said, "seriously jeopardized

19 Heilke, *Eric Voegelin*, 114.

20 CW, 29:706. Voegelin submitted this paper, "Clericalism," for publication in the *APSR* but the editor, Frederic A. Ogg, declined to publish it. HI, 62:18.

not only the immediate publication schedule but also the entire status of the manuscript" and constituted the context for "the breakthrough of 1950."[21] Perhaps even more significant were the implications of three external and unrelated events.

First, early in February 1950 Voegelin received a travel grant from LSU to conduct research in Europe (HI, 23:28). Second and more important for present purposes, on 16 February, Jerome G. Kerwin wrote Voegelin to invite him to deliver a series of lectures about a year later under the auspices of the Walgreen Foundation at the University of Chicago.[22] Voegelin accepted four days later and proposed the title "On Representation." Because, as Kerwin indicated, the Walgreen Foundation was interested in the study of "American Institutions," Voegelin explained that "under the title 'On Representation' I could give a systematic treatment of the problem of representation; and I could give proportionately more space to materials drawn from the English and American tradition. If you have more leeway in fixing the subject, I could talk on the genesis of political science and the idea of right political order in the Greek fifth and fourth centuries—which has become somewhat my specialty." On 25 June, North Korea invaded South Korea and in October Kerwin suggested that Voegelin prepare a series of lectures on Marxism. Voegelin replied that three lectures were already finished "in a form that could go to the printer" and in any event he could not rewrite the series for delivery early in the New Year. However, "the philosophical analysis of Marxism will come into its own because the principles of Marxism, in my opinion, are a variant of medieval Gnosticism" (HI, 38:21). Third, in April, Voegelin learned that his application for a Guggenheim Fellowship was successful (HI, 15:25).

21 Szakolczai, *Reflexive Historical Sociology*, 51. Voegelin also characterized the writing of *The New Science of Politics* as a "breakthrough." CW, 34:91.

22 The Foundation was established by Charles R. Walgreen, the successful owner of a chain of drug stores. It offered scholarships to social science students in part because Walgreen thought his daughter had been corrupted by communist teachers at the University of Chicago. The foundation was also responsible for the publication of a remarkable series of books based on the Walgreen Lectures. For details, see Mary Ann Dzubach, *Robert M. Hutchins: Portrait of an Educator* (Chicago: University of Chicago Press, 1991), 173ff. Hans Morgenthau suggest to Kerwin that Voegelin would be a suitable Walgreen lecturer. Morgenthau to Kenneth W. Thompson, 10 April 1956. Rockefeller [Foundation] Archive Center, RF1.2/2005/531/4539. The terms of the contract were generous. Voegelin received a thousand dollars (nearly ten thousand 2014 dollars) and a generous royalty scale: 12.5% after 2000 copies were sold and 15% after 4000 sales. Kerwin to Voegelin, 16 February, 1950. HI, 38:21.

Voegelin's summer in Europe was important for two reasons. First, as Hollweck observed in his introduction to the second volume of Voegelin's correspondence, he connected or reconnected with European intellectual life (CW, 30:3). Letters to friends during the summer and following his return expressed great excitement at "the great contemporary renaissance of political science" (HI, 39:19). Several times he mentioned his enjoyable and fruitful encounters with old friends in Vienna, including Alois Dempf, but also meetings with Raymond Aron, Hans Barth, Karl Barth, Karl Jaspers, Friedrich Heer, Edgar Salin, Fritz Lieb, and especially Hans Urs von Balthasar. In Vienna he experienced the Cold War first hand.[23] When the Korean War broke out he wrote to Schütz: "The Korean affair makes me sick—but the idiocy of unconditional surrender, the demobilization, and the United Nations must find its revenge sometime" (CW, 30:58–59). That is, the problem of Western confusion, which he had noted in connection with Presidents Wilson and Roosevelt was still present as, of course, was the military threat of the Red Army in occupied Austria.

The second reason why the 1950 summer research trip was important is because it provided a long break from the problems Voegelin was dealing with in the *History*. In chapter one we noted that the interruption that began with the summer trip was continued in the fall as Voegelin completed his lectures. The break and the retheorization of the problems in his Walgreen lectures consolidated the insight Voegelin laboriously worked out in "The People of God," that there was "a kind of structured equivalence between ancient Gnosis and modern ideologies."[24] Moreover, Voegelin explained in *The New Science of Politics* why the "structural equivalence" was real: because the experiences, which in "The People of God" Voegelin identified as political sectarianism sustained by eschatological violence, were equivalent, not to say identical. *The New Science of Politics* added to that insight.

3. The New Science of Politics

Voegelin delivered six lectures in late January and early February 1951 under the title "Truth and Representation." The original subtitle was "An

23 See HI, 63:3 for his initial "Impressions" on his return to Vienna.

24 Szakolczai, *Reflexive Historical Sociology*, 55. Voegelin explained the significance of this interruption on his own terms in a letter to Eduard Baumgarten in the summer of 1951. See CW, 30:95–96. He also explained the significance of his new understanding of myth, which we analyze in chapter four.

introductory Essay." Other titles for the series of lectures included "The End of Modernity" and "An Introduction to the New Science of Politics." There were, moreover, variations in the lecture titles and the chapter titles of the finished book, the effect of which was to give greater emphasis and prominence to the significance of Gnosticism than to the occasions of its appearance (HI, 63:10). The title of lecture four, for example, was changed from "The Third Realm—The Nature of Modernity" to "Gnosticism—The Nature of Modernity" and lecture five was changed from, "The People of God—the English Case" to "Gnostic Revolution—The Puritan Case." Voegelin agreed to the title, *The New Science of Politics* because, he remarked later, it indicated a connection to Vico's *Nuova Scienza*, which in turn was conceived in opposition to Galileo's *Nuova Scienza*; likewise Voegelin's *New Science* was an attempt to restore the meaning of classical political science, in contrast to the dominant methods of positivism.[25] Of course Voegelin had used the term Gnosticism in the *History*. Section 10 of "The People of God" for example drew a parallel between medieval and reformation figures, including Boniface VIII and Luther, and ancient Gnostics (CW, 22:177–201; 235–36). Likewise the discussion of Comte and then Marx drew attention to the "spiritual disease" of the two thinkers expressed in an attitude of "Gnostic revolt" and "spiritual impotence."[26] Even so, the "Gnosticism thesis" was more systematically developed in *The New Science of Politics* than in his earlier work.

Let us begin with Voegelin's initial self-understanding of the book. To Heilman he said it would be his "first systematic study on theoretical politics since my abortive attempts about 1930" in the *Herrschaftslehre*.[27] He replied to a standard publisher's request for an author's account of the intention, content, and prospective audience for his forthcoming book in a seven-page document (HI, 38:21). He began, much as he did in the published

25 See Voegelin's Foreword to the German edition, *Die Neue Wissenschaft der Politik: Eine Einfüring*, ed. Peter J. Opitz (Freiburg and Munich: Alber, 1991), 13. The Introduction, which Szakolczai found to be highly polemical, was written after the lectures had been delivered (see Voegelin to Kerwin, 30 March 1951; HI, 38:21). See also *Reflexive Historical Sociology*, 58 ff., CW, 30:95–96. The original dust jacket bore the title *The New Science of Politics: An Introductory Essay*; the title page, *The New Science of Politics: An Introduction*.

26 CW, 26:236 ff., 368 ff.,' 199–200. See also Walsh's "Introduction," CW, 26:21ff.

27 *Robert B. Heilman and Eric Voegelin: A Friendship in Letters, 1944–1984*, ed. Charles R. Embry (Columbia: University of Missouri Press, 2004), 91.

Introduction, by stressing the destructive effects of positivism on the sciences of man and society. However, during the first half of the twentieth century a movement of restoration of political science had arisen in opposition to positivism. It was based on three constituent elements: (1) classical philosophy and Christianity, (2) a vast increase in historical knowledge, and (3) the experience of contemporary politics. Those who were undertaking this renovation of political science were not necessarily political scientists in the professional sense. They were as likely (or perhaps more likely) to be philosophers, theologians, historians, medievalists, classical philologists and so on. The first purpose of *The New Science of Politics*, then, was to introduce the reader "to his movement of restoration by applying its magnificent results to fundamental theoretical issues of political science in particular to the issue of representation."

At a time when political scientists in North America were debating the applicability of the so-called "scientific method" to the study of political phenomena, Voegelin made what must have seemed an astonishing argument. "Science," he said, was not a matter of method at all but of providing a truthful account to the structure of reality and of human participation in it. A "theoretical orientation" presupposed an explicit elaboration of criteria of "theoretical relevance," which in turn was the result of a philosophical anthropology (CW, 5:91–94; 106).

As Voegelin argued in the *History of Political Ideas*, social self-understanding was not the same as the theoretical analysis of it. On the contrary, as discussed in the previous chapter, the social cosmion "illuminated with meaning from within by the human beings who continuously create and bear it as the mode and condition of their self-realization" typically was in conflict with the meaning developed by the theorist (CW, 5:109). The illumination of the cosmion was accomplished by "an elaborate symbolism, in various degrees of compactness and differentiation" that expressed the internal structure of the cosmion and rendered it intelligible or "transparent for the mystery of human existence."[28] Later in the book, Voegelin reiterated that the creation of the cosmion was "universally human" inasmuch as all human beings and all human societies experienced a "horror of existence"

28 Voegelin discussed the problem of compactness and differentiation in more detail in *Order and History*, and we consider the question explicitly in the following chapter. In *The New Science of Politics* Voegelin simply restated the point made above in chapter one, that the theoretical concepts were not the same as political ideas, which now were identified as symbols, which were constituent elements of political reality.

without meaning and thus were inclined "to extend the meaning of order to the fact of existence" (CW, 5:224–25).[29]

Voegelin reiterated the problem he discussed in the 1940 letter to Max Mintz that was discussed in chapter one. As in the *History of Political Ideas*, Voegelin focused on the conflict in interpretations between an articulated political order, which lived within the social cosmion, and the theorist whose concepts referred to the reality of the cosmion but also were derived from it. Here he identified the previously mentioned process of "critical clarification" with the procedure introduced by Aristotle and the beginning of *The Politics* and related the problem to his philosophy of consciousness (CW, 5:110; 129). In contrast to the self-understanding of the cosmion, "the true order of man . . . is a constitution of the soul, to be defined in terms of certain experiences which have become predominant to the point of forming a character" (CW, 5:138). Philosophy or theoretical analysis amounted to the explication of "the content of a definite class of experiences" that, following Plato, Voegelin identified as an ascent "toward the border of transcendence" and an "anamnetic descent into the unconscious" (CW, 5:140).

The discovery of Plato, moreover, was a discovery about the structure of reality. Corresponding to the discovery of the height and depth was a discovery of the soul as the means by which consciousness became "open" to reality, including the divine beyond and the mysterious depth. The "opening" of the soul or the "differentiation of the soul" as the means by which the beyond and the depth were sensed,[30] were, he said, an "epochal event in the

29 Voegelin began the analysis not by discussing the internal cosmion of meaning but the external or, as he called it, the "elemental" problem of representation. Representation was a fundamental theoretical issue because it referred to a fundamental political act, namely the act by which a society produces a representative to act in its name. The constitution of a representative was a foundational act of power that generated a "we" who thereby became capable of concerted activities. Such societies came into being and disappeared. The "process in which human beings form themselves into a society for action shall be called the articulation of a society" (CW, 5:117). Societies became articulated when they produced such a representative and become disarticulated when, for one reason or another, they were unsuccessful in the attempt to do so. At the extreme, a disarticulated society disintegrated into several smaller (and more or less well-articulated) societies, hordes, tribes, clans, etc. In short, the necessary condition for political existence was articulation that engendered a political representative.

30 Voegelin called the soul the "sensorium" of the beyond and the depth. He continued to work out the implications of this insight until he died. Accordingly, we return to his later discussions in subsequent chapters.

history of mankind" because the experience of a soul open to transcendent reality was a discovery of a source of order superior to the established order of society; and likewise the truth that came to light in the experience was superior to the truth that informed the social self-interpretation of the cosmion. In other words, the experience that Plato symbolized by the phrase "God is the measure" (*Laws*, 716c) marked an advancement in clarity about the structure of reality. Moreover,

> the symbols in which he [the philosopher] explicated his experience formed the nucleus of a theory of social order. And, finally, it was possible to penetrate the mystery of critical clarification. Genetically it proved to consist in the discovery of the psyche and of its anthropological and theological truth, while critically it consisted in the measuring of the symbols in reality by the standards of the new truth." (CW, 5:141–42; 148; 215)

The argument of chapter one of *The New Science of Politics*, therefore was intended to secure the distinction between the truth of the cosmion and the truth of the theorist or philosopher. Furthermore, it established a hierarchy between the two inasmuch as the "critical clarification" undertaken by the theorist provided an insight that was unavailable to those who still lived within the taken-for-granted cosmion. In chapter two Voegelin discussed how "the field of competitive types of truth is historically broadened by the appearance of Christianity" (CW, 5:149). Voegelin's discussion of philosophy and Christian revelation was connected to the problem of the historicity of truth. Here he presented the problem in terms of "the assumption that the substance of history consists in the experiences in which man gains the understanding of his humanity and together with it the understanding of its limits" (CW, 5:151). The assumption entailed a theoretical consequence that Voegelin called a "principle," namely "that a theory of human existence in society must operate within the medium of experiences which have differentiated historically" (CW, 5:151). Furthermore, "since the maximum differentiation was achieved through Greek philosophy and Christianity, this means concretely that theory is bound to move within the historical horizon of classic and Christian experiences" (CW, 5:152). Voegelin had already provided an argument as to why this last proposition was true in the discussion of the process of critical clarification; it was a problem to which we return in later chapters. For the present, let us simply accept the argument as valid.

Voegelin illustrated the conflict between Christian truth and the truth of the cosmion by comparing St. Augustine's experience of reality symbolized by the two cities with that of his Roman antagonists who "live firmly in their political myth" based on "the archaic experience of social order before its dissolution through the experience of the mystic philosophers" (CW, 5:160). Moreover, if we recall that the "substance of history" consisted in experiences by which human beings came increasingly to understand themselves, and that the insights afforded by philosophy and Christian revelation endowed human beings with the capacity "to play the role of rational contemplator and pragmatic master of a nature which has lost its demonic terrors" (CW, 5:151), then the persecutions of the Christians no less than the trial of Socrates, made perfect sense. Just as Socrates was charged with impiety and with introducing new diamonic things, "the Christians were persecuted for a good reason; there was a revolutionary substance in Christianity that made it incompatible with paganism," namely its "uncompromising radical de-divinization of the world." Indeed, de-divinization was "a sedition against the divinity" that animated the cosmos and thus the Imperial cosmion (CW, 5:169).

If the triumph of Christianity in the Roman Empire amounted to the de-divinization of the temporal sphere of power, and if this achievement was a "maximum differentiation" in the sense that Christianity reordered human existence in society by way of "the experience of man's destination, by the grace of the world-transcendent God, toward eternal life in beatific vision" (CW, 5:175), then any effort at "re-divinization" would necessarily entail a retreat from this maximum of insight. This did not, however, mean a recovery or revival of the gods of the Roman Empire but, as we saw in "The People of God" chapter, a revival of sentiments and experiences that had been suppressed by the Church as heretical, particularly eschatological experiences that the Kingdom of God was about to arrive (as distinct from the apocalyptic experience that the Church was the representative of Christ in history).

As noted in previous sections, the medieval political order of Church and Empire or, to use the new terminology, the articulation of Western Christendom into spiritual and temporal orders, represented both the organization of political existence and the representation of transcendent meaning. Moreover, during the period of Germanic invasions, according to Voegelin, Augustine used the term *saeculum senescens*, the old age of the world, to express the sentiment that temporal history was simply waiting for the end times ushered in by the Second Coming of Christ, more or less along the lines of the Book of Revelation. By the twelfth century, however, the Cluniac reforms, the growth of towns, the Crusades, and so on led to changes that Charles Haskins called the renaissance of the twelfth century.[31] The implication, as we argued above, was that the "compromise with the world" undertaken by the Church was no longer bearable. In its place the sentiment was growing that the structure of the world was increasingly blended with the realm not of this world: "the world had entered the realm of God" (CW, 20:109). The first clear and thorough presentation of how to understand the new *saeculum* was made by Joachim of Flora (CW, 20:126ff).

In *The New Science of Politics*, Voegelin provided a synopsis of Joachim's new symbolization.[32] The significance of Joachim's evocation was that it expressed the new sentiment of an "increase in fulfillment within history" as a result of a "new transcendental irruption of the spirit" (CW, 5:185). Joachim did not simply give expression to the new sentiments of the age, he introduced a new theoretical problem, the meaning, *eidos*, or essence of history, which existed neither in philosophy nor in Christianity. As Voegelin summarized the issue: "the problem of an eidos in history . . . arises only when Christian transcendental fulfillment becomes immanentized." More precisely, an ersatz historical eidos could be created by an act of the human imagination whereby the Christian faith in the destination of human life would be postulated as taking place here and now and not by the grace of God after death. In Voegelin's words, "the meaning of history, thus, is an illusion; and this illusionary eidos is created by treating a symbol of faith as if it were an object of immanent experience" (CW, 5:185–86).

Because the attempt to construct a meaning of history looks like a "rather elemental" fallacy, the question immediately arose: why was it done? Voegelin allowed as it was not a matter of stupidity but a "drive" that blinded Joachim and his successors to the fallacy. "On this point there is no doubt. They achieved a certainty about the meaning of history and about their own place in it, which otherwise they would not have" (CW, 5:187). Moreover, this attempt to bring knowledge of transcendence into a firmer possession than could be afforded by the cognition of faith was the essential attribute of "Gnostic experience" (CW, 5:189). As with the earlier discussion of "The

31 Haskins, *The Renaissance of the Twelfth Century* (Cambridge: Harvard University Press, 1927).

32 For a more comprehensive account, see Warwick Gould and Marjorie Reeves, *Joachim of Fiore and the Myth of the Eternal Evangel in the Nineteenth and Twentieth Centuries* (Oxford: Clarendon, 2001).

People of God," whether one chose to call medieval sectarianism ideological or modern ideologies anti-Christian sectarian movements was secondary: "the best course will be to drop such questions and to recognize the essence of modernity as the growth of Gnosticism" (CW, 5:190).

Finally, Voegelin argued, as in "The People of God," that one of the reasons for the growth in the social effectiveness of Gnosticism was the failure of the Church to provide a meaning for the expanding institutions of the West. Gnostic speculation replaced the uncertainty of faith with a clear and certain meaning to action undertaken here and now by endowing human worldly activity with the sentiments that previously were attached to Christian eschatological fulfillment. To the extent that this immanetization increasingly penetrated Western consciousness, "civilizational activity became a mystical work of self-salvation." Historically this "miracle" of self-salvation was imaginatively achieved "by the successive types of Gnostic action that have made modern civilization what it is." Voegelin mentioned the literary and artistic achievement of the humanistic intellectual that secured the immortality of fame, followed by the "discipline and economic success that certified salvation to the Puritan saint . . . the civilizational contribution of the liberals and Progressives, and, finally . . . the revolutionary action that will establish the Communist or some other Gnostic millennium" (CW, 5:193). The historical result has certainly been impressive: "the endowment with the meaning of salvation has made the rise of the West, indeed, an apocalypse of civilization" (CW, 5:194).

Such "miracles" were too good to be true. The more human energy was devoted to self-salvation through intramundane activity, "the further the human beings who engage on this enterprise move away from the life of the spirit. And since the life of the spirit is the source of order in man and society, the very success of Gnostic civilization is the cause of its decline." The limit of civilizational advance and spiritual decline "is reached when an activist sect which represents the Gnostic truth organizes the civilization into an empire under its rule. Totalitarianism, defined as the existential rule of Gnostic activists, is the end form of progressive civilization" (CW, 5:195).

Voegelin was very much aware that the analysis of Gnostic experience—and he reiterated "that the substance of history is to be found on the level of experiences, not on the level of ideas" (CW, 5:190)—resulted in a concept of modernity "that seems to be at variance with the conventional sense of the term" (CW, 5:196). By Voegelin's interpretation, then, the periodization of Western history between medieval and modern needed to be replaced by the notion of a continuous evolution whereby modern Gnosticism came to dominate the earlier discoveries of philosophical and Christian truth. As in "The People of God," Voegelin called the "pneumopathological state" of the Gnostic sectarians "revolutionary." However, "since this program cannot be carried out in historical reality," Gnostic revolutionaries must invariably institutionalize their partial successes in this existential struggle by a compromise with reality. Whatever emerged from the compromise, "it will not be the transfigured world envisaged by Gnostic symbolism." Accordingly, it would be misleading to focus on the various compromises, stabilizations, and tactics because "the essential unity of the variegated Gnostic phenomena would disappear" (CW, 5:201; 211).

The final chapter, "The End of Modernity," made two significant points. The first, which also was made in the Introduction, was that "the building-up of spiritual and intellectual resources against Gnosticism in all its variants" was a significant attribute of contemporary life. "The reconstitution of a science of man and society is one of the remarkable events of the last half-century and, in retrospect from a future vantage point, will perhaps appear as the most important event in our time" (CW, 5:222). This development in the area of philosophical anthropology and the historical sciences was "as yet practically unknown to the general public" as Voegelin had noted on a number of previous occasions (CW, 5:90). That was one of the reasons he called the book *The New Science of Politics*.

The second point concerned the self-defeating character of Gnosticism. Granted that the success in the growth of modern Gnosticism from medieval sectarian activism had shaped the imagery of large numbers of human beings, it was also true that this imagery constituted a "dream world." The premise of the dream world was the nonrecognition of reality. As a consequence, actions that would be considered morally insane because of the real effects they had "will be considered moral in the dream world because they intended an entirely different effect" (CW, 5:226). The identification of the dream world with reality had the secondary consequence of making the rational connection of cause and effect, of means and ends, impossible. Thus when Gnostic leaders were compelled to deal with enemies, instead of a rational response, they undertook "magic operations in the dream world, such as disapproval, moral condemnation, declarations of intention, resolutions, appeals to the opinion of mankind, branding enemies as aggressors, outlawing war, propaganda for world peace and world government, etc." (CW, 5:227).

By way of conclusion to this section, three things immediately stood out about *The New Science of Politics*. The first was that it was a kind of culmination of the approach Voegelin had developed during the late 1940s for handling the enormous volume of historical and textual materials he had mastered. In this respect it was continuous with the *History of Political Ideas*. But second, in developing the "Gnosticism thesis" Voegelin had achieved a genuine new insight concerning the course of Western civilization. As he wrote to his publisher, "the principal achievement of the book is the interpretation of modernity as the rise of political Gnosis since the high Middle Ages, in rivalry with the classic and Christian tradition, and of its destructive effects on western civilization." Voegelin understood his analysis to have been based on "the Platonic-Aristotelian science of politics," notably Plato's understanding of myth as a means for human beings to express the ascent and descent of the soul, and Aristotle's analysis of the process of "critical clarification." And third, the irrationality of Gnostic modernity was not to be understood in terms of "the pessimism of cycle theorists" (cf. CW, 33:41ff). On the contrary, the crisis of modernity was only one component in contemporary civilization. The other, "the remedial forces of the classic and Christian tradition, hold out the promise of recovery" (HI, 38:21).

4. The Reception

The initial reception of Voegelin's book was surprising both to him in the 1950s and is today to persons reading the relevant correspondence and reviews. "Originally," Voegelin wrote several years later, "I had expected it would be a complete flop, considering the state of interest in theory in this country."[33] Many of those who read the book were unquestionably intelligent scholars with solid and well deserved reputations, though they were not, perhaps interested in Voegelin's understanding of theory. Reading their reviews and other remarks on *The New Science of Politics*, however, is often shocking; one wonders how they could be so careless, not to say perverse, in their accounts of what Voegelin said and meant. It is true, of course, that any author's work may be improved, that the progress of science introduces new facts and evidence, and that even Homer nods. *The New Science* was no exception. The value of even misdirected criticism, however, lies elsewhere. First of all, the review of a positivist would illustrate Voegelin's criticism of positivism. By pointing to such miscreant adventures as Voegelin's

33 Voegelin to Roger W. Shugg, Director of the University of Chicago Press, 7 October 1960. HI, 38:21.

toying with metaphysics and theology, a positivist critic scrupulously observed the taboo that, according to Voegelin, was the source of so much irrationality in contemporary political science. Others denounced him in more or less explicit terms for the policy implications they detected, thus confirming Voegelin's analysis of the pragmatic consequences of Gnosticism. Finally critics who disagreed strongly with one or another points in Voegelin's analysis usually did so because they found a crucial turning point in his argument and the implications of it to be unacceptable to their "position" on one thing or another. The importance of such texts attached not to the fact that the author did not like what he (they were almost all men) encountered but that, perhaps inadvertently, the critic had stumbled on something important. In any event, the defective theoretical achievements of most of Voegelin's critics are not our prime concern. The significance of even those defective criticisms is. On the other hand, occasionally a reviewer was adequate to the text or simply praised the author's erudition or achievement. Voegelin doubtless found such responses gratifying, but they are not particularly informative.

We will look first at a sample of contemporary scholarly reviews, then at Voegelin's correspondence, unpublished at the time, and then at accounts in the popular press. We conclude with a brief account of a retrospective analysis half a century after publication and of Voegelin's reflections on the reception of the book.

a. Academic Reviews

It is the nature of academic reviews to appear often years after the book appeared. At their best they provide an analysis of an author's argument and situate it in the context of other literature on the same or related problems. It is a relatively minor matter for a reviewer to provide his or her personal opinions. This does not mean that academic reviewers are discouraged by convention from recording their criticism. On the contrary; but criticism is expected to be based on understanding, analysis, and evidence, often new evidence. We consider only a few of the many reviews collected by the University of Chicago Press and preserved in the Voegelin archive at the Hoover Institution.

The reviews that most conformed to conventional academic standards tended to be favorable. Francis G. Wilson, in the *American Political Science Review* and Michael Oakeshott in *The Times Literary Supplement* were both careful and respectful. Because of Voegelin's historical and philosophical erudition, Wilson wrote, "he reduces the shock to the average political scientist when he is led outside of the presuppositions of liberalism, a shock that is a part both of the process of self-interpretation and self-education."[34] For Oakeshott, *The New Science of Politics* was

> one of the most enlightening essays on the character of European politics that has appeared for half a century." It was, he added, "a book powerful and vivid enough to make agreement or disagreement with even its main thesis relatively unimportant. It cannot fail to instruct even those whom it does not convince. In spite of its comprehensive sweep, it escapes vagueness; and there are reservations enough to make it exaggerations harmless. . . . And if the reader puts it down with the conviction he has been given a new understanding of European politics rather than a glimpse of a New Science of Politics, perhaps that is what was intended.[35]

Hans Aufricht provided a straightforward exegesis and compared Voegelin's analysis to that of Hans Jonas. He disagreed with Voegelin's theological formulations but this misunderstanding was subsequently cleared up.[36] Similarly Martin Wight, John Hallowell, and William L. Lucey combined high praise for Voegelin's achievement and a lucid analysis of his argument. They also all criticized Voegelin's language as "an opaque German-American style," as pedantic, as lacking in "terminological precision and clarity" and simply as "outrageous." On the other hand, A. T Polyzoides considered the book "compact and very readable" because of its "uniformly simple and clear language."[37]

34 Wilson, Review, *APSR* 47 (1953): 542.

35 Anon., "The Character of European Politics," *Times Literary Supplement* (7 August, 1953), 504. The evidence that Oakeshott was the author of this anonymous review is in Luke O'Sullivan, ed., *Michael Oakeshott, Selected Writings*, vol.2, *What is History? And Other Essays* (Luton: Andrews, 2011), 210–14. See also CW, 30:151.

36 Aufricht, "A Restatement of Political Theory: A Note on Eric Voegelin's 'The New Science of Politics,'" *The Western Political Quarterly* 6 (1953): 458–68. See also HI, 7:1.

37 Wight, "Review," *International Affairs* 31 (1955): 336; Hallowell, "Review," *Louisiana Law Review* 13:3 (1953): 525–30; cf. CW, 30:138–41; HI, 16:3; Lucey, "Review," *Social Order* (Feb. 1953): 95; HI, 63:12; Polyzoides, "Review," *The Personalist* 35 (1953): 90. See also Robert Ammerman, "Review," *Philosophy and Phenomenological Research* 19 (1959): 539–40. Herman Finer made essentially the same point in October 1952 in a letter: "You want people to understand you,"

The most instructive, not to say amusing, responses were also those that were highly critical. Of these, the most superficial hardly began to grapple with Voegelin's argument. Hans Kohn dismissed the book as "in no way a new theory."[38] Frank Sherwood was alarmed at Voegelin's "bald authoritarian talk" and his closeness to Henry R. Luce (an allusion to the coverage given the book by *Time* magazine, which is discussed below).[39] George Catlin expressed the same sentiment in a more scholarly tone. "This is a small curious book of great importance," he began. He noted that Voegelin was "a member of the new immigration to America" and that he was teaching at Louisiana State University, "a university which owes so much to the late Senator Long." Like Hans Morgenthau, Voegelin "expresses a specifically Germanic tradition in political thought, as distinct from that American tradition which stems from Locke. In some of his themes the debt is considerable to the *Abendländische Eschatalogie* of Jacob Taubes. He is also especially significant as giving expression to a particular school of Catholic thought." Catlin "happens to share this faith" and so is sympathetic towards Voegelin's "system of values" and his philosophy of history. However, Voegelin, like François Mauriac and Graham Greene seemed to be "infected" by the heresy of Jansenism, "and in the modern vein, 'anxiety,' *Angst*, is lauded at the expense of spiritual assurance and joy." As a result, Catlin declared, Voegelin had no concern for any earthly justice; "I regard Professor Voegelin's treatise as very dangerous in trend—indeed as being as reactionary as anything I have noted in America in my memory." In short, "I suspect that his so-called 'science of order' usually has another less pleasant name."[40]

In his review Julian Franklin combined a plausible summary with considerable confusion that ended in a lively denunciation. Voegelin's method, he said, was "mystic realism," which in due course was applied to "the problem of social representation." This method, transformed into a "view," considered representation to be "the appearance of universals as concrete symbols, and the universal symbolized by society is man." On the basis of this somewhat obscure remark, Franklin deduced that "Voegelin therefore regards society as a collective effort to represent the human essence as a

he wrote. "You know into what comparatively uneducated hands your work may get: why leave it to uneducated teachers to reach your ultimate readers by second hand distortion?" (HI, 12:17).

38 *The Nation* 176:3 (17 Jan. 1953): 57.

39 *Frontier* (April 1953); HI, 63:12.

40 Catlin, "Review," *Political Studies* 11 (1954): 174–75.

concrete historical fact." Voegelin's point in fact was not that the theorist "regards" society one way or another but that political societies understand themselves as representative of a truth that is greater than, or that transcends, their sheer existence. That is why Voegelin used the term "cosmion." According to Franklin, Voegelin "held" that "social institutions, political structures and individual personalities" were the imperfect means by which this representation was to be achieved. Franklin then said that "Voegelin denies, however, that the truth of humanity can ever be embodied in a concrete social order."

In fact what Voegelin "held" or "denied" was not evidence of some idiosyncratic opinion. All the evidence of *The New Science of Politics*, as discussed in the previous section, indicated that no concrete society was capable of embodying the truth of humanity and, moreover, the members of such societies were all well aware of it. This provisional insight regarding "representation and existence," to use the title of Voegelin's first chapter, then led to the problem of "representation and truth," to use the title of the second, which introduced the problem of the criteria of truth for which the example of the opposition of the philosopher and the polis was likely the most well-known. These were, to repeat, evidence-based arguments, not unsubstantiated opinions.

Franklin summarized the last half of the book as "a bitter polemic against the political civilization of the West," that ended with Voegelin's call for "the 'end of modernity,' both in theory and in practice" and a prediction of a "return to theocratic traditions by the more stable nations of the West." Franklin's summary led him to make a final characterization: Voegelin had developed an "antirationalist" philosophy of politics that borrowed from Burke, continental Romanticism, Spengler, and the ultramontanist Donorso Cortes. Moreover, if Voegelin had been astute enough to acknowledge these "forebears" then "he might have clarified the social implications of his own position." Franklin's implication seemed to have been that Voegelin was keeping bad company for indulging in his alleged polemic against the political civilization of the West. His conclusion followed inevitably, more in sorrow than in anger: Voegelin had dogmatically rejected "Western liberalism." Whatever insights Voegelin's argument might have contained—for Western liberalism was not immune to criticism, Franklin allowed—"is lost in a maze of neo-Platonist terminology."[41]

41 Franklin, "Review," *Political Science Quarterly* 68 (1953): 157–58. Incidentally, Martin Wight answered Franklin's criticism that Voegelin was "anti-rational" or

Given the importance of the fact-value distinction in postwar social science, and given Voegelin's criticism of it in the Introduction, it comes as no surprise that the orthodox defenders of this methodological doctrine objected strongly to Voegelin's critique.

The New Science of Politics, Bernard Wand wrote, attempted "on a grand scale to criticize sociology as the science of society, and in its stead to erect a science of politics in terms of a theory of representation." Because it was "a purely descriptive science," sociology had accepted the fact-value distinction "and as a consequence, has been unconcerned with a science of order based on ontology." Wand's summary of Voegelin's argument was adequate, but he took issue with what he saw as its chief implication, Voegelin's apparent inability to distinguish "the rebel who reacts against the injustice of a concrete situation and the revolutionary who would mold the world nearer to his heart's desire." This oversight, according to Wand, stemmed from Voegelin's rejection of the fact-value doctrine: "once grant that it is mere opinion to talk about values but knowledge to have a science of order grounded in the nature of things, then that order must be accepted in all its aspects without challenge." In short, Voegelin, according to Wand, was simply dogmatic. And a good dose of the fact-value distinction would indicate that the so-called science of order is really just an opinion or that, properly speaking, there is no knowledge of social order at all. To claim otherwise was, clearly, to think oneself (wrongly) superior to "mere opinion." Not surprisingly Wand ended his remarks with the comment that "the book is marred by an undertone of intellectual arrogance which too often becomes explicit."[42]

In two reviews, Arnold Brecht provided a more extensive criticism based essentially on the "position" espoused by Wand. Brecht opened his review in *Social Research* with the declaration that "the mid-century revolt against positivism, scientific method, and relativism in political science is making headway." Voegelin's book was a "leading expression" of this revolt. It had been "offered as a challenge, and must be appraised and answered as

even romantic: "The political student with a strong possessive attachment to the word 'rationalist' will no doubt want to dismiss Voegelin as 'anti-rationalist,' but Voegelin takes care of him in several trenchant passages: Voegelin's theory included and explains him with a completeness that his theory cannot do for Voegelin" (*International Affairs* 31 [1955]: 336). Like Franklin, Alan Gewerth combined a plausible summary with a strong denunciation of the implications. See his review in *Ethics* 63 (1953): 142–44.

42 Wand, "Review," *Philosophical Review* 62 (1953): 608–9.

such," even though "the main body of the book hardly refers to the fundamental revolt." Brecht called himself a "scientific value-relativist," a "position" he identified with that of Max Weber and from which he proposed to interpret Voegelin's work. In his own words, he proposed to "cull the particular message of these [six] chapters from the wealth of material with which it is mingled." We consider first Brecht's method of culling, offer an appraisal of the results, and then indicate the reason why they were defective.[43]

Brecht began clearly enough by noting that representation was not confined to democracies. "There is an 'existential' meaning of representation, which must not be overlooked." Brecht did not say what Voegelin meant by existential representation but he did note an obvious consequence. "To introduce democratic representative institutions where existential conditions for their functioning are not present can only aggravate international disorder" (cf. CW, 5:125–26). However, Brecht's next sentence indicated that, in fact, he had not grasped Voegelin's argument: "Existential representation must mirror the 'self-interpretation' of society, in which transcendent elements have always played a significant role." Brecht's *must* is misleading: it would be more accurate to say that an existential representative expressed the self-interpretation of society. That is, so to speak, the purpose of such representatives.

Brecht was correct to stress the "monadic" claim (his term, not Voegelin's) of cosmological empires to represent an order that transcends them; he was also correct in raising the question of a truth that can pierce the claims of the cosmological empires to be the embodiment of order. "Such a truth exists, Voegelin assures us." Voegelin was not the only one to "assure" us, as Brecht indicated in the sentences immediately following: there was for example evidence—from China, India, Persia, Greece and Israel. Brecht then stated, correctly, "the true nature of man was found in his psyche, in his soul, in his relation to God," but proceeded (again) to misdirect Voegelin's argument. "Consequently," Brecht wrote, "the author suggests, the question of the existential meaning of society must be raised to the level where the decisive question is, 'which society represents transcendental truth?'" This "decisive question" was not asked by Voegelin. In fact, it would be senseless to ask it since *all* political orders represent

43 In 1946 Voegelin and Brecht were on a round-table panel at the APSA annual meeting. I discussed the results of the panel in *Eric Voegelin and the Foundations of Modern Political Science* (Columbia: University of Missouri Press, 1999), 82–89.

transcendental truth, as Brecht had already indicated with respect to the cosmological empires. The illustration he adduced compounded the misunderstanding: "The later Roman emperors attempted to organize secular power in such a way that it represented the spiritual destiny of man. But these attempts failed. Instead, the idea of double representation of society by church and empire came to be adopted, and it was preserved throughout the Middle Ages; secular power was becoming 'de-divinized.'" Superficially Brecht's summary seemed plausible. Unfortunately it is plausible only so long as it remained superficial and failed to raise any genuinely "decisive questions."

Let us consider his remarks in some detail. First, to speak of "secular power" in connection with Roman politics is obviously anachronistic. Second, the matters discussed in Section 8 of Chapter Three of *The New Science of Politics* (to which Brecht probably was referring) were considerably more interesting theoretically than any attempt by "Roman emperors" to develop a civil theology. To give but one example: the possibility that Christianity could serve as a Roman civil theology was plausible because the one God of Christianity could be interpreted in light of a metaphysical monotheism that had taken a quasi-doctrinal form as early as Aristotle's *Metaphysics* (1976a) as well as with Philo Judaeus, whom Voegelin discussed at some length. Third, it was surely significant to know *why* this attempt "failed," and Voegelin provided a careful analysis of the reasons, all of which centered on the Christian insight that the spiritual destiny of human beings cannot be represented by any political organization. This is why the institutions of church and empire (which were hardly "ideas," as Brecht had called them) were adopted as more or less adequate vehicles to represent human being in Western society.

Brecht then turned to another topic, Voegelin's terminology: "Professor Voegelin tends to baffle his readers by his use of terms." Brecht chose an example that was not at all baffling: "To divinize secular power means, to him, not to fill it with religious faith and zeal, but to arrogate to it divine qualities. Therefore, in his terminology, it was right for St. Augustine to 'de-divinize' secular power, and it was wrong for the later Gnostics to 're-divinize' it." The implication that Voegelin was using some sort of private language to express a personal preference for Augustine over some unspecified "later Gnostics" was misleading in the extreme. Voegelin provided a careful analysis of Augustine's account of reality experienced and expressed in Christian symbols. Moreover, he contrasted it with the attempts to ignore reality and substitute an imaginary product for it; and finally, Voegelin indicated the motive for undertaking the imaginative constructions. Moreover, Voegelin's analysis of Augustine was a model of clarity.

According to Brecht, Gnosticism "is the term Voegelin uses for all those movements that assert, not that they know God—a claim to which Voegelin would not object—but that they know secular history in advance." Considering the well-known words of Saint Paul (I Cor. 13:12) that in this world we "see through a glass, darkly; but then face to face," it is surprising that Brecht provided no evidence that Voegelin would not object to applying the term Gnostic to all those who claim to know God. Moreover, by confining Gnosticism to the knowledge of "secular history" Brecht looked at one of the consequences of Gnosticism, not at its experiential core.

Brecht found the other consequences, spelled out in the concluding chapters, worthy of attention, "whether or not one agrees with every strong passage." His main objections, however, were directed at Voegelin's argument in the Introduction, particularly the notion that "like other neo-Thomists, such as Jacques Maritain, he [Voegelin] opposes the restriction of the term 'science' to what is now called [by Brecht] scientific (empirico-logical) method. Demanding a 'restoration' of political science in its scholastic sense, which included metaphysics, he calls for its 're-theorization,' and for a 'new craftsmanship of metaphysical speculation.'"[44] This was the core of Brecht's disagreement with Voegelin. He was able to accept certain commonsensical aspects of Voegelin's argument, despite the unspecified "strong passages" to which he registered a *pro forma* objection. However, as a result of Brecht's "position," he distorted or misunderstood the central issues.

Accordingly, Brecht agreed it was important to devote attention "to metaphysical alternatives in scholarly discussions and explanations of the universe." What was utterly unacceptable was to conclude that one or another of these "metaphysical alternatives" was true or false. "But," Brecht went on, "if he wants to imply that the truth of any particular metaphysical

44 In fact, Voegelin did not use the adjective "new." He wrote: "The understanding of ontology as well as the craftsmanship of metaphysical speculation had to be regained, and especially philosophical anthropology as a science had to be re-established." Once that had been achieved, several other conditions could be met or met sufficiently so that it made sense to write of a "restoration of political science." See CW, 5:107. In his review of *The New Science of Politics* in *Annals* 288 (1953): 215–16, Brecht also remarked that "what the author calls a 'new science' is exposed to the rejoinder, certain to be raised by nonbelievers, and not by them alone, that it is neither new nor science, but rather a revival of Thomism and an appeal to unscientific metaphysical speculations. . . ."

speculation can be established, like empirico-logical truth, by some sort of intersubjective demonstration, then we are confronted with an entirely different challenge." In one sense, Brecht was correct: it does take a particularly sensitive consciousness to follow a metaphysical argument, if not exactly a "proof." Moreover, as Voegelin said, "the craftsmanship of metaphysical speculation," such as understanding why the range and variety of souls formed a central element in Plato's anthropology, had to be regained. That was not, however, Brecht's meaning. Indeed, he did not mention philosophical anthropology at all. For him, *the* standard for "intersubjective demonstration" was set by "empirico-logical truth." Other so-called truths were mere, which is to say, empty or imaginary, speculation. For Brecht, this was a question of the greatest importance. "Unfortunately, he [Voegelin] treats this crucial problem, which is at the very base of the modern dichotomy between philosophy and science, rather cavalierly. It does not seem to interest him." Brecht provided a footnote to several of his own articles in order to indicate just how important this "crucial problem" was.

Brecht ended his review by objecting to Voegelin's alleged misrepresentation of Max Weber, but agreed with Voegelin "in desiring that attention be redirected to the deeper levels of human needs, and to a methodical discussion of metaphysical intimations and alternatives—in political science as well as elsewhere in the sciences. In this context, Voegelin's book is a contribution of the highest rank."[45]

The final three responses we consider are almost caricatures of what a scholarly review is. William Anderson began his remarks by declaring that *The New Science of Politics* was not about politics as he understood the term, nor was it scientific. Moreover, "if I know anything about political scientists in the United States, very few of them will come even close to guessing from its title alone the nature and contents of this work." Second, after "having read the work with much difficulty and great expenditure of time I still do not claim to understand it thoroughly." Nor would he attempt to summarize the argument, presumably for the same reason. Having thus disqualified himself as a competent reviewer, he nevertheless pressed on to characterize the book: "I would venture to describe the book as an effort to transmute the study of politics directly into an amalgam of metaphysics and theology." Far from explaining what he meant by amalgamating metaphysics and theology, Anderson explicitly refused: "I have no competence in those fields." He did, however, claim competence to "pass upon," that is, to judge,

45 Brecht, "A New Science of Politics," *Social Research* 20 (1953): 230–35.

the validity of the claim Voegelin made regarding science. Regrettably, "I cannot accept this work as a work on the science of politics." Words have meanings, according to Anderson, and one cannot simply make metaphysics, theology and philosophical anthropology "into science or into political science, merely by calling them that." Nor was there anything new in *The New Science of Politics* except in the sense that "any scholar who traverses the literature in a field can turn up with an individualized subjective interpretation, and with some items of topical interest not emphasized in other writers." Worse than containing nothing new, "the emphasis is distinctly upon ancient and medieval writers," though Comte and Marx, it was true, "receive a considerable amount of adverse attention."

Immediately after having declared the book neither new nor scientific nor really dealing with politics either, Anderson summarized quite accurately Voegelin's point regarding the restoration of political science during the previous half-century. He seized upon Voegelin's remark that these developments were "practically unknown to the general public," and triumphantly declared that he knew nothing about them either. The balance of his review attempted to summarize Voegelin's argument regarding representation and Gnosticism. Perhaps the kindest thing one could say about the results would be that they confirmed Voegelin's own observation that "the attack on metaphysics can be undertaken with a good conscience only from the safe distance of imperfect knowledge" (CW, 5:103).

Even relatively straightforward aspects of Voegelin's argument were beyond Anderson's understanding. For example, we quoted in the previous section Voegelin's remark that, because political societies "do not exist as cosmic fixtures from eternity but grow in history[,] this process in which human beings form themselves into a society for action shall be called the articulation of society." As a result of this "political articulation" we find rulers who are capable of acting on behalf of society. "Articulation, thus, is the condition of representation. In order to come into existence, a society must articulate itself by producing a representative that will act for it" (CW, 5:117; 120). According to Anderson, however, this comparatively simple observation by Voegelin meant that: "While men receded into the background, society articulates itself" and did so "I judge, by establishing symbols and a representative ruler or system of rule which give meaning, or 'transcendent truth,' to the society, and thus prepare it 'for action in history.' The ruler represents not only the society but also the will of God in the world." Now, there are modes of articulation that conform to the characterization of a ruler representing an articulated society and the will of God in the world, and Voegelin discussed them (CW, 5:132–35). However Anderson drew the odd conclusion that "the ruler of an articulated society represents truth, order, faith, and civilization, in a transcendent sense beyond the power of man's puny reason to criticize or deny."

Anderson then illustrated his objection by referring to "the history of the Lombards who 'articulated' themselves under a king, and then went out and destroyed all their enemies and took their possessions," which he said "is given as an apparently approved example of how the articulating process works." Given that Anderson subsequently noted that, in the medieval world: "An amalgamated Christian-classical tradition and order then prevailed, and, such as it was, it seems to have the approval of the author," he seemed to imply that Voegelin "approved" of the Lombard practice of warfare (see CW, 5:124–25). Anderson's account of Joachim of Flora was equally bizarre. Joachim "is the expounder of a heresy," called Gnosticism, which Anderson also called with measured sarcasm, "this wicked cult and all its works." In any event, it was to Joachim "the author most fully pays his mordant respects. Gnosticism, or the belief of the people in their ability to rule themselves by reason, in disregard of the traditional order, is to the author the fatal sin and weakness of all modern politics." As evidence Anderson pointed to Voegelin's criticism of "mistakes of recent politics," which he instead identified with "attempts to govern by human reason." Anderson concluded: "Thus a work started out to present 'The New Science of Politics' ends up in a strident exhortation for repression, and a warning to the world to mend its ways or go to its doom. The scientist has been transformed into a preacher, his work into a jeremiad."[46]

In the same vein of slightly malicious bewilderment, Robert Dahl attempted to be witty but succeeded only in being supercilious in comparing *The New Science of Politics* with David Easton's *The Political System*. "The two authors," he said, "conflict over the elementary meaning of words." Although Voegelin had an "offhand unconcern with definitions," he was nevertheless conceded "his freedom to choose his own definitions; the modern right to redefine science dates back at least to Mary Baker Eddy." Dahl made the by now expected complaint that Voegelin used unfamiliar terms. *The New Science of Politics* "is written in an extraordinary awkward, polysyllabic language only distantly related to the one normally used in written discourse in English-speaking countries." According to Dahl, Voegelin never informed his readers with any precision what he meant by "modern Gnosticism" nor

46 William Anderson, "Review," *The Journal of Politics* 15 (1953): 563–68.

what he meant by a "critically tenable concept." In fact, Voegelin explained both in considerable detail in chapter two of his book. But, since the problem escaped the reviewer, it didn't exist. Because it revealed the uncultured ignorance and sheer inability to read of a major figure in American political science, a celebrated president of the Association (1966–67), and a man who received a Guggenheim the same year as Voegelin (1950), it is embarrassing to read Dahl's words today.[47]

As a final example of the genre of pseudo-ironic assertion, one might mention the review of Joseph S. Roucek. "At no point," wrote Roucek, "does 'the new science of politics' emerge from the deep and involved verbal gymnastic. A simple summary would help this ignoramus-sociologist to appreciate at least what it is all about." Lacking such a simple summary, Roucek supplied his own: "Voegelin has tried to return 'the science of politics' to the fold of the church by granting the primacy of theology over all thinking."[48]

b. Unpublished Responses

Apart from the sustained epistolary discussion between Voegelin, Alfred Schütz and Aron Gurwitsch discussed below, most of the unpublished responses to *The New Science of Politics* that I have been able to discover were brief and allusive. For example, Hannah Arendt registered her disagreement with Voegelin's argument even while she supported his application for support from the Rockefeller Foundation. Leo Strauss said of this same application "there can be no doubt that he belongs to the leading men in this field both in the United States and Europe. You know me too well to take this statement to imply that I agree with Voegelin's approach and results. I wish to make it clear that I thoroughly disagree, both with his approach and results. But I regard it as both stupid and illiberal to judge men by their opinions."[49] Similarly Carl Friedrich wrote to Voegelin:

47 Dahl, "The Science of Politics, New and Old," *World Politics* 7 (1955): 479–89.

48 Roucek, "Review," *American Sociological Review* 19 (1954): 494–95. A more moderate and sensible expose of what Voegelin's criticism of positivism entailed is Lee Cameron McDonald, "Voegelin and the Positivists: A New Science of Politics?" *Midwest Journal of Political Science* 1 (1957): 233–51. There is, in addition, a lengthy 1954 review by Hans Kelsen that remained unpublished until 2004. I discussed this document in *Beginning the Quest: Law and Politics in the Early Work of Eric Voegelin* (Columbia: University of Missouri Press, 2009), 219–26.

49 Rockefeller [Foundation] Archive Center, RF 1.2/2005/531/4539. 7 April 1956; 12 April 1956. In *On Revolution* (New York: Viking, 1965), 19 n. 7, Arendt said she doubted that Voegelin's argument was valid. Strauss evidently read *The New Science*

> I also recently read your book on the science of politics. I could not disagree [with] you more, as they say, and I wish there were a chance to discuss the various matters at length and in person. Having always considered myself in the same camp with you, as far as the role of metaphysics and all that sort of thing is concerned, and even rather close to the Thomistic position which I surmise you still favor, I was really puzzled by this book. Dante, incidentally places Joachim in Heaven. I hear you say: you see. (HI, 13:16)

In contrast to the critical disagreement of these distinguished political philosophers, Marshall McLuhan gave Voegelin his enthusiastic support and mentioned how English literature and the arts generally were riddled with Gnostic themes and sentiments. Voegelin replied that "Gnosis is an all-pervasive phenomenon in the modern age, and perhaps in the arts even more so than in politics." In reply, McLuhan reiterated a previous observation about secret societies and Gnosis with a flood of examples—from T.S. Eliot and Ezra Pound to Coleridge and Jane Harrison. "Pardon my haste and starkness of characterization," McLuhan wrote. "I'm really very tentative in my mind about these things even though I sound dogmatic. In poetry I really know the ground in detail. But a person feels like an awful sucker to have spent 20 years of study on an 'art' which turns out to be somebody else's *ritual*. To have studied it as an art is to have been taken in by the vulgar or exoteric façade." He concluded by raising the question of what "strategies" could be adopted to deal with the problem.

Voegelin replied that "what interests me most is the fact that you have hit on the problem at all." Working through the problem was not a waste of time, even if it took McLuhan twenty years. And as for strategy, it "is a rather simple one: to know so much more, in a plain technical sense, than the others that they will be afraid to molest you. In detail you will probably soon discover what I have discovered, that it is a lot of fun to bait the ungodly when they get impertinent."[50] As we have seen in the previous section, the

of Politics with some care and provided notes that recorded his disagreement with Voegelin's argument. See "Leo Strauss' Anmerkungen zu Eric Veogelins *The New Science of Politics*, übertragen und mit Anmerkungen Versehen" by Emmanuel Patard, in *Glaube und Wissen: Der Briefwechel zwischen Eric Voegelin und Leo Strauss von 1934 bis 1964*, ed. Peter J. Opitz (Munich: Fink, 2010), 129–48.

50 HI, 25:3; CW, 30:173. There is also a letter from McLuhan to Voegelin, 25 July 1952 in the Voegelin library in Erlangen in Voegelin's copy of McLuhan's book, *The Mechanical Bride* (Boston: Beacon Press, 1951).

"ungodly" could certainly be impertinent and unimpressed by Voegelin's erudition.

In the "Documentary Appendix" to a second *Festschrift* for Voegelin, Gregor Sebba wrote of the aforementioned epistolary conversation between Voegelin, Schütz and Gurwitsch: the argument of *The New Science of Politics* "came as a shock; nothing had heralded this sudden appearance on the scene of a radical philosophy whose extraordinary truth claim was implicitly stated, without any anchoring in a systematic exposition of its ground. This, and not the sharp attack on modernity was a rebellion against this truth, was indeed the heart of the matter." Or rather, it was the heart of the matter for Voegelin's "philosophical friends."[51]

On 2 November 1952 Gurwitsch wrote both Schütz and Voegelin. To Schütz he observed that Voegelin's "phenomenological approach" to "historically active societies," and especially his distinction between political self-interpretation and the conceptual language of political science was "surely the only possible" way of "pursuing *politics* as *science*." To Voegelin he repeated his praise with respect to Voegelin's phenomenological astuteness, including his parallel discussion of the distinction between *doxa*, opinion, and *episteme*, science. "But," he added, "as soon as the 'soteriological truth' appears, I find myself confronted with insuperable difficulties. That 'transcendence' makes a counter-movement to man, that there is a reciprocity of 'God' and man, and even *amicitia*: where does that come from?" It is not from the Greeks, Gurwitsch said, but from "the whole mass of Jewish-prophetic motifs and ideas," which Voegelin ignored because of "the logic of your problematic," namely the question of representation in the Roman Empire. But in fact, "the logic of the history of political ideas required a concern with the God who reveals Himself and was concerned with human salvation as a mere matter of empirical or indeed phenomenological

51 Sebba, "Documentary Appendix," in Peter J. Opitz and Gregor Sebba, eds., *The Philosophy of Order: Essays on History, Consciousness and Politics* (Stuttgart: Klett-Cotta, 1981), 431–33. The letters were collected in several places: *Briefwechsel über Die Neue Wissenschaft der Politik*, ed. Peter J. Opitz, (Munich: Aber, 1993) contains excerpts from the original German letters. Translation of the Schütz-Voegelin correspondence is in *A Friendship that Lasted a Lifetime* and of the Schütz-Gurwitsch exchange is in Richard Grathoff, ed., *Philosophers in Exile: The Correspondence of Alfred Schütz and Aron Gurwitsch, 1939–1959*, trans. J. Claude Evans (Bloomington: Indiana University Press, 1989), 183–233. We usually follow the English translations and refer in the text to the dates of the letters of the German and English editions.

observation." For Gurwitsch, "that is something that breaks into the cultural world from without." He then suggested that "as a layman," that he "would like to risk the thesis that the Gnostic elements are embedded and motivated by the idea of the Messiah." The Greek and messianic elements Gurwitsch added, were quite distinct because "logos does not care for man."

On 9 November 1952, Schütz wrote Voegelin a self-described "fan letter" filled with praise. Next day he wrote Gurwitsch that he agreed with the latter's "heretical" objection. "The turning point of the entire critique of Gnosticism is the dogma, which is asserted without proof that every attempt to search for an eidos of history involves making the Christian transcendental *eschaton* immanent and is *therefore* a 'fallacy.' That is a gigantic *non sequitur*. Why shouldn't it be possible in Gnosticism (in Voegelin's sense) too that the soul open itself to transcendental experience?" Later in the month (the letter is simply dated "November") Schütz made the same observation to Voegelin in the course of a long letter.

Specifically, Schütz said he didn't understand how the reintroduction of eschatology amounted to the re-divinization of politics; second, he said, as he had done in his letter to Gurwitsch, that he considered Voegelin's remark that "an immanentist hypostasis of the Christian eschaton was a theoretical fallacy" to be a *non sequitur*:

> I cannot see why an immanent hypostasis of the eschaton should be a theoretical fallacy; nor can I see why you concluded from this that history can have no eidos since the course of history extends into the unknown future. I cannot see why, for this reason, the meaning of history should turn out to be an illusion. Your belief is evidently that this illusionary eidos is created by treating a symbol of faith as if it were a proposition concerning an object of immanent experience. This sentence is the only one I can find in the whole book that could be regarded as proof of such a "fallacy."

Accordingly, Schütz wrote, "I should be grateful if you would clarify under what circumstances Gnosticism must lead to a fallacious construction of history and under what circumstances it need not." He then wondered: "can there not also be non-Christian experiences of transcendence, just as there are non-Euclidian geometries? Does the appearance of soteriological eschatology render the metaphysical theories of Plato and Aristotle invalid? Does it prove them to be fallacies?" And without irony he asked whether raising such questions might appear to Voegelin as evidence of Schütz's "Gnostic thinking." He closed by remarking that he thought Voegelin's concept to Gnosticism was "both too broad and too narrow." It was too broad because codifying doctrine as "Koranic" writings and prohibiting questions were common to all kinds of power organizations, not just to Gnostics, and too narrow since "why should an open soul and access to an existential truth be impossible to a Gnostic philosophy?"

Voegelin replied on New Year's Day, 1953, and continued his response ten days later in two long letters. He emphasized (twice) that there was no misunderstanding between Schütz and himself. Their apparent differences simply reflected their different objectives: Schütz wanted to work out a general social theory, Voegelin a specific theory of politics. Schütz's questions were well taken and more explanation was needed, but a lecture format imposed restrictions. Schütz's questions concerned "issues that are part of the background of the book but could not be presented there, so you are quite right in asking about them."

In reply to Gurwitsch, Voegelin said that he treated Christianity as something that had to be examined in the context of a history of ideas. As for Schütz's "decisive question: Is theory possible only within the framework of Christianity? Quite obviously not." The work of Plato and Aristotle proved that. Moreover, if "the essence of philosophizing" is "the interpretation of experiences of transcendence," then as a matter of "historical fact" theories existed independent of Christianity.[52] There was, however, one "essential" qualification. Since philosophizing must take account of "the maximally differentiated experiences," the philosopher cannot ignore them—hence "the problem of the history of ideas" that Voegelin had to deal with in terms of the historicity of truth. And with Christianity, "a decisive differentiation has occurred," namely the experience of grace with the "intervention of transcendence into human life" that had attracted Gurwitsch's attention. Plato expressed this experience in the relatively compact myth, image, or parable of the Cave. Someone or something turns the first person around, the *periagoge* or *conversio* of Republic 514–17. This philosophical experience of grace, Voegelin wrote "is new. And it has an important philosophical-technical consequence in that today no one would think of developing a theory of mystical experience in the form of a Platonic myth." This was a problem to which he returned in his later work.

52 Indeed, as Voegelin wrote to Schütz on 17 September 1943 discussing Husserl: "problems of philosophical transcendence" were "the decisive problems of philosophy" (CW, 6:61).

In Maimonides and Bodin, for instance, the symbol of the prophet appeared rather than a prisoner who was dragged up into the sunlight and then was compelled to return to the darkness. Institutionally, a school such as the Academy was not a church. If a philosopher were concerned only with logic or with "the constitution of the external world in consciousness," these questions would never arise. "As a political theorist, I have no choice: questions of this kind are present in the historical material and I have to analyze them—and in the direction I have outlined." Voegelin was not, therefore, "inclined to jettison Christianity" but this refusal was burdened by the problem of the relationship of Gnosticism to Christianity. Historically, Christianity contained two components, "the Gnosis of historical [i.e., intramundane] eschatology" and what Voegelin now called "essential Christianity." Since some sectarians and Protestants, for example, identified the two and considered what Voegelin meant by essential Christianity to be a corruption institutionalized by the Catholic Church, "this can easily lead to misunderstandings." Voegelin reiterated the argument made in the *History of Political Ideas*, that Christianity became historically effective "through the Pauline compromises with the order of the world," including the political order of the empire, by toning down the eschatological expectations that the world would soon come to an end, and by transforming these expectations into the historical mystical body of Christ (cf. CW, 19:169–72; 22:206–7).

Voegelin then discussed four major "achievements" of "essential Christianity:" Christology, the Trinity, Mariological dogma, and a critical understanding of theological speculation, that were essential for political science and philosophy. But all four had largely been ignored.

Christology was important not in the sense of the divinity of Christ since there were plenty of god-men around in Jesus' day and in Hellenistic and imperial Egyptian times as well. What was unusual were: (1) Jesus social status and (2) his mediating function for all humanity. That is, Jesus as the Christ was not a king but a common carpenter and he performed his mediating purpose not for a specific society but for humanity. Moreover, he was the incarnation of God, not a god, as were all the other god-men. In pre-Christian civilizations the experience of divine help that "was symbolized polytheistically and national-pluralistically, was reduced by Christology to its essence and made humanly universal." This interpretation of human existence in society was, Voegelin said, "a critical tidying up of the first order."

A second, equally important achievement of Christianity was "the dogma of the Trinity" because it combined in one theological symbol "religious experiences that must remain differentiated if speculative fallacies are to be avoided." The first experience consisted on the "radical transcendence" of God. The second, symbolized in the second person of the Trinity, was of "the divine transforming intervention into 'nature,'" which is to say, grace. Third was the experience of the spirit in "the community of the faithful," namely the Church.

A third achievement was "the complex of Mariological dogmas." Voegelin had in mind not only the Immaculate Conception and the Assumption but the doctrine that Mary was co-redemptrix and mediator of all graces. In this, Voegelin said, he agreed with Karl Barth that the creature participated in the work of grace. "Again this is one of the basic human experiences that must be symbolized." And this too tidied up an important problem. Not that human beings by themselves could simply take an active hand in their own salvation, but that they did participate in it at a minimum by being open to the possibility. "Just as Christ marks the end of the gods, Mary marks the end of superhuman vessels of the divine. In both instances the symbolism restored the balance between man's splendor and possibilities, and his limitations."

A fourth achievement was "the critical understanding of theological speculation and its meaning" and especially the "analogy of being" as developed by Saint Thomas. For example, "God is almighty" combined a transcendent subject with an infinitized intramundane predicate, which was meaningless as a proposition if taken literally but made sense "if the predicate is added analogically to the extrapolated subject of the experience of faith." That is, Voegelin did not simply say that Thomas would agree with the philosophers of the Enlightenment, that Christian dogmatic statements are meaningless because they cannot be verified as statements about sense perception, but that that was "the very starting point of Christian theology." Dogma, Voegelin said, "is a symbolic web that explicates and differentiates the extraordinarily complicated religious experiences" into a descriptive and evocative, not an axiomatic and rational, order. It was "a storehouse of more than a thousand years of religious experience" that had been thoroughly analyzed and differentiated by Church thinkers.

All of this "critical tidying-up" had been conducted within the context of "essential Christianity," which was not quite the same thing as Catholicism, as Strauss had discerned. Accordingly, while all important Christian thinkers saw eschatology as symbolism of the experience "of the eternal presence of Judgment," they were also quite willing to make remarks about the transfiguration of creation in terms of sensually perceivable phenomen Besides, he said, notwithstanding the efforts of neo-Thomists, Thomas had no doctrine of the Church.

The New Year's Day letter dealt with Voegelin's understanding of Christianity and the Church. The second one dealt with Gnosticism. Voegelin assured Schütz that by no means did he consider Schütz's questions to be evidence of a "Gnostic disposition." Rather, they were evidence of a "justifiable desire" to hear more about a complex issue than could be presented in a lecture. He began by considering Schütz's questions about an *eidos* of history since it appeared to be the easiest to answer. There could only be an *eidos*, a form or essence, for things that are experienced. There could be no *eidos* for something that was not experienced, and, since history was experienced only to the extent it had unfolded, the whole of history could not be experienced. Here he agreed with Karl Löwith that there could be meaning *in* history but no meaning *of* history.[53]

Only in Judaic and Christian symbolization was there a problem of meaning of history as a perfection that extended beyond experienced history. Sometimes it was an immanent perfection in history and sometimes it was transferred to the transcendent beyond, as in Augustine. "This gave rise to the distinction between sacred and profane history," with profane history continuing the pre-Christian attributes of the rising and falling of political powers. Sacred history, the history of salvation, reached its earthly summit with Christ and continued historically as a term of faith, which was precisely *not* an object of intramundane experience. Thus the "immanetization of the eschaton" was a "hypostasis" because the term that "designates an experience of faith oriented to transcendence is set within intramundane reality." It was a fallacy similar to Whitehead's fallacy of misplaced concreteness because "an expression, only meaningful for interpreting an experience of transcendence, is used in intramundane speculation."[54]

As for non-Christian or Christian-related Gnosticism, "this point has not been treated fully enough in the lectures." Nor did he properly discuss the problem of redivinization or a "major complication," namely that the new Gnosticism was not the ancient cosmological Gnosticism, prior to the "differentiation of the transcendence complex." Modern Gnosticism was burdened with a "bad conscience" because of two thousand years of intellectual insight that humans were not gods. As a result, the introduction of new gods was difficult. "He who denies God knows very well who God is and that he is not God." Hence Voegelin called modern Gnosticism

53 Löwith, *Meaning in History* (Chicago: University of Chicago Press, 1949), 3f.

54 A. N. Whitehead, *Science in the Modern World* (New York: Macmillan, 1925), 52ff.

pathological, which term would not apply to ancient Gnosticism "insofar as it was still naïve, compact-cosmological."

He agreed with Schütz that all societies prohibit some questions, produce "Koranic" dogmas, and so on. But so far as the truth and the order of the human soul was concerned, it was inadequate simply to observe the formality of a "position" and a "counter-position." "It is not immaterial whether a development proceeds from the compactness to the differentiation of experiences of transcendence, or from differentiated transcendence to immanentizing Gnosticism." That is, one must move from a general observation to the content of a particular "position." In the example of Socrates and the Athenians, in order to avoid historical relativism, "here one must decide: Socrates was right, Athens was wrong." Moreover, one could make that decision precisely because of the more differentiated consciousness of Socrates with which one can imaginatively identify.

When Schütz shared Voegelin's account with Gurwitsch, the latter wrote back to Schütz that: "We are in complete agreement here—which is hardly surprising. Especially with regard to the methodological orientation of his [Voegelin's] book. Aside from what would have to be said about the details, the orientation of his book is one of the best vindications of phenomenological thought. Historical interpretation must do justice to what the historical structures and societies have understood themselves to be. Voegelin has done this to a degree which has—so far as I know—hardly ever been reached in historical studies."[55] Apart from the courtesy these three friends showed one another, the most notable aspect of these exchanges is that Schütz and Gurwitsch were both more eager for clarification of what Voegelin meant than in creating division among themselves and their respective "positions." No one was concerned with scoring points. Unlike so many of the published reviews, these exchanges were models of scholarly conversation.

A similar generosity of spirit was found in the comments of John Hallowell and in Voegelin's reply.[56] Hallowell said that he considered *The New Science of Politics* "a little masterpiece" that nevertheless "raised a number of questions in my mind" and in particular "the relationship between Christianity and culture." Specifically, Hallowell explained: "Granting that the Kingdom of God is not of this world, is there no sense at all in which Christians can work for the approximation of that kingdom in this world?"

55 Gurwitsch to Schütz, 24 January 1953.

56 Hallowell's letter is in HI, 16:3; Voegelin's answer is in CW, 30:138.

Accordingly, it was not clear to him "what you conceive the relationship between God and civilization to be." Second, he wondered whether Voegelin agreed with Löwith's thesis in *Meaning in History*. Third, a point raised by Schütz as well, if Gnosticism is salvation by knowledge, how does "any philosophical inquiry" escape being Gnostic? And finally, what did Voegelin mean by "civil theology"?

Voegelin replied that, indeed, the question of Christianity and culture was central to any philosophy of history. If the two were radically distinguished, Christianity became completely "other-worldly," whereas historically, whatever the "essence" of Christianity may be, the Church had its concern with radical transcendence, leaving Christians to conduct themselves in "this world." But it would be "fatuous to pretend that the course of Western civilization has not been profoundly affected by Christianity." In fact, "historically all religions are formative cultural influences wherever they spread."

Regarding Löwith, Voegelin agreed that there were two main types of historical speculation, the cyclical and the eschatological, which transcended "the immanent process of history." The first was based on the experience of "transcendence into the infinity of rhythmical order in the cosmos" and the second "on the experience of transcendence into transmundane perfection. And that is all there is." However, Voegelin went on, the real problem did not concern speculative principles at all because "speculative principles extrapolate experiences; and . . . the substance of history had to be found in the experiences themselves, not in their symbolization." In that case, history "becomes the description of experiences from compactness to differentiation," as Bergson clearly, but Löwith less clearly, grasped.

Third, on principle "philosophy is not Gnosis" because philosophy, as Plato indicated, was not wisdom but love of wisdom. Moreover, "there is no 'salvation' for Plato, but only the orientation in the right direction through Eros. Eros, not knowledge, is the core [experience] of Platonic philosophizing."

Finally, "civil theology" is a term used by Varro (as Voegelin discussed in chapter three of *The New Science of Politics*) and referred to the social self-understanding of any society independent of the "natural theology" of the philosophers. The distinction between the two corresponded to Voegelin's distinction discussed above between cosmion and theory or philosophy. "In philosophy symbols of political theology are unacceptable, because a political philosophy must be based on a theory of the nature of man," which is to say, a philosophical anthropology.

c. Popular accounts and Voegelin's Response

Apart from the discussion with friends and colleagues such as Hallowell and Schütz, many of Voegelin's responses to the reception of *The New Science of Politics* were mediated by the coverage the book received in *Time* magazine on the occasion of its Thirtieth Anniversary edition.[57] Voegelin several times remarked to friends that he was surprised by the coverage in *Time*. As he wrote to Harry D. Karl at the University of Chicago Press, "the book certainly has [had] an odd reception. Setting aside a few positivists, everybody seems to consider it very important, though nobody knows exactly why." A couple of years later he remarked to Elizabeth Scott, also at the University of Chicago Press, that he was pleased to learn the demand for the book was still strong. "It is more than I had expected of this *livre de circonstance*" (HI, 38:21).[58] It may be worth noting that however much the article in *Time* helped sales of the book and perhaps even Voegelin's public profile, compared to the coverage of the German edition of the book, the popular press in the Unites States all but ignored it.[59]

The article in *Time* was commonsensical and reasonably accurate. It devoted considerable emphasis to the application of Voegelin's theoretical argument to American foreign policy, a topic that featured prominently in the closing pages of the book. *Time* also pointed to the behavior of Senator

57 "Journalism and Joachim's Children," *Time*, March 9, 1953, 57–61. Voegelin was impressed by the scholarly tone of the article, which referred to several sources not discussed in the book. "I was in particular intrigued by the quotation from Fra Salimbene, which I had not known myself." He asked who wrote the piece so that he might make his acquaintance (CW, 30:154). It was written by the Senior Editor, Max Ways (HI, 63:14). In 1979, to mark the twenty-fifth anniversary of the publication of *The New Science of Politics*, Andrew Baird prepared an essay for *Fortune*. To a letter from Baird, Voegelin replied that apart from a few minor factual errors, "on the whole, your interpretation looks correct." Baird said that his "main worry" was that "the article will be a little too highbrow for the type of magazine *Time* and *Fortune* have become in the past twelve years." He was right inasmuch as the essay never saw publication. See HI, 7:7.

58 The University of Chicago Press was also "pleased" with sales (HI, 38:21); see also *A Friendship that Lasted a Lifetime*, 186. Voegelin reiterated in his Foreword to the German edition that he was surprised at the attention the "little book" received. *Die Neue Wissenschaft der Politik*, 14.

59 See Price, *Eric Voegelin: International Bibliography*, 175–83. By my count, the American edition was reviewed in around 15 non-academic places and the German in 45. Sebastian de Grazia pointed out to Voegelin how coverage in *Time* "elected [him] to prominence" (HI, 15:16).

Joseph McCarthy in the context of the inevitable failure of Gnostic politics and praised the thinking of Reinhold Niebuhr. One might sum up *Time's* version of Voegelin's argument: "The mood that holds material progress unworthy and moral progress impossible is produced by frustration and disappointment at the collapse of Gnostic visions."

Over the next few weeks, *Time* published 35 letters to the editor. They ranged from lavish praise to this, from Michael Callaghan of Minot, N.D.: "Garbled nonsense. This Voegelin is just another egghead." Gordon Wilkinson of Las Cruces, N.M. called it "queasy pseudophilosopical slumgullion."[60] In his own letter to the editor, Voegelin expressed his pleasant surprise at the successful application of "theoretical propositions . . . to the concrete questions of our time." He added, mischievously: "Of course, theory should be applicable if it is any good; but I did not over-emphasize this point because your article will help even professionals in the field of political science to understand the pragmatic value of my analysis" (CW, 30:154).

He expanded his last observation in a short note to Schütz:

> The article in *Tine* was a surprise. The world situation must really be worse that even I thought if a magazine of this kind takes note of one of my books. The "nuisance value" of the article is great and enjoyable: A whole series of scoundrels in our branch that call themselves professors without doing the work of a scholar, and who would have never in their lives looked at the book, find themselves forced at least to take notice of it—if it's in *Time*, there must be something to it. I've even heard of an upcoming salary increase in the fall. (CW, 30:149)

In fact, the Hoover Institution Archives contain several letters from various political scientists around the country and overseas who treated Voegelin to their views.

Here is a sample: Charles B. Hagan, Professor of Political Science at the University of Illinois told Voegelin he was not "persuaded" by the argument in *The New Science of Politics* (HI, 16:1). Voegelin replied: "that is most regrettable personally, but . . . there is not much I can answer to this statement of an autobiographical fact. All I can say is, the book was not written to

60 The noun referred to a beefy, tomato-based macaroni stew; the etymology is from two English dialect words: slum = slime; gullion = mud or cesspool.

persuade you, or anybody else, but in order to advance true propositions in political science. And whether that purpose has been achieved or not can only be determined by examining the subject-matter and the theoretical argument," which Hagen had not done but which Voegelin invited him to do (CW, 30:254).

Voegelin made the same point in response to the "kind review" in the *APSR* by Francis Wilson. Did Voegelin's analyses "hold water"? Were the propositions true or false? It was Voegelin's view "that it contains a substantial improvement in the following two points: (1) it advances from theologizing to science and replaces symbols of political theology with critical concepts; and (2) it advances from the historical type concepts, which still are the bane of Max Weber's work, to ontological type concepts based on a philosophical anthropology" (CW, 30:170–71). Several of Voegelin's' correspondents seemed unaware that the significance or, as he said, the "substance" of the book was "an ontology of political societies" (CW, 30:141, 150). But, he also noted that "it was practically impossible to convey the idea, because it is so utterly at variance with the conventional treatment of political theory. In a future publication, when the present book has sunk in a bit, perhaps I can dare a theoretically correct title" (CW, 30:156).

The *Time* article also inspired several people to write Voegelin. As one example, Ernst Krenek, an American-Czech-Austrian composer wrote him an appreciative letter recollecting their previous meetings in Vienna and at Harvard.[61] Another unsolicited communication came by Western Union from J. Paul Morris Jr. He said on the basis of *Time's* "synopsis that:

> I RACH THE CONCLUSION THAT LOUISIANIANS DO NOT HOLD THE BOROAD INTERPRETATION OF THE WORD DREAM WHICH WAS HELD BY THE FOUNDERS OF THIS NATION IN THE 17TH AND 18TH CENTRUES I AM MUCH INDEBTED TO BOTH YOU AND TIME FOR THIS NEW INTERPRETATION OF THE WORD DREAM. I WOULD SUGGEST TO YOU AS WELL AS TO TIMES EDITORS THAT AN INTELLIGENT PERUSAL OF BOTH THE BIBLE AND SOME OF THE WRITINGS OF ARNOLD TOYNBEE MIGHT REFRESH YOUR MEMORY TO THE PRACTICAL APPLICATION OF CHRISTIANITY TO LIFE.

61 This letter is in the Voegelin library at the University of Erlangen; it was placed in the fly-leaf of one of Voegelin's copies of *The New Science of Politics*. If Voegelin answered, there is no evidence in the Hoover Institution Archive.

Voegelin replied with exaggerated courtesy, thanking him for his "lengthy telegram favoring me with your opinions about Louisiana, dreams, Christianity and sundry subjects." He pointed out that he had nothing to do with the *Time* article and could not be held responsible for what others said about him. If he were interested in what Voegelin actually wrote "about Gnostic dreams and their murderous consequences" he might purchase the book at a price "less than the expense of your telegram" and then he might consider actually reading it. "Finally, I inform you herewith that you have no business to molest a scholar with your opinion about his ideas without knowing what they are. In view of the fact that you have not read the book, your telegram is an impertinence."[62]

Regarding Voegelin's response to the reviews by his academic colleagues, he was polite to those, such as Wilson and Hallowell, who were fundamentally supportive but nevertheless asked them why they did not consider what Voegelin thought was as the fundamental question: was what he said true? As for the likes of Dahl and Franklin, he maintained silence.

He did have a few things to say regarding the reviews of Brecht and Thomas I. Cook. In September 1953 he wrote to Schütz that "the 'New School' has succeeded in arousing my displeasure. It gave Brecht the review of *The New Science of Politics*, which in itself is a misdeed but, as a presumably unavoidable one, to be forgiven. However, in addition, Brecht has sent me the review so that I can thank him for not having understood what the book is about."[63] In a letter to Brecht Voegelin objected that he was not, as Brecht had said, a neo-Thomist. Brecht semi-apologized and, in his later book, *Political Theory,* indicated explicitly that Voegelin was not a neo-Thomist.[64]

62 HI, 63:14. Another equally impertinent letter advised Voegelin: "Our God who is the Lord Jesus Christ is imprisoned by the DEVIL, say this prayer as often as you can and liberate Him. LORD JESUS CHRIST, THY WILL BE DONE" (HI, 63:11).

63 *A Friendship that Lasted a Lifetime*, 185–86.

64 HI, 8:39. See Brecht, *Political Theory: The Foundations of Twentieth-Century Political Thought* (Princeton: Princeton University Press, 1959), 272. When asked by John D. Lewis, book review editor of the *APSR* to review Brecht's *Political Theory* Voegelin declined on the grounds that he was too busy with *Order and History* and "somewhat out of sympathy" with Brecht's position of value-relativism (CW, 30:390). Brecht was hardly alone in suspecting that Voegelin harbored "professional Catholic tendencies." But, as Voegelin wrote Jacob Taubes, "this suspicion, I can assure you, is unfounded" (CW, 30:18). As late as 2007 he was called "the Catholic political philosopher" who "alongside Leo Strauss (1899–1973) [is considered] to be a founding father of neo-conservatism" (Yotam Hotam, "Gnosis and Modernity:

As a final example of Voegelin's courtesy combined with directness, consider his response to Thomas I. Cook, whom Voegelin knew well. In his review Cook said he had "every feeling of personal kindness toward the author" and Voegelin said of Cook (and his wife) that "Both of them are truly better than that which one generally finds in academic circles" (CW, 30:180). Cook's review, while not as appalling as those of Anderson or Dahl, indicated that he was just as bewildered as they were.[65] As Voegelin wrote to Taubes about Cook's review: "One can only cry—there's no point in arguing" (CW, 30:180).

Cook summarized his criticism of Voegelin's "position" with the observation that he did not accept the "premise" of Voegelin's theology and metaphysics (HI, 9:28). Voegelin replied, after having recovered from an operation, that he found Cook's letter "illuminating" because on the basis of it he thought he could understand the grounds of their misunderstanding. The difficulty, Voegelin wrote, seemed to be Cook's opinion that metaphysics or theology could be a "premise." Voegelin found this attitude "utterly strange" and wondered where it had come from. Voegelin's objection to Cook's "position" had nothing to do with Cook's religious faith or its absence, nor with Voegelin's. Metaphysics, he explained, was not a premise of anything, "but the result of a process in which a philosopher explicates in rational symbols his various experiences, especially experiences of

A Postwar German Intellectual Debate on Secularization, Religion, and 'Overcoming' the Past," *Totalitarian Movements and Political Religions* 8:3–4 [2007]: 592). This characterization of Voegelin was, no doubt, aided by well-meaning but misguided efforts by Voegelin's "conservative" supporters. William Buckley, for example, replied to a sixteen-year-old correspondent, Edward H. Vazques, who enquired about the meaning of the phrase "to immanentize the eschaton." As was evident from his discussions with Schütz and Gurwitsch, a similar phrase appeared in *The New Science of Politics* where, as we saw, Voegelin said the attempt expressed a "theoretical fallacy" (CW, 5:185). Buckley was aware that the attempt to do so was a denial of God and of transcendence, but he also seemed to convey the impression that such attempts could succeed, and referred to a famous slogan, "Don't let THEM immanentize the eschaton," which was printed on a button issued by the Young Americans for Freedom. See Buckley, *Execution Eve and Other Contemporary Ballads* (New York: Putnam, 1975). On November 14, 1975, the Philadelphia Society held a debate: "Resolved: This House Would Immanentize the Eschaton." Madsen Pirie and Gordon Tullock spoke in favour; M. Stanton Evans and Michael Uhlmann spoke against. Presumably their tongues were firmly in their cheeks. See HI, 29:2. Voegelin's response to the Yaffers' button is in CW, 30:548, 590.

65 Cook, "Review," *The Hopkins Review* (Spring-Summer 1953): 191–96. HI 63:12.

transcendence." And likewise Christian theology was the expressive result of specific concrete experiences.

More to the point so far as political science was concerned, such experiences were "constituent elements" of social order and thus "facts of political history." Accordingly, political science had to consider them on their own terms, namely as experiences of transcendence that were expressed in metaphysics and theology. Thus, he went on, he was not operating with any "premise" but "with a proposition which certainly is empirically testable" namely that experiences of transcendence and their metaphysical and theological expression "are ordering facts in history." In order to recognize this you need not be a theologian or a believer "any more than you have to be a great artist in order to write a competent study on Rembrandt." You do, however, have to have an "adequate" theoretical instrument to theorize about or even intelligently discuss these empirical facts, and, not surprisingly, the most adequate such instruments happened to be "the theoretical articulations provided for such experiences by the men who had them." Thus, in order adequately to understand philosophy and Christianity, "the theories developed by Plato or St. Augustine will prove considerably more adequate than the theories developed by such comparatively provincial thinkers as James or Dewey." Not that a skeptical or pragmatic interpretation of philosophical or revelatory experience was impossible, but that no one had done it successfully yet and Voegelin considered it doubtful that anyone could (CW, 30:187–88). Voegelin's responses to questions from students were both polite and substantive.[66]

5. Concluding Remarks

Voegelin's initial description of the purpose of *The New Science of Politics* was to introduce his readers to the intellectual movement of a restoration of political science to its full status as a science of human being in history. In later formulations, Voegelin stressed that he was constructing an "ontology of politics." It became increasingly clear as Voegelin was asked to clarify one of another aspect of his argument, particularly in response to friendly

66 See, for example, the exchange between Arthur Fine, whose honours paper at Harvard was being directed by William Y. Elliott, one of Voegelin's early supporters, or Voegelin's response to Russell Nieli's "huge dissertation" on Voegelin written under the supervision of Manfred Halperin and Paul Sigmund at Princeton. See HI, 12:16; CW, 30:212–13; HI, 27:12.

questions, that the chief implication of his political science was that the substance of politics was to be found in experience. Of course, traces of that insight and even linguistic formulations close to it could be found in the *History of Political Ideas* and especially in the chapter on "The People of God." This is why many of Voegelin's explanations to Schütz or Hallowell amounted to a conceptually precise reiteration of arguments made in this then still unpublished document.

As we argue in the following chapters, the consequences of the importance of experience as the substance of politics were worked out in much greater detail in the early volumes of *Order and History*. Whether Voegelin's deepened understanding of the implications of his argument was assisted by the experience of illness and convalescence as Szakolczai suggested we may leave an open question.[67] What seems uncontroversial is that Voegelin learned a great deal about how not to be understood. The taking of "positions," for example, meant that there was nothing anybody could learn from anybody else and that agreement or even honest disagreement became impossible because positions were derivative, not substantive.

67 Szakolczai, *Reflexive Historical Sociology*, 61.

CHAPTER THREE

THE DIFFERENTIATION OF CONSCIOUSNESS

In chapter one we discussed the publication history of the large manuscript that started out as the *History of Political Ideas* and ended up as *Order and History*. In October 1953 Voegelin wrote encouragingly to Macmillan that the prospects of publishing the big book, now called *Order and Symbols*, had improved. "My 'New Science of Politics,' distinctly a difficult, theoretical work, has sold 1500 copies within a year. People are just waiting for that sort of thing. (Toynbee's 'Study of History' sold only 2000 copies within the first twelve years)" (CW, 30:183). The implication was clear: Voegelin expected his multi-volume *Order and Symbols* to surpass in sales Toynbee's multi-volume *Study*. The final rejection by Macmillan came in February 1955; by the spring Voegelin had signed a publication contract with LSU Press.

That summer he received a second Guggenheim fellowship and spent the time in Europe discussing various "problems" with Rudolf Bultmann, Gerhard von Rad, Carl Schmitt, Max Horkheimer, and many others. That fall he put the finishing touches on what he called at various times the "Israel" or the "Exodus" volume, which became *Order and History*, volume one, *Israel and Revelation* (CW, 14). Typesetting began early in 1956; it was published in the late summer of 1956. The argument developed in the first volume of *Order and History* reflected Voegelin's most recent research; the arguments dealing with the Greeks, discussed in volumes two and three (CW, 15–16), seem to have been essentially what had been written for the *History* only slightly recast in light of Voegelin's having jettisoned the format of a linear history of political ideas attached to the great names of the Western tradition.

1. The Exodus from Cosmological Order

The Preface to *Israel and Revelation* began with a kind of restatement of the opening words of the *History of Political Ideas*: "The order of history emerges from the history of order. Every society is burdened with the task, under its concrete condition, of creating an order that will endow the fact of its existence with meaning in terms of ends divine and human" (CW,

14:19). Voegelin used the term order in a number of different ways.[1] Not surprisingly after the reception of *The New Science of Politics*, Voegelin's locution was often misunderstood.[2] In his *Autobiographical Reflections* Voegelin summarized and simplified the question: "By *order* is meant the structure of reality as experienced as well as the attunement of man to an order that is not of his making—i.e., the cosmic order" (CW, 34:101). In the first volume of *Order and History* Voegelin advanced the concept of order as process: "Order is not an eternal status of things, but a transition from chaos to cosmos in time. Once created, order required attention to its precarious existence, or it will relapse into chaos" (CW, 14:348).

The "history of order," then, meant the intelligible account of the several attempts to endow the fact of the existence of the political cosmion with meaning—a problem discussed in chapter one above. As distinct from the history of the accounts of the successive evocations of successive cosmia, which was the formulation of the *History of Political Ideas*, the "order of history," by Voegelin's later argument, only gradually came into focus. Initially it referred to the intelligible connection of the sequence of temporary and imperfect symbolizations used to express the meaning of successive cosmia. In order to make an intelligible connection between the several political cosmia to be found as the "content" of the history of order, one must develop a defensible philosophical anthropology along the lines of the argument developed in chapter one. In *Order and History*, the problem of the historicity of truth was recast in terms of the problem of compactness and differentiation of experience, symbolization, and eventually of consciousness as well.

In other words, the order of history was initially understood by Voegelin to mean an advance toward or a defection from "an adequate symbolization of truth concerning the order of being" of which social and political order was a constituent. This did not imply the existence of a "simple pattern of progress or cycles" so much as a pattern of intelligible struggle for "true

1 See Paul Grimley Kuntz, "Voegelin's Experiences of Disorder Out of Order and Vision of Order Out of Disorder: A Philosophic Meditation on His Theory of Order-Disorder," in E. Sandoz, ed., *Eric Voegelin's Significance for the Modern Mind* (Baton Rouge: LSU Press, 1991), 111–73. See also Jürgen Gebhardt, "Epilogue" to *Order and History*, vol.5, *In Search of Order*, CW, 18:125ff.

2 William Foxwell Albright thought it was a "surrogate" for the *Geist* of Hegel ("Review of *Israel and Revelation*," *Theological Studies* 22 [1961]: 270–71). Carl Friedrich thought it was "inspired by a deep-seated antagonism to democracy, as commonly understood" (Friedrich, "Symbols of Order and History?" *Jewish Frontier* 25:12 [1958]: 9).

order." The order of history thus could be found in no specific society but rather could be discerned "retrospectively in a flow of events that extends, through the present of the observer, indefinitely into the future" (CW, 14:19). What could be known, as we saw in the brief discussion of the argument of Karl Löwith in the previous chapter, was only that part of the process that had unfolded in the past, and even that part could be known only "to the extent to which it is accessible to the instruments of cognition that have emerged from the process itself" (CW, 14:20). Voegelin clarified this meaning to the term, the order of history, later in the book in connection with what he called the "form" of a civilization (CW, 14:91–102), and in subsequent work he modified it further (we shall consider his modifications in subsequent chapters).

The Introduction, called "The Symbolization of Order," contained what Bernhard W. Anderson quite properly called the "presuppositions of Voegelin's analysis."[3] The Introduction opened with the announcement: "God and man, world and society form a primordial community of being" that was a datum of experience "insofar as it is known to man by virtue of his participation in the mystery of its being" but was not a datum of perception akin to the perception of objects in the world. That is, human beings were not so much spectators as actors, participants "in the drama of being" simply by virtue of their existence.[4] But they remained ignorant of their role in the drama and of who wrote the play, if anyone did. Voegelin took the

3 Anderson, "Politics and the Transcendent: Voegelin's Philosophical and Theological Exposition of the Old Testament in the Context of the Ancient Near East," in William M. Thompson and David L. Morse, eds., *Voegelin's Israel and Revelation: An Interdisciplinary Debate and Anthology* (Milwaukee: Marquette University Press, 2000), 20.

4 Again, Voegelin modified his understanding of participation in his later essays. Here participation meant what Wilfred Cantwell Smith called engagement or commitment. See Smith, *Faith and Belief* (Princeton: Princeton University Press, 1979), 6–11. In many respects participation seemed akin to the "unfocussed" consciousness of infants. See Alison Gopnik, *The Philosophical Baby: What Children's Minds tell us about Truth, Love, and the Meaning of Life* (New York: Farrar Straus and Giroux, 2009), 109–25. More directly, Paul Caringella argued that Voegelin's evocation of a participatory cosmos was written in opposition to the "disenchantment" argument of Max Weber. See Caringella, "Crisis and Exodus: Eric Voegelin's 'Anamnesis,' Voegelin's Way from Weber and Husserl through Schütz to Anamnesis as the Method of History," in Kurt R. Leube and Andreas Pribersky, eds., *Krise und Exodus: Österreichische Sozailwissenschaften in Mittelleuropa* (Vienna: WUV Universitätsverlag, 1995), 203. See also CW, 7:103.

image of a play most immediately from Johan Huizinga's *Homo Ludens* and more remotely from Plato. Having such a role in such a drama was "disconcerting," to say the least, and human beings often preferred "the less bewildering routine" of ordinary and everyday life.

But that was just the problem. "Participation in being" was not partial or optional but committed the whole of existence "for participation is existence itself," which is to say there was no external vantage point outside existence where one could contemplate the meaning of the whole drama. Accordingly, there was considerable uncertainty with respect to the play and the role humans were called upon to enact. Uncertainty, however, did not mean total ignorance because "man's participation in being is not blind but is illuminated by consciousness."

In other words, the sentence "man or human being, in his or her existence participates in being" was not a proposition denoting an entity, called "human being" that "participates" in "being" the way a human being might or might not participate in a baseball game. Rather, within human being there was something capable of a fundamental act of evocation, of calling forth, and of the experience of itself as participant and of calling this experience "consciousness" and "human being." But this complex evocative act "is not itself an act of cognition." Why not? Because the experience of participation depended on a whole such that the perspective of participant necessarily excluded the possibility of cognition of the whole. One participated, so to speak, from the inside; one did not perceive being as a phenomenal entity. As a result, if knowledge of the whole was precluded, so too was complete knowledge of the part, namely of the human being that experienced the participation. "This situation of ignorance with regard to the decisive core of existence is more than disconcerting: It is profoundly disturbing, for from the depth of this ultimate ignorance wells up the anxiety of existence" (CW, 14:40). And yet, just as uncertainty was not total ignorance, neither did anxiety induce paralysis.

First of all, we do know *that* we participate in being, even if we do not know why or whence. Moreover, we are aware of the "quaternarian structure" of being—the divine, cosmic, human and social fields of being. Following Henri Frankfort, Voegelin characterized this quaternarian structure as consubstantial.[5] By consubstantiality was meant a single ordered "stuff,"

5 See Frankfort et al., *Before Philosophy: The Intellectual Adventure of Ancient Man, An Essay on Speculative Thought in the Ancient Near East* (Baltimore: Penguin, 1946), 71–78.

a "substance" that was at once divine, cosmic, political and anthropological. Within a consubstantial order, the glorification of God would also be the glorification of the people, the rulers, the land, and so on. As Voegelin once put it, consubstantiality can be visualized as a single homogeneous cosmic pudding (CW, 33:187).

Within that somewhat inchoate awareness of consubstantiality, second, "is the preoccupation with lasting and passing" of the several partners that, notwithstanding their consubstantiality, exhibited differing degrees of durability. Individuals perished more quickly than societies; societies more quickly than the world, which may well have been created by the even longer-lasting gods. This hierarchy of durability furnished additional information about human participation in being. The more lasting existences "provide by their structure the frame into which the lesser existence must fit" or be extinguished. That is, success in existence for humans depended on their "attunement" to the more durable elements of society, world, and gods (CW, 14:41–42). The imagery of drama, participation, and attunement, as William M. Thompson observed, emphasized respectively, mystery, action and passion.[6] The drama was a mystery play; our participation was active; our attunement presupposed a reality to which we are passively attuned.

In other words, we may not know why or how we come into existence, but we do know that so long as we exist we are mysteriously consubstantial with the being to which we return.[7] Moreover, we know that we need to attune ourselves to the more comprehensive elements of the quaternarian structure of being. Attunement, that is, is experienced as an obligation. Just as we may not fulfill our obligations, so we may lose by default our attunement of consciousness with reality. Anxiety in this context, thus, meant more than fear of death because, for humans, existence has already been bounded by death, by pre-existence as much as by post-existence. Anxiety, therefore, amounted to a horror at losing the precarious foothold that human existence enjoys as a partner in being that we experience so long as we exist. "In existence we act our role in the greater play of the divine being that enters

6 Thompson, "Voegelin's *Israel and Revelation*: The Reception and Challenge in America," *Occasional Papers*, XXVII (Munich: Eric-Voegelin-Archiv, 2001), 7–9

7 Or as Voegelin once mischievously said, "It is impossible to die unless you are immortal." (*The Cavalier Daily* [University of Virginia], 29 September 1977 [HI, 82:3]). To Thomas Hollweck he said: "There is no after life. Immortality is the Presence of the Divine in life. We are Immortal because we are mortal" (Hollweck, "Conversations with Eric Voegelin," [HI, 112:330, 23]).

passing existence in order to redeem precarious being for eternity" (CW, 14:43).

A third feature of the process of symbolization was "the creation of symbols that interpret the unknown by analogy with the really, or the supposedly, known." Gradually what was essentially unknowable could be distinguished or "differentiated" from what was knowable.[8] Accordingly, "the history of symbolization is a progression from compact to differentiated experiences and symbols" (CW, 14:43). This did not mean that differentiated experiences were permanent achievements, but it did mean, as with the People of God and the Gnosticism thesis, that any attempt to avoid the implications of differentiated consciousness would be attended by considerable difficulty, incoherence and irrationality.

There were, Voegelin argued, two basic forms of symbolization. The first expressed the meaning of society and its order as an analogue of the cosmos and cosmic order. The second did so by analogy with the human being who was well attuned to the order of being, which included but was not necessarily limited to the cosmos. Society as microcosmos was historically the earliest symbolic form because "earth and heaven are so impressively the embracing order" into which human existence must fit itself in order to survive. Thus the cosmos and its order suggested obviously enough the model of all order, including that of human and social existence. Accordingly, "vegetative rhythms and celestial revolutions function as models for the structural and procedural order of society" (CW, 14:44).

The second form, society as macroanthropos, tended to emerge when cosmological societies, particularly empires, disintegrated, which undermined humans' trust in cosmic order. On such occasions symbolization shifted towards the cause, origin, or "Ground" of the visible world, which was somehow sensed to be more lasting, durable, stable and ordered than the visible existing world and its evidently unstable and unreliable order. At any particular time, this actual pragmatic order may be in deep disrepair; during periods of imperial disintegration, Toynbee's "time of troubles," the

8 Bernard Lonergan used the term "differentiation" in a manner very close to that of Voegelin. See his *Insight: A Study of Human Understanding* (New York: Longmans, 1957). See Thomas J. McPartland, *Lonergan and the Philosophy of Historical Existence* (Columbia: University of Missouri Press, 2001). See also Glen Hughes, *Transcendence and History: The Search for Ultimacy from Ancient Societies to Postmodernity* (Columbia: University of Missouri Press, 2003), 183ff.

surrounding society may be chaotic. If nevertheless sensitive individuals could apprehend a source of order and meaning beyond the evident disorder of the day, the "site" of this experience, Voegelin said, was the soul of the human being, the *anthropos*, who experienced the shift away from the world toward a reality usually symbolized as divine, an "unseen god" or to use Voegelin's preferred philosophical term the world-transcendent Ground of Being.[9]

A fourth typical feature was an awareness of the analogical character of symbolization and of symbols, along with awareness that the order of being could be symbolized in several different ways. This "tolerance" ended when the insight was achieved that "no symbolization through analogues to existential order in the world" was adequate to the world-transcendent Ground of Being or to the divine partner on whom the community of being depended. Typically the shift was from competition between stronger and weaker gods to an opposition between true and false ones (cf. CW, 17:202–3). When such a shift occurred, the very order of existence was altered. The symbols based on cosmic analogues, which used to be experienced as adequate, were suddenly "unseemly," to use a term of Xenophanes (B16; CW, 15:240–43). Plato spoke famously in this context of a *periagoge*, a turning-around or conversion, in his image of the cave near the middle of the *Republic* (515c; CW, 16:168–69). The conversion (and Plato's was not the only one) was more than an insight into the structure of reality or knowledge of the order of being. "It is a change in the order itself" because the structure was altered insofar as consciousness became aware that its new partnership with the divine ground of being had broken with the prior consubstantiality and relegated the mundane participation in the being of the world to a decidedly secondary rank. "The more perfect attunement to being through conversion," Voegelin said, "is not an increase on the same scale but a qualitative leap," a "leap in being." Moreover, it was experienced not as a consequence of human activity but as a passion, "a response to a revelation of divine being" (CW, 14:48).

9 The genesis of Voegelin's use of the terms, Ground, and Ground of Being, has been ascribed variously to Tillich, Scheler, Dilthey, Schelling and Kant. Voegelin said he translated Aristotle's *aition*, which is usually rendered as "cause," by the term "Ground" (CW, 11:225–26; 12:42ff, 271; 33:202). As he explained in his 1965 essay, "In Search of the Ground" (CW, 11:224–51), he was looking for a general term that could be applied to all cultures and civilizations, notwithstanding the distinct language in which the "search for the Ground" was expressed.

The "leap in being" is a term that does not occur outside *Order and History*.[10] It is clearly a metaphor; Voegelin indicated that he borrowed the image of a leap from Kierkegaard.[11] As Thomas Hollweck said, it is "a term obviously intended to illuminate something that seems to have resisted the author's analysis."[12] Both Alfred Schütz and Gregor Sebba had questions about Voegelin's use of the term, chiefly because the most significant connotation of the metaphor was discontinuity.[13] In Voegelin's words, the "leap in being" referred to the new and unprecedented experiences of divine being as world-transcendent and as the Ground of all other being. Moreover, since the experience occurred in the soul or consciousness of a human being, the soul developed "in parallel with the understanding of a transcendent God." Whenever the event took place, the articulation of the experience required a coming to terms with the mystery of death and immortality, a mystery that was expressed easily enough within the symbolism of the cosmological myth where, for example, a New Year festival was a ritual repetition of creation as well as a memorial (CW, 12:281). A mystery, in this context, referred to an experience of consciousness that may be desecrated but never fully understood. This element of mystery, furthermore, was, as Hollweck said, intended to illuminate rather than enhance the act of analysis. No wonder Schütz and Sebba wanted clarification.[14]

10 As John J. Ranieri observed, Voegelin focused more on the structures of consciousness to describe human participation in reality, especially after the publication of *Anamnesis* in 1966 (CW, 6). See Ranieri, *Disturbing Revelation: Leo Strauss and Eric Voegelin and the Bible* (Columbia: University of Missouri Press, 2009), 71.

11 See Soren Kierkegaard, *Concluding Unscientific Postscript*, trans. David F. Swenson and Walter Lowrie (Princeton: Princeton University Press, 1941), 90. The term was also used by Lessing (upon whom Kierkegaard commented) and Schelling. See also CW, 34:105.

12 Hollweck, "Cosmos and the 'Leap in Being' in Voegelin's Philosophy," Paper delivered at the 2010 Annual Meeting of the APSA. Subsequent references are to this paper.

13 See *A Friendship that Lasted a Lifetime: The Correspondence between Alfred Schütz and Eric Voegelin*, trans. William Petropulos, ed. Gerhard Wagner and Gilbert Weiss (Columbia: University of Missouri Press, 2011), 190; 194. Sebba, "Prelude and Variations on the Theme of Eric Voegelin," in *The Collected Essays of Gregor Sebba: Truth, History and the Imagination*, ed. Helen Sebba *et al.* (Baton Rouge: LSU Press, 1991), 218–19.

14 Some of Voegelin's readers thought they knew all too well what he meant. H. J. Muller considered it "a slander on the whole history of civilization" (Muller, Review, *New Republic* 135 [29 October 1956], 19). Albright saw it as a combination of Augustine's "leap of faith" and the contamination of certain "Hegelian notions"

In terms of the argument developed in the previous chapter, the leap in being amounted to an increase in precariousness. To the "seemliness" of the new symbols was added the fact that "the leap upward in being is not a leap out of existence" (CW, 14:49; see also CW, 17:56–58, 291–302). The experience of a new partnership with the divine Ground of Being did not, because it could not, abolish the reality of mundane existence, including the cosmos and society. Accordingly, new conflicts and tensions arose between the newly experienced and symbolized relation of human being to the Ground of Being, and the surrounding context. The problem of "unseemliness" did not disappear, but was balanced by an awareness of the need to compromise, similar in principle to the compromise of the Church discussed in the previous chapter. In short, the new insight or new truth did not abolish the old but was added to it along with awareness that a forceful attack on the seemliness of the old cosmion and its symbolization carried with it the danger that it would destroy what order existed, even if it was expressed in unseemly symbols. In short, "it is better to see the truth obscurely than not at all" because "imperfect attunement to the order of being is preferable to disorder" (CW, 14:50).

Hollweck speculated about the genesis of the term:

> The notion of a "leap in being" probably came to Voegelin in the course of a meditative process in which he was actually searching for as precise a term as possible to describe what was taking place in the consciousness of a relatively few human individuals when they became aware—either through a direct revelatory call or at the end of a meditative process—that the source of cosmic order was not located within the cosmos itself but "beyond" the cosmos, even though it was experienced by a human being within the cosmos, who had thus become privileged and elevated as a human being and had thus ceased to be just like the other cosmic "things" with which he shared his habitat. Indeed, this was a "differentiation" of reality, occurring in the psyche and thus making the psyche aware, that is, conscious of its own status in the structure of reality. Voegelin wanted to indicate unmistakably that this event was not simply a matter of "cognition," that

(*Theological Studies*, 271). Moses Hadas notoriously thought it was Voegelinian code for fascism. See his astonishing review of *The World of the Polis* in the *Journal of the History of Ideas* 19 (1958): 442–44.

> it was not merely *Erkenntnistheorie* [theory of cognitive knowledge] but an ontic event. The concept of the "leap in being" suggested itself as the best possible linguistic solution to this problem.

The term itself, wherever it came from, was, Hollweck said, a symbol "for a mystical kind of event that recurred in the past of humanity in different places and at different times." It was "an event in which something happens that is interpreted by those to whom it happens as a break in the continuity of cosmic time." Voegelin sometimes symbolized this event as the "flash of eternity into time," which certainly suggested discontinuity. The leap in being, Hollweck concluded, "is not a leap forward or backward but a leap *in being*, that is a disturbance of the primordial field by something that is experienced as other than any of these things that made the field."[15] There was, therefore, no hint of progress in moving from compact to differentiated consciousness except, perhaps, for the pilgrim's progress towards fulfillment through divine grace after death. In short, the leap in being was a mystical symbol, not a concept, which was why existence for those who experienced it and for the surrounding society into which the symbolism was defused, grew more not less precarious.[16]

Voegelin developed the argument summarized in the Introduction to the first volume of *Order and History* on the basis of the historical materials contained in the rest of the book. *Israel and Revelation* was organized in four parts, beginning with an account of the cosmological order of the ancient Near Eastern empires and proceeding through the successive differentiations of Israelite symbolism.

"The societies of the ancient Near East," he wrote, "were ordered in the form of the cosmological myth." This form of myth "so far as we know, is generally the first symbolic form created by societies when they rise above the level of tribal organizations" (CW, 14:51–52). As an empirical observation regarding the state of science in the early 1950s, this was an adequate description of reality. Two generations later it was accurate neither with respect to modern tribal societies—North American aboriginal societies, for

15 This is why Pierre Hassner translated the term as *saut ontologique*, an "ontological leap." See his review in the *Revue française de Science politique* 10 (1960): 714.

16 In his later writings Voegelin emphasized the "consciousness of epoch" that accompanied the experience symbolized here as the leap in being. See CW, 12:192–95; 265–67; 17:385–89.

example—nor with respect to early, pre-imperial societies.[17] We cannot consider the implications of the past two generations of anthropological and paleo-science on this occasion since our present concern is with Voegelin's account.[18]

Voegelin began the discussion of the cosmological order of Mesopotamia with the sentences: "To establish a government is an essay in world creation.[19] When man creates the cosmion of political order, he analogically repeats the divine creation of the cosmos" (CW, 14:55). The earliest political form known to Voegelin in the 1950s was "far from primitive." It consisted of city-states, "an agglomeration of temples with large land holdings, each owned by a god and administered by the god's tenant farmer." The several Mesopotamian cities belonged to a common civilization insofar as they were united by a common religion or, to be more precise, by common ritual practices and myths, which Voegelin called cosmological symbolization. Such myths and rituals expressed the participation "of the order of society in the divine being that also orders the cosmos" (CW, 14:61; 66). That is, the order of society was consubstantial with that of the cosmos.

But even in Mesopotamian society, Voegelin said, "experiences and symbols are exposed to the pressures of reflective analysis."[20] Accordingly, lines of rationalization began to appear that eventually led to the differentiation of intramundane pragmatic reality and world-transcendent divine reality. At the same time, however, "it is hard to abandon the gods who so convincingly reign in the sky with their splendid presence" (CW, 14:75; cf. Rev. 12:1). The "strict sense" of cosmological symbolization was an expression of cosmic analogies without concern for "the pressure of reflective analysis." Cosmological

17 Even at the time Albright criticized Voegelin for having ignored archaeological evidence as well as alternative interpretations (*Theological Studies*, 275–76). Later criticism has emphasized how the "shortcomings and doubtful, even erroneous interpretations" had been exposed by a half-century of scholarship. This was hardly surprising. See Klaus Vondung, "Rereading Eric Voegelin's *Order and History*," *International Journal of the Classic Tradition* 11 (2004): 80–94.

18 As indicated in the Preface above, the application of Voegelin's philosophy of consciousness to the Upper Paleolithic and Neolithic materials is the subject-matter of a subsequent volume or volumes.

19 This sentence clearly echoed the 1940 Introduction to the *History of Political Ideas* discussed above in chapter one: "To set up a government is an essay in world creation" (CW, 19:225).

20 A point decisively emphasized by Peter Machinist, "Mesopotamia in Eric Voegelin's *Order and History*," *Occasional Papers*, XXVI (Munich: Eric-Voegelin-Archiv, 2001), 30–31; 35–37. See also CW, 12:265.

symbolization consisted in the expression of experiences that the life of human beings and the life of society were ordered by the same forces of being that ordered the cosmos. Cosmic analogies "both express this knowledge and integrate social into cosmic order. The rhythms of the seasons and of the fertility of plant and animal life, as well as the celestial revolutions on which these rhythms depend, must be understood as the order that furnishes the analogies" (CW, 14:78). By the same analogy that understood political order as a reflection of cosmic order, the celestial sphere was the scene of political events. Moreover, the Mesopotamian ziggurat, like the Pythian *omphalos* at Delphi, was the physical mediation between the two.[21]

Voegelin's discussion of Egyptian symbolism was preceded by a brief analysis of an interpretative dispute between Henri Frankfort and Arnold Toynbee. Voegelin centered his analysis on the problem of the interpenetration of institutions and experiences, which previously he had discussed in terms of a political cosmion; Frankfort called the blending of pragmatic organizations and the experiences of order the "form" of a civilization. Institutions rise and fall and rise again within the same form "unless there has also occurred a revolutionary change in the experience of order." That is, formal stability could endure despite institutional degradation and change. The problem of form, Voegelin argued, "can be clarified theoretically, and its phenomena made intelligible, through the use of principles that govern the compactness and differentiation of the experiences of order." Voegelin's three principles of interpretation were: (1) the nature of man is constant; (2) the range of human experience is always present in the fullness of its dimensions; (3) the structure of the range of experience varies from compactness to differentiation (CW, 14:99; cf. 12:195). Accordingly, so long as the experiences of order remained within the cosmological form, the institutional vicissitudes of, for example, Egyptian society would appear "subdued" rather than revolutionary.

Voegelin concluded that "the intelligible order of history" or "the ultimate constants of history" could not be found or described on the basis of Weberian type-concepts based on phenomenal regularities. Such patterns were simply reflections of manifestations of the constants of human nature as expressed historically in terms of the range of compactness and differentiation.

21 This "mediation" was later developed by Voegelin on the basis of Plato's use of the common Greek preposition, *metaxy* or "in-between" as a noun to describe human being. See also Steven Shankman, *In Search of the Classic* (University Park: Pennsylvania State University Press, 1994), 21–26.

Moreover, civilizations were not "self-contained units" that repeated a pattern of growth and decline. On the contrary, Voegelin said:

> A civilization is in the form in which a society participates, in its historically unique way, in the supracivilizational, universal drama of approximation to the right order of existence through increasingly differentiated attunement with the order of being. A civilizational form has historical singularity, never to be absorbed by phenomenal regularities, because the form is an act in the drama of mankind that unknowably is enacted into the future.[22]

Turning to the civilizational form of ancient Egypt, Voegelin argued that the pharaoh was the manifestation of a god, a mediator by virtue of the divine presence in him to the members of Egyptian society who "participated in the divinity of the order that emanated from the pharaoh; the divinity of the pharaoh radiated over society and transformed it into a people of the god" (CW, 14:112, 114). The stability of the cosmological form of Egyptian society was evident as much in the longevity of its institutions as it was in the stability of its myths. Jan Assmann elaborated this difference between institutions and myths by distinguishing two ways that the remote and hidden Egyptian gods manifested themselves: by inhabitation and by incarnation. The gods "inhabited" the divine images and temples and, through ritual, could be persuaded to leave the heavens, the underworld and the past and "inhabit the here-and-now of the temple." In contrast, the gods, or at least the god Horus, was incarnate in the Pharaoh.[23] This did not mean that Egyptian speculation was devoid of "intellectual movement," but that such movement towards differentiation as occurred took place firmly within the experience of consubstantiality.[24]

22 CW, 14:102. This is the first occasion, so far as I know, where Voegelin used the term drama of mankind. See CW, 33:174ff. His argument, essentially reiterated his understanding of Vico's *corso*. See CW, 24:82ff.

23 See Assmann, *The Mind of Egypt: History and Meaning in the Time of the Pharaohs*, trans. Andrew Jenkins, (New York: Holt, [1996] 2002), 407.

24 Voegelin provided a kind of *via negativa* to indicate "what type and degree of differentiation is *not* to be found in Egyptian civilization" (CW, 14:122). Specifically, "the myth in its compact form . . . contains both the experiential bloc that was developed by the Ionians and their successors into a metaphysics of world-immanent being and the other bloc, disregarded in such speculation, that developed into the faith in a world-transcendent being" (CW, 14:124). See also CW, 12:62ff; 169.

Egyptian differentiation consisted in a speculative exploration of the structure of consubstantiality. To use the later language of scholasticism, the techniques of both the *theologia negativa* and the *analogia entis* were used to present and discuss a content that was at the same time a cosmogony, a theogeny and a political myth. Voegelin summarized the famous Memphite Theology, for instance, as: One God, One World, One Egypt. Even during the Egyptian "time of troubles" with the end of Dynasty VI (ca. 2200), the mediation of divine substance through the pharaoh had broken down but there was no break with the cosmological form.[25] Until Egypt finally was conquered by the Persians in the sixth century and then by Alexander in the fourth, the "political" and "religious" crises of Egypt were understood as cosmic events decreed by the gods.

Voegelin's discussion of the cosmological empires of the ancient Near East has quite properly been challenged and corrected by contemporary specialists.[26] Likewise, his account of "the historical order of Israel" has been challenged by contemporary members of the Jewish community. The reason for this opposition becomes clearer in the course of the present analysis of his argument. In principle, the conflict in interpretations was an example of the difference between the self-interpretation of a community and the analysis of its symbolization by a political scientist.

The pragmatic exodus of several Hebrew clans led by Moses did not appear in Egyptian records. For desert nomads, Egypt was a house of bondage despite the attractions and comforts of daily life in a stable empire. Had nothing further happened than an escape of an ethnic group from the institutions of Egyptian power, the result would have been inconsequential.

> But the desert was only a station on the way, not the goal; for in the desert the tribes found their God. They entered into a

25 The text Voegelin pointed to was the famous "Dispute of a Man who contemplates suicide with his Soul" in *Ancient Near Eastern Texts Relating to the Old Testament*, ed. James Pritchard (Princeton: Princeton University Press, 1950), 405–7. See also CW, 14:158; 12:58ff. In this text, to which Voegelin returned several times, was likely autobiographical. The author planned to commit suicide to inform the god in the afterlife that the pharaohnic order had fallen apart on earth, and, by delivering the message, effect a return to order. Contemporary Egyptologists date the Memphite Theology about 1500 years later, though deliberately written in an archaic style—which confirms Voegelin's point.

26 See, for example, the remarks of Vondung, "Rereading Eric Voegelin," 83ff, or Assmann, *The Mind of Egypt*, 206.

> covenant with him and thereby became his people. As a new type of people, formed by God, Israel conquered the Promised Land. The memory of Israel preserved this otherwise unimportant story, because the irruption of the spirit transfigured the pragmatic event into a drama of the soul and the acts of the drama into symbols of divine liberation. (CW, 14:153)

For political science, "the major theoretical issues arising in a study of Israelite order have their common origin in the status of Israel as a peculiar people" (CW, 14:157). In volume four of *Order and History* Voegelin remarked that "the case of Moses and the Chosen People merits attention as the only case before the rise of ecumenic empires wherein a differentiated advance beyond the cosmic analogue has succeeded in creating a new type of order both pragmatically and spiritually" (CW, 17:205). True, the Biblical narrative indicated that God had chosen Israel, but equally important was that, in their response the Israelites were able to take the "leap" toward more perfect attunement with divine transcendent being. For Voegelin the political scientist, the Israelite response was the focus of the analysis.[27]

Because the Israelites were illuminated by a new spiritual experience, the narrative of Exodus transformed the pragmatic house of bondage, Egypt, into the house of spiritual death. Egypt, and the cosmological order it embodied, became the realm of the dead, *Sheol.* But the exodus from the spiritual *Sheol* led only to the strenuous and uncomfortable life of desert nomads. The desert thus became a symbol "of the historical impasse," the "eternal impasse of historical existence in the 'world,' that is, in the cosmos in which empires rise and fall with no more meaning than a tree growing and dying, as waves in the stream of eternal recurrence." When the world became a desert, human beings must find their bearings beyond the world. In the solitude of the desert, one could hear the "voice of the spirit" that had already effected the rescue from *Sheol* (CW, 14:153).

The spiritual meaning of the exodus was well understood but it was not entirely differentiated from the actual escape of the Israelite tribes from imperial Egypt nor was the Kingdom of God entirely distinguished from the

27 This is one reason why Voegelin's reading of the Biblical texts has been criticized. See, for example, John J. Ranieri, "Taming Israel: Voegelin and the Problem of Israelite Order," in Thompson and Morse, eds., *Voegelin's Israel and Revelation*, 211–12. On the other hand, see Gerhardt von Rad, *The Problem of the Hexateuch and Other Essays*, trans. Oliver and Boyd (London: SCM Press, 1966), ch. 1, 3.

pragmatic military conquest of Canaan. Accordingly, the subsequent spiritual renewals of the Israelites "had to assume the literary form of additions to the Instructions" first given to Moses on Mount Sinai as the Ten Commandments. In this way, the Word of God delivered to humanity by way of Israel became the sacred scripture of a particular ethno-religious community. "The nature of Israelite compactness can be summarized, therefore, as a perpetual mortgage of the world-immanent, concrete event on the transcendent truth that on its occasion was revealed" (CW, 14:208). The metaphor of a "mortgage" has also been controversial.[28] Perhaps the simplest way to understand what Voegelin had in mind would be to contrast his interpretation with conventional progressive histories concerned with the development of "monotheism."

According to the progressivist "model," any society was supposed to start out with a "primitive" religious life consisting of rites, rituals and myths and then "advance" slowly (if at all) to a spiritually sophisticated religion oriented towards transcendence. "It is not supposed to start where a respectable society has difficulties even ending." And yet, Israel began its history with the radical leap in being of the Mosaic revelation, "and only after the people had been constituted by that initial experience did it acquire, in the course of centuries, a mundane body of organization to sustain itself in existence" (CW, 14:365–66). That is, Israelite history, as it were, went backwards, gradually retreating from the initial leap in being back to the *Sheol* of the world, a process that by Voegelin's interpretation was resisted by the prophets.

Particularly important in this respect was Voegelin's interpretation of Deuteronomy as standing "on the borderline between the orders of Israel and of the Jewish community." An era had ended when Yahweh was changed from the author of a community to the author of a book, and especially when the book took on a life of its own. "The fundamental fact that the Bible was never the book of Israel lies so deeply below the historians' consciousness that today it is practically forgotten" (CW, 14:423). This remarkable observation was followed by several more: "The exegetes and historians of religion are interested in the Torah not as the entombment of Israel, but as the

28 See, for example, Anderson, "Politics and the Transcendent," 27ff; Aaron L. Mackler, "Voegelin's *Israel and Revelation* after Forty Years: A Jewish Perspective," in Thompson and Morse, eds., *Voegelin's Israel and Revelation*, 105–39; David L. Morse, "The Problem of Metastasis: Eric Voegelin's Reading of Isaiah," in Thompson and Morse, eds., *Voegelin's Israel and Revelation*, 166ff.

transmitter of its spirit to Judaism and Christianity" (CW, 14:424). Voegelin, following Gerhard von Rad, considered the spiritual atmosphere of Deuteronomy "relaxed" insofar as the words of the text were not the words of God to Israel but of a mythical Moses who reminded the Israelites that they could live in fulfillment of their duties by following the rules: "a permanent peace of mind had replaced the existential anxiety of the fall form being (CW, 14:425). "It looks," wrote Voegelin, "as if in Deuteronomy we were touching the genesis of 'religion,' defined as the transformation of existence in historical form into the secondary possession of a 'creed' concerning the relation between God and man" (CW, 14:427). As with all such compromises, survival in the world of the order of the spirit was purchased at the price of an "experiential thinning out." The process is recognizably equivalent to the compromise of the Church as discussed in the previous chapter.[29] It should be pointed out that Voegelin's remarks regarding Israel, no less than his discussion of the Greeks, appear odd, remarkable, or controversial only because his focus was on the experience that symbolized by way of the Biblical (or Greek poetic and philosophical) texts rather than on the literary meaning of these texts as independent or self-subsistent phenomena.

Having argued that the spiritual order of Israel came to a dead end in the religion of the Jewish community, Voegelin returned to the substance of that order, the experience first of Moses, then of the Israelites, and finally of the prophets. The first element of the analysis was relatively straightforward: "The order of Israel has its origin in Moses; and the order in the soul of Moses has its origin in the leap in being, that is, in his response to a divine revelation" (CW, 14:453).

The second element was the Exodus narrative, which for Voegelin was *the* historical drama insofar as it brought "the order of existence into historical form" by means of the human response to divine revelation. Nothing was predetermined. Moses accepted the leadership of his people and visited the pharaoh, who in turn agreed to let the people go; the people agreed to leave and enter the service of Yahweh. At any point the drama could have ended with a human refusal—but it didn't. "The new dispensation will after all be the order neither of Moses nor of the pharaoh but of the people under

29 See however, Marie L. Baird, "The Movement toward Personalism in *Israel and Revelation* and Emmanuel Levinas' Ethics of Responsibility: Towards a Post-Holocaust Spirituality?," in Thompson and Morse, eds., *Voegelin's Israel and Revelation*, 140–47.

God; and the people resists," as did the pharaoh and Moses. The drama continued with "the actual establishment of the new dispensation" by way of the Covenant. This was not, finally, a "happy ending but the very beginning" of the endless rhythm of defection from and return to "the order of human existence in the present under God" (CW, 14:469–70).

A third significant element of the order of Israel was the Decalogue, the Ten Commandments. The Commandments "are not general rules of conduct but the substance of divine order to be absorbed by the souls of those who listen to the call" (CW, 14:478). Especially significant were the first two Commandments, which prohibited other gods and images of gods (Exod. 20:3–4). God revealed himself when he wished and how he chose. Thus he must not be made manifest by the work of human hands because images would obscure the reality of God as hidden and thus alter the relationship between God and human beings. "Behind all attempts to image God in the likeness of anything within the visible cosmos . . . there lurks the desire to bring God within the reach of man" (CW, 14:479; cf. 5:311). The Decalogue was not therefore a collection of moral instructions as much as an expression of the constitution of human existence in society under God.

These reflections brought Voegelin to the problem of the prophets. From the middle of the eighth century until the fall of Jerusalem in 586, the prophets expressed Israelite order as a discrepancy between the conduct of politics in the Kingdom of Israel and the message from Sinai. They experienced and expressed this discrepancy as a defection from the Covenant that was bound to be followed by divine punishment. In the event, there was no return to the ways of God and the prophets could do nothing to avert the destruction of the kingdom by the Assyrians. The dynamics of this act of the drama were particularly significant for the creation of symbols that had significant subsequent historical consequences.

By the prophetic interpretation Moses was the first of a line who "in the present, under the revelatory word of Yahweh, continued to bring Israel up from Egypt into existence under God" (CW, 14:481). That is, the successors to Moses would continue to ensure the drama of the Covenant continued, first by reminding the people of the response of their predecessors to God's revelation through Moses and second by reminding them "of the fact that its continued existence depended on its continued response to Yahweh's revelation through the prophets. . . . The historical form of the people unfolds in time; but it remains historical form only as long as the people, while lasting in time, lives in the tension of response to the timeless, eternal revelation of God" (CW, 14:482). Defection from the order of Israel could be measured by the comprehensive order of the Decalogue. In all instances it amounted to a refusal to listen to the voice of God.

Prophetic existence or, if you like, prophetic recollection of the meaning of the Covenant, could prove to be dangerous. Thus, for instance, by raising the issue of the order of Israel and of the defection of Israel from it, the prophet Jeremiah was in danger of being killed (Jer. 26:11–15). The parallel with Socrates, who was not reprieved, raised a common problem that was also more fundamental than the fate of either man. "The comparison should make us aware that we are dealing not with contingent events but with essential processes of experience and symbolization." More specifically, the comparison of Jeremiah and Socrates indicated "that the relation between transcendent and mundane order, when it reaches the level of conscious experience in prophets or philosophers, will become articulate in closely related symbols; and when the man in whose experience the problem lives becomes a force in community life, the response will be so closely related that the pattern of action will become a symbolic play, acting out the drama of revelation" (CW, 14:489). Between prophets and philosophers, as with the compromises of the Church and the order of Israel, there is an equivalence of meaning, experience, and symbolization (see CW, 12:115ff).

Prophets were not, however, philosophers. The Decalogue required that the people have no other god in the face of Yahweh. Jeremiah knew that by violating the Commandment the people had not simply broken the rules but showed that they loved other gods (Jer. 2:11–12). For Jeremiah the cosmic gods were "useless" but the people preferred them to a world-transcendent God who may not be useless but certainly was remote or was in some other way experienced as defective. As Voegelin put the matter: "it became clear, in brief, that Israel, while it did not mind being a Chosen People, did not care to be chosen at the price of ceasing to be a people like the others" (CW, 14:493). In terms of political science, the problem was one of finding a suitable compromise between the mundane world of politics and human order on the one hand, and the spiritual substance of divine order on the other. The problem can be posed by analogy with Socrates: for both the philosopher and the prophet, revelation was not a private affair "but the entrance of God, at a specific time, through the prophet, into the public order of the people" (CW, 14:490). However, there was no positive prophetic articulation of the soul oriented toward the invisible God. That experience, the foundation of philosophy, was never distinguished in Israelite history "from the compact collectivism of the people's existence" (CW, 12:492). Voegelin argued, however, that in the prophecies of Jeremiah, Israelite symbolism closely approached that of philosophy.[30]

The historical context may be summarized as follows: during the eighth century the prophet Isaiah formed a group of disciples, a "remnant," when the king did not accept his advice. They were entrusted with an understanding of the true order, but nothing further was heard of the disciples until after the exile. About a century later, Jeremiah was called by God to be a prophet not only to Israel but to the nations. The message from Sinai, by way of Moses, constituted Israel as a holy omphalos to humanity even though the Covenant and the Decalogue applied only to Israel. The wars with its neighbours, the conquest, and the exile made it clear that humanity beyond the Israelite order was rather significant. In response to the threat of the Philistines, the Israelites organized themselves as a kingdom "like the other nations" (1 Sam. 8:20), but the new political organization proved ineffective against the larger imperial battalions of Egypt, Assyria, and Babylon. If the kingdom could fall, then the existence of humanity in history under God did not take the form of an imperial Israelite political order, even if it were successfully organized as a kingdom.

Politically, the issue was straightforward. If the message from Sinai revealed the order of history, it did not follow that the actual wording was "the last word in the history of order." Even for Amos, if "Israel" remained the holy omphalos, the "nations" of the Near Eastern world were also somehow included; by the time of Jeremiah, since the nations and Israel were both in a state of disorder, the omphalos "had contracted into the person of Jeremiah" (CW, 14:543–44), in much the same way that Socrates became the only statesman in Athens (*Gorg.*, 521d–e).

Even without having to be concerned with the actual survival of Israel as a political and historical entity, as we noted above, prophetic existence struggled against the "law," understood as the externalization of existence into doctrinal rules of conduct. More important for the dynamics of political order, if one could not reconcile the order of Israel with ordinary politics, perhaps it would be possible to transfigure politics into the work of Yahweh. Voegelin discussed this possibility in terms of what he called "metastatic prophecies."

30 The closeness of Jeremiah to philosophy and the similarity of his fate to that of Socrates was no doubt why he was Voegelin's "favorite prophet," a characterization he made at Notre Dame at the 20th anniversary celebration of the publication of *The New Science of Politics* (HI, 44:6).

In the face of a serious public emergency, the wars with Syria and Assyria, what would the prophet, in this case the "first" Isaiah, advise the king? He told the king to trust in God, not in the army and its weapons (Isa., 7:6–9; 31:1–3). Building on von Rad's discussion,[31] Voegelin called this expansion of God's work in history an eschatological war "that requires no human synergism, especially no military action" (CW, 14:503). The problem, however, was commonsensical: how can anyone think that prophetic utterances are a substitute for weapons? This, Voegelin said, was magic (CW, 14:503–4).

Isaiah's advice was premised "on the fact that the divine plan itself has been brought within the knowledge of man inasmuch as Isaiah knows God wants the survival of Judah as an organized people in pragmatic history" (CW, 14:504). And if one asked how Isaiah came by his remarkable knowledge of God's plan, Voegelin concluded that what was visible in the making was reminiscent "of the later phenomenon of Gnosis." In the analysis of Voegelin's Introduction, we noted that the leap in being was not a leap out of existence. "Isaiah, we may say, has tried the impossible" (CW, 14:505). Voegelin discussed the "magic component" of the "Isaianic problem" with several Old Testament scholars (including von Rad) who expressed their misgivings at his use of the term magic. Lacking an appropriate conventional term to describe Isaiah's consciousness, Voegelin introduced the term metastasis "to signify the change in the constitution of being envisaged by the prophets."[32] But in reality the constitution of being is what it is and cannot be changed by somebody's fantasy. In the language of the Israelite revelation, "the will to transform reality into something which by essence it is not, is the rebellion against the nature of things as ordained by God" (CW, 14:506).

31 Gerhardt von Rad, *Holy War in Ancient Israel*, trans. and ed. Marva J. Dawn (Grand Rapids: William B. Eedermans Publishing Company, 1991 [1951]), 101ff. See also David L. Morse, "The Problem of Metastasis: Eric Voegelin's Reading of Isaiah," in Thompson and Morse, eds., *Voegelin's Israel and Revelation*, 164–90.

32 CW, 14:505–6. Voegelin explained his new term in a letter to Peter Fleiss: "I have solved at last the great methodological and terminological problem for classifying ideas which operate with a change in the nature of the world. The origin lies in the Prophets; and the term found is *metastasis*. That ought to make everybody happy who balked at Gnosis. That is now a great relief, because I have the conceptual instruments to handle such phenomena as Gnosis and Marcionism; and especially the modern ideas" (HI, 12:25). See also Voegelin's discussion at the 1959 Rheinfelden Conference: "The West and the Meaning of Industrial Society" (CW, 33:90ff).

Metastatic transfiguration was imaginary and philosophical attunement to the invisible God by way of the right-ordered soul was beyond the range of prophetic experience. Even so, there was a significant development within the compact prophetic symbolism by Jeremiah. Jeremiah's complaints were not simply a pointless jeremiad. In chapter 31:29–30 the prophet introduced, within the collective existence of the people, the notion of individual responsibility and individual punishment. In chapter 17:1, he introduced the image of the "heart" upon which the tablets of the Decalogue were written, and in the "climactic prophecy" of chapter 31:31–34 he wrote of a "new covenant." Unlike the one that brought the Children of Israel from the land of Egypt, it would be written not as law but will be placed "within them," because God will "write it in their hearts." For Voegelin, Jeremiah's discovery of the law written in a person's heart was as close to a philosophical insight as could be accomplished within the symbolic order of Israel.

Looking back, therefore, he argued that the action of Jeremiah was in continuity with the initial Covenant. Yahweh made Israel his own on condition that God's people hear his voice and keep his Covenant—now written in the hearts of the Israelites. The significance for human consciousness was clear: "The cosmic-divine order of Egypt was to be superseded by a new order of history under the world-transcendent God who had revealed himself at Sinai" (CW, 14:511). But at the same time the Covenant of Sinai had degenerated into the Deuteronomist rules for pious living and the now defeated kingdom. Voegelin emphasized both aspects of this single drama.

First, the revelation of God had entered history on the occasion of Moses' response at Sinai. It simply could not be thrown out of history because humans tried later to ignore it by turning it into rules. The response of the prophets proved Voegelin's point. They recalled the original Covenant but did so under altered circumstances, namely that the Chosen People had chosen to forget about it. And yet the experience of revelation was ontologically present in the "hearts" of the prophets—whatever the response of the people. The prophets knew, because their personal existence was conducted in historical form, in this instance within the tension and conflict between the divinely willed and humanly realized order of history, that "in whatever manner the empirical Israel conducts itself, the divinely revealed order is beyond doubt the immutable order of history; what God wills cannot be undone by the doings of man" (CW, 14:515). That is, history really does structure the existence of the human being who responds to divine revelation, which was what Voegelin meant by saying it was "ontologically real." Again the evidence was present in the words of the prophets who would not let

Israel "forget" that the people still lived in the present under God. Accordingly, Voegelin argued, revelation "carries with it the irreversible direction from compact existence in cosmological form toward the Kingdom of God. 'Israel' is not the empirical human beings who may or may not keep the covenant, but the expansion of divine creation into the order of man and society" (CW, 14:518). The prophets might suffer because of the defections of the people, but they could not doubt the order of history as the revealed will of God—which, incidentally, also happened to make sense of their suffering within the empirical Israelite society.[33]

The second aspect of the drama followed directly from the position of the prophets in the midst of the empirical Israel. The prophet was called in his response to the defective empirical Israel to recover the original Israel in his own life because "the holy omphalos of history had contracted from the Chosen People into his personal existence. . . . The Chosen People had been replaced by the chosen man" (CW, 14:520), in this instance, Jeremiah, who thus became "the sole vicar of God" (CW, 14:523). Correspondingly, the concern of the prophets, beginning with Amos (9:7), was for "the nations" as well as for the Chosen People. It could hardly be otherwise if Yahweh were experienced as the universal God of history.

This new insight brought additional problems with it. "The recognition, in Amos, that Yahweh is the God of the nations as much as of the Chosen People does not abolish the peculiar status of Israel as the center from which radiates the order of history" (CW, 14:525). But if the original Mosaic message had been ignored and if the prophetic reminders were met with hostility, what then? Where was the historical omphalos? And what if the kingdoms of Israel and Judah were extinguished, who would be the carrier of historical order even in its defective form? By historiographical convention, Voegelin said, this was referred to as the "Messianic problem," notwithstanding its anachronistic Christian connotation. In the prophetic context,

33 William M. Thompson remarked, quite properly, that Voegelin was able to understand that "there are times, when the divinely willed order is realized nowhere but in the faith of solitary sufferers" (CW, 14:542ff) because Voegelin himself had experienced just such suffering. See Thompson, "Voegelin's *Israel and Revelation*: The Reception and Challenge in America," 61. Similarly Geoffrey L. Price remarked that "it is as if he himself were a second Jeremiah, that Voegelin undertook his own effort to rebalance the consciousness of his own age" (Price, "Recovery from Metastatic Consciousness," in Glenn Hughes, Stephen A. McKnight, Geoffrey L. Price, eds., *Politics, Order and History: Essays on the Work of Eric Voegelin* [Sheffield: Sheffield Academic Press, 2001], 204).

the "Messiah" was the Anointed, which is to say, the king. That is, the prophets were concerned chiefly with the conduct of their kings who were to live righteously in fear of God if they were to avert the political disaster that otherwise would be visited upon the empirical Israel.

There was always the option of the metastatic vision of Isaiah, as in chapter 11:1–9, where a transfigured Israel became the embodiment of world peace.[34] God would judge the nations and "they will beat their swords into ploughshares" (Isa. 2:4). In short, the vision of Isaiah was for divine rule over the world without the bother of any political institutions at all. As Voegelin observed, "when the metastatic experience had been explored to its limits by Isaiah, prophetism had arrived at an existential impasse" (CW, 14:534). That is, Isaiah's vision could not be fulfilled by any pragmatic or empirical institutional establishment: all one could do is await the miracle, perhaps for several generations.[35]

When prophecy was resumed by the anonymous Deutero-Isaiah (Isa. 40–45) in the mid-sixth century, the symbols used reflected not only the Isaianic tradition but that of Jeremiah as well. Jeremiah, as noted, was concerned with the untransfigured present, not a future that never became or could become a present. What Jeremiah took from Isaiah was the insight that the order of society in history was constituted by human beings who challenged the disorder that surrounded them on the basis of the order that they experienced as real within themselves and articulated as the Word of God—whether to the people or to their own disciples. What Jeremiah rejected of Isaiah was his projection of a metastatic transformation to take place sometime in the future. That is, with Jeremiah, "the order of Israel was complete in the present again," only now it was contracted into the personality of the prophet who "enacted the fate of the people while carrying the burden of the Anointed" (CW, 14:537). Or as we noted above, Jeremiah was a divinely chosen, one-person holy omphalos.

34 "And the wolf shall dwell with the lamb, and the leopard shall lie down with the kid; and the calf and the young lion and the fatling together; and a little child shall lead them" (Isa. 11:6, King James Version).

35 In a footnote (CW, 14:535), Voegelin made the observation that how long one must wait was a recurring problem for metastatic visions, whether they were to be accomplished by God or, as in the modern world, by human action. Where humans were understood to be the agents, as with "progressives" of various kinds, the expectation of world peace, for example or of some other desideratum, which would inevitably be followed by disappointment at its non-actualization, could be managed by reinterpretation and assuaged by pointing to "installments."

Jeremiah suffered the spiritual disorder around him in the reality of an empirical Israel that disobeyed God and threatened him physically for pointing out the Israelites' disobedience (18:18), to which Jeremiah replied by imploring God to deal with the conspirators and their families with violence and death (Jer. 18:21–23). This attack on Jeremiah, and his violent response to it, was not simply a personal disagreement. Granted the Israelite officials may well have considered Jeremiah a pest, much as the Athenians looked upon Socrates. Jeremiah, however, saw the Israelite action as an attack on God and on God's justice. "The prophet of Israel," Voegelin wrote, "could not condone an attack on the life that served Yahweh" (CW, 14:540). But was Jeremiah then asking for simple retaliation? And if so, when would it end? A partial answer was found in the "dialogue" of chapter 12, where Jeremiah both acknowledged the mystery of iniquity and suffering of humans and the even greater suffering of God (12:7ff). "Prophetic existence," Voegelin wrote, had become "participation in the suffering of God" (CW, 14:542).

Voegelin then considered the two responses of Isaiah and Jeremiah together. After Isaiah's advice was rejected by the king, he invoked a future order of Israel where the "remnant" would constitute the spiritual center of a world living in metastatic peace. Jeremiah moved beyond the isolated order of Israel to the contemporary world of Israel and the nations at war. The world might someday be at peace, but for the present, the order of God was concentrated in his person. "Both prophets, thus, had in common the tendency to move away from the order of the concrete Israelite society towards an indeterminate goal" (CW, 14:544). One way or another, the concern of the prophets went beyond the Chosen People articulated as a kingdom like the other nations and thus subject to the vicissitudes of political power. So, what sort of a society were they talking about? Obviously, the metastatic vision of Isaiah was of a nonexistent or imaginary expectation. The prophetic suffering of Jeremiah as participation in the suffering of God gave him "at least a glimpse of the terrible truth: that the existence of a concrete society in a definite form will not resolve the problem of order in history, that no Chosen People in any form will be the ultimate omphalos of the true order of mankind." Voegelin then summarized the Israelite history of order as follows:

> When Abram emigrated from Ur of the Chaldeans, the Exodus from imperial civilization had begun. When Israel was brought forth from Egypt, by Yahweh and Moses his servant, and

> constituted as the people under God, the Exodus had reached the form of a people's theopolitical existence in rivalry with the cosmological form. With Isaiah's and Jeremiah's movement away from the concrete Israel begins the anguish of the third procreative act of divine order in history: the Exodus of Israel from itself. (CW, 14:545)

The last exodus, Voegelin said, was lived through in the anguish of the anonymous prophet designated Second or Deutero-Isaiah by modern conventions. Three aspects of this new mode of prophecy were noted by Voegelin. First, the guilt of Israel had been atoned and the prophet was bringing the news of redemption. Second, the appeal to the Israelites was to accept that they had been redeemed by God. Third, the interest of the prophet had changed from the order of the Chosen People living under the Covenant to "an order under the Redeemer God" (CW, 14:553–54).

Voegelin again summarized the history of Israelite order, only now from Moses to Deutero-Isaiah:

> From the imperial order of cosmological form emerged, through the Mosaic leap in being, the Chosen People in historical form. The meaning of existence in the present under God was differentiated from the rhythmic attunement to divine-cosmic order through the cult of the empire. The theopolity, supplemented by kingship for survival in pragmatic history, however, still suffered under the compactness of its order. The order of the spirit had not yet differentiated from the order of the people's institutions and mores. First, in his attempt to clarify the mystery of the tension, Isaiah split the time of history into the compactly unregenerate present, and a quite compactly transfigured future, of the concrete society. Through Jeremiah this unregenerate present then gained its existential meaning, inasmuch as the prophet's participation in divine suffering became the omphalos of Israelite order beyond the concrete society. And through Deutero-Isaiah, finally, there emerged from existential suffering the experience of redemption in the present, right here and now. The movement that we call the Exodus of Israel from itself, the movement from the order of concrete society toward the order of redemption, was thus completed. The term *completion* must be properly understood. It means that the order of being has

> revealed its mystery of redemption as the flower of suffering. It does not mean, however, that the vision of the mystery is the reality of redemption in history: The participation of man in divine suffering has yet to encounter the participation of God in human suffering. (CW, 14:555)

The participation of God in human suffering was, precisely, the differentiation achieved by Christianity.

An outline of the problem of order and history in the Christian context could be discerned even in the notion of an Exodus of Israel from itself. The Chosen People could last as a symbol of order so long as the surrounding empires maintained their military effectiveness. But the crumbling of Assyria, Lydia, and Babylon within a century impressed not only the spiritually sensitive with the insight that beyond the rise and fall of empires "the word of our God shall stand forever" (Isa. 40:8). The Israel to whom the revelation from Sinai was given may have been constituted as the Chosen People, but then, when both the empires and the Israelite kingdoms had fallen into disorder, "Israel" had come to mean the people to whom the revelation to humanity happened historically to have come first and who thereby were given the task of communicating the new order to the nations. The new Israel was the new Covenant and the light to the nations (Isa. 42:6); its task was to spread the Word of God to the ends of the earth (Isa. 49:6).

There were, however, several pragmatic difficulties. The society of Israel had dissolved into a leaderless population living in the vicinity of Jerusalem, the exiles in Mesopotamia, and a massive diaspora of refugees. When Herodotus wrote his inquiries a century later, no one mentioned Israel or Judah or even Jerusalem. Moreover, the end of Babylon was emphatically not the end of empire, notwithstanding the experience of Isaiah that empires wither like grass under the breath of Yahweh (Isa. 40:7). Five centuries later, in Roman times, Luke resumed the question of Israel as the light to the nations (Luke 2:29ff).

The spiritual insight of Deutero-Isaiah remained alive, though evidently suspect in the minds of canonical and rabbinical authors. One thing however seems unequivocally true: the exodus from the compact cosmic-divine order of empire was completed. The history of Israel as a people living under God was completed in the vision of a representative sufferer for humanity. The meaning of the drama of the suffering servant was of a movement from the relatively compact symbolism of the Covenant towards the logos of God.

> When man is in search of God, as in Hellas, the wisdom gained remains generically human; when God is in search of man, as in Israel, the responsive recipient of revelation becomes historically unique. Since the human experience of revelation is an event in the history constituted by revelation, historicity attached to the recipient of revelation, to the very historicity of Christ. (CW, 14:550)

Let us now consider the genesis of this "generically human" wisdom.

2. From Myth to Metaphysics

We begin with some preliminary observations:

1. In the discussion of Voegelin's Introduction to *Israel and Revelation*, "The Symbolization of Order," which we undertook in the previous section, we noted Voegelin's remark that the two basic forms of symbolization of society were as microcosmos and as macroanthropos (CW, 14:43–45). We noted further that the second form typically succeeded the first when trust in the cosmic order had eroded or disappeared under the all-too-obvious disorders of the day. Searching for what was more lasting than the empirical disorder around them, "the invisible divine being . . . can be experienced only as a movement in the soul of man; hence the soul, when ordered by attachment to the unseen god, becomes the model of order that will furnish symbols for ordering society analogically in its image" (CW, 14:44).
2. Philosophy, understood as "the experience of the soul and its right order through orientation toward the invisible God" (CW, 14:492), did not develop in Israel, Voegelin argued, because of "irresolution" over the status of the soul. Within Israelite symbolism, the individual soul had not disengaged itself from the mediation of clans and tribes so that the experience of community with other human beings established through individual but common participation in the divine proved impossible. "The personal love of God cannot become the ordering center of the soul" until the soul was personalized. In Israelite order, the spirit of God was present in the community and in individuals as representatives of the community, but not in terms of a personal relationship to God (CW, 14:286–87).
3. Turning to Greece, the theory would then direct Voegelin to look for

evidence of a breakdown in the cosmological order among the peoples living in the Aegean civilizational area later called Hellas. We know the *terminus ad quem* is the philosophy of Plato and Aristotle, but where is the beginning? Even though Augustine seriously considered the possibility that Plato had read Moses (*The City of God*, 8:11), there was, in fact, no Greek house of bondage from which a Moses or a Plato led his people; nor was there the suddenness of a revealed message. "The telos of Platonic philosophy," Moulakis said, "determines—and, it must be said, overdetermines—the selection and interpretation of materials" by Voegelin (CW, 15:27).[36]

4. Lacking any external criteria by which the Greeks could be construed as an intelligible unit of study (cf. CW, 15:193ff), Voegelin, so to speak, worked backwards from Plato. Of course there were independent poleis that understood themselves as meaningful cosmia, but no documents expressing a pan-Hellenic political order.[37] Instead, working back from the pragmatic crisis experienced by Plato in terms of the "war like no other," on the one hand and the execution of Socrates on the other, one finds a recollected and meaningful past.

One may summarize the foregoing observations, which constitute the presuppositions of Voegelin's argument in the second volume of *Order and History*, called *The World of the Polis*, as follows: the Greeks living in the Aegean area, as did the peoples living in the ancient Near East, existed in the form of the cosmological myth. The Hellenes emerged from this cosmological form into the pragmatic order of the polis along with the symbolic form of philosophy (CW, 15:53). The study of "Polis and Philosophy," Voegelin said, was parallel to the study of "Israel and Revelation," with the difference that the Greek story took two volumes to tell, likely because

36 Moulakis was making a critical remark. Its force was considerably reduced however if we recall that Voegelin was not providing a textual explication of "Greek" history but developing a philosophy of history and philosophy of consciousness.

37 Moulakis noted that Voegelin paid little attention to what were arguably pan-Hellenic rituals expressing a cultural unity. Nor did he concern himself with the visual arts, sculpture or architecture such as the Parthenon, which was clearly an expression of Athenian self-understanding. See CW, 15:38, 46. A very similar criticism has been made of Voegelin's treatment, or rather, of his lack of treatment, of Israelite ritual. See Moshe Idel, "Voegelin's *Israel and Revelation*: Some Observations," in Hughes *et al.*, eds, *Politics, Order and History*, 311, 324; Vondung, "On Reading Eric Voegelin's *Order and History*," 84.

Voegelin described his work as a "philosophical inquiry" (CW, 14:24; 15:53).

Voegelin's Introduction to *The World of the Polis* was called "Mankind and History" and discussed many of the problems analyzed in *The New Science of Politics*. Hellas was not a sequel to Israel but an independent occurrence of the leap in being sufficiently distinct in terms of experience as to require a different symbolism. As in *The New Science of Politics* and in *Israel and Revelation*, the primary field of order was a society organized to act and maintain itself in existence but also devoted to the creation of a cosmion that attuned human being to the order of being. Moreover, "this order can be understood by man and realized in society with increasing approximations to its truth" (CW, 15:68). The struggle for order was "the substance of history" and as societies succeeded one another, a single society transcended itself as a "partner in the common endeavor of mankind," which extended indefinitely into the future.

Such a reflection introduced a problem for philosophy of history. On the one hand, as in *The New Science of Politics*, there was no eidos to history because history was understood to be a process by which human being articulated its own nature, the dimensions and limitations of which could not be known before they were experienced. "Only when man advances from the truth of cosmic-divine order to the differentiated experience of transcendent-divine order does the order of human existence in society acquire luminosity of conscious historical form," as, for example, in the response to Mosaic revelation that constituted the Chosen People.[38] This too was a problem for philosophy of history because humanity or mankind, which was supposed to have a history, was not given to human experience or experienced by human beings. "All that is really given are the concrete societies whose members experience themselves in historical form by virtue of the leap in being."[39] And yet, when the leap in being took place it transformed prior societies and their succession into the past of humanity. As we have seen with *Israel and Revelation* and *The New Science of Politics*, the leap in being did not entail the possession of a final truth or an ultimate order of humanity. On the contrary, the struggle was more, not less, precarious.

38 CW, 15:69. This is, so far as I know, the first time Voegelin publically used the term luminosity with respect to consciousness.

39 CW, 15:69. This is a problem that Voegelin revisited in volume four of *Order and History* and in his later essays. We discuss it in chapter six below.

Moulakis has argued that there were three differences between the Hellenic and the Israelite leaps in being: (1) the Hellenic has a different *structure* "insofar as it represents a reaching up from the human psyche towards a transcendent *agathon*," which is to say the Hellenic leap was primarily a movement from the human rather than the divine side; (2) the Hellenic leap in being had a different evocative *effect* insofar as the Sinaitic revelation led to the constitution of Israel as a people under God, whereas the polis was unaffected by the presence of philosophers and certainly did not achieve any institutional durability on their account; and (3) the Hellenic leap in being had a different *genesis* insofar as there was no sudden break with the cosmological myth but rather a series of "intermediate steps," well known to generations of students of classical sources, that were antecedent to Plato (CW, 15:25).

For a philosophy of history, however, both the Israelite and Hellenic leaps were essential. "Without the [Israelite] leap in being that brings God and man into their mutual presence" and that created history as the inner form of Israelite society in opposition to the cosmological form of order, there would be no problem of the history of humanity. And without "the discovery of the logos in the psyche and the world," there would be no philosophy and "history would not be a philosophical problem" (CW, 15:73).

Following his discussion of "Mankind and History" Voegelin turned his attention to "Hellas and History." The problem sketched above was that the Greek experience of order had its place in the history of humanity or the history of mankind not because of any pragmatic activity by the Greek poleis but because of philosophy; philosophy, however, "never formed the institutional order of any concrete polis." Here Voegelin drew a parallel with Israel: philosophy as a universalist symbolization nevertheless arose in a polis, a concrete society, much as Deutero-Isaiah arose with in the concrete Kingdom of Israel (CW, 15:95).[40] If Plato was, as has been suggested, the *terminus ad quem* of Voegelin's analysis of Hellenic order, we still need to discover the *terminus a quo*. Here Voegelin argued, "if memory be accepted as a guide," and with comparatively thin philological and archaeological

40 At the time Voegelin considered the eventual expression of these two universalist orders to take imperial form in the Hellenistic, Roman, and Christian empires (CW 15:95). This development was initially expressed in the original title for volume four: *Empire and Christianity*. By the time the actual volume four was published (1974), Voegelin had modified his original plan, as we discuss in chapter six.

evidence, then Greek order extended into a pre-Hellenic past that included Minoan and Mycenaean civilization. Memory *could* be accepted as a guide because what was held in memory "is not an indifferent collection of knowledge, but the experience of certain events as factors that constitute the society as it exists in history at the time of the remembering historian and philosopher" (CW, 15:100). That is, remembrance, retrospective by definition, recalled (as with Voegelin's own anamnetic experiments) what was important. His brief survey of Herodotus, Thucydides, and Plato indicated that they (and Voegelin as well) took it for granted that Cretan society was part of Greek society and that Mycenaean and Minoan civilizations were part of the "course" of Hellenic history *because* it was recollected that way by the Hellenic historians and philosophers.[41]

As to the motive for organizing the memory of Hellas in various historical and philosophical texts, Voegelin pointed to the experience of crisis, first in the struggle against the Persians (Herodotus), then in the great convulsion of the Peloponnesian war (Thucydides), and finally in the disintegration of order that made Athens unfit to unite Hellas (Plato). The "central issue" in all three was the conception "of the historical course of a society as a cycle with a beginning and an end" (CW 15:115). The conception of a cycle in history, Voegelin said, "is a new symbolic form" (CW, 15:117). The imperial societies of the ancient Near East, he argued in 1956, never developed the conception of a society with a historical beginning and end but remained part of a compact cosmic-divine rhythm. Israel certainly had a beginning in historical time but could have no end because Israel was created by divine will as the omphalos of humanity. Hellenic consciousness of history, in contrast, was motivated by the experience of crisis, temporary resistance to it, followed by eventual or anticipated disintegration. Thus the society and its course from beginning to end were constituted in retrospect from its disintegration, not from its beginning, as with Israel.

In terms of "direction" therefore, one could say that Israelite and Hellenic symbolizations were contrary to one another. The Hellenic experience of disorder led to the understanding of order; the Israelite revelation or knowledge of order was a beginning that needed to integrate the reality of

41 Voegelin modified the significance of such retrospective interpretation in volume four of *Order and History* when he introduced the concept of historiogenesis. Here he was content to rely on the term "course," which, as noted above, was borrowed from Vico and first discussed at length in the *History of Political Ideas*.

defections. The Israelite word of God fully revealed the spiritual order of existence and left to the prophets the discovery of the recalcitrance of world-immanent reality to conform to it; "the philosopher's love of wisdom slowly dissolves the compactness of cosmic order" until it too became a world-immanent order beyond which was sensed but never grasped the world-transcendent divine measure (CW, 15:118). The principal stages of the Greek differentiation from the postulated cosmological myth of Cretan society, Voegelin argued, were: (1) the Homeric myth, (2) the Hesiodian speculation, and (3) the philosophers' break with the myth.

Voegelin's discussion of the evidence regarding Cretan and Achaean societies was cautious. He was explicit about the assumptions and probabilities that informed his argument. Moulakis quite properly drew attention to the difficulty with Voegelin's sources (CW, 15:28ff). Notwithstanding these qualifications, Voegelin concluded that "since the Cretan order found its expression in symbols similar to the Near Eastern, we can recognize the general type as cosmological."[42]

Second, Voegelin argued that if a society "is to reach effective participation in the history of order," it must be organized as a town- or city-dwelling population. Not that tribal cultures cannot create empires, but their pragmatic success was not matched by "their role as participants in the search of mankind for the truth of order." In this latter respect, the participation of tribal empires was "peripheral."[43] Town-based culture, which was present in Cretan and Achaean societies, was the matrix for experiences of a common humanity beyond a "biologically determined group" such as a kinship-determined tribe (CW, 15:120, 127–28).

Third, he argued that, notwithstanding the interruptions of the northern invasions of around 1950, and of the Assyrian, Hittites, and Dorians in later centuries, the Achaean aristocrats accomplished "the astonishing feat" of maintaining "civilizational continuity" with the Mycenaean and

42 CW, 15:123. Voegelin had in mind here the symbols of the bull, the labyrinth, the double axe (*labrys*) used to sacrifice the bull, and so on. In this respect, Voegelin's assumptions have been confirmed by paleoscientists, including paleoastronomers, a science that scarcely existed when Voegelin was writing this book.

43 The pragmatic success of the empire of Genghis Khan was certainly undeniable, but it remained a "barbarian" and relatively undifferentiated cosmion. In this respect, Voegelin's comparison of it to the imperial organization of the Soviet empire in *The New Science of Politics* was particularly critical of the latter. See CW, 5:134. I have discussed Voegelin's analysis of Mongol constitutional law in *Eric Voegelin and the Foundations of Modern Political Science*, ch. 7.

through the Mycenaean with the Minoan phases of Greek history (CW, 15:133–34).

A new historical phase, by Voegelin's argument, was achieved by the Homeric epic, which "converted" Mycenaean civilization "into the past of the Aegean-wide society that now was growing from the center in Ionia" (CW, 15:136). "Homer," for Voegelin, was not a singer of songs or a literary author so that the conventional debates concerning the traditional "Homeric question" were scarcely mentioned. Rather, Homer created "a symbolism that expresses a new experience of human existence under the gods, of the nature of order and the causes of disorder and of the historical decline and fall of society" (CW, 15:139–40). Homer and the poets who followed him were "prophetic singers who experienced man in his immediacy under the gods." They made articulate the gulf between divine wisdom and human misery. "That was less than the Mosaic insight that placed the people under God; but it was more inasmuch as the singers appealed to the psyche of every man singly." The experience of the divine essence of order in the soul or to the immortal core of existence "was still bound by the cosmos as were the gods" so that there was no movement toward anything like a beatific vision. Humans could, however, place themselves "before the gods forever by action that entered the streak of Memory through the song of their prophets" (CW, 15:143). For the Hellenes, Homer was the man who first transfigured their past into memorable song.

As for the contents of Homer's song, the divisions among humans as expressed in war reflect "a disturbance in the Olympian order of the world" just as the divisions among gods were evidence of a disturbance in human order. From this experience of disorder and even of disaster, the poet-prophet "wrested his insight into the order of gods and men, from the suffering grew wisdom when the fall became song." By transfiguring suffering and misery into song, "the poet transcended Achaean society and created the Hellenic symbolic form." It was akin to the "style" of the Israelite exodus from the form of cosmological civilization because the poet's self-transcendence opened a future that was based in the past but that moved beyond it. "The Hellenic society did not have to die as did the Babylonian or Egyptian, the Cretan or Achaean. Hellas could transcend itself into Hellenism; and it could transcend the symbolic form of the Olympian myth, in which it had constituted itself into philosophy as the symbolic form of mankind" (CW, 15:144). Voegelin argued, in other words, that initially the poet transcended the mute experience of suffering by singing about it. Homer thereby transfigured suffering into the source of wisdom. In this way the Achaean experience became Hellenic and eventually attained the symbolic form of philosophy.[44]

That Homeric society was disordered was evident to Voegelin by posing two commonsense questions: (1) why was Achilles not willing to accept the generous offer of Agamemnon to atone for having taken Briseis? and (2) why did the Trojans not return Helen with suitable apologies and reparations? Voegelin provided an incisive and elegant analysis of both the wrath (*cholos*) of Achilles and of the eros of Paris and Helen and concluded provisionally that the problem of disorder in Homer could be traced to the council of the gods as its ultimate source "and that is as far as the *Iliad* goes." There was no taking stock of the results so that the purpose of the divine assembly seemed to be simply the destruction of Mycenaean civilization, which "is odd to say the least" (CW, 15:167). The opening of the *Odyssey*, where Zeus reflected on the source of evil in the world, has often been compared to a theodicy. According to this interpretation, the gods were somewhat more divine or more pure in the later poem. For Voegelin, however, Homer was not concerned with, as it were, improving the gods with the passage of time just because the dramatic date to the *Odyssey* was a decade later than the *Iliad*. According to Voegelin's analysis, Homer was concerned with the truth of the source of evil experienced as both divine and human.

That is, the gods were not simply self-contained entities that sometimes behaved rather disgracefully and so received a Homeric rebuke but were "power complexes in the order of being that also embraces man" so that greater insight on the part of the gods would entail an increase in insight among humans. It was not therefore morality that was at issue, but the structure of reality so far as its order and disorder were concerned. Considered ontologically, gods and men "are not fixed entities but more or less clearly discerned forces in an order that embraces them both. The primary experience is that of being that permeates man and transcends him" (CW, 15:170).

44 The relationship of Homer to Plato has been undertaken in detail by Zdravko Planinc in "Homeric Imagery in Plato's *Phaedrus*," in Planinc, ed., *Politics, Philosophy, Writing: Plato's Art of Caring for Souls* (Columbia: University of Missouri Press, 2001), 122–59, and Planinc, *Plato through Homer: Poetry and Philosophy in the Cosmological Dialogues* (Columbia: University of Missouri Press, 2003). The arguments of the latter book, in particular, enabled Planinc to develop a critical assessment of Voegelin's discussion of the *Timaeus* and *Critias*. See Planinc, "The Significance of Plato's *Timaeus* and *Critias* in Eric Voegelin's Philosophy," in Hughes, *et al.*, eds., *Politics, Order and History*, 327–75.

Homer also introduced the problem of existential authenticity or of a "true self" that was oriented towards a rational understanding of reality. The behavior of Achilles, for example, at the height of his wrath, was never quite disconnected from the awareness that he was doing something wrong (or stupid). Or Paris, after having been whisked away from death at the hands of Menelaus, Helen's husband, by Aphrodite and transported back to Helen's boudoir, explained to her that he was obsessed with eros. He then ignored his own insight and acted on the "blindness" of his obsession, which may be taken to be the very definition of stupidity.

Homer's dramatic presentation of such questions, along with the overarching disorder of gods and humans, obviously left a lot of loose ends to be accounted for. On the one hand, as Zeus said, humans created more evil than they needed to and the gods were not to blame for it. On the other, the question of evil for which humans were not responsible remained to be accounted for. Even Zeus exercised limited jurisdiction since he did nothing to bring order to Poseidon's realm or to the underworld. Besides Olympian jurisdictional disputes and domestic problems among the gods, Moira, Fate, had an independent impact on humans. Homer did not try to reconcile these problems nor to explain, beyond the "distinctly odd" decision of the Olympians to destroy Mycenae, the pattern or configuration of social decline. He did, however, recognize the problem.

Voegelin's reflections on Homer were part of his reflections on the experience of order and history, not separate political or literary studies. To recapitulate: at the center of the leap in being, whether from cosmological myth to revelation or from myth to philosophy, was the discovery of cosmic-transcendent divine order or the Ground of Being. Radical as the leap in being may have been both in Egypt and in Hellas, it was prepared for by experiences and symbolizations that "loosened up" the cosmological myth. In *Israel and Revelation* Voegelin discussed the "Memphite theology" and the reforms of Akhenaton as symbolic achievements that made the cosmological myth sufficiently transparent for an inchoate awareness of the cosmic-transcendent Ground of Being; that not a few historians of religion have called these formulations "monotheistic" speculations (CW, 14:46, 74, 125–26, 477 n. 27).

In Hellas this "preparation" or "loosening up" was undertaken by the poets. Thus Homer created a human present under the monarchically organized Olympians and with it a heroic past and a future that could survive in his song. Hesiod, in contrast, *began* from what Homer had achieved. For him the Olympians were a given to which rational speculation could be applied in order to examine its truth. But Hesiod's speculation, unlike the Egyptian efforts at "loosening up" the cosmological myth, was not applied to a cosmological but to a Homeric historical form where the disintegration of Achaean order became the past of Hellas. "The poems of Hesiod," Voegelin said, "are a symbolism *sui generis* inasmuch as they establish a genuinely transitional form between myth and metaphysics" (CW, 15:196).

Two things may be said to distinguish Hesiod's speculation from Homer's epic. The first was that Hesiod was motivated by his personal distress at suffering injustice. For the first time the poet appeared as an individual in opposition to the accepted order of things and thereby also opposed his personal truth to the untruth of society (CW, 15:199). Second, Hesiod gave voice from a position of "lower-class" opposition to existing social order by using a stock of images and metaphors common to the eastern Mediterranean and beyond. His famous "ages of the world," for example, or his "ages of man," evoked parallels from Indian speculation. More important than the available range of material that enabled Hesiod to express his experience of decline and disorder, however, was that his account "is not inspired by the clear conception of a cycle in the cosmos in which the sacred order deteriorates until the cosmos perishes with its law" (CW, 15:215). This intermediate position of Hesiod's speculation was of continuing interest to Voegelin as was evident by his returning to the question in later volumes of *Order and History*. In this volume, however, Voegelin was more concerned with the implications of Hesiod's "individuality" as an opponent to existing social order and the significance of this opposition for philosophy.

As Voegelin argued later in this volume and in volume three of *Order and History*, philosophy was more than an intellectual exercise practiced with success by a number of clever Greeks: "it was a symbolic form that expressed definite experiences of order in opposition to the polis" (CW, 15:238). The personal order of the individual soul, in its orientation towards the cosmic-transcendent Ground of Being, relied not on community, political, or sacerdotal institutions but on the experiences of autonomous individuals.

As noted, in Israel, the leap in being took the form of the historical existence of a people under God or chosen by God; in Hellas it took the form of personal existence under God. Moreover, as in the Israelite symbolization, where the conquest of Canaan was called by Voegelin a "mortgage," in the sense of a symbolic burden, so in Hellenic symbolization philosophy carried the symbolic burden or "mortgage" of the polis. That is, notwithstanding the universality of the truth of God's revelation to humanity, the occasion of that revelation was interpreted in terms of a specific concrete event, namely the chosenness of God's people, the Israelites. When the accent was shifted to the people chosen and away from the divine chooser, the transparency of God's revelation was burdened, in this instance, by the ethnic and religious articulation of Judaism.[45] Likewise in Hellas, the philosophers remained citizens and Hellenic philosophy became to a considerable extent the articulation of "true order" within and in opposition to the empirical order of the polis. This is evident in the pre-philosophic texts of the poets as well, which led Voegelin to make the obvious distinction: "philosophy as a symbolic form is distinguished from myth and history by its reflective self-consciousness" (CW, 15:239).

"Reflective self-consciousness," which is to say, being aware of your being aware, was evident in the "pre-Socratic" philosophers as much as it was in Socrates, Plato, and Aristotle. We have already mentioned Xenophanes, for example, who was as concerned with the issue of true order as were Homer and Hesiod, but also with the "seemliness" of the symbols used to represent the divine by the prophet-poets. The reason was not "a banausic aversion to poetry" but a rejection of the public authority of poets and the form of the myth that had become an obstacle to an "adequate understanding of the order of the soul" (CW, 15:240–41). The actual content of Xenophanes' criticism of the poets (as was also true of Plato) was that the poets portrayed the gods as behaving disgracefully—as in the aforementioned example of Aphrodite's saving Paris from punishment at the hands of Menelaus. Such behavior, however, was disgraceful for humans, which is to say that the human critic of divine behavior, in this case Xenophanes, demanded that the gods lived up to what he, in his psyche, had discovered as being a proper (or "seemly") standard of behavior.

Voegelin generalized Xenophanes' concern about "seemliness" to a concern about how to represent a universal god analogically with human being. That is, the representations of the gods may have been "unseemly" but their divinity was not, so the problem of how to represent divinity was brought into sharper focus. The dynamics of the problem were familiar from the examination of the position of the prophets in *Israel and Revelation*. First came a conflict between the philosopher and the surrounding society

45 In his later work, Voegelin used consistent metaphorical imagery and spoke, in contexts such as the present one, of "opacity" in contrast with transparency rather than of a burden.

regarding human excellences as well as the representation of the gods and divinity. Second, there was the demand by the philosopher, in this example, Xenophanes, for public recognition—not for himself but for his insight.[46]

The reason for this demand was that Xenophanes had discovered new areas of experience that actualized what all human beings had in common. Traditional polis culture had not risen to the occasion, but Xenophanes sensed that it was the duty of citizens, *polites*, to do so. Voegelin then drew the conclusion that "the discovery of transcendence, of intellectual and spiritual order, while occurring in the souls of individual human beings, is not a matter of 'subjective opinion.'" Once the discovery was made, the experience was authoritative so that the philosopher or prophet appealed to every human being to actualize it in his or her own soul. Hence the conflict with the surrounding society and its "unseemly" order. Here Voegelin touched upon a fundamental insight: the prophet or philosopher could not compel those who refused to actualize their hitherto dormant potentialities, but neither did the surrounding society have a right to remain ignorant.[47]

The logic of the succession of discoveries about the structure of the soul through Parmenides, Heraclitus, and the tragedians to Plato and Aristotle pointed, eventually, to an awareness of a supernatural destiny. The "ways" of Parmenides, Voegelin argued, led to the "border" of transcendence with his speculation on Being. Moreover, "the vexing problem of the soul" became part of philosophical speculation, particularly in Heraclitus' work, because "the soul is a sensorium of transcendence."[48] Voegelin detected in Heraclitus' break with the earlier connection of immortality with the divinity of the soul an affinity with Zen Buddhism and "the basis for a critical philosophical anthropology" (CW, 15:296). He concluded his analysis of Parmenides and Heraclitus, who, following Jaeger, he called mystic philosophers, with the observation that they were able to break with the

46 In this respect Xenophanes acted rather like Jeremiah threatening the Israelite officials.

47 CW, 15:256–57. Hence Xenophanes' ridicule of the Olympic victors (B2) and their being held in esteem by their fellow citizens. In Plato's *Apology of Socrates* the demand to be heard had become ironic. Socrates knew he would not be heard (twice he had to quieten the jury), which made his demand that he be maintained in the Pryteneum (which sometimes was a reward given to Athenian Olympic victors) particularly (and deliberately) offensive to the jurors.

48 CW, 15:293. In *The New Science of Politics* the soul was called "*the* sensorium of transcendence" (CW, 5:148, 215). The meaning of *sensorium* in Voegelin's later works is discussed in chapter seven. Here it is not distinguished from the "site" where human consciousness experiences transcendence.

Homeric myth "because they have discovered a new source of truth in their souls."[49] The gods of Homer and Hesiod would henceforth be "unseemly," and their writings turned into mere poetry as compared to the more differentiated but unseen harmony enacted within "the drama of the soul [of the philosopher] with its intangible, silent movements of love, hope, and faith toward the *sophon*."[50]

The challenge to the order to the polis-cosmion was obvious: it could not be unquestioned when the philosophers were developing an anthropology "that identifies humanity with the life of the common logos in every soul" (CW, 15:311). The problem (once again) was that the differentiation of the soul as a, or the, sensorium of transcendence was a perilous experience. "The many need gods with 'shapes.' When the 'shapes' of the gods are destroyed with social effectiveness, the many will not become mystics but agnostics. The agnostic empiricist, if we may define him historically, is an enlightened polytheist who is spiritually not strong enough for faith" (CW, 15:312). Even the mystic philosophers understood themselves in competition with existing conventions for the inner formation of the polis, which led to entirely new problems of political organization. Accordingly, the Hellenic manifestation of the spirit in the leap in being of the mystic philosophers could not be ignored because it was the structure of the soul. Social order thus depended on the public effectiveness of their spiritual insights and the transmission of those insights over succeeding generations.

49 CW, 15:311. See Werner Jaeger, *The Theology of the Early Greek Philosophers* (Oxford: Oxford University Press, 1947).

50 CW, 15:311. Voegelin found something "very close to the symbolism" of the Pauline trio of love, hope, and faith in Heraclitus (CW, 15:300). In *The New Science of Politics* (CW, 5:140), he made the same observation, which was the subject of an epistolary exchange with Tibor Horvath, S.J., who was not persuaded. Voegelin replied that the passages in *The New Science of Politics* and *The World of the Polis* "deal with the development of certain experiences from compactness to differentiation." Of course, the *formulations* of Saint Paul were not those of Heraclitus, nor the other way around. That would "make nonsense of the whole inquiry." He then rather condescending referred Horvath to Nygren's celebrated *Eros and Agape* and to his own discussion of "The Pauline Vision of the Resurrected" in *The Ecumenic Age*. He concluded the correspondence: "If however you should find it simply improper that a thinker like Heraclitus should have become aware of the experiences of love, hope, and faith and their function in the cognition of divine reality, I recommend that you rely on the chapter on "Heraclitus" in Werner Jaeger's *Theology of the Early Greek Philosophers* where such improprieties as the passages which I have quoted are mentioned" (HI, 18:32).

And this was just the problem. The order of the soul discovered by the mystic philosophers, "and still more the Christian revelation," were not some kind of cultural achievement "on which one can sit down and be happy ever after" (CW, 15:312; 329). The discovery of the transcendent order was "sensed in the orienting movements of the soul" and was in no way a world-immanent order that somehow realized itself in society independent of the life of the soul. And yet the "mortgage" of the polis was undischarged, even in Plato's symbol of the philosopher-king, which evoked a new order where the spirit would be connected to power, but not, as has sometimes been argued, so that philosophers should not be murdered, but because of what Voegelin called Platonic patriotism. Plato's "science of order" was developed in part at least in response to the catastrophe suffered by the Athenians' defeat in the war with the Spartans (CW, 15:312–13). As we shall see in the following chapter, Platonic patriotism had a limit.

Part Three of *The World of the Polis* was called "The Athenian Century." The spiritual problem for the Hellenes may be summarized as follows: (1) the Homeric myths had disintegrated as sources of order because of the discovery of the soul and its authority as the sensorium of transcendence; and (2) there was not a people in existence who would or perhaps could live in accordance with the insights of the mystic-philosophers. In order for philosophy to become more than an irritation to the polis performed by various odd personalities, there had to be a response by society at large akin to the love of the *sophon* experienced in the psyche of the philosopher. According to Voegelin, this "Great Awakening" occurred in fifth-century Athens, the Athens of Marathon, tragedy, and sophistry, an intellectual and spiritual change that coincided with the rise and fall of Athenian political power in the eastern Mediterranean.

The "Athenian Century" from the Persian Wars to Plato, was therefore both an empirical achievement and the creation of a "spiritual and community substance" that created a "golden hour" when "power and spirit were linked" (CW, 15:315ff; cf. CW, 5:144). In fact, as Moulakis pointed out, this interpretation was "a topos that goes back to ancient Athens itself" (CW, 15:45). The "glory that was Greece" that has become the standard fare of modern college courses in classics departments, was perhaps the most lasting consequence of Pericles' famous funeral oration. Voegelin's treatment of this topos was highly selective for the obvious reason that his purpose was not to provide a survey and exegesis of Athenian history but to contextualize the achievement of philosophy and "Platonic patriotism." His concern was not with Athenian history in the conventional sense at all but with

Plato's response to Athenian iniquity and his recovery of the prophetic authority of the pre-Socratic philosophers under new spiritual conditions established by the tragedians, the sophists, and the historians.

The spiritual and intellectual significance of these three groups was quite different. Voegelin analyzed *The Suppliants* of Aeschylus, as he did in *The New Science of Politics*, to bring into focus two aspects of this expression of the acme of Athenian democratic order. The first was that Pelasgus, king of the Argives, followed Dike, Justice, in his decision to admit the fugitive daughters of Danaus who were in flight from the sons of Aegyptus who sought to compel them into an unwanted marriage. He was able to persuade the demos, the assembly of the people, that this was the right course, even if it meant war with the Egyptians. The second equally important aspect of the drama was that the position of Dike in the greater world was precarious indeed. It required the "saving counsel" of Pelasgus to discern and persuade the demos, and it required the willingness of the demos to take the risk of war and make military sacrifice to defend Dike. The polis of Aeschylus, Voegelin said, "unlike the people of Moses, does not exist freely under God through the leap in being, but approaches such existence through the tragic efforts of its people to descend to the divine depth of Dike. The Dionysiac component in tragic existence precluded the irruption of a divine revelation from above" (CW, 15:338). This observation was not a criticism of Aeschylus because "the revelation of God to man in history comes where God wills" and not where humans might wish it (CW, 15:338).

The second element, the sophistic movement, was a pragmatic consequence of the Persian Wars, the hegemony of the Delian League led by Athens, and the concomitant retreat of Sparta to the Peloponnese. Athens ceased to be a provincial backwater and became the seat of an empire and the cultural and intellectual center of Hellas. Pericles praised Athenian democracy before an audience of Athenian democrats following an insignificant infantry skirmish during the war with Sparta as "the school of Hellas" (Thuc., 2:34). Athens the empirical polis was itself schooled by the so-called sophists. As Aristotle observed in *The Politics* regarding the baneful effects of teaching people to play the flute:

> those in earlier times rightly rejected the use of it by the young and free, even though they used it before. For when they came to have more leisure because of their wealth and became more magnanimous in the measure of their excellence (*arête*), and further, being full of confidence on account of their deeds both

> before and after the Persian Wars, they began to pursue every kind of learning without discrimination but reaching out in every direction, they introduced flute-playing among the kinds of learning. (1341a25–33)

One of the consequences of the Athenian Empire, then, was the ability of the Athenians to support "foreign" teachers. As we discuss in the following chapter, Plato did not think the combination of imperial expansion and sophistry was desirable.

Voegelin provided a splendid exegesis of Plato's discussion of two of the big four sophists, Hippias and Protagoras; Gorgias, a third, was discussed in volume three of *Order and History*, *Plato and Aristotle*, and the fourth, Prodicus, was pretty much ignored. Voegelin also discussed several sophistic fragments. His focus was less on the personnel involved than on the subsequent reaction to them by Plato. The effect of the sophistic movement, apparent even in Aristotle's criticism of teaching the young and free to play the flute, was further to erode the traditional piety that ordered the generation of Marathon. The significance in particular of the remaining late sophistic fragments adhered not to their spiritual or intellectual penetration but to their having "created a new theoretical situation and found the symbols for expressing it." They were, Voegelin said, "symptoms of disintegration" within the old order as well as badly formulated signposts pointing to the new. That new order would have to deal with

> the quest for the nature of man that is the same for all human beings, the problem of the inequality of men within the amplitude of their equal nature, the search for a common order that will harmoniously hold together the unequals without destroying excellence, and the historical diversification of national civilizations. The sophists see these problems even though their solutions are clumsy and inadequate. (CW, 15:399)

In a word, with "the disintegration of the primary experience of the cosmos the sophists discovered the problem of philosophical anthropology, which made them "brothers under the skin" with the philosophers; it would take a philosopher, however, to deal adequately with the anthropological problems expressed by sophistic writings (CW, 15:29–30).

The third group, the historians, was discussed in Voegelin's last chapter, "Power and History." Appropriately enough, it began with a summary of

The World of the Polis. As was indicated above, volume two of *Order and History* began with reflections on the significance of memory during the Aegean "classical period" in Greek history. It was expressed initially in the Homeric poems and that expression was retained in the "historical consciousness" of Herodotus and Thucydides where it was transformed into explicitly historical categories. By the end of the fifth century the drama of the conflict between the Achaeans and Trojans had been replaced by the drama of the conflict between Hellas and Persia, Greeks and barbarians. As in Homer's time, this conflict among Aegean powers was a constituent of a continuing "drama of mankind" (CW, 15:406). And with the widening drama came a consciousness of equality between the protagonists and thus of the "dramatic unity of mankind" (CW, 15:407).

Voegelin stressed this aspect of the historical symbolism because it was less obvious than it was in the symbolism of the Homeric epic where the conflict between Trojans and Achaeans, as Voegelin argued, was a common fate that attended the disintegration of a common (and *ex hypothsei*, cosmological) Mycenaean civilization. Perhaps equally significant, Voegelin argued that the symbolism of history constituted a symbolic form alongside the epic, tragedy, and philosophy. The historical symbolism was not as clear on this point as was Homer or the tragedians and philosophers because of the absence of any Olympian world government of humanity. Instead, "the historians try to preserve the sense of a common drama in a world without gods by expressing it in philosophical categories."[51] Their task grew increasingly difficult as the pragmatic stage narrowed from the conflict of Europe and Asia described by Herodotus to the intra-Hellenic conflict discussed by Thucydides—notwithstanding the latter's effort to downplay the drama of Herodotus and to insist that his description of the war between the Spartans and the Athenians was of much greater importance (Thuc., 1:23).

Herodotus' description of geographic detail was part of the story because the whole of the known world was the stage on which this drama unfolded historically. The Persian Wars turned out to be just an episode that began with the earliest memories of humans. Herodotus was writing therefore about a war of humanity, and did so, he said, so that the "things done"

51 CW, 15:407. See, for example, the detailed analysis of Herodotus by Seth Bernadete, *Herodotean Inquiries* (The Hague: Martinus Nijhoff, 1969) or Leo Strauss' discussion of Thucydides in *The City and Man* (Chicago: Rand McNally, 1964), ch. 3 or "Thucydides: The Meaning of Political History," in Thomas L. Pangle, ed., *The Rebirth of Classical Rationalism* (Chicago: The University of Chicago Press, 1989), 72–102.

would not be obliterated with the passage of time. History was ordered, he said, like a "wheel of human affairs that, in turning, does not suffer the same human beings always to prosper" (Hdt., 1:207). Humans, moreover, were bound by a "purposeless necessity" (Hdt., 9:16) that compelled them to expand their dominion until they were defeated "without hope of escape." Humans, Voegelin said, knew "how it all happens but the why remains a mystery" (CW, 15:413). We seem to be at once in a world of imperial overreach, motivated by a Machiavellian desire to acquire more for its own sake than anything else, but leading inevitably to defeat because for his own mysterious reasons the God "loves to bring low that which rises too high" (Hdt., 7:10). "The turning of the wheel," Voegelin said, "is inexorable" (CW, 15:418).

In contrast to Herodotus' notion of an inexorable wheel, Thucydides wrote of an upheaval or crisis, a *kinesis* that was larger and more important than anything before (Thuc., Book One). "Thucydides," Voegelin said, "takes a particular pride in the greatness of the disaster" as compared both to the Trojan War and to the wars with Persia (CW, 15:426). This also meant that Thucydides rejected the claim of Herodotus that he was discussing the war of humanity, of which the Persian wars were just a recent episode. Rather, he argued that the war between Athens and Sparta, which involved the acme of Hellas, which was the acme of humanity, must necessarily be a "war like no other" in its significance if not in its nevertheless impressive body-count. Moreover, unlike both Homer and Herodotus, Thucydides claimed his account was reliable, whereas theirs were just poetry, legend, and hearsay. His argument, he said was based on an understanding of human nature and thus "a possession forever" rather than an ephemeral performance (Thuc., 1:22).

Voegelin argued that Thucydides "was strongly influenced" by the medical school of Hippocrates who also spoke of a crisis, a *kinesis*, in the course of a medical condition, and of his search for the *eidos* or *idea* of a disease (CW, 15:429). That is, according to Voegelin, Thucydides was the first person to attempt to turn his empirical knowledge of politics into a science by analogy with Hippocrates' science (and art) of medicine, which served as a model. This effort "raised grave problems for the future of political science" because Thucydides, like Hippocrates, was focally concerned with disease rather than health. Accordingly, "the political science of Thucydides was a model study of the suicide of a nation but hardly a study of successful political order" (CW, 15:431). For Thucydides as for Herodotus there was no solution to conflict, though things might have gone differently for the

Athenians. For both "historical" writers, necessity led only to the bleakness of disorder. In Voegelin's words, Thucydides "created the empirical science of the lethal disease of order; Plato created the other half of politics, the empirical science of order" (CW, 15:432).

This relationship between Thucydides and Plato was important, Voegelin reminded his readers, because it was sometimes said that, had political science followed the path begun by Thucydides rather than the "idealist" Plato, things would have turned out much more agreeably. One still hears this argument in the context of "realism" and even "neo-realism" in the political science subfield of international relations. Such a position made no sense even in the context of interpreting Thucydides because for him war was more than diplomatic moves and military operations in pursuit of the interests of any given political community. It also had an element of meaning that extended to the problem of moral disintegration. Even the most superficial reading of Thucydides' text would bring to light the intimate connection between Athenian ruthlessness in establishing and maintaining its hegemony and the pusillanimity and lack of imagination of its (former) allies. But Thucydides acknowledged as well that the aggressive expansion of Athens also sustained magnificent architectural and cultural achievement and was driven by a kind of internal necessity that in part the Athenians deliberately chose. No one, least of all the adversaries of the Athenians, ever expected them to scuttle their fleet and abandon their empire in a gesture of courteous goodwill. The Hellenes at least were not tempted by metastatic hopes for a change in the structure of reality.

"There is no solution to the conflict" of justice and political necessity (CW, 15:436). In order to retain the empire the Athenians by necessity had to behave atrociously, and atrocity was not excused by the beauty of the Parthenon. Indeed, unjust action in the execution of foreign policy was a beginning that had a similar effect on domestic politics. For Voegelin the result was almost foreordained because "the sphere of power and pragmatic rationalism is not autonomous but part of human existence, which as a whole included the rationality of spiritual and moral order" (CW, 15:438). If morality and spiritual insight broke down then the selection of pragmatic ends for the pursuit of political action would likewise disintegrate and goals would be chosen not on the basis of their reasonableness or even the commonsense feasibility that they might be achieved, but on the basis of emotions, passions, and even imaginary fears and dreams, all of which were amply discussed by Thucydides.

The path of decline may not be inevitable, but its course was certainly likely. In historical reality it has been taken time and again.

> When the corrosion of reason has reached a certain degree in depth and has befallen a sufficiently large proportion of the people, effective leadership in terms of reason becomes difficult and perhaps impossible, even if the man at the head under more favorable conditions could exert such leadership; in a further degree of corrosion a man of such qualities will, precisely because he possesses them, find it impossible to reach a position of leadership; and in a final degree the society by its corruption may prevent the formation of a man of such qualities even if by nature he should not be lacking in gifts. This connection between corruption of society and the impossibility of rational leadership Thucydides was unwilling to admit. (CW, 15:438)

That is, Voegelin argued, there simply was no hope of a "miraculous" succession of Periclean personalities as Thucydides seemed on occasion to wish for. And even if a new Pericles did emerge, there was no chance, under the new conditions that were the consequences at least in part of the original Pericles' actions, that the new Pericles would be able to lead the city. It was unlikely, Voegelin concluded, that Thucydides ever thought that "a first-rate man would not care to be the political leader of Athens and would turn to a less nauseating pursuit" (CW, 15:438).

By refusing to obscure the dilemma of power and justice as well as by his refusal to rationalize it, Thucydides could be considered "the true heir to the tragic tradition." At the same time, he marked the end of tragedy because "the tragic sentiment had withdrawn from the people into single individuals who as contemplators preserved the meaning of order in measuring the surrounding disorder by the memory of its standards" (CW, 15:439). An age of political culture ended with Thucydides' analysis of the disorder of the war. A new one began with the order evoked by Socrates and Plato, which connected the world-immanent order of society to the world-transcendent origin of that order in the *Agathon*, the Good.

CHAPTER FOUR
Myth and Nature

The preface to volume three of *Order and History: Plato and Aristotle* is identical to the one provided for volume two. In them, Voegelin explained that, as was discussed in the previous chapter, the Hellenic polis and the symbolic form of philosophy emerged from the cosmological myth and the pragmatic order of empire, much as did the pragmatic order of the Chosen People and the symbolic form of history in the present under God. Accordingly, he said, the study of the polis and philosophy "matches" the study of Israel and revelation in terms of the organizational structure of *Order and History*.[1] Only because of the bulk of the second study, on the polis and philosophy, was it treated in two volumes (CW, 16:43).

In addition, however, the study of the polis and philosophy attained the length it did because it dealt, as Voegelin said in *Israel and Revelation*, with "generically human" wisdom that was gained from the human search for God (CW, 14:550). In contrast, as we saw, revelation was invariably particular: God revealed Himself to Moses on a specific occasion and Moses brought God's message to his particular people, the Israelites. By Voegelin's argument, philosophy was "generic" because all human beings were endowed with what the Greeks first discovered or differentiated and called reason, *nous*. This philosophical insight formed the basis for Voegelin's assumption noted above, that human nature is constant, notwithstanding the historical differentiations of experiences and symbolizations. Furthermore, and as noted in the previous chapter, because *Order and History* was "a *philosophical* inquiry" concerning the chief types of pragmatic order and the corresponding symbolic forms (CW, 16:43), it should occasion no surprise that the philosophical analysis of the genesis of philosophy was extensive enough to fill two volumes.[2]

1 The "matching" was not elaborated further. Later Voegelin introduced the concept of equivalence of experience and symbolization to analyze these two pragmatic-and-symbolic complexes.

2 Even so, *Israel and Revelation* was about 70% of the size of the two-volume treatment of philosophy and the polis.

1. Plato and Myth

a. Introduction

Voegelin began his discussion abruptly with an account of Plato's genealogy. This was followed by an analysis of the motivations for Plato's involvement in politics and then his disillusionment, first with the regime of the Thirty, which tried to involve Socrates in their criminal activities, and then with the restored democratic regime, which executed him for impiety.[3] Philosophy and the founding of the Academy were Plato's responses to the same disorders so clinically analyzed by Thucydides. In this context, Plato continued the tradition of the mystic philosophers and Hesiod in resisting the untruth or conventions of society on the basis of his own differentiated experience of truth, but now under conditions aggravated by the intervention of the sophists.

Plato's pragmatic conclusion was obvious: if the purpose of politics was to establish a just order, participation in the politics of the day was senseless. One consequence was that in the early dialogues dealing explicitly with politics, starting with the *Euthyphro*, there was invariably a comic element present. Another was that it would take "an almost miraculous effort" along with good luck, as he said in the *Seventh Letter* (326a), to renew the order of Hellenic civilization or, to use political language, to restore some semblance of justice to it. Plato's effort to do so constituted what Voegelin earlier called his "patriotism" (CW, 15:312–13).

The result of Plato's patriotic and "almost miraculous" effort was a pragmatic failure because no Hellenic empire led by a hegemonic polis informed by the spirit of the Academy ever came into existence.[4] On the other hand, his dialogues, written within the Academy and studied by his successors, "created the symbols of the new order of wisdom, not for Hellas only, but for all mankind" (CW, 16:60). Hence Voegelin's description of philosophy as "generically human." Voegelin first discussed the generically human experience of the philosopher in a paper presented to the American Political Science Association in 1952.[5] The philosopher, Voegelin said,

3 See also Debra Nails, *The People of Plato: A Prosopography of Plato and Other Socratics* (Indianapolis: Hackett, 2002); P. Krentz, *The Thirty at Athens* (Ithaca: Cornell University Press, 1982); Danielle Allen, *Why Plato Wrote*, (Oxford: Wiley-Blackwell, 2010).

4 This is not to say that Plato and his pupils did not make the attempt. See CW, 16:68–77 for details.

5 Voegelin, "Political Science and the Intellectuals," HI, 64:13.

> is the man who lives in partnership with what is common to all men, that is, with the divine *Nous* or reason that transcends them all. Through participation in what is common, men become a community; and since the transcendent *Nous* is the universally common, men through participation in it become members of universal mankind. With regard to the universal common, before God, all men are equal; through participation in the common, man gains the essence of his humanity; he realizes himself as a finite being capable of transcendence.

Intellectuals, the contemporary version of Plato's sophists, have lost or ignored or otherwise eclipsed the experience of transcendence. Thus, for example, Condorcet's discussion of immortality based in the extrapolation of actuarial tables was "ridiculous" and we know it "only because we know about human finiteness through experiences of transcendence." Or there was the example of "social contract" imagery, which had things exactly backwards. Any such "contract" already must presuppose a common understanding and a common bond among human beings; it did not constitute it.

> The common bond between men must exist in reality and be experienced as existing, in order to make mutual declarations concerning future conduct intelligible as agreements with binding force. The binding force of [a] specific agreement derives from the ontologically pre-existent common bond; one cannot derive the common bond from the agreement.

And what was common to all human beings was symbolized by philosophers as the divine Nous. When experiences of transcendence were lost, human beings "have suffered the loss of an important segment of reality" and so were unable to order their own personalities through orientation towards transcendent reality.

In *Plato and Aristotle*, Voegelin began his substantive analysis of this problem with the early transfer of the authority of Athenian order from the polis and its conventions and myths, which he called the "people's myths," to Socrates (and more importantly, to the creator of the dramatic Socrates, namely Plato). The transfer began in the *Gorgias* (521d) and was completed in the *Laws*, where the order of wisdom differentiated by Plato was presented as a cosmic analogue. Between the two lay the *Republic* and the eventual authentication of the paradigm of right order in that dialogue by way of his "philosophy of myth" set forth in the *Timaeus* and *Critias*. Preceding the analysis of Plato's initial effort in the *Republic*, Voegelin provided a prefatory chapter on its double origin, an account of the life and death of Socrates, and of Plato's political activities.

Behind Socrates' insults to the jury at his trial and his mockery in the *Apology* of the whole proceeding, the story of the genesis of Socrates' "mission" (*pragma*) as a result of Chaerophon's alleged questioning of the oracle at Delphi also symbolized the transfer of the Hellenic omphalos to Socrates. Dramatically, as generations of political theory students have been amazed to discover, there existed a perennial conflict between the philosophers who were aware of that they were ignorant and the non-philosophers who were unaware of their ignorance. This source of the comedy of the conflict between the philosophers and the non-philosophers was balanced by the philosopher's awareness that the pride of pretended wisdom on the part of the non-philosophers was nevertheless a threat. In the *Apology*, as Voegelin noted, "Socrates speaks as the representative of the divine power of Hellas; and he stresses the irony that he, the only Athenian who believes in the gods to such an extent that he follows their orders and risks his life, is accused of impiety by the very men whose disbelief in things divine is the reason for decay" (CW, 16:62–63).

The drama of Socrates' life and death, Voegelin argued, was "a symbolic form created by Plato as the means for communicating, and expanding, the order of wisdom founded by its hero" (CW, 16:64). In addition to Socratic comedy, there could also be found the element of tragedy, and the problem of the persuasive imposition of right order, Dike, on disorder and passion, which Plato borrowed from Aeschylus. The *Suppliants*, discussed briefly in the previous chapter, was "a liturgy of Dike, and in particular it was a cult of political Dike" (CW, 16:65). However, like any cult, it could lose its meaning when the people for whom the drama was written became incapable of experiencing imaginatively in their own souls what the playwright intended.

The *Apology* was clear evidence that the tension of Dike and disorder that had been present and expressed in the action of the *Suppliants* had evaporated. Henceforth the conflict between the Athenians and Socrates was the subject-matter of the drama—or, more broadly, between the non-philosophers and the philosopher. In this context the Platonic dialogue "was in the history of Hellenic symbolic forms the successor of Aeschylean tragedy under new political conditions" (CW, 16:65). The reason for such a succession was found in a common presupposition of Aeschylean and Platonic drama: the psyche was understood by them as both the site of order in society and the site at which the influence of society and its conventions might in turn influence the order of the psyche. The conflict or struggle among these influences constituted the drama of the soul and of the polis.

For Plato, philosophy was "an act of resistance" by the soul to its destruction by the conventions of society that was "illuminated by conceptual understanding." Moreover, Plato's experience of resistance to conventions that aimed to destroy his psyche was the origin of the "insight that the substance of society is psyche" (CW, 16:123). Accordingly, the disorder of convention was experienced in the psyche of the philosopher as a reality to be resisted and, in resisting and diagnosing the source of disorder, the philosopher also analyzed the health and disease of the substance of society. Conceptually Plato expressed this insight in the principle that the polis was the human being written in large letters (*Rep.*, 368d–e). Thus a well-ordered city was ruled by human beings with well-ordered souls and it was disordered when the souls of the rulers were disordered.[6]

Only when the new order of wisdom and justice was conceptually established and the dramatic conflict had simmered down "can its expression assume the form of a static dogma or a metaphysical speculation" (CW, 16:65). The theoretical or speculative triumph of the new order came, however, at the cost of a diminution of dramatic conflict or struggle with disorder. The struggle could be maintained as existentially viable—as drama—only by way of a dialogue, "the symbolic form of the order of wisdom," as distinct from speech-making (CW, 16:66).

Both the *Gorgias* and the *Protagoras* indicated that dialogic partners could not be compelled and that conversation could easily turn into prolix speech-making (*makrologia*). To forestall the ultimate futility of the dialogue as a symbolic form, Plato introduced the psychic force of Socratic death, *Thanatos*, that ordered the souls of the living. The experience of Thanatos in the psyche enabled one to distinguish the soul from the body, psyche from soma, and to grasp the nonsomatic, psychic or spiritual connections of psyche and *cosmos*, or order (CW, 16:96). As Voegelin summarized the point:

6 In commonsensical language, the type of personality of the ruler influenced the kind of people with whom he or she surrounded himself so that the character of the rulers helped constitute the regime, the *politeia*, which was the Greek title of Plato's *Republic*.

"the soul is immortal; and death is the incision in its existence that permits the readjustment of station after the earthly period has given the soul its chance for development" (CW, 16:67). In terms of the dialogue, then, its drama continued in the beyond of life, in death. Hence the myth of judgment in the *Gorgias* was understood as the first of the "Platonic poems that concern a philosophy of order and history." This dialogue and its concluding myth or poem was dramatically effective because of its "elemental terseness and its closeness to the experiences expressed in it." In the later dialogues, *Republic*, *Statesman*, and *Timaeus*, the meanings expressed in the *Gorgias* poem were expressed in a more differentiated symbolism that took into account the connection between the psyche and the cosmos as well as between the psyche and the surrounding contemporaneous political society.

On the other hand, when the conversation was conducted among Socrates, Plato, and their friends, then the psychic force not of Thanatos but of Socratic Eros was in play. Whereas Thanatos could purge the psyche of all unessential appearance and of all that was neither noble nor just, Eros expressed the desire for the Good awakened in successive generations, from Socrates' animation of Plato right down to the present, when teachers awaken an echoing desire for the Good in their pupils. The two forces in the psyche were closely related: in the *Phaedo* philosophy was called the practice of dying; in the *Symposium* and the *Phaedrus* the *Eros* in the psyche of the Idea created the community of philosophers living among other human beings. Now let us consider the details that Voegelin emphasized.

b. Gorgias

The specific drama of the *Gorgias*, with which Voegelin began his textual exegesis, can be indicated briefly. In the opening scene, the migratory sophist, Gorgias, appeared tired from a long day exhibiting his rhetoric at an open house hosted by the democratic politician, Callicles. Socrates showed up with Chaerophon who conducted an inconclusive debate with Polus. This was followed by a comic discussion between Polus and Socrates and the enacting of an erotic confrontation between Socrates and Callicles, representing the conflict between the philosopher and the political representative of the city. It led to an impasse where Callicles reminded Socrates that philosophizing might get him killed. Callicles then developed his own account of Dike as the self-assertion of the stronger.

Callicles' position, however, was based on the unexamined and inarticulate assumption of a pre-established harmony between the good and the strong. Moreover, he was sufficiently conventional still to hold to a somewhat hazy view that some virtues (courage, for example) were superior to others (cowardly self-preservation, for example). Socrates first demolished the pre-established harmony and then drew the implications of the reality of a hierarchy of virtues.

The point of the discussion with Callicles was not so much political as existential. For Callicles the meaning of existence was exhausted in getting more than one's share (*pleonexia*) and keeping it. Socrates, in contrast, maintained that the price of such an acquisition and the defence of it may be too high. Hence his famous summary position: suffering injustice is bad; doing injustice is worse; doing injustice and avoiding punishment is worst of all. Given the self-important manliness of Callicles, Socrates' comic touch was perfect: "who is the real man (*aner*)?" he asked. Only an *anthropos*, a wimpy human being, would want to prolong his life at all costs (*Gorg*., 511b–12c).

In terms of simple political conflict, the result also displayed a comic dimension. Callicles was just one of many politicians and would likely be caught in the morass to which his way of existence contributed. Socrates, however, introduced the notion of the *politikos*, the statesman, who was good if the citizens were improved under his guidance and bad if they grew more existentially disordered. Applying this standard to the great politicians of recent Athenian history—Themistocles, Pericles, Cimon, and Miltiades—he found them deeply defective for filling the city with junk (*phlyrion*) and leaving no room for justice or moderation (*Gorg*., 517c).

When Callicles replied that the consequence of such an attitude for Socrates might prove fatal, Socrates agreed. Moreover, he explained why it was likely he would be killed: he was one of the few, perhaps the only, statesman in Athens, which is to say, he practiced the true art of politics (*Gorg*., 521d).

This particular formulation in a political context was as important for Voegelin's argument as the experience of the prophets was in the Israelite context. Specifically, Socrates replaced Callicles in the drama as the proper representative of public order. For Plato, the actual author of the dramatic text, it declared that politicians, represented by Callicles, who were overcome by love of the people, the *demos*, were in fact adversaries, not to say enemies (*antistasiotes*, *Gorg*., 513c) and that he, Plato, through his character, Socrates, represented the authoritative order. "Surprisingly," Voegelin wrote, "Plato's claim has proved historically quite sound. The order represented by Callicles has gone down in ignominy; the order represented by Plato has survived Athens and is still one of the most important ingredients in the order of the soul of those men who have not renounced the traditions of Western civilization" (CW, 16:92). Just as with Jeremiah or Isaiah, Voegelin's focus was on the concrete experience of the actual individual, Aristocles, son of Ariston, known to history as Plato.

For Plato to make such a claim, which implied that the Athenians had lost the dramatic meaning of their existence, their reason for being, was revolutionary. The drama of Socrates' trial indicated that the law courts could kill but their action had no authority and so was not, properly speaking, punishment. An obvious question followed: where did Plato get the authority to displace the political leadership of Athens? The answer, Voegelin said, was found in the myth of judgment that ended the dialogue. In response to Callicles' repeated warnings that he was likely to be killed for maintaining his "mission" or his "business" (*pragma*), namely philosophizing, Socrates replied that the last and worst of all evils would be to die with a soul filled with injustice (522e). The reason for holding that position he set forth in a story, a mythos or "poem" as Voegelin called it, in order to distinguish its form from logos or rational account (cf. *Apol.*, 40a).

Socrates warned Callicles that the myth was true, even if Callicles thought it was no more than a pretty story, which is to say the symbols found in the myth translated "the experiences of the soul that they articulate" (CW, 16:94). Voegelin then provided an exegesis of the myth centred on Plato's experience of the life and death of Socrates. On the one hand, the philosophers were the ones "who let their souls be penetrated by the experience of death and thus, have achieved life *sub specie mortis* in freedom from somatic passion." This experience of Thanatos had imaginatively entered the philosophers' souls. On the other hand, "the soul of Socrates was oriented toward the Agathon [the Good] through its eroticism; and the Agathon invaded the soul with its eternal substance, thereby creating the autonomous order of the soul beyond the passions of the body." The life of Socrates, Voegelin continued, "was the great model of the liberation of the soul through the invasion of death into earthly existence; and the *imitatio Socratis* had become the order of life for his followers, and above all for Plato" (CW, 16:96–97).

What about those who did not experience the presence of Thanatos in their souls or who were not oriented by desire toward the Agathon? "On this question hinges the problem of history as meaningful order, i.e., as the process of revelation," Voegelin wrote. "The revelation of divinity in history is ontologically real. The myth of the people and the poets is really superseded by the myth of the soul. . . . The order of the soul as revealed through

Socrates has, indeed, become the new order of relations between God and man." The authority of the new order was "inescapable" and everyone, including the dramatic Callicles, knew it, whatever his "sulkiness and recalcitrance" (CW, 16:97). Indeed, his sulkiness and recalcitrance were evidence, if any more were needed, that Plato was not formulating a dogma regarding purgative punishment in postexistence for souls who refused to let themselves be ordered by the imaginative experience of Thanatos. Even those who sought to evade the authority of the Socratic soul must first acknowledge what they tried in vain to deny.

c. The Republic

The discussion of the *Gorgias* was followed by an analysis of the *Republic*. Voegelin's "magisterial treatment of a much-misunderstood classic," as Dante Germino called it (CW, 16:9). Granted that Voegelin's analysis of the structure of the text, and his interpretation of specific passages can all stand on their own, our concern is with what Voegelin took from the *Republic* (as from the *Gorgias* and the other dialogues) in the construction of his own philosophy of order.[7] For example, the descent to Piraeus, which was indicated in the first word of the dialogue, was balanced by the descent of Er into the underworld in the myth of judgment at the end of the book, which Voegelin called the epilogue. "The myth of cosmic order," Voegelin wrote, "completes the study of right order in the individual psyche of the philosopher, as well as in the polis of the idea. The order of man and society is part of the embracing cosmic order" (CW, 16:105). The actual procedure Voegelin used in his interpretation, as in his earlier work, was to trace the "dominant problems" in the text by "following the order of their appearance in the chain of motivating experiences" (CW, 16:106).

The most significant of these experiences were found in the subheadings of Voegelin's chapters. For example, the equality of citizens and

7 As with *The New Science of Politics*, the reception of the first volumes of *Order and History* was mixed, especially by classicists and professors of philosophy when they examined volumes two and three. Dante Germino discussed many of these unsympathetic appraisals in his "Introduction," CW, 16:29–36. What they had in common, including the reviews that praised Voegelin's scholarship and interpretive achievement, was that they viewed the study as a kind of conventional "history of ideas" rather than a philosophical anthropology that made use of historical predecessors. This may be understandable since Voegelin was not always clear about his purpose, but it made for some remarkably thoughtless, not to say plain insulting and stupid results.

foreigners in the Piraeus taking part in the cultic practice of the festival of Bendis was balanced by the equality in death of all persons as expressed in the story told by Er, the Pamphylian, a "man of all tribes." Or there was the theme of descent and ascent. Socrates descended to the Piraeus and ascended with the saving tale that he recounted next day as the dramatic text written by Plato, the *Republic*. Or there was the story of Er, the messenger (*angelos*) from Hades who told his story to Socrates. And finally, to deal with only the most obvious symbol, there was the Parable of the Cave, midway between the opening descent by Socrates and the closing ascent by Er.

This well-known structure or set of parallels in the *Republic* carried with it the "disquieting" realization "that the truth of human existence can be found both by descent and by ascent. The truth brought up from the Piraeus by Socrates and his discourse and the truth brought up from Hades by the messenger Er are the same truth that is brought down by the philosopher who has seen the Agathon" in the Cave story (CW, 16:114). The creation of all these symbols and of their relation to one another was motivated by the experience of Plato, and that remained Voegelin's focus: the philosopher-poet who wrote the dialogue that told of the messenger from Hades whose "saving story" was told a day later by Socrates of a fictional conversation with friends. By writing it down as the text of the *Republic* Plato transformed this fictional audience into "mankind."

Likewise, Voegelin argued, the "friendly advice" that the young Athenian aristocrat was, *ex hypothesi*, likely to have received from his own friends and family was rejected for a life of philosophy. Plato expressed this experience, using the imagery of the Cave, in terms of having been turned around and dragged up to the light. But whereas Er was sent *up* to earth from Hades to deliver his message, the philosopher was sent back *down* to the Cave. Hence the "disquieting" realization of Voegelin mentioned above.

If it be granted that the major dramatic symbols of the *Republic* expressed Plato's experience of resistance to the spiritual death and political disorder of Athens, symbolized by the Piraeus, and by the awakening of a new order in the psyche, there remained several unanswered questions to consider. To use the imagery Plato employed, from where did the spiritual strength come to Plato that enabled him to resist the spiritual death of the polis? Who or what turned around the prisoner in the Cave, namely Plato, and dragged him up? Who were the judges that sent Plato with his message to humanity in the saving myth of judgment? Voegelin argued that such questions would take his readers beyond the text of the *Republic* both to other Platonic texts and, for even greater clarity, beyond Plato to

Neoplatonic mystical union with God and to Christian experiences and symbols as well.

Plato, however, was neither a Neoplatonic mystic nor a Christian. His experience and symbolization of reality, Voegelin said, "remains bound by the compactness of the Dionysiac soul." Indeed, Plato's philosophy was not "a" philosophy "but *the* symbolic form in which a Dionysiac soul expresses its ascent to God" (CW, 16:116; 125). As we noted in chapter three, just as the prophets had to struggle with the "mortgage" of the Chosen People so did Plato struggle with the mortgage of the polis. In the *Republic* this mortgage took the form of articulating a very pragmatic resistance to political corruption by means of paired symbols that contrasted the truth and untruth of existence, which, as noted, continued the resistance by the mystic philosophers under new political and spiritual conditions created by the public success of their "brothers under the skin," the sophists (CW, 15:29–30).

Within the *Republic* there were three major complexes of symbols that expressed the philosophers' resistance to corruption. The first was found in the paired notions of justice and injustice, health and sickness, and minding one's own business and minding everyone else's business. The second, "political," dimension contrasted the rule by politicians and the rule by "true philosophers" who looked with admiration on the truth and who could see the one idea in the many instances and so could act and judge prudently in different circumstances. Third was the opposition of truth and lie with respect to the gods, a continuation of Xenophanes' concern with the "seemliness" of stories discussed in the previous chapter and motivated by the experience of the discovery of a universal humanity that was recognizable in light of its relation to a transcendent Ground of Being. "The one, unseen, greatest god, who is the same for all men, is correlative with a sameness of men that is now found in the sameness of their transcendental experiences. Plato, finally, introduced the 'types of theology' as the conceptual instrument for clarifying the issue" (CW, 16:121–22).

These various complexes of experience and symbolization were summarized by the pair: philosopher and sophist. As indicated above, the resistance of the philosopher to the destruction of his psyche motivated the insight that the substance of order was psyche in the sense that a well-ordered polity was comprised of human beings with well-ordered souls. Hence the general observation noted above that any political order reflected the psyches of its dominant members written in large letters.

Following the survey of sophistic opinions regarding justice, Glaukon and Adeimantos asked Socrates what justice and injustice truly were and why the former was the greatest good and the latter the greatest evil. And thus began the inquiry, the *zetema*, that constituted the bulk of the book. The focus of the inquiry was not on Plato's "ideals," as is still occasionally maintained today, but "the reality of order in the soul and society." In keeping with the symbols just discussed, it began in the dark and aimed for the light. More precisely it began in the "depth of existence" where the soul sensed only a vague direction, indicated in part by pre-Platonic philosophical language as well as by existing stories and commonsense use. The zetema proceeded by clarification by the psyche of its own situation and analysis of given experiences that, in consequence, brought into focus new experiences and thereby refined the initial, vaguely sensed direction, into conceptual clarity. This enormously difficult process of clarification, Voegelin said, was "undertaken in the *Republic* for the first time in history." Despite the difficulties of clarification of experiences by the psyche this "first philosophy of order is still the classic work of its kind" (CW, 16:136–37).

The zetema itself may have resulted in conceptual clarity, but its unfolding consisted in symbols "evolved by the soul when it engages in the exegesis of its depth." There was no object to be interpreted prior to the inquiry itself, which brought "levels of consciousness" into the light, "as the logos of the experience becomes victorious over its darkness." The concepts created by the philosopher in the course of the inquiry became the "building blocks of the substantive stature into which the soul grows through its inquiry." The beginning was not unrelieved darkness because there was also present a sense of an alternative, a kind of light that expanded as consciousness grew increasingly aware of the way out of the depth. Voegelin again used the term "luminosity" to describe the "self-illumination of the soul through augmentation of its logos." These "zetetic symbols," as Voegelin called them, chiefly "draw their meaning from the experience whose logical luminosity they are" (CW, 16:138–39). Since within the dialogue, the zetema led from the depth and darkness to the light of the logos, one might say that the zetema was itself "luminous" without being the light.

Again Voegelin emphasized that there was no "doctrine of order" in the *Republic* but a series of stages of clarification of the meaning and structure of order. The highest experience in the *Republic* was found near the end of Book IX where Plato returned to the problem of statesmanship and the possibility of actualizing the best polis. Socrates told Glaukon that the right order of the soul would be gained by "establishing a politeia within them, as in a polis."[8] A wise man would keep his eye fixed on the politeia within his psyche. Glaukon then remarked that such a person would not willingly take part in politics and Socrates prefaced his response by swearing "by the Dog," and asserting strongly that such a person would indeed take part in politics, "though not in the city of his birth." Glaukon understood Socrates' meaning as referring to the polis they had just founded in speech, *en logois*, that existed nowhere on earth, to which Socrates replied: "Perhaps there is a paradigm set up in heaven for him who desires to look on it and so looking to settle in it. It makes no difference whether it is anywhere now or ever. To the things of that polis would he be concerned and none other" (*Rep.*, 592b).

This exchange between Socrates and Glaukon Voegelin called an "artistic miracle." The zetema into the best politeia was transfigured into an inquiry into human existence beyond any political regime. "The leap in being, toward the transcendent source of order," Voegelin said, "is real in Plato; and later ages have recognized rightly in the passage a prefiguration of Saint Augustine's conception of the *Civitas Dei*" (CW, 16:146). But again, this did not mean Plato was a Christian: "a prefiguration is not the figuration itself." It did, however, dissolve the paradox of the philosopher-king: for the philosopher, participation in politics "now means concern with the transcendent politeia that is set up in heaven and will be realized in the soul of the beholder" (CW, 16:146). The psyche had become a one-person polis and the philosopher was the "statesman" who watched over its politeia. At the same time, participation in the politeia in heaven did not ease the disorder of any actual city on earth. Human beings may indeed experience the growth of the psyche into the transcendent politeia, but they remained nevertheless still citizens of the city of their birth, a prefiguration indeed of Augustine's two cities.

The disintegration of the best polis, starting in Book VIII, has not usually been understood as part of the initial zetema. Voegelin argued that it was as much a part of the inquiry as was what he called the polyogeny by means of which the best polis was generated in speech. But in neither instance was Plato evoking a historical course. Both the construction and the disintegration of the best polis, including the version of the politeia in heaven, took place within the "time of the tale" which was, following Mircea Eliade who introduced the term, a "time of mythical narration" rather than of pragmatic history (CW, 16:171–72).

8 *Rep.*, 590e–91a. *Politeia*, in this context, referred to the common spiritual substance linking the best person to the best polis.

The actual Greek polis was comprised of families, so Plato had no available experience of personal membership in the community of the spirit. Hence the otherwise curious proposal of a community of women and children. True, the philosophical schools began to erode the importance of family-based citizenship, but it was no more than a beginning. The possibility of a spiritual community united by a common vision of the Agathon was obviously an option, but one that Plato did not pursue. "The enduring concern about the somatic basis [of the polis in the *Republic*] . . . reveals the degree to which the Platonic notion of spirituality is still embedded in the compact myth of nature" (CW, 16:172–73). This was why Plato made a "mock-Homeric" appeal to the Muses (*Rep.*, 545d–e) who answered by enunciating the principle of cosmic mystery: everything generated must perish.

The resumption of the "old quarrel" with poetry (*Rep.*, 607b) reflected the leap in being achieved by Socrates and recollected by Plato. As we saw in the previous chapter, the Homeric epic was itself a critical analysis of a civilizational crisis. From Homer to the mystic-philosophers, Hesiod, and Aeschylus, the dramatic myth of the soul superseded the epic myth. For Plato, fifth-century tragedy and comedy likewise were experienced as untrue.

> The discovery of the soul, as well as the struggle for its order, thus, is a process that extends through centuries and passes through more than one phase until it reaches its climax in the soul of Socrates and his impact on Plato. The attack on mimetic poetry from Homer to the time of Socrates pronounces no more than the plain truth that the Age of the Myth is closed. In Socrates the soul of man has at last found itself. After Socrates, no myth is possible.[9]

The new symbolic form was hinted at three times in the Epilogue. First, "dear Homer" (599d) was replaced by "draftsmen who use the divine paradigm," namely the philosophers (600e) who have associated themselves with divine order (500c–d). And who could be meant but Plato, draftsman of the

9 CW, 16:187. In light of Voegelin's understanding to Plato's myth of the myth developed in the *Timaeus* and *Critias* discussed below, this last statement might better be qualified as: "After Socrates, no simple myth, or myth of the people, was possible, but only the philosophers' myth of the myth."

divine paradigm in the text of the *Republic*? The second hint was provided when Plato allowed the best polis no poetry but only "hymns to the gods and encomia of good men" (607a). The examples, Voegelin indicated, were obvious: "The Pamphylian Myth, at the end of the Epilogue, is a hymn to the gods who are guiltless. And the *Republic* is the encomium of a noble man—Socrates" (CW, 16:188).

d. Phaedrus

At the end of Book VII, Plato suggested the comic impossibility of philosophers actually coming to rule a polis. The first thing they would do, after being compelled to rule by the non-philosophers, would be to expel everyone over ten years of age and then raise the children according to philosophical laws or conventions (*nomoi*). Since this was impossible because neither the philosophers could be coerced nor could the non-philosophers either make the attempt or be able to tolerate their own expulsion, to say nothing of leaving the children behind, the point was, clearly, to indicate to the potential and actual philosophers who happened to read the *Republic* that actualizing the Socratic politeia, apart from doing so in the psyche of the individual philosopher, was a daydream.

Voegelin argued that the abandonment of the philosopher-king did not mean the end of the relations among Plato, the Idea of right order, and history but its revision, which initially took place in the *Phaedrus*. In terms of the Cave parable/image/myth, the philosopher was required to return to the world of the non-philosophers. "Plato has discharged this duty through the *Republic*," after which "he has left the cave for good." The *Phaedrus* was written from the position of revision: the parallel between psyche and polis receded into the background to be replaced by the relation between psyche and the Idea of right order—so closely related, Voegelin said, "that the two seem to merge" (CW, 16:190).

"All that is psyche is deathless," Plato wrote, and the soul was deathless insofar as it saw and participated in the Idea (*Phaed.*, 245–47). There was, on the one hand, a distinction between psyche and the Idea of right order such that the psyche could participate in the Idea; but on the other, there was an identity because psyche now was not so much an individual soul as "a cosmic substance."

> The cosmos as a whole thus is an entity, engaged in a pulsating movement of perfection and decline through its psychic articulation. Hence, the "participation" of the individual soul in the

> idea means the rank of perfection that this specific particle of the total psychic substance holds at the moment in the pulsation of the world.
>
> The Idea has the character of a dynamic principle that determines a pulsating movement of the cosmos in psychic expansion and contraction. The rank of the member-souls of this total soul is, therefore, no longer determined by the vision of the Agathon [as in the *Republic*], but through their psychic tension or tone, the higher or lower intenseness of their animation by the cosmic fundamental force.

But even as the distinction between soul and the Idea was necessary, it was also inadequate because "the process should be understood as an impersonal pulsation of the cosmic force, a flow and ebb of the cosmic rhythm in that a particular part of the total psychic substance that for the time being gives form to a particular human body" (CW, 16:190–91). A number of implications followed from this additional dimension of a "cosmic substance" to Plato's Idea of right order.

First, the impersonality of the cosmic force displaced the previously central problem of embodying the Idea of right order in the polis. Henceforth the Idea would be embodied wherever possible, and especially in the souls of philosophers. "In the history of Athens, the *Phaedrus* is the manifesto that announces the emigration of the spirit from the polis" (CW, 16:193). Plato was still, of course, an Athenian, but henceforth he was relatively indifferent to the fate of his polis. His "patriotism" had become diluted to the extent that, as he came to understand that if the polis had no use for the best human beings, they, and more particularly, he, Plato, had no use for the polis. One may say, therefore, that the mortgage of the polis had been discharged in Plato's later work.

The individual human being named Plato still lived in Athens, but this "coexistence of a public order and a civilizational force that it does not represent is what may technically be called the state of disintegration." That is, the Idea of right order, which was once represented in Athens as the Aeschylean "liturgy" and "cult" of Dike, had departed the polis but lived on in the souls of individuals—in this instance Plato and his school. The Academy was not however Augustine's *civitas Dei*, nor even a Church but a *civitas naturae* that was articulated in a myth of nature. Plato had removed from the polis its ontological status as ultimate reality and in so doing introduced a new ontology. The Idea of right order was "reborn and the position of the philosopher is authenticated, through the communion with a nature that is psyche. That is, the ontological foundation for Plato's late political theory, and the communion [with a nature that is psyche] is the source of the 'truth' of the mythical poems in which the late Plato symbolizes the life of the Idea" (CW, 16:194–95).

The cosmos and nature were ensouled (*empsychos*) according to this new ontology so that the hierarchy of souls, from the human to the cosmic, introduced a new understanding of a transition from human to divine nature. This imaginative achievement, Voegelin said, was emphatically pre-Christian: the life of the soul was conducted in nature and the life of nature was conducted in the soul. As the late work of Plato emphasized increasingly, the ascent of the erotic souls to the divine cosmic pole and the dissociation between those souls and the actual city "engenders a tension of such sharpness that the common bond of humanity between the lost souls and the manic souls is almost broken." The difference between the two types of souls tended toward expression in terms of lower animal and upper semi-divine beings, "which seems absurd in the realm of Christian experience," but which, nevertheless "is inherent in the logic of the myth of nature." Absent an experience of creaturely equality before a transcendent God, such a differentiation seems inevitable.[10]

e. Theatetus and Statesman

By Voegelin's argument, the *Phaedrus* acknowledged the irreparable separation of the Idea of right order and the polis that was only hinted at in the *Republic*. In the trilogy, *Theatetus*, *Sophist*, and *Statesman*, Plato developed his analysis of politics from the perspective of disintegration indicated in the *Phaedrus*. The three dialogues, Voegelin said, were characterized "by a strong undercurrent of violence" as the implications of the irreparable split of semi-divine manic souls and beastly lost souls were made more evident. All that kept the parties to the conflict together—a more intense version of the conflict of philosophers and non-philosophers in the *Gorgias* and the *Republic*—was the historical contingency that they were all Athenians. But make no mistake: the conflict was deadly. This was indicated dramatically by Plato's description of Socrates' partner in the first dialogue, Theatetus, as both the representative of the hopes of the younger generation, and as dying of wounds received in battle for a city that had no use for his

10 It recurred, for example, with the reintroduction of a myth of nature in the Renaissance as, for example, with Bruno. See CW, 23:168ff.

soul but happily made use of his body in war. This dramatic situation, Voegelin said, expressed "the cold rage of Plato, who is compelled to live in obedience to a government of the beast, which makes the best die by the beast [Socrates] and for the beast [Theatetus]" (CW, 16:197).

Plato expressed the new position of the philosopher in the city of non-philosophers in the "diversion" of *Theatetus*, 172–77. The meaning was similar to the parable of the Cave, with the difference that the implicit appeal of the *Republic* had been rejected and the philosopher was under no obligation to return below. What in the parable of the Cave had been seen as a temporary situation had in the diversion become permanent. Even so, "rejection" of the actual polis was not an "escape" from it (CW, 16:197). Nor had the contingency of historical rejection of the Idea of right order by the polis invalidated either the Idea or the authority of the philosopher whose soul had been ordered by it. Instead, the "inimical reality" became an integral, even a preponderant, part of a larger zetema, much as Plato's account of politics was "enlarged to encompass the reality that is not ordered by the idea" (CW, 16:201). The philosopher, Plato said, dwelt in the polis "in body only" (*Theat.*, 173e) whereas his thought (*dianoia*) roamed far and wide, considering what was beyond the heavens and below the earth (cf. *Apol.*, 19c). And as for the non-philosophers who lived in the "most wretched godlessness" (*Theat.*, 176e), the philosopher was unsure whether they are "human or some other kind of creature (*thremma*)" (*Theat.*, 174b).

Politics as established by the diversion was a field where the reality of the Idea of right order and the reality of disorder apparently coexisted. The *Statesman* began from this situation and developed a "philosophy of history" that further contextualized the conflict between the philosopher and the non-philosophers within a transitory moment of cyclical cosmic change. Necessarily such a transition opened the possibility of future improvements. Because the possibility of revolutionary transformation had already been closed in the *Republic*, any attempt to read such an option into the *Statesman* would, in principle, be an error. Accordingly, Voegelin argued, Plato ensured that the actual meaning of the *Statesman* was deliberately made obscure.[11]

11 Certainly the commentaries on the *Statesman* are obscure. See, for example, Stanley Rosen, *Plato's Statesman: The Web of Politics* (New Haven: Yale University Press,1995) or Seth Bernadete, *The Being of the Beautiful: Plato's Theatetus, Sophist, and Statesman* (Chicago: University of Chicago Press, 1984). Regarding Bernadete, Rosen wrote that his "style" had "descended . . . into a willful obscurity and mannerism that seems to be somehow modelled on Plato's own baroque prose while capturing only the eccentricity" (p. 193).

Again, however, it was not Voegelin's interpretation of the *Statesman* that is of interest but what he took from it for his own work.

On this question there can be hardly any doubt: Voegelin's study of the obscurities of the *Statesman* and his argument concerning the reasons for them all centred in the significance and importance of myth in Plato first of all and then in Voegelin himself. As Voegelin wrote in an early version of the Plato chapter in the *History of Political Ideas*, "the myths of Plato are the key for the understanding of his political work," a problem that had concerned Voegelin from the 1930s.[12]

To summarize Voegelin's argument rather brutally in order to expand the previous paragraph: the tension between the Idea of right order and the actuality of disorder was permanent so that nothing was to be gained by embracing a nostalgia for a golden age or hope for a future revolutionary transformation. "Civilization and its order are the work of man," not of God, notwithstanding the "people's myth" that claimed the opposite. So far as the "philosophers' myth" was concerned, the One God did impose order on chaos and maintained or restored order as well. However, this God was not omnipotent. Chaotic matter had its own force as did Innate Desire (*symphytos epithymia*, which could also be translated as Innate Lust) that, when followed also reverted to chaos (*Polit.*, 272e). And finally, there was Destiny or Fate, *Heimarmene*, which governed the temporal rhythm of order and disorder. Beyond this trinity "lies the mystery of iniquity" (CW, 16:208), and the equally mysterious reversal of the cycle. The reversal was not an automatic act of Fate but required as well "the man who is the vessel of the idea" (CW, 16:211). Such a one was a royal ruler who mediated between the divine reality of the Idea of right order and the people. This ruler did so by means of the rejuvenation of the old order and the curing of souls in order to create a new spiritual community substance (*homonoia*) (*Polit.*, 311c). This homonoia was not the salvation of humanity as in Romans 15:5, but a return to the early Cosmos that would, under the inevitable disposition of Heimarmene, be followed by a new decline.

That the philosopher and the non-philosophers were opposed to one another was clear. So too was the means by which the philosopher expressed his opposition to the non-philosophers: by not worshipping the gods of the polis in the *Apology*, for example, to opposing the "people's myth" in the *Republic*. From the *Statesman*, Voegelin concluded that Plato discovered that the philosopher also must "use a new set of mythical symbols in order

12 HI, 56:10. See also his letters to Strauss, CW, 29:338ff; 30:75ff.

to express his authority" because, he said, "the soul is neither a subject nor an object, but an entity, illumined with consciousness from within, that explores its own nature by means of the zetema." That is, the soul existed between an awareness of the depth from which it moved to the height to which it aspired, which Voegelin identified with Heraclitus and Parmenides respectively; the soul was aware of the universality of the order of the psyche (Xenophanes), and the necessity of "attunement" to the order that comes from the depth (Aeschylus). And finally, with Plato, the soul discovered itself "as the entity whose experiences are expressed by the symbols of the myth" (CW, 16:224). Moreover, the greater awareness the soul had acquired with respect to its own depth and the other dimensions of its participation in reality constituted the experience that enabled it to declare the lower or more opaque degrees of awareness—in the people's myths, for example—to be "untrue." Thus the conflict between the myth of the fully conscious philosopher and the non-philosophers' myths was "radical."

To this insight, which was obviously shared by many other interpreters of Plato, Voegelin added a second: that "the philosopher discovers that the myth is the ineluctable instrument for communicating the experience of the soul; for he must himself develop mythical symbols in order to express his discovery both as a process and as a result." Voegelin then translated this summary of what he took from the *Statesman* into the language of his own philosophical anthropology: "through that opposition of his conscious myth to the less conscious forms, he becomes aware that the old myth also expresses the truth of the soul, merely on a less differentiated level of consciousness. The soul as the creator of the myth, and the myth as the symbolism of the soul, is the center of the philosophy of order."[13] According to Voegelin, Plato discussed the "center of the philosophy of order" in the *Timaeus* and the *Critias*.

f. Timaeus and Critias

In January 1947, Voegelin wrote to William Y. Elliott at Harvard with, *inter alia*, the information that he had been "writing entirely new the section of Plato in my 'History'" following his analysis of Vico and Schelling (CW, 29:496). Specifically, he argued that the cycles introduced in the *Statesman*, the *Timaeus* and the *Critias* constituted (as just indicated) the substance of Plato's "philosophy of history." In principle, he said, "the Hellenic cycle

13 CW, 16:224. In a letter to Strauss of April 22, 1951, Voegelin explained this same understanding of Plato's use of myth. See CW, 30:75ff.

theory corresponds functionally to our Western eschatologies."[14] By Voegelin's reading, the key to understanding the relationship between the *Timaeus* and the *Republic* was to interpret the *Timaeus* "as a drama within the soul of Plato" (CW, 16:232). In place of the impasse of the *Republic*, with the paradigm set up in heaven and present only in speech, Plato introduced the Atlantis myth that was present in his soul as what Voegelin called the "collective unconscious" of the anonymous Athenian, of humanity, and of the cosmos itself.

Voegelin has been criticized for using the Jungian term, "collective unconsciousness." He used it in volume five of *Order and History* as well, but in a more restricted sense (CW, 18:74ff) because, by then, he had developed the concept of historiogenesis to describe such myths as that of Atlantis and other similar stories. Planinc was obviously correct to note that "Plato's unconscious is not available to us at all."[15] However, Voegelin was not concerned with psychoanalyzing Plato so much as finding a term to express a more or less impenetrable depth from which the symbols constituting such stories as the Atlantis myth were drawn. They did, after all, come from somewhere. Once they had been drawn from the depth into the story they were no longer "unconscious." Moreover, Plato drew up the Atlantis story from the depth by way of recollection, *anamnesis*, along with the stories of Solon, Critias, the archaic Athens and so on, right back to the primordial life of the cosmos from which humans and gods sprung. In "the life of the soul" of Plato, as expressed in the later dialogues, "the solitude of contemplation is now in harmony with the transpersonal rhythms of the people, of the human race, and of the cosmos" (CW, 16:233). In the later dialogues Plato was "the

14 CW, 29:496. I have discussed some of these problems, which Voegelin published as "Plato's Egyptian Myth," *The Journal of Politics* 9 (1947): 307–24, in *Eric Voegelin and the Foundations of Modern Political Science* (Columbia: University of Missouri Press, 1999), 416ff. There were a few minor changes between the article version and the later version published in *Order and History*.

15 Zdravko Planinc, "The Significance of Plato's *Timaeus* and *Critias* in Eric Voegelin's Philosophy," in Glen Hughes, Stephen A. McKnight, Geoffrey L. Price, eds., *Politics Order and History: Essays on the Work of Eric Voegelin* (Sheffield: Sheffield Academic Press, 2001), 326ff. See also the remarks of Tilo Schabert, "Reaching for a Bridge between Consciousness and Reality: The Languages of Eric Voegelin," *American Catholic Philosophical Quarterly* 20 (2014): section II. See also CW, 29:496ff and *A Friendship that Lasted a Lifetime: The Correspondence between Alfred Schütz and Eric Voegelin*, trans. William Petropulos, ed. Gerhard Wagner and Gilbert Weiss (Columbia: University of Missouri Press, 2011), 104, 200–1.

poet of the myth." He was not, however, a Homeric poet "in the third remove from reality" (*Rep.*, 599a) but "the poet of the idea itself" (CW, 16:234). Plato could sing the poem of the Idea of right order because his own soul had undertaken the anamnesis expressed in the *Timaeus* myth. The substantive harmonies just indicated were existentially present in the psyche of the man, Plato. The use of the term "unconscious," modified by the adjective "collective" or not, was intended to indicate a dimension of what Voegelin would later call "It-reality" that was, if not exactly impenetrable, at least was not perceptible, and so did not appear before the light of consciousness. From this insight, it seems to me, Voegelin developed his argument regarding what he called "the philosophy of myth" (CW, 16:237ff).

In the *Timaeus* this philosophy was presented "in the form of an intricate myth of the myth" rather than a theory or discursive account of the myth such as Voegelin presented in the section under discussion. The *Timaeus*, he said, "marks an epoch in the history of mankind insofar as in this work the psyche has reached the critical consciousness of the methods by which it symbolizes its own experiences." As a result, any "philosophy of order and symbols" (an interim title for *Order and History*, we recall) must absorb Plato's philosophy of myth into its own principles of analysis.

Voegelin summarized his interpretation of Plato's philosophy of myth with a rather gnomic statement: "the *Republic* projects the soul on the canvas of society. The *Timaeus* projects it on the still larger canvas of the cosmos." Where in the *Republic* the soul of the philosopher provided a model for the order of the polis, in the *Timaeus* the soul of the philosopher provided a model for the order to the cosmos that, as it were, encompassed the order of the polis and of human being.[16] Such a new development or expansion raised a new problem so far as political order was concerned: the embodiment of the Idea of right order in historical reality, which was already doubtful in the *Republic*, became effectively impossible when the psyche was

16 We have been focused on Voegelin's interpretation of Plato's experiences rather than the "systematic" or "dramatic" relationship of the *Republic* to the *Timaeus*. Voegelin summarized that relationship as follows: "The order of the soul, in the *Republic*, was authenticated well enough through the ascent from the Cave to the intelligible realm of the Idea. The *Republic* had not, however, authenticated the paradigm of the good polis in the form of society in history. That second step required the insight into the consubstantiality of the soul and society, and ultimately of the cosmos. The myth of the soul can be the myth of the polis only if both individual soul and the polis in history can be embraced in the psyche of the cosmos" (CW, 16:253).

projected on an even larger scale than the polis. "For the cosmos is not a datum of immanent experience; the philosopher, as a consequence, cannot advance verifiable propositions concerning the psychic nature of its order. That is the difficulty Plato solves by means of the myth" (CW, 16:238). Hints of what Plato had in mind were present in the myths of judgment at the end of the *Gorgias* and the *Republic*; matters were made more explicit in the anamnetic-historiogenetic Egyptian myth of the *Timaeus*.

That is, the "truth" of the myth was already present in the unconscious, whether it was described as the collective unconscious of the Athenians or the "generic unconscious" of humanity or the deepest part of the soul that was in communion "with the primordial forces of the cosmos." The essential experiential aspect of this myth, as with the earlier myths of judgment, was that they both expressed a primary participation of consciousness in a meaningful reality that only subsequently, by means of what Voegelin later called "reflective distance" (CW, 18, 109–10), was consciously acknowledged as true. This conscious conception of a cosmic *omphalos*, where the depth of the soul was unconsciously part of, which is to say, a participant in, the order of the cosmos, gave explicit, philosophical expression to "the myth as the medium of symbolic expression, endowed with an authority of its own, independent of, and prior to, the universe of empirical knowledge constituted by consciousness in attention to objects" (CW, 16:238). Voegelin was here making the point discussed in chapter three concerning the priority of participatory consciousness over perceptual or constituting consciousness—and thus of the immediacy of a meaningful myth over the scientific acknowledgement of its truth.[17]

Adopting not the participatory exegesis of the myth from within but rather the scientific and descriptive or philosophical perspective of the contemplative, the aforementioned "reflective distance," Voegelin described the two-fold function of the omphalos. First, the omphalos was experienced in the psyche as the source "of the forces, of the sentiments, anxieties, apprehensions, yearnings" that well up from the depth of the cosmos and "roam"

17 The question returned in Voegelin's discussion of space and time in connection with the speculation of Henry Margeneau. See chapter six, below. Voegelin later discussed the truth of myth as lying in its ability to keep the field of what he later called non-existent reality present in a story and symbol. The purpose or function of myth was to keep existential consciousness ordered by maintaining the openness of consciousness to its non-existent Ground. This truth of the myth, moreover, like the truth of reason, was acquired in meditative articulation and not as information. See below, chapter six and CW, 28:90.

around in the unconscious of the individual human being urging the individual to find an appropriate expression of these experiences "in the imaginative order of mythical symbols." Second, the openness of the psyche towards the cosmos, which was experienced in the pre-theoretical depth of the psyche, provided the "subject-matter" of the myth. Because the experience of the depth was boundless or infinite (and could be expressed only through some kind of negative metaphor), but because as well human existence was finite, this "subject-matter" was divided into categories. Typically the experience of the depth evoked such problems or mysteries as: birth and death, return to origins or rebirth, individuation and depersonalization, union and reunion with transcendent reality whether mediated by erotic, group, or spiritual ecstasies, suffering through separation from the Ground of Being or redemption through a return to eternal communion with the Ground, and so on. The immediacy of the myth in experience "authenticates its truth because the forces that animate its imagery are at the same time its subject matter." Accordingly, "a myth can never be 'untrue' because it would not exist unless it had its experiential basis in the movements of the soul that it symbolizes" (CW, 16:238–39). That was why, to use the myths of judgment as an example, Socrates said they were not "beautiful myths" or "beautiful stories" but *logoi* (*Gorg*., 522–23; *Rep*., 612b–21d).

Although a myth could not be "untrue" so long as it retained an experiential basis in the movements of the soul that it symbolized, it could become historically untrue either through further differentiation of spiritual self-consciousness or through changes in the relationship of human consciousness, however differentiated, and the understandings by human beings of the surrounding environment. "The myth-creating forces of the soul," Voegelin said, "while retaining the identity of their origin and subject matter, have to express themselves in symbols that correspond to the level of spiritual consciousness, as well as to the degree of differentiation that the self-understanding of man in his environment has reached" (CW, 16:239).

In the Hellenic example, Voegelin detected four "levels" or "degrees" of differentiation of the myth. The most archaic and compact was the enactment of mythical forces in rites and rituals. At a second level, the myth appears as a story, the origin of which was anonymous, that interpreted the rites as "peoples' myths." On a third degree of differentiation, the anonymity and collective nature of the story was transformed by an identifiable and specific person into an instrument to express specific movements in the soul of that person. Finally, when the archaic symbolic materials could be freely and deliberately manipulated to meet the exigencies of personal experiences of the order of reality, we have reached Plato who retained the seriousness of the truth of the myth at the same time consciously engaged in "an imaginative play."[18]

Voegelin considered "the new dimension of conscious play" to be the distinguishing characteristic of Plato's myth, though the constituent elements were prefigured even in ritual play. Two conditions, Voegelin argued, needed to be present in mythic creation no matter what the degree of compactness or differentiation. First, the myth (or ritual) must be understood by the creator as the appearance of psychic forces from the unconscious that attained a communicable and tempered form when they were expressed.[19] This condition, Voegelin thought, was present at the most archaic level because of the "range of imaginative play" even in ritual, to say nothing of "the bewildering richness of the play on the level of the mythical tale." What Plato achieved in his use of myth was an "inner freedom" or "distance" that resulted from the increased differentiation of the personal psyche after the sixth century. This freedom or distance destroyed the immediacy or naiveté of the myth by turning it into a work of art, but one that "must not destroy the 'truth' of the myth." Hence the second condition: the conscious play must be based on the premise that, although one myth could supersede another, "no other human function, for instance 'reason' or 'science,' can supersede the myth itself" (CW, 16:240). The myth alone could express the fundamental movements of the psyche and order the self-conscious personality of the philosopher.

18 CW, 16:239–40. Voegelin based his analysis of these stages on the early work of the original "Cambridge School" of Jane Harrison, F. M. Cornford, Gilbert Murray, etc. I have discussed some of these problems in "Two Tellurian Themes in Plato's *Republic*," in Zdravko Planinc, ed., *Politics, Philosophy, Writing: Plato's Art of Caring for Souls* (Columbia: University of Missouri Press, 2001), 80–121. During the early 1920s Voegelin attended Murray's lectures at the University of Oxford. He later reported that the impact of this "introduction to the style of distinguished English scholarship at its best" was "overwhelming" (CW, 34:55). The "playful seriousness" of Plato was discussed in Johan Huizinga's *Homo Ludens: A Study of the Play Element of Culture* (Boston: Beacon, 1955). See also CW, 13:160ff; CW, 16:311f.

19 Voegelin wrote here that the expression of these unconscious forces was "assuaged" by being expressed. So far as I know, he did not use the expression anywhere else. See CW, 16:238, 240. The meaning seemed to be that the raw, immediate anxieties and sentiments of the unconscious were tempered by communicable intelligibility when they were expressed symbolically.

Voegelin then went out of his way to emphasize the resultant degeneration in human self-understanding when freedom toward the myth turned into freedom from the myth. Such an attitude invariably led to misunderstanding if symbols were supposed to be meant "literally," as referring to phenomenal objects or verifiable propositions rather than being expressions of the unconscious. "The myth has a fundamental function in human existence and myths will be created no matter what anybody thinks about them"—as evident, for example, by someone calling myths "primitive" or "unscientific." The result would be a pseudoscientific myth—scientism.[20] Consequently, "we cannot overcome the myth, we can only misunderstand it" (CW, 16:241). The movements of the cosmic depth were felt or sensed in the soul of the conscious subject but did not become objects for it. "Hence, the symbols of the myth, in which the reverberations [of the movements of the cosmic depth] are expressed, can be defined as the refraction of the unconscious in the medium of objectifying consciousness" (CW, 16:246). This was so because whatever entered human consciousness had to assume the "form" of an object, even if it wasn't one. Accordingly, symbols did not turn unconscious reality into objects; they were "the unconscious reality itself, broken [that is, deformed] in the medium of consciousness."[21]

So far as Plato was concerned, his use of myth had several distinct purposes. First, as has been noted, it superseded the "people's myth." Second, it opposed the warped personalities of sophistic enlightenment that tended to discount myth in any form. And finally, "it regains the truth of the myth on the new level of the differentiated consciousness of the mystic." Particularly the last purpose must be emphasized: here the imagery of the earlier more compact myths was available to be used by the mystic-artist because they expressed authentic movement of the soul. "The wider and more grandiose perspective that has opened in the soul [of the mystic poet-philosopher, Plato]

20 See Voegelin's "Origins of Scientism" (1948) in CW, 10:168ff., the discussion of space and time in "The Moving Soul," CW, 28:163ff., and the discussion of "Phenomenalism," in the *History of Political Ideas*, CW, 25:178ff. See also Voegelin's notes on a 1980 discussion with Victor Weisskopf (HI, 98:4).

21 CW, 16:246. In his later work, Voegelin referred in this context of analysis to "non-existent reality." The argument here, to simplify somewhat, was that, when unconscious reality, however symbolized, breaks through to consciousness, that breaking-through also rendered the unconscious reality "broken," because it necessarily presented non-existent reality as an existent phenomenon or "object." This problem is discussed at greater length below in chapter six.

does not abolish the reality of the archaic experiences; it will embrace them but relegate them to a humbler distance" (CW, 16:242–43).

At the same time, however, the philosopher-poet, no more than the sophist or the contemporary positivist, could simply create a science of myth. The meaning of the myth is intelligible but its intelligibility could not be specified by a phenomenalist epistemology that accounts for our knowledge of the external world. To develop a theory of myth, the philosopher must accept the reality of the unconscious, including the reality of the relationship of consciousness to its own unconscious Ground. Moreover, the philosopher cannot accept this relationship "on any other terms than its own, that is, on the terms of the myth. Hence a philosophy of the myth must itself be a myth of the soul." There was, therefore, in Plato "even in the moments of a most awesome intimacy with the cosmic mysteries the veil that separates the myth from knowledge" (CW, 16:247). Returning to the *Timaeus*, Voegelin then provided an account of Plato's myth of the myth: "the theory of the myth is itself a myth; its truth is not the truth of the intellect but the self-authenticating truth of the psyche" (CW, 16:252). The use of the term "unconscious" in this context also expressed Voegelin's understanding of the ineffable Ground of Being. As noted above, in his later work Voegelin developed a more precise vocabulary to describe this experience of participation in an unknown reality.

g. Laws

The last text of Plato that Voegelin discussed was his "religious poem," the *Laws* (CW, 16; 282, 309). As he indicated in his discussions of the *Timaeus* and *Critias*, the *Laws* provided Plato's "evocation of the polis as a cosmic analogue" (CW, 16:257). He brought these two interpretive themes together in a complex and elegant argument that Plato had changed his position from the "heroic appeal" of the *Republic* to one of "ecclesiastical statesmanship . . . within the boundaries drawn by the myth of the cosmos." In this last text Plato developed a theocratic conception of order "because he does not advance to the distinction of spiritual and temporal order." There was a universalism of the spirit in the *Laws*, Voegelin argued, but it remained "just beyond the horizon; but the last step was never taken—and was not taken without revelation" (CW, 16:281). Because philosophy could not move "beyond the horizon" and still remain a zetema, Voegelin's discussion of this last expression of Plato's conception of order, despite the great attention to detail, did not, because it could not, pursue Plato's philosophy of myth, and with it his philosophy of consciousness, farther than it had been taken in the *Timaeus* and *Critias*.

2. Aristotle and Nature

a. Plato and Aristotle

Differences of style and content between Aristotle's *Politics* and, say, Plato's *Gorgias* are apparent to anyone who reads these texts, but specifying what had changed and why is not as easy. As with his discussion of the Prophets, Voegelin began by noting the succession of generations. When Aristotle entered Plato's Academy in 367, Socrates had been dead for thirty years and Plato was more than sixty. Accordingly, Aristotle "did not enter only into the way of life of the philosopher; he also entered into the debate on its results," a debate that was conducted by way of "doctrinal symbols" rather than mythic ones (CW, 16:325–27). No less than Plato was Aristotle conscious of a new epoch. The difference, however, was that, for Plato, the era of the people's myth as articulated in the poets was drawing to a close and Plato "experienced himself as the inaugurator and royal ruler of the new age," whereas with Aristotle "the experience has become objectified: he knows about the epoch and he knows that it is marked by Plato. The epoch has become a historical fact and its nature can now be discerned as an incision in spiritual history" (CW, 16:338). By spiritual history Voegelin meant the spiritual achievements of Plato as expressed in his dialogues, which obviously were distinct from the pragmatic history of the Athenians.

In other words, what for Plato had been an existential and deadly conflict between the philosopher and the Athenians played out in the trial and execution of Socrates and dramatized in the *Apology* and in the *Gorgias* (521d), was for Aristotle a series of events of which several aspects could be analyzed and discussed. One of those aspects was Plato himself. Plato's philosophy, Voegelin said, had "completely changed" the "proportions of the problems." Accordingly, for Aristotle, "the accents of the crisis will no longer lie on the misery of Athens; they will lie on the new life that begins with Plato" (CW, 16:342–43). Voegelin summed up the difference between the two with the observation that "Plato had authenticated his insights, drawn from the unconscious, through the myth of the cycle; the descent to the cosmic omphalos of the soul assured us of the truth of the myth. For Aristotle the myth of the cycle has become a doctrine, and the unconscious as a source of truth is replaced by the memory of the species that can be recovered through historical studies" (CW, 16:346).

Voegelin called Aristotle's "formalization" of Plato's symbolization an "intellectual thinning out" or an "intellectualization" of philosophical experience. "I am speaking," Voegelin wrote, "of the transformation of symbols developed for the purpose of articulating the philosopher's experience into topics of speculation" (CW, 16:330–31, 336 cf. CW, 29:339). The problem with this transformation, he explained, was "simplicity itself." First of all, the leap in being "differentiated world-transcendent Being as the source of all being, and correspondingly attaches to the 'world' the character of immanence." Since such experiences of transcendence must rely on language terms that had their origin in the world of sense experience, and since the language terms that referred to the experiences of transcendence also must rely on language terms that had their origin in the world of sense experience, the language terms that nevertheless referred to the experiences of transcendence "must be understood analogically, whether they be symbols of the myth, of revelation, or of philosophy" (CW, 16:331–32). Such an analogical understanding of metaphysical speculation, Voegelin said, did not receive "an approximately satisfactory formula" until the elaboration of the analogy of being by Saint Thomas in the *Summa Theologica*. For his part, Plato "hypostatized transcendental being into a datum as if it were given in world-immanent experience." Voegelin characterized Plato's act, in the *Laws* for example, as one of "theocratic compactness" (CW, 16:330, 347). Even though Aristotle quite properly criticized Plato for "duplicating" being in his account of the Ideas, Aristotle only achieved clarity on this point at "the great price of eliminating the problem of transcendent form along with its speculative misuse" (CW, 16:330). Both "errors," however understandable, followed from the absence of the Thomistic *analogia entis* or any approximation of it.

In a footnote to a draft of this chapter Voegelin expanded on the relationship of immanent and transcendent reality in the context of revelation. He did not have in mind any specific revelation such as the Mosaic or the Christian, but "the structure of spiritual experiences as they become differentiated in the fourth century B.C." There were aspects of this structure, he said, that were "not accessible to immanentist speculation" but that required a revelation in order to achieve a "meaningful completion." His task was to make the connection between the zetema and the "completion" intelligible. Accordingly, it was not a question of whether any specific revelation were true in any dogmatic sense but rather whether "as a historical phenomenon" it "can be accepted by men as meaningful." No revelation can be historically effective unless it "makes sense to human beings," which was a restatement of the argument regarding the historicity of truth discussed in chapter one. In the context of philosophy, Voegelin was concerned with "an experiential structure which requires revelation as a 'solution.'" In the event, no such revelation took place so the resulting symbolizations could be characterized as "makeshift." It took several centuries before revelation could become socially effective, as when the various salvation religions began to spread throughout the Roman Empire. It was intelligible to say that Mediterranean humanity awaited those religions "in the sense that the experienced structure that made them meaningful had undergone a ripening of several centuries."[22] Such an understanding of the relationship of philosophy and revelation obviously had more appeal to the philosopher than to one thirsting for the truth of salvation. This was a problem that recurred in connection with Voegelin's discussion of the Gospel in his later work, which we consider in chapter six.

b. Political Science

The result, notwithstanding its doctrinal form, was not negligible. The order of the soul, as articulated through Socrates by Plato, and "intellectualized" by Aristotle became the *bios theoretikos*, the "best" way of life because it led to the greatest *eudaimonia*, happiness. Voegelin insisted that the link to Platonic problems was never broken by Aristotle, but also that, within that continuity, Aristotle reformulated the mystical knowledge of the Athenian stranger in the *Laws* into "standards" and he devised ways and means for the maximal realization of them under varying conditions. That is, Aristotle was interested in a different complex of problems than Plato, but his approach to them was deeply informed by his own ability to recover and reactualize Plato's philosophical experience.

The contrast between the two philosophers could be brought out clearly by considering one of Aristotle's criticisms of Plato (CW, 16:347ff). In the *Politics* (1265a 10–18), Aristotle objected to the size of the polis advanced by Plato in the *Laws* (771a 5 *et seq.*). It was too big, Aristotle said; it would need to include as large a territory as was found in Babylon if it were to support 5000 warriors along with their women and servants. Plato's number in the *Laws* was 5040; it was chosen for its numerical and astrological or zodiacal properties as a reflection of the mythic numerical structure of the cosmos (CW, 16:303). Indeed, it exemplified Voegelin's point regarding

22 HI, 68:1, pp. 582–83.

Plato's mythic integration of cosmic and political order. However that may be, by rounding off a cosmological symbol, 5040, into an approximate population statistic, 5000, from which he drew some critical and commonsensical conclusions, Aristotle ignored or destroyed the playful meaning Plato sought to convey.

At the center of Plato's consciousness of epoch was his effort at spiritual renovation; at the center of Aristotle's was not an act of creative will but analysis of the distinct realities that Plato held together within this "theocratically compact" vision. Aristotle's consideration of the distinct aspects or constituent elements of Plato's vision should not be considered a failure on his part but, as indicated, a new and contemplative attitude developed toward a society that was still in crisis but, for Aristotle, beyond saving (cf. *Rep*. 621c). All that remained of Plato's Idea of right order was preserved by Aristotle in terms of explicit criteria by which existing political orders may be classified, judged, and perhaps therapeutically and marginally influenced, which was indeed a "thinning out."

This "intellectualized" version of Plato's myth of the philosopher served as the basis for Aristotle's philosophical anthropology beginning with the first book of the *Nichomachean Ethics*, which discussed the true nature of human being and various human excellences. The argument that the *bios theoretikos* was the best life was akin to one made in defence of Socratic philosophy by John Stuart Mill.[23] It was both abstract and not entirely convincing, so Aristotle added that discussion of such matters was properly conducted only among *spoudaioi*, a term that is usually translated as "good men" or "decent men" but according to Voegelin "mature," "serious," or "weighty" men is preferable (EN, 1113a 23–35; 1176a 15 *et seq*.; CW, 16:354). These reflections by Aristotle, Voegelin said, "are perhaps the most important contribution to the epistemology of ethics and politics that has ever been made" (CW, 16:354). The implication was clear: analysis of human excellences could be undertaken only by human beings who knew the material they analyzed and they could know human excellences only by possessing them.

So far as pragmatic history was concerned, neither the Platonic philosopher not the Aristotelian spoudaios was the ordering force of society, as Aristotle, quoting Hesiod, perfectly well knew (EN, 1095b 10ff). That is, the

23 Mill, *Utilitarianism*, Ch. 2 in *Essays on Ethics, Religion and Society*, ed. J.M. Robson, *The Collected Works of John Stuart Mill*, vol. x (Toronto: University of Toronto Press, 1969), 211–13.

validity of the standards was not at issue; their social acceptability was. It may be, as Voegelin said, that the *Ethics*, which upheld the authority of the spoudaios "asserts itself through the ages, beyond the accidents of politics,"[24] but it was also true that the philosophers were increasingly disinclined to take part in political life. This "a-politic tendency," Voegelin said, was "a new factor."[25] It necessarily disrupted Aristotle's understanding of political science insofar as it implied that even though the polis may be the most comprehensive form of human existence, true eudaimonia was not found in political life but only by transcending politics in the practice of the dianoetic virtues (CW, 16:359). In an early draft of this section Voegelin wrote of the "separation of spiritual and moral authority from the authority that is embodied in contingent political authority" that began with Plato and "found its millennial fulfillment in the creation of the church as the institutionalized authority in matters spiritual and moral beyond the sphere of temporal power. The *Nichomachean Ethics*, like the *Laws*, is one of the authoritative scriptures in the spiritual church of mankind" (HI, 68:1, p. 500).

For Voegelin this apolitical tendency was also evidence that the polis was a finite unit, as Aristotle knew as well as Plato, in the great "process" of human history. "And the complicated problems of structure in this process—which are the subject matter of the present study [*Order and History*]—can obviously not be resolved by declaring one of the sub-units [such as the polis to be] the unit with ontological status and by appointing its structure as an essence." This observation raised the obvious question: why did Aristotle do it? "The answer must be," Voegelin wrote, that the relevance of the rise and fall of Greek poleis and even the civilizational continuity of Hellenic with Achaean and Cretan societies "could not become visible within the Hellenic experience of order. The *episteme politike*, the science of the order of the polis, could expand into a science of order and history

24 CW, 16:358. Ephesian (C. E. Bechhofer Roberts), *Winston Churchill* (London: Mills and Boon, 1927), 102 told a story of how Churchill was "once lent a copy of Aristotle's *Ethics* by an enthusiastic admirer of the philosopher. Churchill returns it with an expression of his delight, adding simply, 'But it is extraordinary how much of it I had already thought out for myself.'"

25 In chapter three we noted that in Voegelin's discussion of the spiritual consequences of the Peloponnesian War one of them was that "effective leadership in terms of reason" eventually became impossible, a consequence that Thucydides "was unwilling to admit" (CW, 15:438). By Aristotle's day these consequences were obvious.

only where existence in historical form had been established, i.e., in the orbit of Mosaic and Christian revelation" (CW, 16:387–89).

Voegelin then elaborated the absence of a historical dimension in Aristotle, notwithstanding his observation of the course of any particular polis, as well as the end of the independence of the poleis at the armed hand of Alexander. The motive for Aristotle's position with respect to attributing ontological status to the polis must be sought, Voegelin said, not simply in the *absence* of Mosaic or Christian revelation but in the very real presence of a focal concern with the nature, the physis, of the polis. Aristotle was concerned with the best order of a polis; his conclusion was that it was a polis governed by spoudaioi. Such a position was intelligible and defensible provided that two assumptions be granted: "(1) the nature of man has achieved its full actualization in the type of the spoudaios who cultivate the bios theoretikos, and that (2) the full unfolding of human nature is possible only in a society of the polis type." Neither assumption was acceptable in the light of a Christian anthropology, which in this context served to delimit Aristotle's analysis as "a search for perfection, within the more compact experience of physis, which in Christianity is conducted under the assumption that perfection lies in the beyond." Because Aristotle was convinced that perfect order can be achieved within history, the order *of* history was "theoretically irrelevant." The order of history could become of "absorbing interest" as it was for Voegelin in his study, "only when perfection is recognized as a symbol of eschatological fulfillment beyond history." The rise and fall of poleis as well as the discovery of the spiritual epoch marked by Socrates and Plato remained events within the Heimarmene, the Fate of the cosmos. "The philosopher's leap in being has set free the paradigmatic physis of man and society, but has not disengaged, as has the Mosaic and prophetic leap in being, the order of history from the myth of the cosmos" (CW, 16:390).

c. Philosophical Anthropology

Aristotle's philosophical anthropology developed a theory of human nature common to all human beings but maximally actualized only in a few spoudaioi who habitually practiced the bios theoretikos. Both inclination and habituation were required to attain the practical wisdom of a prudential political science, which meant it was not a question of information alone but also entailed the cultivation of the soul. Aristotle's study of human nature revealed it to be not a possession but a potentiality that may or may not be actualized during the course of a life. "And if such actualization is not too successful, the carrier of human potentiality is still a man" (CW, 16:413). However, the existence of such an overwhelming number of non-spoudaioi had the consequence of turning the representative of the bios theoretikos into one of several options or "characters." Given a common human nature, "one might even say that the differentiation of the contemplative type has resulted in the sharper characterization of the noncontemplative types and added to the legitimacy of their existence." And this, Voegelin said, constituted a "serious impasse" because the imperfect characters, the non-spoudaioi, "become actualizations of their specific types" and thus were to be "respected and preserved." By comparison, Plato was more consistent because he refused to legitimate the non-philosophers and instead called "for repentance and submission to the theocratic rule of the incarnate Truth." As a result, the imperfections of the actualizations of both the spoudaioi and the corresponding regimes "tend to become essences in their own right, forming the manifold of reality" (CW, 16:417).

Voegelin characterized this problem in Aristotelian political science by the same term he used in the *History of Political Ideas*: "historicity of truth." To recapitulate: the truth of philosophical existence was discovered in the experiences of Socrates and Plato. The cathartic experience of Thanatos and the enthusiastic experience of Eros opened the psyche to transcendent reality and became effective in the soul when the soul was re-ordered through Dike. Truth, accordingly, was not understood as a collection of timeless propositions about worldly phenomena but "the world-transcendent *summum bonum*, experienced as an orienting force in the soul, about which we can speak only in analogical symbols." This transcendent reality, the *summum bonum*, Truth, could not be an object of cognition for the by now obvious reason that it did not share with human beings the finite and temporal mode of a now differentiated immanent or intramundane existence. "It is eternal, out-of-time; it is not co-temporal with the experiencing soul. When, through the experiences of the Socratic-Platonic type, eternity enters time, we may say that 'Truth' becomes 'historical'" (CW, 16:418).

In the context of Socrates and Plato, the experiences of the philosophers and the symbolization of those experiences by way of Thanatos, Eros, and Dike amounted to a more differentiated expression of the realities previously symbolized through the people's myth. The advance in insight, the differentiation of experience and symbolization, was part of the historical process. Hence Voegelin's summary formulation: "By 'historicity of Truth' we mean that transcendental reality, precisely because it is not an object of world-immanent knowledge, has a history of experience and symbolization" (CW, 16:418).

The history of experience and symbolization has been played out within the psyche of specific human beings who have come to know themselves not only as existing in the world but as open to world-transcendent reality. Historically, human beings attained this second kind of self-knowledge "only historically in the degree of differentiation that . . . [their] experiences and their symbolization have reached." The self-understanding of human beings, therefore, has been conditioned and limited by the development of human existence toward transcendence. This meant that the "nature of man" as the subject-matter of metaphysical inquiry was also informed by the presence of transcendence. Accordingly, "when the philosopher explores the spiritual order of the soul, he explores a realm of experiences that he can appropriately describe only in the language of symbols expressing the movement of the soul towards transcendent reality and the flooding of the soul by transcendence. At the border of transcendence the language of philosophical anthropology must become the language of religious symbolization" (CW, 16:419).

Aristotle's discussion of this "border problem," notwithstanding its limitation in light of Christian anthropology, nevertheless developed a terminology that was successfully taken over by Christians from St. Paul to St. Thomas. Aristotle's "fundamental hesitation" was his inability to recognize the formation of the soul through grace, which he expressed in terms of the impossibility of *philia*, friendship, between humans and God owing to the ontological inequality of divine and human being (EN, 1158b 35ff). It was true that Aristotle allowed that the gods did love humans (EN, 1179a 23ff), "but their love does not reach into the soul and form it towards its destiny." That is, there was no "heightening of the immanent nature of man through the supernaturally forming love of God." For Aristotle, the nature of man remained an "immanent essence" that was actualized within the world; even though the noetic self was the most divine part of human being, its actualization and fulfillment remained immanent. Accordingly, "transcendence does not transform the soul in such a manner that it will find fulfillment in transfiguration through Grace in death" (CW, 16:419–20).

Aristotle's metaphysics, Voegelin said, was therefore "technically inadequate." To summarize the points made in the previous paragraph, Aristotle was unable to symbolize his genuine experiences of transcendence in a way that took into account the question of supernatural fulfillment, which experiences of transcendence would "technically" require. A similar problem was discussed in chapter two when, towards the end of the Middle Ages, political thinkers, starting with Joachim, began to evoke the notion of intramundane realization of perfected human existence that could be achieved by proper organization and the judicious application of violence. Aristotle's argument could have taken a similar course, but his "spiritual sensitiveness and . . . magnificent realism" precluded such a "catastrophic derailment." Instead, "the conflict between transcendental spiritualism and immanentist metaphysics worked its confusion only at the theoretical stage. The immanentist construction of the best polis, to be sure, compelled Aristotle to classify all empirical constitutions as perversions, but it did not induce him to make war on the perversions in the name of Truth" (CW, 16:420).

d. Physei Dikaion *and Nature*

In the mid-1960s Voegelin published two articles dealing with Aristotle that complement the treatment given in *Plato and Aristotle*. When they were re-published in *Anamnesis* (1966), Voegelin called them empirical and historical studies that illustrated the "close empirical continuity between the analysis of consciousness and the phenomena of order" (CW, 6:34). The two essays were "Natural Right in Political Theory" (1963) and "What is Nature?" (1965), both of which dealt with "the Aristotelian problems of a consciousness of the Ground." The first was reprinted as "Right by Nature,"[26] and began with a disarmingly simple statement: "In classical philosophy 'right by nature' was a symbol, with the help of which the philosopher interpreted his noetic experience of right human action" (CW, 6:140). Regarding this symbol, namely Aristotle's *physei dikaion*, attention to the context where it originated, the *Nichomachean Ethics* (1134b 18ff), revealed that it had nothing to do with the modern notion of "natural law" in the sense of "a body of norms claiming to possess eternal and immutable validity."[27] "Natural law" in that sense was what Voegelin (following Aristotle) called a "topic" or *topos*, a way of thinking and arguing that had as its purpose the prohibition of the kind of questions that eventually led humans to engage with experiences of transcendence (CW, 6:306–9). These two

26 There is also an outline for a talk in the Voegelin Archives (HI, 71:7) with the title "Physei Dikaion – Das Rechte von Natur" that contains nearly all the references to the published version and in some respects is easier to understand than the exegesis and interpretation printed in *Anamnesis*. Also helpful is the discussion that took place at the original conference on natural right in political theory, especially the exchanges between Voegelin and his former teacher, Hans Kelsen. See CW, 33:112–49.

27 CW, 6:140. "Natural right" as used by Leo Strauss, however, retains some of the original Aristotelian sense of flexibility.

essays also illustrate by example what Voegelin meant by the historicity of truth.

Since justice could not be defined dogmatically, the purpose of Voegelin's analysis of right by nature was "to probe the background of the topos of dogmatic philosophizing and to reconstitute the symbol of noetic exegesis," which is to say: to recover its original experiential meaning. Aristotle's term was especially apt for such an analysis because "it is the first of its kind" so that Aristotle must have had a pretty clear idea why he wanted to use the term. In other words physei dikaion was a symbol that expressed a particular human experience, in this case, Aristotle's. Moreover, Aristotle explicitly indicated that, rather than being a "natural law" that was the same always and everywhere, physei dikaion was at the same time everywhere and always changeable, *kineton mentoi pan* (EN, 1134b 30), which raised an obvious question: "How can this be?" or: "How can the same term refer to a reality that is both universal and contingent?" Voegelin's answer required a detailed exegesis of Aristotle's text.

He began by summarizing a set of distinctions from *The Politics* (1253a 37ff): (1) justice (*dikaiosyne*) is a politikon, which Ernest Barker translated as something that "belongs to the polis;"[28] (2) for dike is the order (taxis) of the political community (*politike koinonia*);[29] and (3) dike is the determination (*krisis*) of what is dikaion.[30] Despite Voegelin's misreading of dikaion for dike in line 37, it seemed tolerably clear that "Aristotle wanted to establish an essential connection between the polis and questions of justice and of what is right" (CW, 6:142). Given the ontological status of the polis in Aristotle's argument, as we discussed in the previous sub-section, this was to be expected.

Aristotle's *Ethics* contained a similar argument. Because justice, properly speaking, must be political, it pertained to non-political domestic relations only as a "resemblance" or "analogue" (*homoion*, *EN*, 1134b 10). Political (not domestic) right was the focus of Aristotle's analysis, but

28 Barker, *The Politics of Aristotle* (Oxford: Clarendon Press, 1948), 6. Likewise Carnes Lord interpolates: "[The virtue of] justice is a thing belonging to the city" (Lord, *Aristotle: The Politics* [Chicago: University of Chicago Press, 1984], 38).

29 Here Voegelin substituted *dikaion* for Aristotle's *dike*.

30 Even the authoritative W. L. Newman had difficulty with this passage, which he rendered: "Justice is bound up with the State [i.e., the polis], for adjudication, which is the determination of that which is just, is the ordering of political society" (Newman, *The Politics of Aristotle*, vol. II, *Prefatory Essays, Books I and II, Text and Notes* [Oxford: Clarendon, 1887], II, 131).

politikon dikaion, as distinct from the domestic analogues that were qualified as *despotikon*, which pertained to the relation of masters and slaves, or as *patrikon*, which pertained to fathers and children, or finally as *oikonomikon* which pertained to husband and wife, was also divided into what is by nature (*physikon*) and what is by convention (*nomikon*), the latter being concerned with such peripheral matters as whether speed limits are posted in miles or kilometers per hour or whether fuel is sold in gallons or liters. Only the physikon dikaion "is concerned with essentials" (CW, 6:142; EN, 1134b 20).

Aristotle then restated the problem: physikon dikaion had the same validity everywhere and did not depend on our opinions. Of course, some people think that justice was simply *nomikon* because, unlike fire that burned by nature the same way here and in Persia, justice seemed to be changeable. But this observation would not apply to the gods, and even if it were true that what was just changed among humans, it was still true that there was a physikon dikaion. Indeed, Aristotle said, it was "easy to see" what was by nature just and what was by nature unjust even though justice and injustice were not absolute, or invariant, much as the right hand is "naturally" stronger than the left, though it is possible to become ambidextrous (EN, 1134b 35).

Voegelin clarified this observation by arguing that Aristotle used the word nature and natural in different ways but he did not clearly distinguish his meanings. What "is valid everywhere," Voegelin argued, referred to the "divine substance" of justice; what is changeable referred to "its realization in a concrete situation" (CW, 6:145). In the passage that followed, Aristotle explained that conventions, *nomika*, were based on utility (miles and gallons or kilometers and liters), which was also true for the *dikaia*, the legislation or judicial decisions, that were human (*anthropina*) rather than natural (*physika*) because even regimes (*politeiai*) were not everywhere the same even though there was only one politeia that is by nature (*kata physin*), namely the best (*ariste*) (EN, 1135a 3–6). Now, the actual content of the best regime was described in books seven and eight of *The Politics* so that the question of the physei dikaion referred to the fundamental question in Aristotle's political science, the question of right order in the political community.

In his useful exegesis of Aristotle's "substantively paradoxical" symbol, physei dikaion, James M. Rhodes provided a useful modern and almost commonsensical example to illustrate what Aristotle had in mind.[31]

31 Rhodes, "Right by Nature," *The Journal of Politics* 53 (1991): 318–38.

> Assume (a) that you read the history of Hitler's "final solution," and (b) that you learn that a man has tortured, raped, and murdered a little girl. Are you, to various extents, outraged? If so, do you think it truer to assert that you *know* that the offending acts were wrong, or that you merely *opine* it, such that you could with equanimity see the deeds declared right by social contract and done routinely? My bet is that, although you do not have certainty, because we are not discussing material or mathematical realities, and, although you are no fanatic, you experience something inside you that never will tolerate the crimes. I offer this as evidence of physei dikaion. At the level of common sense, these straightforward cases are sufficient to establish the existence of some universal principles. If you also ponder a third example, that of waging war on the Third Reich, and if you concur in the conclusions that the allied policy was just, and that a bombardier could have killed a child accidentally in the prosecution of this war without being guilty of immorality, we have arrived at a variability of the principles, and the argument from common sense is finished.[32]

This was not, Rhodes said, an example of circular reasoning. It is true, of course, that we could doubt all kinds of things, including the morality of murderous rape or genocide, "but Aristotle would tell us that we are being silly, because, for us, these kinds of facts are starting-points (EN, 1095b 6). It is fallacious to try to deduce everything from something higher, as if there could be an infinite regress of highers."[33] To be sure, like Don Quixote, we could be "silly" but a commonsensical Sancho could point this out as well. In other words, "some ethical cases are clear and more fundamental than life-style. Others are hard, permitting reasonable disagreement. We need only to consider the former to get to the physei dikaion."[34]

Granted, then, physei dikaion was not a dogma that consisted of correct propositions. It existed, rather in the concrete experience of a human being who understood "what is right" (and what is right is the same always and everywhere) *and* it existed in this particular human being under these particular circumstances (*hekasta*) which meant "what is right" was actualized

32 Rhodes, "Right by Nature," 332.
33 Rhodes, "Right by Nature," 332–33.
34 Rhodes, "Right by Nature," 333.

in a changeable and different way all the time. "What we have here," Voegelin said, "is an existential tension that cannot be resolved theoretically but only in the practice of the man who experiences it" (CW, 6:147). In order to mediate between what is always and everywhere right and the actual circumstances of a here and now required what Voegelin called an "existential strength" (*einer existentiellen Kraft*), faculty, or capability that Aristotle called phronesis, conventionally translated as prudence or good sense.

Voegelin stressed, first, the concrete particularity of the experience and its actualization in prudent action, which in turn was always changeable (*kineton*). Thus did the problems surrounding phronesis parallel those between the right and the actual order of the polis. And just as the best polis was rare, so too was the human being who actualized phronesis, whom we have already encountered, namely the spoudaios. Such a person was able to see the truth in concrete circumstances (*hekasta*) and not simply come to a correct decision on the basis of commonsense because such a person was open to the full amplitude of reality, including the Divine Ground. This openness, furthermore, Voegelin characterized as an "event" rather than a proposition that enabled the prudent spoudaios to speak about the right order of human being (CW, 6:15; EN, 1113a 30–35). Such a person, in other words, not only acted rightly but could speak rightly about his right action. The spoudaios, in short, was an "intermediate link" between what was contingent and what was universal.

The second study of classical politics, "What is Nature?," "complements" the analysis of "Right by Nature" because it was necessary to be clear about the meaning of "Nature" if it was to legitimate the "Right" just discussed (CW, 6:35, 157). Unfortunately, neither Aristotle's text nor the secondary analyses of it were especially clear. There was, of course, broad textual evidence to indicate Aristotle lived within a tradition that included Plato, the tragedians, and the "pre-Socratic" philosophers and "that he expected to be understood when he spoke about nature." For Voegelin it was clear from the context within which the term appeared that it referred "to constant structures in the movement of being, comprising gods and men, organic and inorganic matter—in other words, to something like a constitution of being" (CW, 6:157). This was all very well, but terms such as "constitution of being" (*Seinsverfassung*) were hardly self-explanatory either.

Voegelin first looked to the "philosophical dictionary" in Book Five (Delta) of the *Metaphysics*, which turned out to be conceptually clear but still a "disappointment" because the discussion of form and matter did not seem to be pertinent to the question of "man and society, where the question is one of right order," which was the question discussed previously in the analysis of physei dikaion (CW, 6:157). Moreover the discussion in the *Politics*, Book Three, in terms of the continuity of the "matter" of Athens when it was re-formed with a new regime (politeia) simply led to an aporia, as Voegelin had already discussed in *Plato and Aristotle* (CW, 16:369ff). Similar difficulties followed in the *Metaphysics* when the psyche was construed as the form of the body. Voegelin therefore made a preliminary conclusion: "If we mean by nature the constants of the order of being, the nature of man and society obviously comprises much more than a complex determined by the form-matter schema" (CW, 6:160). Specifically, the notion of form did not take into account the "constants of motion" or change (*Bewegungskonstanten*). This problem looked like a repetition of the impasse that arose with the dogmatization of physei dikaion into a permanent, stable natural law.[35]

On the grounds that Aristotle expected to be understood when he spoke about nature, Voegelin then looked to the first discussion of the nature of things, *peri tes physeos*, in the "historical survey" in the first book of the *Metaphysics*. Thales was the first to raise the question of nature, physis, and he declared water to be the *arche*, the origin, of all, *to pan* (*Meta*., 983b 20). Before him the poets gave the same answer in the myth of Oceanus and Tethys, which Aristotle called "theologizing" a term first used by Plato (*Rep*., 379a; *Meta*., 983b 30). Voegelin concluded from this (and had argued at length in *Plato and Aristotle*) that the older form of accounting for the nature of things, which we would call mythology, was followed by philosophizing, but that, insofar as both were enquiries into the nature of things, they were simply different "configurations" regarding the "question of the Ground of Being." Moreover, when Voegelin compared the Ionic philosophical accounts provided by Aristotle with the Egyptian cosmogonic myths, the parallels were obvious. The myths of Re or Atum, Khnum, Amon, and Ptah centred on the cults that flourished at Heliopolis, Elephantine, Thebes and Memphis corresponded to the Ionic archai of fire, water, air, and earth.

The Egyptian cosmogonic myths, Voegelin said, "arose from the primary experience of the cosmos" whereas the philosophical variants

35 Much of what follows in Voegelin's essay dealt with the "philosophical inadequacy" of Aristotle's distinction of form and matter and where it came from. Our concern is more with the principles and the results of Voegelin's analysis than with the cogency of his criticism, much of which was already discussed in the analysis of *Plato and Aristotle*. Moreover, in this essay, he made many of the same points in connection with *physei dikaion* as both constant and changing.

excluded the polytheistic gods. Accordingly, philosophy dissociated the order of things from the divine order, though the relationship between the two remained hazy. The problems that arose in the wake of this "dissociation" fell into three "complexes," a term implying interconnectedness of apparently distinct entities that Voegelin used with increasing frequency in his later work. First was the connection of philosophy to cosmogonic myths and its separation from them; second was the relationship of the divine to the order of non-divine things; and third was the relationship of human being to the divine and to the order of things.

The first "complex" was relatively simple. Much as Hesiod reflected on the Homeric myths, so the Ionians borrowed from the cosmogonic myth the form of a story or narrative about events in the cosmos. This fundamental experience of the nature of being as coming-to-be, Voegelin called the primary experience of the cosmos. The change made by the Ionians was to posit an arche that was no longer one of the gods but that, standing at the beginning of the coming-to-be, took the place of a cosmogonic god who gave impetus to a chain of events that ended up with the events experienced here and now. Accordingly, the form of the myth as a story imposed on the Ionian notion of being the character of coming-to-be, of genesis. But once the investigation of being had begun, the investigator experienced not just the flow of genesis but patterns that recurred and endured, in the phases of the moon, for example, or the movement of the night sky. Obviously, these phenomena had long been observed. But the achievement of the Ionians, and then of Aristotle, in this context, was to have understood these phenomena and their coming-to-be as "transparent" for a mode of being that was not simply coming-to-be or genesis. One could "see through" the phenomena to apprehend a pattern that was not simply genesis—hence the usefulness of the metaphor of "transparency." In other words, "the nature of being as becoming must necessarily be supplemented by its characterization as abiding and recurring form" (CW, 6:162). From such experiences of enduring patterns came speculation about being as eternal and unchanging that then could be reinforced by the experience of a vision of a beyond that was beyond even unchanging being. This "beyond of being," sometimes simply symbolized as "the Beyond," or *epekeina* in Plato's terminology, was what Voegelin meant by the Ground of Being (*Rep.*, 508–9).

Following this first dissociation of the order of Being from a narrative of the cosmogonic gods, the second "complex" came into focus. One option would postulate an unmythical god as the origin of being. This god would "relieve" the elements—earth, air, fire, and water—of the responsibility of assuming the role of arche. This was, Voegelin said, expressed in the symbols of Parmenides who recognized a divine Beyond in comparison to which the world of coming-to-be was "immanent" in the sense of existing on "this" side of God. Once the experience of the separation of immanent and transcendent had received approximately adequate language to express the experience, "there is no more need for the divine to release being mythically and genetically into its becoming." Instead, the divine assumed the position of a "transcendent-creative demiurge" (CW, 6:163), as in Plato's later dialogues.

The new intellectual clarity regarding the structure of being engendered new problems of interpretation inasmuch as "the divine" and "the worldly" were not "things that lie on this side or that side of a spatial dividing line." The reality Voegelin identified as the primary experience of the cosmos was not obliterated or eclipsed simply because the experience of the structure of reality was expressed or symbolized in more adequate language: the sun still comes up in the east, and does so every morning. Rather, the aforementioned clarity brought new interpretive problems with it. Specifically, the terms immanence and transcendence were merely "indices" that pointed to the dissociation or differentiation achieved by the experience of transcendence. Being, therefore was symbolized as "a network of ordered relationships" that had previously been a datum of the primary experience of the cosmos. In other words the dissociation of the primary experience of the cosmos (initially expressed in cosmogonic myths) did not dissolve the bond or "network" between God and the world, which was still the cosmos characterized by various rhythms, but now experienced in terms of the aforementioned indices (CW, 6:164–65).

The third "complex" of problems emergent from the experience of the structure of being was concerned with the relationship of the newly differentiated immanent-transcendent order with the human being who was cognizant of it. The logical options included the possibility that the order of being was unintelligible or that humans might simply and arbitrarily impose their own notions on chaos and call it order. However, the literary evidence indicated "a remarkable conformity between the order of thought and the order of being" (*eine bemerkenswerte Übereinstimmung von Denk- und Seinsordnung*) (CW, 6:166). The reason, very simply, was that the original undifferentiated experience, the aforementioned primary experience of the cosmos, never was lost. Human beings remained "consubstantial with the things of their surroundings" and understood their place in the cosmos as one of participation and partnership. This is why, as we saw with Aristotle's spoudaios, such a person "is in the highest degree permeable to the cosmic-divine movement of being, and who, by virtue of this quality, is a creator of ethics, passing down to society the knowledge about what is right by nature" (CW, 6:166–67).

What began with the Ionian dissociation of the cosmos was completed by the separation of the cosmos into partners, a world of more or less autonomous things, and a Divine Ground of Being beyond the world. Between the two was to be found human being, the locus where the dissociation took place and where the respective indices, God and world, nevertheless encountered one another in the manifold of experiences expressed by terms such as hope, love, turning-around, turning-toward, and so on. These experiences could also be analyzed, as we discuss in later chapters of this study. The present insight that Voegelin stressed in his discussions of Aristotle was that the differentiation of experience and symbolization did not abolish the reality of the more compact experiences, here identified as the primary experience of the cosmos.

Voegelin then provided a summary of his analysis of the question, "what is nature?" When the question of the "autonomous nature of the existing things of the world" has been differentiated in human consciousness, "the question of the nature of God also arises without whom, understood as transcending the world, there could not be any world of things this side of God, endowed with autonomous natures." On the contrary, prior to the dissociation there was only the primary experience of the cosmos as undifferentiated or consubstantial. Moreover, such experience contained no differentiated problem of human being either. That is, there was no being who experienced himself as the one who experienced order and so was concerned with its truth and thus with the truth of human nature. "This ontological complex makes sense only as a whole. Philosophizing becomes senseless if it isolates one of its components without regard for the others" (CW, 6:168). That was why several elements or "indices," namely divine, worldly, and human being expressed in principle "the indivisibility of the ontological complex" that was not to be butchered into several autonomous *disjecta membra*. Voegelin summarized the problem as follows:

> The differentiating achievement of the experience of being rests precisely on gaining clarity about the *attunement* of the reality of the order of being with the truth of knowledge, of *einai* [being] with *noein* [thinking], of the divine creation of the order

> of being with human participation in it through a knowing ordering of man's own being. The ordering of man and society through right action is a part of the ordering that governs the cosmos throughout. (CW, 6:169)

The spoudaios, as noted above, was the creator of ethics because, precisely, of his attunement with the Divine Ground of Being (CW, 6:170).

Voegelin's argument and interpretation of Aristotle cleared up a number of problems that have persisted to this day and that might suitably be mentioned by way of conclusion. First of all, the differentiation of the "this-side-of-the-divine," which we called the world or the world of existent things, removed the question of the arche from consideration. If nevertheless we persist in asking about the origin of the world in the sense of a beginning in time, we have already introduced a hypostatization of the order of being into an existing thing, the world. That is, "we have forgotten that there is no 'being' and 'world,' but that being and world are ordering relationships pertaining to the cosmos in which we are living, now as before." This is because the whole question of arche made sense not in terms of philosophical differentiation but in terms of the pre-philosophic primary experience of the cosmos (CW, 6:172).[36]

A second matter clarified by Voegelin's analysis of Aristotle was the matter of equivalence, which here can be taken to mean the similarity in meaning of distinct symbolic "configurations." In the sphere of myth, Voegelin said, the question of the world and being

> takes on the form of cosmogonic speculation, in the symbolism of revelation it figures as the divine creation out of nothing; in philosophy, as the question of the Ground of Being of the world. What is newly differentiated in philosophizing is the concomitant experience of man as the entity who experiences the order of being and his own order as something in attunement with it. (CW, 6:172)

In short, the question of the beginning, the arche, was reformulated by philosophy into a concern with the integration of human being into the divine

36 In his *Confessions*, XI.12, Augustine raised and dismissed a similar question: what did God do before He created the world? His "jocular" answer was: He was preparing Hell for people who ask such stupid questions.

order of being by attunement of the "most divine" part of human being, which Aristotle identified with human reason, with divine reason.

3. Conclusions

The development of noetic consciousness in the psyche, particularly in Aristotle's philosophy, articulated the full range of human nature. It was an event in history, not an idea or the start of a tradition. The language symbols Aristotle developed on this occasion were true in the sense "that they intelligibly articulate the experience of existential unrest in the process of becoming cognitively luminous" (CW, 12:287), which is to say illuminated from within rather than lit up from the outside by the light of intentional cognition. In the context of human being, we have already argued that consciousness could be intentional and "light up" the phenomena of the world by directing itself toward an object or phenomenon or that it could be "luminous" as the meditative awareness or "apperception" (as distinct from intentional perception) that consciousness participated in reality and was aware of its participation.

This problem, which Voegelin discussed in his exchanges with Schütz during the 1940s, received greater clarification following Voegelin's analysis of Aristotle. As we quoted Voegelin above, it referred an internal clarity regarding the attunement of being and thinking. The two terms, luminosity and consciousness of epoch, reinforced one another insofar as once one was conscious of Reason, or, historically speaking "once man's humanity had become luminous for its order," there could be no going back; "one could not return from this meaningful advance of insight to less differentiated modes of experience and symbolization" for the self-evident reason that the luminosity of human existence was experienced as true and that the concern for human beings to live in truth became significant, even pressing (CW, 12:265–66). To the extent that humans are yet concerned with living in truth, they still live in the epoch opened by the discovery and articulation of Nous. Starting from the resistance to disorder, of which the previous analysis of physei dikaion was an example, the philosophers—specifically, Socrates, Plato, and Aristotle—experienced directly a "force" that enabled them to resist. This "force" they called Nous, Reason.

In Plato's *Theatetus* (155d) one could still sense the "shock of the transition" from pre-philosophical to noetic consciousness. Here Socrates said that "philosophy has no other beginning" than wonder, *thaumazein*. A generation later, with Aristotle, the shock had apparently worn off sufficiently that he could open the *Metaphysics* with the statement "all human beings (*anthropoi*) desire to know" (*Meta*., 980a22); we should stress: all human beings, not just philosophers, where "all human beings" meant not a head-count but that the philosopher's response of the *Theatetus* has become humanly representative or representative of humanity.

Second, Aristotle reiterated Plato's point that through wonder human beings first began to philosophize as they do today. Initially they would wonder at obvious perplexities, such as changes in the moon and the rising and setting of the sun and then about greater things such as the planets and stars and about the genesis of all things (*tou pantos*). When one wonders, one does so because of the indubitable experience of ignorance and "unrest" with respect to one's ignorance. Occasionally this experience of ignorance was "luminous" enough to be understood in consciousness as reflecting a more profound ignorance regarding the meaning of existence.

Some people, Aristotle continued, expressed this experience of ignorance and unrest that sought to understand both the experience of ignorance and that of which the ignorant one is ignorant in terms of myth. Accordingly, he said, "the *philomythos* is in a sense a *philosophos* because myths are comprised of wonders" (*Meta*., 982b 15–20). In a sense the *philomythos* was also not a *philosophos* because the language used in philosophy to express the experience of wonder was more "coherent" (CW, 12:269). The question of coherence or, more broadly, of differentiation and compactness of experience and symbolization, did not affect the identity of the structure of our integral humanity.

It did affect the validity of the more compact or less coherent symbols of the myth once the philosopher recognized that the experiential source of the validity of the symbols originated in the psyche. Under these latter conditions, the human being who asked questions about the meaning of existence, its source, and the Divine Ground about which the human being realized the questions were asked, this human being would "merge in the experience of questioning as a divine-human encounter and reemerge as the participants in the encounter that has the luminosity and structure of consciousness." In other words, for the philosopher the act of questioning unrest, or searching for the meaning of existence (or the Divine Ground of Being) contains already a kind of answer because the human being "is moved to his search of the Ground by the Divine Ground of which he is in search." In short, "the Ground is not a spatially distant thing but a Divine presence that becomes manifest in the experience of unrest and the desire to know" (CW, 12:271).

The implications of such an understanding of philosophy, which Voegelin found in Aristotle, were significant. It was obvious first that philosophy was not a set of ideas or opinions mysteriously dispensed to a somewhat otherworldly human being who decided to call himself a philosopher. Rather, philosophy was both an active and responsive pursuit of the experience of questioning unrest and wonder regarding the divine source that initially aroused the wonder in a psyche that was passive. The experience of philosophy was therefore both active as a search and passive as a response to a source beyond the activity of the psyche. Moreover the psyche became aware of itself, or became "luminous," to use Voegelin's image, as an active movement toward the Ground that was experienced passively in the psyche as its mover.

The Ground can be apprehended or apperceived "by the meditative ascent through the *via negativa*." As we noted above, the Ground is *not* to be found among worldly phenomena and *not* to be found among the purposes of hedonistic or even political action but "lies beyond this world" of phenomena and purposes (CW, 12:272). Put another way, human being is ignorant but not entirely ignorant since we are aware of our ignorance; but neither are we ever entirely self-conscious. This movement back and forth between the things of the world and their source or meaning, which Voegelin also called the Divine-human encounter, constituted a "unit of meaning" that Voegelin called "man's tension toward the Divine Ground of existence" (CW, 12:273). To summarize: if we begin in wonder, confusion, and ignorance, we also and thereby begin a quest for understanding or knowledge. This movement beyond sheer wonder is guided by human awareness that we exist from a Ground that is not ourselves, which is the first step in our discovery of the intelligibility of reality.[37]

Such true insights concerning Reason or insights concerning true Reason were gained by the philosophical resistance to the personal and social disorder of the day—and to which we must add the disorders today regarding the meaning of history. The achievement of the philosophical understanding of human nature was not some sort of prophylactic against personal, social, or historical disorder regarding the structure of reality but a new "level of critical consciousness concerning the order of existence"

37 In this context, for example, Michael Polanyi spoke of "tacit" knowing and "tacit" knowledge. So far as I can see it was equivalent to the famous Socratic awareness of ignorance, which was neither sheer ignorance nor knowledge, which would be the absence of all ignorance.

(CW, 12:288). Hence the awareness of epoch noted above. But an awareness of epoch, even for those philosophers such as Aristotle, did not reduce prior symbolizations and experiences to a mere prelude. The continuity was illustrated by a story Voegelin told of Aristotle. Towards the end of his life Aristotle is supposed to have said, "The more solitary I become the more I become a lover of myths" (*philomythoteros*).[38] The *philomythoteros* remained a *philosophos*.

38 Quoted in CW, 6:356. See also Werner Jaeger, *Aristotle: Fundamentals of the History of his Development* (Oxford: Oxford University Press, 1962), 321 n. 1. The original is found in Valentin Rose, ed. *Aristotelis qui Fere bantur Librorum, Fragmenta* (Leipzig: Teubner, 1886), Frg. 668 and another translation in *The Complete Works of Aristotle*, ed. Jonathan Barnes (Princeton: Bollingen, 1984), vol II, 2461–62.

CHAPTER FIVE

THE PROBLEM OF POLITICAL REALITY

Following the publication of *The New Science of Politics*, Voegelin continued to develop the "Gnosticism thesis" in lectures and in publications. Over the next twenty years or so he came to rework the original argument developed in "The People of God" partly as a response to the publication of new materials on ancient Gnosis and partly as a response to his own developing philosophical anthropology. As Voegelin remarked in his *Autobiographical Reflections*, he had to revise his position with respect to "the application of the category of Gnosticism to modern ideologies." So far as it went, the original application was valid, but "in a more complete analysis . . . there are other factors to be considered" as well. Here he included "metastatic apocalypse" deriving directly from the Israelite prophets and Saint Paul's letters, the immanetization of consciousness in the revival of Neo-Platonism in fifteenth-century Florence and its aftermath, which Voegelin later called an "egophanic revolt," and "magic" or "sorcery."[1] All of which, he argued in later writings, were independent factors contributing to a properly scientific understanding of modern politics and to modern self-understanding. In this chapter we begin with an analysis of the development of the Gnosticism thesis after *The New Science of Politics*. We then consider the concept of "second reality" introduced in his inaugural lecture at the University of Munich and conclude with a discussion of political reality that both the Gnosticism thesis and second realities were intended to eclipse.

1. Gnostic Politics

In August 1952, Voegelin included in a letter to Leo Strauss a copy of "a German article—the first I have written since 1938," called "Gnostic

1 CW, 34:93ff. See also Voegelin, "Magic Politics," (16 October 1980) (HI, 84:20); Peter Cangelosi and John William Corrington, "Philosophies of History: An Interview with Eric Voegelin," *New Orleans Review* 3:2 (1973): 135–39.

Politics."[2] It covered many of the points made in *The New Science of Politics*, "The People of God," and in the chapters on Bakunin, Marx and positivism that he had published during the 1940s and early 1950s (CW, 6:280ff; 10:168ff; 26:251ff). Yet, as Szakolczai remarked, the article "has certainly not received the attention it deserves."[3]

Voegelin began with a summary of the radical wing of the seventeenth-century Puritan movement: "The saints of the Lord, led by the Son and filled with the Spirit, did battle for state power, not to inaugurate a new political era, but to allow a new Gnostic eon to succeed the old era that was marked for destruction."[4] The Saints relied on Biblical symbolism, particularly the oracular prophecies of "Trito-Isaiah" (Isa. 65:17–19) announcing the creation of "new heavens and a new earth" along with a new Jerusalem filled with delight and pleasure where "no more shall be heard the voice of weeping or the sound of crying." The textual references, Voegelin said, were well known, but their significance as a "decisive phase in the evolution of modern politics" had often been overlooked.

The reason for this oversight was two-fold. First, the comparative triumph of the Gnosis of the Puritan revolutionaries and their secular successors "in a period of mass democracy" had induced an insensitivity to the "oddity" of attempting to establish the Kingdom of God by military force. Second, the ability of philosophers, theologians, and scholars to provide sufficient "critical distance" to enable a rational analysis of the phenomena had had "little weight" because of this same triumph of mass democracy, which in this context amounted to irrationality and philosophical illiteracy. As a result, such analysis "has lost its status as a public force" (CW, 10:224). In the seventeenth century however, it was still necessary for the radicals to make their case against a Christian tradition present, for example, in the souls of Cromwell's army chaplains.

For this purpose the radicals stuck closely to the Biblical language, but interpreted it as directly describing phenomena rather than interpreting Christian symbols in light of the analogy of being. A typical misinterpretation might

2 *Faith and Political Philosophy: The Correspondence between Leo Strauss and Eric Voegelin, 1934–1964*, ed. and trans. Peter Emberley and Barry Cooper (University Park: Penn State University Press, 1993), 92.

3 Arpad Szakolczai, *Reflexive Historical Sociology* (Abingdon: Taylor and Francis, 2000), 158.

4 CW, 10:223. Voegelin provided a context for his use of the term Gnostic with reference to Simone Pétrement, Hans Söderberg, Hans Urs von Balthasar, and Jacob Taubes.

begin by drawing a distinction between "earth" and "world." Of course, Christ's kingdom is "not of this world" (John 18:36), but this statement had to be interpreted by way of another, that God "hast made us unto our God kings and priests: and we shall reign on the earth" (Rev. 5:10). On the basis of the distinction between "world" and "earth" Thomas Collier preached a sermon in 1647 in Cromwell's headquarters arguing that there was a new and an old world and a new and an old creation but both were on earth and existed historically. The earth therefore could be a world of darkness or a world of light, God's kingdom or Satan's. "This is the classical break with Christianity. The Christian world, as God's creation, is not a realm of darkness," even though it may have been darkened by the Fall. It was also "ennobled" by the Incarnation "as the locus of fulfilled humanity within the limits of creaturely being." The "Christian tension" between created and divine being, between the limits to existence and its "transfiguration by grace in death" was "dissolved into an immanent historical process that embraces world and superworld as temporally unfolding eons." Heaven, likewise, was transfigured from the mystery of the beatific vision to a material paradise to be realized historically.[5]

Voegelin then introduced an ontological assumption that originated with Aristotle and has ever since been a major constituent element in Western philosophy: "The nature of a thing is that by which it is this kind of thing and not another in its essence."[6] Accordingly, and *ex definitione*, a nature is immutable, notwithstanding the fact that "Gnostic politicians" seek to alter the nature of reality. But since in fact it is impossible to alter the nature of reality, any political program based on the premise that reality can be altered is bound to be impossible. So how was it possible that there were those who thought otherwise and tried to act on their impossible assumption? Voegelin explained that the condition for embracing an impossible assumption and acting on it was that such individuals had become spiritually disturbed. They were pneumopaths rather than psychopaths.

Here Voegelin made an explicit distinction between the language of classical philosophical and Christian experience and the Gnostic use of this

5 Voegelin's interpretation of the Puritans has been criticized by John J. Ranieri, *Disturbing Revelation: Leo Strauss, Eric Voegelin, and the Bible* (Columbia: University of Missouri Press, 2009), 147–48.

6 CW, 10:226. Voegelin made explicit the same ontological assumption in his exchange with Hannah Arendt regarding her use of the term "human nature" in *The Origins of Totalitarianism*. See CW, 11:15–23. I have discussed the problem in *Eric Voegelin and the Foundations of Modern Political Science* (Columbia: University of Missouri Press, 1999), 148–49.

same language. Philosophical language, he said, came in three types: "As ontological language it grows out of theory, of the contemplation of being and its order; as metaphysical language, it grows out of the attempt at a speculative extrapolation [of theory] toward the Ground of Being; as theological language it grows out of the exegesis of experiences of transcendence." The point of such language was to attempt to understand the order of the world and of reality, and of the place of human beings within it. Such language could not address the nonsensical or imaginary evocations of Gnostic programs because such programs bore no relation to reality. All philosophical language could do was "treat these programs, actions, and linguistic expressions as symptoms of a sickness" and in that capacity could "verify at what point the break with reality or the derailment (as Jaspers named this phenomenon in the case of Nietzsche) occurs."[7]

The distinctive uses of language by philosophers and by Gnostics pointed to a more fundamental problem: "the linguistic confusion regarding *reality*." Here Voegelin made conceptually precise what he had previously assumed or alluded to indirectly: there is a real distinction or a distinction within reality between the reality of which the philosopher seeks knowledge and the "dream reality" of the Gnostic who imagined that he could change and transform the nature of things by an imaginary act that was made plausible to him as a consequence of his spiritual disorder.

This early formulation of the problem did not achieve the clarity of his later analysis; nevertheless, his meaning seemed to be plain enough. Regarding the dream reality, we could not experience it as real nor could we bring it about by action. Even so, Gnostics spoke about the dream reality as if it were experienced by them and as if it could be the product of action that might bring it about. This problematic led to two further questions. First: "How can a picture of dream reality be constructed so that it bears features of reality and stays on 'earth' and yet still suggests the transfiguration into the condition of light?" And second: "How can a program for action be constructed so that the actions run their course in reality, yet have as their goal not reality but dream reality?" (CW, 10:227).

Both questions expressed the Gnostics' dilemma. They "are sick in spirit, but they are not stupid; they desire the impossible, but they know

7 CW, 10:226–27. Karl Jaspers, *Nietzsche: An Introduction to the Understanding of his Philosophical Activity*, trans. Charles F. Wallratt and Frederick J. Schmitz (Chicago: Regnery, 1965), 449ff. See also CW, 25:259. Jaspers was even more emphatic regarding the *Entgleisungen* by the Nazis in their interpretation of Nietzsche.

what they want." They wanted to break through to a dream, which they knew was a "different sort" of reality than the "normal reality" and precisely those attributes that made the dream reality different were those that could never emerge from the experience of normal reality. One response would be simply to ignore the first question and declare that (however it might be happening), "It's happening!" Others found personal solutions that reflected their temperament, consciousness and intelligence.[8]

The philosopher with a modicum of prudential foresight would understand that political action undertaken on the basis of dreams "cannot be realized and that the dream operation, if it is undertaken, leads, after terrible disturbances of the existing order to a new condition of reality that has nothing to do with the intended dream reality." The philosopher, in Jaspers' language quoted above, was concerned with the derailment from reality into the Gnostic dream. An insightful Gnostic who might share the philosopher's foresight would consider this same outcome not as inevitable but as a dangerous possibility, namely "that after the deed is accomplished, they will be proven to be people as unholy as the rest and will have brought about the sacrificial destruction for nothing" (CW, 10:230–31). The Gnostic, in short, feared derailment from the dream back into reality, which he had never escaped anyhow.

Moreover, for the philosopher the direction in which this "unholy derailment" developed was clear enough. As Hobbes and Hooker diagnosed with respect to the Puritans, "the dream images are the expression of a wild lust for domination freighted with resentment." The victorious Saints were to constitute a new upper class of rulers. On commonsense grounds if nothing else, the destruction undertaken during the course of a Gnostic revolution was likely to ensure a rule of "exquisite brutality." But there was another factor to consider as well: because the violence of the victorious Saints was justified "as a spiritual penal action" against the forces opposed to the light, the previous rulers were not understood to be political opponents so much as cosmic opponents that existed within the dream fantasies of the Gnostics. Thus a "cosmic judgment" against them was entirely appropriate.

There was a problem with the dream reality, however, and that was: it's just a dream. Dreams could not be realized and reality could not be eliminated. The dream struggle of the Saints or of the Vanguard against the imaginary old world had to take place in reality. This posed a problem since,

8 CW, 10:227. Voegelin used the by now familiar examples of "A Glimpse of Sion's Glory" and Bakunin. See CW, 22:145–48; 5:206–8; 6:280ff; 26:251ff.

again in reality, all that actually happened was a lot of violent destruction when the old institutions (though not the old world, which existed only in the dream reality) were destroyed. How long could an orgy of destruction continue before it became evident to everyone that something had gone massively awry and that no transfiguration was happening? By foreseeing the possibility of continued oppression, it was a relatively simple matter to build the answer into the dream. Voegelin illustrated this possibility with the example of Marx: the government of the Saints, now identified with the proletariat, "is a transition period from the old to the new world. The period of transition may last an indeterminately long time, perhaps centuries, so that uncomfortable questions cannot arise about whether it lengthiness may not be construed as a failure" (CW, 10:234).

In this context, "the inevitability of gradualism" and similar liberal and progressive slogans served the same purpose. It also indicated "that pathological Gnosis has penetrated far beyond revolutionary activism into modern politics."[9] The gradualist progressives were living just as much as the revolutionaries in a dream; the only difference was that they were reluctant to resort to violent destruction. Perhaps the dream would realize itself? The absence of violence—in foreign policy, for example—might at first blush look attractive. Who could be against "peaceful change" or "soft power"? The problem with such a position, however, was that it mistook the violent Gnostics for reformers and claimed to be able to achieve the same goals, absent the need for violence, destruction, and revolution. This was, Voegelin said, an "evil mistake," not an innocent one (CW, 10:235–36). Whether one embraced the inevitability of gradualism or the inevitability of violent revolution, the pathological nature of Gnostic politics remained intact.

The essence of Gnostic politics was and is the ever-futile attempt to achieve a dream reality in normal reality. Because this was impossible, Gnostic action took the form of an endless fight against existing human beings, institutions, and ideas that, inevitably to the Gnostic, appeared as obstacles to be overcome. "From this standpoint of reality the problem of Gnosis is therefore not the advent of a new eon but the struggle against the mortal threat of pathological dreamers" (CW, 10:237–38). Because of the comprehensiveness of the Gnostic dream, in reality Gnostic action provoked

9 This in 1815 the liberal journalist Charles Comte wrote of the "*révolution permanante*" which in the twentieth century was appropriated by Trotsky. For Voegelin, this was additional evidence that revolution, whether gradual or not, was "the mental and spiritual condition of an act that has no rational goal" (CW, 11:89).

(and provokes) an equally comprehensive alliance in response. Voegelin then reiterated the conclusion he drew at the end of *The New Science of Politics*, a conclusion that, as we saw in chapter two, provoked considerable critical comment from progressives. He did so, moreover, in much clearer language: "The real danger of contemporary world wars is not the global extent of the theatre of war but their character as wars between worlds in the Gnostic sense that can only end with the annihilation of the counter-world" (CW, 10:239). And in a conflict where both "worlds" were equipped with weapons of mass destruction, as they were in 1952, the pragmatic possibility of massive violence was likely to overshadow the essential meaning of the conflict.

Voegelin concluded by reiterating that the sources of modern Gnostic politics lay in a millennium of Western intellectual and spiritual decay following upon the public respectability of heretical movements with which the Church had been powerless to deal. In addition, Voegelin drew attention to several urgent questions that were not discussed: "What are the intellectual and spiritual processes that lead in individual cases to this pathological development? What are the historical conditions under which this derailment swells up into mass movements? When and why has this derailment entered upon the scene at all and with such social effectiveness?" (CW, 10:239). Some of these questions were discussed in *The New Science of Politics* in terms of the drive for certainty in a Christian world where uncertainty with respect to the meaning of history, of the cosmos, and of the place of human beings in both was gained only by the "tenuous bond of faith," which most human beings found impossible to endure (CW, 5:187). In his later reflections on Gnosticism, Voegelin devoted greater attention to the motives of Gnostics and to Gnostic consciousness.

2. Munich

The publication of the first three volumes of *Order and History* along with the success of *The New Science of Politics* meant that Voegelin might reasonably expect to be courted by major national universities. Voegelin may have been approached by Johns Hopkins,[10] but I have been unable to find any definitive documentation in the Voegelin Archive at the Hoover

10 Patrick Johnston, "Silence is Not Always Golden: Investigating the Silence Surrounding the Thought of Eric Voegelin," *Voegeliniana: Occasional Papers*, No. 72 (Munich: Eric-Voegelin Zentrum für Politik, Kultur und Religion, 2008), 20.

Institution.[11] In May 1956, Voegelin wrote to Robert Heilman that "I am still looking for a professorship in a European University."[12]

Despite spending much of the summer of 1956 at Harvard completing the research for *The Nature of the Law*,[13] he was at the same time actively exploring the possibility of moving to Munich, an option that had been raised several years earlier by Alois Dempf. By early 1955 the Bavarian Ministry of Culture had taken the decision to establish a chair in political science at Ludwig-Maximilian University (LMU) in Munich. Later, funding was also approved for the establishment of an institute. In the summer of 1955 Voegelin was visiting Germany and Dempf again raised the issue of his coming to Munich (HI, 10:4; CW, 30:282ff). Voegelin expressed his interest and, with Dempf's assistance, received an offer by the end of 1956. By the spring of 1957 the details had been worked out to the satisfaction of Voegelin and the Bavarian authorities and he was named to the new chair on May 16, 1957.[14] On February 4, 1958 the Voegelins left New York for Bremerhaven on the S.S. *United States* and by February 12 they were in Munich. He taught his first courses on the revolution of modernity and on the political philosophy of the Greeks in the 1958 summer semester. On November 26 he delivered his *Antrittsvorlesung*, his official inaugural lecture, published in 1959 as *Wissenschaft, Politik und Gnosis*.

Before considering the text of Voegelin's lecture, let us examine his reasons for leaving the United States for Germany. In his *Autobiographical Reflections* he listed three. First, he could organize a new institute and train young scholars, an opportunity largely denied him at LSU; second, he would

11 Voegelin was invited by Thomas I. Cook to give a talk at Hopkins in February 1952 on "Political Gnosis" and by Fritz Machlup, whom he had known since his Vienna days, to talk on the ancient and modern discovery of the soul to the History of Ideas Club the next day, but nothing further came of these invitations. Voegelin combined this trip to Baltimore with a visit to St. John's College, Annapolis, where he spoke on "The Wrath of Achilles" and "The Nature of Modernity." See HI, 64:9–11.

12 Heilman and Voegelin, *A Friendship in Letters, 1944–1984*, ed. Charles R. Embry (Columbia: University of Missouri Press, 2004), 147.

13 CW, 27. Voegelin was supported in this research by the Rockefeller Foundation on the recommendation of Hanna Arendt, M. A. Fitzsimmons, H. A. Rommen, Hans Morgenthau, Erich Hula and Leo Strauss. Rockefeller [Foundation] Archives, 1.2/2005/531/4539.

14 For details see Peter J. Opitz, "Stationen einere Rückkehr: Voegelins Weg nach München," *Occasional Papers*, No. 12 (Munich: Eric-Voegelin-Archiv, Ludwig-Maximilians Universität, 1999), 14–31.

receive a pay hike;[15] and third, it would be congenial to see and discuss problems with scholars such as Dempf. "Besides, the spirit of American democracy would be a good thing to have in Germany" (CW, 34:115–16). In a letter to Kenneth W. Thompson of the Rockefeller Foundation, the main purpose of which was to determine if the Foundation might match the grants of the Bavarian government in support of the Political Science Institute, Voegelin added that the Bavarians sought to make LMU "not only the best University in Germany, but to restore it to European rank" and to that purpose both Voegelin's Institute and the Max Planck Institute were being established in the city. In addition, he said, Munich now had a million inhabitants and "acquired a distinctly metropolitan character." It is, "in fact, on the way to becoming the cultural capital of Germany" (CW, 30:298–99). However attractive the offer and the locale, as Manfred Henningsen observed, he remained an American citizen and never considered taking out German citizenship. "Voegelin's move to Munich was not a homecoming" as Opitz's account suggested. It was "an academic career decision" that provided an opportunity to confront the aftermath of the Nazi revolution that forced him and his many Jewish friends into exile twenty years earlier.[16]

The delivery of an inaugural lecture is a formal academic occasion and usually follows a conventional structure.[17] As Sebba said to Phyllis Burke, "custom required a brief survey of the literature in the Preface to help the

15 See Voegelin's letter to Heilman informing him of his new address, March 7, 1958 in *A Friendship in Letters*, 172ff.

16 Henningsen, "Eric Voegelin and the German Intellectual Left," *Voegeliniana, Occasional Papers*, 63 (2008): 11.

17 The production of the English text was complex. Henry Regnery obtained a copy of the German publication in 1962 and contracted to have it translated (HI, Regnery Papers, 76:4; Regnery to Ivan Bierly, 22 May 1962). Regnery's translator, William J. Fitzpatrick, produced a "conscientious" but literal and thus unidiomatic translation, Voegelin said (HI, Voegelin Papers, 18:2; Voegelin to Regnery, 5 August 1966). The following February Voegelin informed Regnery that he had no time to revise the translation so he was to "proceed therefore with the publication as you see fit." In June he suggested to Regnery that Gregor and/or Helen Sebba revise it (HI, Voegelin Papers, 18:2). Sebba then offered to assist with revising the translation or undertake a new one. Several misunderstandings seem to have arisen but the manuscript was published by Regnery in their "Gateway" series in 1968. The correspondence between Sebba, Voegelin, and Phyllis Burke of Regnery and Company is in HI 35:7. Other relevant correspondence—over changing the title from *Science, Politics, and Gnosis* to *Science, Politics, and Gnosticism*, for example—is in HI, 69:2 and HI, 69:3.

university audience place the thesis in its scholarly context" (HI, 35:7). Voegelin followed this conventional *Sitz im Leben* in some respects, but as Henningsen said in his editor's introduction to the *Collected Works* edition, the result was in fact unconventional. Voegelin was the first political scientist to occupy a chair at LMU since Max Weber in 1920. The significance was not lost on Voegelin. As Henningsen explained, Voegelin had criticized Weber "for his intentionally 'value free' teaching of politics after World War I, at the same university in the same lecture hall" and "blamed Weber for effectively surrendering to the irrationality of the ideologues among his students." Voegelin therefore "refused to make the same mistake and, with the inaugural lecture, set the tone for his teaching during the eleven years of his tenure in Munich" (CW, 5:3). We examine first the rhetoric Voegelin used on this occasion and then analyze the structure of his argument, in which he further developed the "Gnosticism thesis."

The published version began conventionally enough by contextualizing Voegelin's use of the term Gnosticism as a category within which modern political thinkers and modern political movements were to be understood. Until the middle decades of the nineteenth century it was "well understood" that the Enlightenment and what was conventionally called German Idealism existed in intelligible continuity with ancient Gnosticism. During the last half of the nineteenth century the combination of liberalism and positivism eclipsed this traditional learning so that "when the Gnostic movement reached its revolutionary phase its nature could no longer be recognized" because "Europe had no conceptual tools with which to grasp the horror that was upon her" (CW, 5:251–52).

There were, of course, the separate disciplines of church history, the science of post-Westphalian sovereign governments, and even the beginnings of a sociology of power and authority independent of sovereign states, but no scientific way of dealing with the non-Christian and non-national intellectual and mass movements. Since the end of the Second World War, however, scholarly work on ancient Gnosticism and its applicability to the modern political expression of Gnosticism had increased enormously so that "one can say we are living in one of the great epochs of Western science." For the "general public" however, this good news was practically unknown and in this respect not much had changed since the publication of *The New Science of Politics*. Voegelin then listed the major postwar publications in the area of Gnosticism studies (CW, 5:252–53).

The origins of Gnosticism were to be found in what Voegelin later was to call the ecumenic age, which was the title of volume four of *Order and*

History, on which he had begun working. Beginning in the seventh century B.C., from the time of the Persian to the Roman, Parthian and Sassanian empires, Voegelin detected a generalized violence directed against institutions, civilizations, and ethnic communities and populations, notably the Hellenic and Phoenician. Unlike the conditions described in *The New Science of Politics*, namely the expansion and growing self-confidence of European civilization that was no longer content to exist in anticipation of the end of time, during the ecumenic age the overwhelming experience was one of widespread material and spiritual insecurity. On the surface, therefore, there was a significant difference between ancient and modern Gnosticism (cf. CW, 18:51).

Voegelin's initial concern in *Science, Politics, and Gnosticism* was with the ancient variety. He argued that experiences of alienation, violence, and meaninglessness led to new efforts to find meaning in existence: Stoicism, slave cults, Hebrew apocalyptic, Christianity, Manichaeism, and "as one of the most grandiose of the new formulations of the meaning of existence," Gnosticism. Common to the many varieties of ancient Gnosticism was a "central element," namely "the experience of the world as an alien place into which man has strayed and from which he must find his way back home to the other world of his origin." The world was neither the Hellenic cosmos nor the world created by the Biblical God and found to be good: it was a prison from which human beings sought to escape. The speculative mythopoems of Gnosticism all dealt with the questions of the origin of the prison, of the condition of having-been-flung into it, and of the means by which the escape could be accomplished (CW, 5:253–55).

For human beings to be delivered from the world, the world must be a place from which deliverance is possible. In the ontology of ancient Gnosticism, this operation was effected by means of faith in the alien God who showed humanity the way out of the prison that the evil God of this world had constructed. In contrast, the ontology of modern Gnosticism assumed that one or another process in historical reality would do the trick. In both varieties, the Gnostic human being must cooperate with the forces of deliverance by abandoning this world, conventionally called the world of the soul, *psyche*, in an attempt to embrace the world of the spirit, *pneuma*. One way or another, as Voegelin argued in *The New Science of Politics* and in "Gnostic Politics," the old world must be destroyed in an effort to effect passage to the new. The instrument of salvation always was the Gnosis, the knowledge, that would dispel human entanglement with this world that had been brought about by ignorance, *agnoia*. As with previous formulations of the problem of Gnosticism, Voegelin ended his introductory remarks with a warning:

> Self-salvation through knowledge has its own magic, and this magic is not harmless. The structure of the order of being will not change because one finds it defective and runs away from it. The attempt at world destruction will not destroy the world, but will only increase the disorder in society. The Gnostic's flight from a truly dreadful, confusing, and oppressive state of the world is understandable. But the order of the ancient world was renewed by that movement that strove through loving action to revive the practice of "serious play" (to use Plato's expression)—that is, by Christianity. (CW, 5:255–56)

Voegelin reiterated several of the problems discussed in the previous chapter. Specifically, he noted again the Platonic example from the *Gorgias* that indicated that political science was concerned with the truth of existence and, to the extent possible, with persuading those who hold false opinions of their own spiritual disorder. The treatment of this complex of problems in *Science, Politics, and Gnosticism*, however, was undertaken from a greater reflective or analytical distance. Voegelin's theoretical argument was less embedded in the textual narrative than it was in "Gnostic Politics," in *The New Science of Politics*, or in "The People of God."

In *Science, Politics, and Gnosticism* the "Gnostic problem" could be summarized as consisting of three elements or "positions:" (1) reality, the actual world, was either misunderstood (ancient) or was a mess (modern); (2) the Gnostic could fix reality either through speculative or through political action; (3) the program to fix reality consisted of either escaping it (chiefly ancient Gnosticism) or changing it (chiefly modern Gnosticism). Posing the Gnostic problem in this way raised, again, the obvious question: how can this be possible? In his previous analyses Voegelin simply declared what was, to commonsense as well as to philosophy, almost self-evident: changing reality was simply preposterous. End of story. What changing reality actually meant, as with his remarks quoted earlier on changing human or other nature, was *destroying* the reality of existing institutions, traditions, and so on. Voegelin's new focus raised a new question: granted that reality is what it is, what must be the state of consciousness of someone who conceives of changing reality?

Voegelin approached this problem indirectly. In contrast to the limited effectiveness of philosophical therapy, which depended upon an openness to the course of the *logos*, the conversation or discussion, in order to apprehend the reality indicated above by the term "truth of existence," modern Gnostics in particular began precisely by prohibiting philosophical questions. They did so, moreover, to move from the confusion of the first position indicated above to the solution, which in the modern era has usually been called "science," which constituted the third position. To the extent that the prohibition of philosophical questions was successful, rationality was eclipsed and, with its eclipse, so was any attempt to restore order from disorder, as remained a possibility, however remote, in such philosophical documents of antiquity as the *Gorgias*.

That is, the possibility of simply prohibiting philosophical questions did not occur to the Greeks. "This is not a matter of resistance to analysis—that existed in antiquity as well." Nor was it simply a matter of tradition, irrationality, or emotion. "Rather, we are confronted here with persons who know that, and why, their opinions cannot stand up under critical analysis and who therefore make the prohibition of the examination of their premises part of their dogma. This position of a conscious, deliberate, and painstakingly elaborated obstruction of *ratio* constitutes a new phenomenon."[18]

Voegelin then analyzed the problem of the prohibition of questions by considering as examples texts written by Marx, Nietzsche and Heidegger. The point was not simply to undertake a textual exegesis but to illustrate how the spiritual disorder expressed in these texts could be resisted. That is, the analysis was philosophically therapeutic as well as interpretive.

Marx, Voegelin said, was a "speculative Gnostic," which is to say he undertook an argument with respect to substantive problems as if he were discussing phenomenal relationships. So, for example, he postulated "nature" as a process that in the course of its development brought forth human being. If, nevertheless, the "particular individual," as Marx called him or her, raised questions about the origin of nature—the arche of the Ionian philosophers—Marx replied that such questions were "abstract" and so were not to be raised. Indeed, Marx said "for socialist man" such questions became "a practical impossibility" (CW, 5:362–63). The problem, however, was that human beings actually did raise questions about the origin of all

18 CW, 5:261. Voegelin discussed other aspects of the problem in "Necessary Moral Bases for Communication in a Democracy," (1956), CW, 11:47–58; "John Stuart Mill: Freedom of Discussion and Readiness for Rational Discussion," (1959), CW, 6:297–311; and "On Debate and Existence," (1967) CW, 12:36–51.

things, including themselves and nature, and that such questions could not be silenced by Marx or by anybody else blandly declaring that the matter was settled by invoking the doctrine of spontaneous generation.[19]

Voegelin next noted that Marx was not alone in prohibiting questions, nor was the practice a harmless idiosyncrasy. Comte likewise, in the opening lecture on "The Aim of This Work" in his *Positive Philosophy*, said he would ignore such idle questions as the nature and destiny of human being in order to discuss the laws of social phenomena. And finally Voegelin quoted Rudolf Höss, the Kommandant at the Auschwitz extermination camp. Deliberation over the orders he received, Höss said, "was just completely impossible," a position, Voegelin observed, "quite close" to the wording Marx provided for "socialist man" for whom questions of the origin of all things was "a practical impossibility." Quoting Höss in the context of a similar sentiment expressed by Marx, as Henningsen observed, was done deliberately "in order to infuriate the detached intellectual reader," particularly the leftist intellectuals of 1958 Munich (CW, 5:13).

The next paragraph was, to many in Voegelin's audience, equally provocative. He began blandly enough by noting that the suppression of questions was "a very complicated psychological phenomenon" that could be analyzed by raising three related questions. First, Marx was fully aware that his "construct" would collapse as soon as anyone raised a "basic philosophical question." Did this knowledge, Voegelin asked, "induce him to abandon his untenable construct?" Not at all; to protect it, despite its untenability, was the very reason why he prohibited questions in the first place. But then, second, the prohibition raised a further question: "was Marx an intellectual swindler?" Voegelin rather coyly raised the possibility that this second question "will perhaps give rise to objections." How could a thinker of "considerable rank," whose lifework attracted a mass following and inspired a

19 Voegelin made explicit references to Marx's texts, available in English in T. B. Bottomore's edition and translation of Marx's *Early Writings* (New York: Macmillan, 1964), 164–67; 206–7. Anyone who compared Voegelin's analysis with what Marx actually wrote cannot but be persuaded of the soundness of Voegelin's interpretation. On the question of "spontaneous generation" of nature or *generatio aequivoca*, Kant had already in 1790 declared it to be "unheard of," which is to say against both reason and experience. In *The History of the Race Idea* (1933) Voegelin observed that Kant's objection "still applies word for word today" (CW, 3:144). See also John H. Zammato, "'This inscrutable *principle* of an original organization': Epigenesis and 'looseness of fit' in Kant's Philosophy of Science," in *Studies in History and Philosophy of Science* 34 (2003): 73–109.

political world power, the Soviet Union, advance an argument based on an intellectual swindle? Would no one have noticed? Despite the improbability of such an interpretation, the evidence was there. "Yes, Marx *was* an intellectual swindler," which raised a final question: "What can prompt a man to commit such a swindle? Is there not something pathological about this act?" (CW, 5:264–65). To answer these questions, Voegelin turned to another speculative Gnostic, Nietzsche, who happened to be "a more sensitive psychologist than Marx," particularly regarding his own motivations.

Nietzsche explained that the motivation for intellectual deception, which may also be self-deception, originated in the will-to-power.[20] The boundless expansion of the will-to-power meant that it also must master the act of deception, and did so by becoming aware of its own deception. That is, from the surface of deception, consciousness sought its own point of origin and there discovered that it really had committed an intellectual swindle. In the case of Nietzsche, as Voegelin later explained in his Hitler lectures, he was fully aware of the difference between will as *libido* and will as *voluntas*, in the classical and Christian sense. The latter term referred to "the rationally ordered will" that combined "the power of existence" with "reason and spirit." Where the power of existence separated from reason and spirit, one would not speak of *voluntas* but of *concupiscentia* and *libido*. Accordingly, "when Nietzsche speaks of the will-to-power, then he intends the *libido*; he is still aware of that. '*Libido*' is the Pascalian expression towards which he orients himself." That is, Nietzsche's will-to-power is Pascal's, and before Pascal, Augustine's *libido dominandi*.[21] It might be more accurate to say that Nietzsche oriented himself *away* from the Pascalian distinction between *libido* and *voluntas*. As we shall see with Marx's discussion of Aeschylus, the awareness of reality was acknowledged precisely in order for it to be denied.

The final step of gnostic consciousness in its path of deception/self-deception, Voegelin said, consisted in an act "where revolt against God is revealed to be its motive and purpose." Voegelin therefore distinguished three

20 *Beyond Good and Evil*, aphorism 230.

21 CW, 31:107. In his study of "Nietzsche and Pascal," CW, 25:251–303, Voegelin dealt with this problem at great detail. Of particular significance is Pascal's *Pensée* 458, which analyzed the remarks of the first epistle of *John* 2:16, on the three elements of "lust of the flesh, lust of the eyes, and the pride of life." All were variants on *libido/concupiscentia*, Voegelin remarked, and permitted Pascal "to develop a systematic theory of human nature and of the principal character types" of which Nietzsche was fully aware but which he ignored (CW, 25:272).

levels of deception. First was Nietzsche's will to deceive, which served as the primordial will-to-power. Were it not deliberate it would be indistinguishable from error. Second was the intellectual swindle where the speculator was aware of the untruth of his speculation but persisted anyway, fully conscious of the untruth of his deception. Third, as the intellectual swindle was pursued in full awareness of its untruth, only now the motive, namely the revolt against God, transformed the intellectual swindle into "demonic mendacity" (CW, 5:267–68).

Given that the purpose of Gnostic speculation was to change reality, the progression from deception to revolt against God was inevitable inasmuch as, in order to change or control reality, which in this context embraced the entirety of Being, it was necessary to destroy what was outside human control, the Divine Ground of Being, the arche that, in the example of Marx, was dismissed as an "abstraction." This is a problem to which we return below. Voegelin then showed how Marx, in his doctoral dissertation, misquoted Aeschylus in order to claim that "philosophy" confessed with Prometheus to hate all gods. Since Marx had, in fact actually read Aeschylus' play but omitted the observation of Hermes, that Prometheus was suffering from *nosos*, a spiritual sickness, Marx was simply exercising "demonic persistence" in his own revolt against the better judgment of Aeschylus and against his own understanding of what Aeschylus actually meant—in the same way as Nietzsche had deliberately ignored the distinction between *libido* and *voluntas* (CW, 5:270). Nietzsche may have been a more sensitive psychologist than Marx, but he was not a more honest one.

The third constituent in the modern Gnostic consciousness was the replacement of reality with a new and presumably improved version. As noted above, the solution to the problem of an unsatisfactory reality could be achieved chiefly by modern Gnostics under the symbol "science," which corresponded to the Gnosis of antiquity. Marx borrowed his understanding of science from Hegel who argued that the "true form" in which truth existed could only be "the scientific system of it."[22] When philosophy attained the form of science in the system, it could then rid of itself the name "love of knowledge" and become "actual knowledge." That is, for Hegel, *philosophia* can become Gnosis when it attained the form of the scientific system.

22 G. W. F. Hegel, *Phänomenologie des Geistes*, ed. J. Hoffmeister (Hamburg: Meiner, 1952), 12. CW, 5, 272. See also CW, 12:213–55. I have discussed this problem in *The End of History: An Essay on Modern Hegelianism* (Toronto: University of Toronto Press, 1984), esp. 336ff.

To see what was implied by this seemingly innocuous formula Voegelin returned to Plato and the *Phaedrus* (278d) where Socrates distinguished between a *sophos*, a wise one, and a *philosophos*, a lover of wisdom. Only God, Socrates said, was properly speaking wise. In the context of the *Phaedrus*, the *philosophos* would also be a *theophilos* insofar as the philosopher loved what God is, namely wise. In summary, "philosophy springs from the love of being; it is man's loving endeavor to perceive the order of being and attune himself to it. Gnosis desires dominion over being; in order to seize control of being the Gnostic constructs his system. The building of systems is a Gnostic form of reasoning, not a philosophical one" (CW, 5:273).

Once again one encountered the by now familiar problem: the Gnostic could dominate being only if being lay within his potential control. So long as the *arche*, the origin of being or the Ground of Being lay beyond the being of this world, "the construction of a system will be impossible." Hegel's answer to this problem was simplicity itself: if he could build the system, the truth of the premise of the system was thereby established. "The system is justified by the fact of its construction; the possibility of calling into question the construction of systems, as such, is not acknowledged. That the form of science is the system must be assumed as beyond all question" (CW, 5:273–74). In other words, the connection between the suppression of philosophical questions and the construction of a Gnostic system was essential, not accidental.

Let us summarize the analysis so far. Voegelin focused on Marx's prohibition of questions because Marx was brutally clear and forthright about what he was doing. This intellectual deception, motivated by will-to-power, transformed itself into self-deception. The ostensible aim of these activities was to destroy the order of reality, which was experienced as imperfect and unjust, and replace it with a perfect and just order. From compact to differentiated symbolism, however the order of reality is symbolized, it is a given order and so not subject to human control. One requirement of attempting to create a new order was that the given order must be reinterpreted as being under human control. In order to take control of the order of reality, the transcendent source of order must be obliterated. This act requires the "decapitation of being—the murder of God" (CW, 5:278). This consideration brings us again to the point previously noted in passing: the murder of God turned out to be the chief motivation for the will-to-power that led to the initial deception/self-deception.

The trick was simple enough: God was to be understood as a work of the human imagination. In fact, for the Gnostic, it turns out that God always had been a human creation, which explained why God could be retrospectively speculated into non-existence, which is to say, speculatively annihilated, in order for human being, now seen as the true human being, to emerge. "The murder of God, then, is of the very essence of the Gnostic re-creation of the order of being" (CW, 5:279). Voegelin then provided in a short essay on "The Murder of God," a straightforward analysis of Nietzsche, Feuerbach, Marx, and Hegel, as might be anticipated. But for greater clarification of the problem he also discussed a couple of versions of the Kabbalistic golem legend. The difference between the golem legend and the German speculation was that, with the former, the adept was able to undo the magical murder of God, whereas with Nietzsche, for example, the murderer stood by his speculative act and aspired to become God. What in the golem story was a warning (because in reality human beings could neither murder nor become God) with Nietzsche the murderer moved on, looking to become the Superman.

> The madman [in *Gay Science*, aphorism 125] is therefore looking for man, but not the man of the philosopher. He is looking for the being that springs from the magic of the murder of God. It is necessary to elucidate this symbolism, for, in the conscientious efforts in behalf of Nietzsche's "philosophical" intentions, it is all too often forgotten that the interpreter of a magic *opus* need not, to put it bluntly, be taken in by the magic. It is not enough to examine the symbol of the superman on the basis of the texts and determine the meaning Nietzsche intended; for the symbol occurs in a context of magic. What really takes place in the order of being when this magic is practiced must also be determined. (CW, 5:284)

In fact, we already know what takes place in reality when adepts try magically to destroy reality and create a substitute: "Man cannot transform himself into a superman; the attempt to create a superman is an attempt to murder man. Historically, the murder of God is not followed by the superman, but by the murder of man: the deicide of the Gnostic theoreticians is followed by the homicide of the revolutionary practitioners" (CW, 5:284).

To return to Voegelin's *Antrittsvorlesung*, the final version of the Gnostic enterprise he discussed was found in Heidegger's *An Introduction to Metaphysics*. Whereas Hegel assumed that philosophy would progressively turn into wisdom as history achieved its goal, and whereas Marx constructed his progression of man into "socialist man," Heidegger claimed that his authority derived from his being the herald of Being, where Being was interpreted by him as coming-into-presence, *parousia*, from the future. As with Hegel, Marx, and Nietzsche, being was a closed immanent process as it was for his nineteenth-century predecessors. "But Heidegger has reduced this complex to its essential structure and purged it of its period-bound versions of the future. Gone are the ludicrous images of positivist, socialist and superman. In their place Heidegger puts Being itself, emptied of all content, to whose approaching power we must submit" (CW, 5:276). Thus did Heidegger substitute the power of Being for the power of God and the parousia of Being for the Parousia of Christ.[23]

Henningsen, we noted above, drew attention to Voegelin's intent to be provocative. The reception to *Science, Politics, and Gnosticism* would not therefore have disappointed him. The Munich newspapers expressed their disapproval that Voegelin would describe Hegel, Marx, and Nietzsche as intellectual swindlers or dismiss Heidegger as abruptly as he did.[24] *Die Zeit* called it an "astounding piece of demagoguery" written "less by a critic than an inquisitor."[25] Judging from the correspondence, the book seems to have been accepted by Voegelin's friends with greater equanimity that was *The New Science of Politics*.

There was, however, an important difference between the two treatments of Gnosticism. First, Voegelin improved upon the textual analysis undertaken in his earlier work by employing a more precise terminology. His commonsensical description of Gnostic movements included such things as progressivism, positivism, psychoanalysis, communism, and National Socialism. Not all were political; none began as a mass movement so much as small intellectual movements. Second, he examined the motivation of the Gnostic speculators with greater attention than he had done previously. Central to the motivation of Gnostic speculation, as we have seen, was will-to-power. The Gnostic speculator did not merely wish to provide, for example, an up-dated Joachistic three-phase schema of history, as did Marx and

23 In this context Stanley Rosen argued that Heidegger's notion of "resoluteness" and "submission," both of which were gifts of being, corresponded in reality or historically to the politics of the day. Heidegger was "resolute" with the Nazis and "submissive" under allied occupation. See his *Nihilism: A Philosophical Essay* (New Haven: Yale University Press, 1969), 119–36.

24 See *Münchener Merkur*, 285 (28 November 1958); *Süddeutsche Zeitung*, 286 (29–30 November 1958), in HI, 124:4.

25 *Die Zeit*, 9 April 1959), in HI, 101:1.

Comte; in addition, the modern Gnostic also wished to be present at the transformation of reality and to direct its course in accord with his own "scientific" account. These two summary points reinforced one another. Because will-to-power could overcome commonsense and ordinary humility with respect to the order of being, but could not in reality overcome the order of being, the result was not the domination of reality but a "fantasy satisfaction" (CW, 5:309). Third, when Voegelin drew out the implications of the term "second reality," which he introduced on this occasion, the impossibility of the Gnostic speculator ever being entirely unaware of his own willful self-deception, and thus of the untruth of his entire enterprise, was demonstrated conclusively. Let us consider this new issue.

3. Second Reality

During the course of his exegesis of Marx's *Early Writings* Voegelin discussed the passage where Marx admitted that the "tangible experience" of human beings was a clear indication of the dependence of human beings on "another." The context of Voegelin's remark was the "third phase" of Gnostic speculation, the rebellion against God.

> But reality must be destroyed—this is the great concern of Gnosis. In its place steps the Gnostic who produces the independence of his existence by speculation. It would indeed be difficult to find another passage in Gnostic literature that so clearly exposes this speculation as an attempt to replace the reality of being with a "second reality" (as Robert Musil called this undertaking). (CW, 5:269; cf. 280)

In a letter to his friend Robert Heilman (23 February 1957), written soon after his return to America following the second round of negotiations with the Bavarian authorities in Munich, Voegelin mentioned his transatlantic passage, various trips by rail, and his having caught the flu and a viral infection. His illness was a problem, he said, because it was so debilitating and he was unable to do much "concentrated work." As a result,

> besides writing letters, I did a good deal of reading these days. Above all, two new novels by Austrians: Doderer's *The Demons*, and Musil's *The Man without Qualities*. You remember Broch's *Death of Virgil*? Now there are two men of similar stature. . . .

> Both authors [Doderer and Musil] deal with the problem of "second reality" as they call it, which in its variegated forms of sexual perversions, dream worlds, political ideologies, etc. superimposes itself on the "first reality" which furnishes the frame of human existence. The conflicts and catastrophes, arising from the clash between the two realities, are studied, by Musil, in the Austrian society immediately preceding the first World War, and by Doderer, in the events of 1926/27 which led to the minor revolution in Vienna in July 1927. Both men are incredibly careful observers of reality, as well as masters of the intellectual problems involved. To give you an idea: Lissy said of Doderer, that he is what Faulkner would like to be: The spiritual chronicler of a dying society. (CW, 30:306)

In *Der Mann ohne Eigenshaften*, Musil used the term "second reality" synonymously with the term "the other condition," which is to say a condition of "unreality" created by the character Ulrich, "the man without qualities" of Musil's title.[26] Ulrich lived in an ambiguous relationship with himself because he did not recognize his own qualities as belonging to him but rather to the role he adopted according to given circumstances. Complementing the man without qualities were qualities without a human being to whom they may be attributed. In this imaginary world, there was no meditative or erotic center; Ulrich lived as if he were devoid of human spirituality.[27] In this way he could adopt whatever qualities seemed at the moment

26 Robert Musil, *Der Mann ohne Eigenschaften*, ed. Adolf Frisé (Hamburg: Rowohlt, 1960), 1129. Translated by Sophie Wilkins and Burton Pike, *The Man without Qualities* (New York: Knopf, 1996.) See also Philip Payne, *Robert Musil's 'The Man Without Qualities': A Critical Study* (Cambridge: Cambridge University Press, 1988), ch. 6; and David S. Luft, *Robert Musil and the Crisis of European Culture, 1880–1942* (Berkeley: University of California Press, 1980). Musil provides a discussion of the "other condition" in a 1923 essay, "The German as Symptom," in his *Precision and the Soul: Essays and Addresses*, ed. and trans. Burton Pike and David S. Luft, (Chicago: University of Chicago Press, 1980), 184–91.

27 Hannah Arendt's study of Rahel Varnhagen brought into focus two real-life individuals, Friedrich Gentz and Karl Finkelstein, who embodied Ulrich's fictional characteristics. Count Finkelstein "was nothing; stripped of his title of nobleman he had nothing he could represent." He "has come to her as the representative of everything from which she was excluded. Because he was personally nothing, it was possible for him to represent everything." And of Gentz, Arendt wrote, "he would have been able to oppose to reality a second reality so strange, so unique, so

to be desirable, and never accept any personal responsibility for his choice. This was possible, according to Musil, because Ulrich could not summon up any sense of reality, even in relation to himself.

In a conversation with Diotima, a character developed by Musil from several Viennese ladies, Ulrich explained that "in reality there is hidden a meaningless craving for unreality." Diotima then asked Ulrich what he would do if he were able to rule the world for one day. "There would be no choice for me except to annihilate reality." He added that he was not sure what he meant by that but was confident that we overvalue the present, which was constantly abolishing itself. "So you see," he said, "that reality is annihilating itself."[28] Given that, at the time, Diotima was standing on a grassy mound surrounded by mud and alpine melt-water, her elegant shoes wet and ruined, Ulrich's unconcern for her present discomfort was also evidence that he could live in a second reality of bizarre intellectual constructions completely detached from the person Diotima and unconcerned with her actual condition.

A more extensive and explicit discussion of the problem can be found in the work of Heimito von Doderer, particularly in his novels *The Demons* and *The Merovingians*.[29] In the latter novel, Doderer established the analogy between the spiritual decline of the modern world with that of the late Middle Ages in order to establish the continuity between the second reality of witchcraft and that of ideological politics in general and of National Socialism in particular. The existential story of *The Demons*, very simply was: if you are incapable or unwilling to experience the divine beyond, then you may as well believe in demons, which are, if nothing else, a "beyond in this life" that exist within the second reality created by the imagination.

complete with itself, that the true world would scarcely have surpassed it." See Arendt, *Rahel Varnhagen: The Life of a Jewish Woman*, rev. ed., trans. Richard and Clara Winston (New York: Harcourt Brace Jovanovich, 1974), 38, 42, 87. I owe this reference to Amanda Achtman.

28 Musil, *Der Mann*, 288–89; trans. 310–11.

29 Doderer, *Die Dämonen: Roman; Nach der Chronik des Sektionsrates Geyrenhoff* (Munich: Biederstein, 1957); trans. Richard and Clara Winston, *The Demons* (New York: Knopff, 1961); *Die Merowinger, Oder die Totale Familie* (Munich: Biederstein, 1962). See also Elizabeth C. Hesson, *Twentieth Century Odyssey: A Study of Heimito von Doderer's Die Dämonen* (Columbia: Camden House, 1982); C.E. Williams, *The Broken Eagle: The Politics of Austrian Literature from Empire to Anschluss* (London: Elek, 1974).

Doderer did not, however, leave the matter of demonology and witchcraft as a kind of postmodern option that one can take or leave at will: the choice of trying to live in a second reality, he said, was the consequence of "a refusal to apperceive reality," an *Apperzeptionsverweigerung*, precisely because one had already placed a second reality in front of a "first reality" that was openly and receptively experienced. In Doderer's political science, "the consolidation of the refusal to apperceive reality, which is thus a second reality," was called "the total state."[30] Doderer also indicated that "anger is the catastrophic form of *Apperzeptionsverweigerung* that finally would sneak about in one of many hundred forms of stupidity."[31] Anger was an acute form of *Apperzeptionsverweigerung*, "a panic-stricken flight from life, a weird kind of suicide where instead of killing oneself, one wants to kill everyone else. One wills that there be no life."[32] The significance of anger was particularly important for someone such as Hitler who deliberately chose to whip himself into a state of histrionic anger until he was quite willing to believe what he knew to be false. By Voegelin's analysis, outbursts of rage were inevitable because the libidinous fantasy of the person living within the second reality was bound to be disappointed precisely because of a lack of contact with reality. In this respect, Doderer's discussion of rage was connected to Musil's discussion of stupidity (CW, 31:255). This connection was presupposed in Voegelin's analysis of Hitler and the Germans.

Voegelin knew Musil but not Doderer.[33] Occasionally Voegelin added Albert Paris Gütersloh to the two novelists as having introduced the term

30 Doderer, *Die Wiederkehr des Drachen: Aufsätze/Traktate/Reden*, ed. Wendellin Schmidt-Dengler (Munich: Biederstein, 1970), 293.

31 Musil also discussed "stupidity" (*Dummheit*) at length in "On Stupidity," in *Precision and the Soul*, 268–86. See also Luft, *Robert Musil and the Crisis*, 283–86. As we discuss below, Voegelin initially approached the problem of Hitler and the Germans by way of Musil's discussion of stupidity. See also Hans Joachim Schröder, "Apperzeption und Vorurteil," *Beiträge zur Neueren Literaturgeschichte* 28 (1976): 71–89; Eberhard von Lochner, "Eric Voegelin und Heimito von Doderer: Politische Wissenschaft und Literatur im Kampf gegen die 'Zweite Realität,'" in Kai Lührs-Kaiser and Gerald Sommer, eds., *Flügel und Extreme: Aspekte der geistigen Entwicklung Heimito von Doderers* (Würtzburg: Königshausen und Neuman, 2000), 46ff.

32 Doderer, *Die Merowinger*, 230–31.

33 CW, 30:756; 762–63. See also HI, 26:11 and Musil, *Briefe: 1901–1942*, ed. Adolf Frisé (Hamburg: Rowohlt, 1981), I, 789.

second reality.[34] Voegelin relied on the language and insights of these novelists and creative personalities (and often included references to Thomas Mann and Karl Kraus) because they were reliable witnesses to the disorders of the age. The *locus classicus* can be found in Voegelin's 1964 lectures on *Hitler and the Germans*. As with the previous discussion of Voegelin's "sources" in *Order and History* such as Plato or Jeremiah, our concern is with what Voegelin made of his sources and not whether he provided a proper interpretation of them.[35]

"The central German experiential problem of our time," Voegelin said, was "Hitler's rise to power. How was it possible? What consequences does it have today?" (CW, 31:52). The theoretical approach was indicated by a term used in *The New Science of Politics*. Voegelin would apply Plato's "anthropological principle" to the German problems in order to analyze what sort of persons the Germans were to have chosen an individual such as Hitler to represent them (CW, 5:136–38). As indicated above, Voegelin initially formulated the problem in terms of "stupidity."

Voegelin began his analysis by considering the response to a discussion by Albert Wucher in the *Süddeutsche Zeitung* of the attempt by Percy E. Schramm, a celebrated professor of medieval history, to present an account of Hitler in the pages of *Der Spiegel*. Wucher summarized Schramm's effort as one of excluding systematically relevant facts and interpretations that would allow readers to understand Hitler's personality. Wucher wondered why Professor Schramm proceeded in this fashion, which provoked a number of responses as letters to the editor of the *Süddeutsche*. Wucher was right, wrote one man, and Schramm was naïve: the real problem was that Hitler was elected and that he was popular. Voegelin agreed. That *was* the real problem. Another wrote that he did not consider millions of Germans to be stupid (*Dummköpfen*) but that is just what Wucher implied. Voegelin remarked: "If Hitler was stupid or a criminal, and the people voted for him in droves, then they too must have been stupid and criminal. But that is not possible, so Hitler was not stupid and no criminal" (CW, 31:56). Some other

34 CW, 12:16; 34:122. See also Frank Trommler, *Roman und Wirklichkeit: Eine Ortsbestimmung am Beispiel von Musil, Broch, Roth, Doderer und Gütersloh* (Stuttgart: Kohlhammer Verlag, 1966). The correspondence between Doderer and Gütersloh and the editor's introduction are also helpful. See Heimito von Doderer and Albert Paris Gütersloh, *Briefsweschel, 1928–1962*, ed. Reinhold Treml (Munich: Biederstein, 1986).

35 See Jürgen Gebhardt, "On the Critical Understanding of Politics: Voegelin on Austria, Hitler and the Germans," *Review of Politics* 65 (2003): 263–77.

explanation therefore had to be found for Hitler's success. The letter-writer refused to consider seriously the possibility that Wucher was correct and that a very great number of Germans were in fact extraordinarily stupid. Voegelin called this resistance to considering such a question, let alone answering it properly the "Buttermelcher Syndrome" named after a Munich street, Buttermelcherstrasse, where the letter-writer lived.

A few weeks later Wucher reported on a panel discussion on the theme "Hitler as Alibi," which included Schramm, sponsored by the Congress for Cultural Freedom. Here the learned participants discussed several alternative explanations for Hitler's success. Perhaps Hitler was just an "accident;" or perhaps he had a "demonic personality." Perhaps a lot of other things, but one way or another, it seemed, the Germans had to be absolved from responsibility. One of the panelists, Wlademar Besson, a political scientist from the University of Erlangen, raised the possibility that Hitler was not so much a demonic personality as an "idiot." To this possibility Schramm replied that it would be a "frightening" realization for 70 million Germans to have followed an idiot. Such resistance by Schramm, Voegelin observed was further manifestation of the Buttermelcher Syndrome. Moreover, there was "something" to Besson's characterization, "for this problem of the idiot ultimately is related to the problem of the *stultus*, the fool in the technical sense" (CW, 31:60). The problem that caught Voegelin's attention was how Hitler could be a stultus and a successful, even a brilliant, politician.

In order to understand the stultus, Voegelin explained, this human type must be examined in light of philosophical anthropology, or an "idea of man," the most adequate accounts of which were discovered in Hellenic and Israelite societies. Voegelin then summarized the first three volumes of *Order and History*: "In the Hellenic society, man was experienced by the philosophers of the classical period as a being who is constituted by the Nous, by reason. In the Israelite society man is experienced as the being to whom God speaks his word, that is, as a pneumatic being who is open to God's word." Methodologically, then, reason and spirit were the two modes in which human being was constituted. "That seems to be the definitive discovery" (CW, 31:86). Whether as reason or as spirit, human being experienced itself as a being that participated in the divine, whether zetetically or by an encounter with the word. Such experiences, Voegelin said, constitute the basis of human dignity.

It followed that the loss of human dignity arose from the denial of human participation in the divine. And because such participation was essential to the constitution of human being, "dedivinizing is always followed by dehumanizing," much as the speculative Gnostic murder of God was followed by the activist Gnostic murder of human beings. Once a person had closed himself off from the noetic or pneumatic divine, and refused to participate "there occurs a loss of reality, insofar as this Divine Being, this Ground of Being, is indeed reality too" (CW, 31:87). Hence the significance of the murder of God discussed above. The typical manifestation of the loss of reality has been, historically, to substitute a diminished or shrunken human reality for the Divine Ground of Being.[36]

A number of consequences followed. First, because of a loss of reality, a human being becomes unable properly to orient his or her action in the world. Accordingly, he acts stupidly. In the language of Psalm 14, "the fool (*nabal* = *stultus*) hath said in his heart, There is no God." In the language of Plato, the stupid person was *amathes* (*Rep.*, 350c; 409d; 467c). Because the fool acted on the basis of his defective image of reality, he caused disorder. Second, once having lost the experience of certain sectors of reality, such a person also has lost the language to characterize and evoke reality. "That means that parallel to the loss of reality and to stupidity there is always the phenomenon of illiteracy" (CW, 31:90). There followed Voegelin's witty demonstration of the illiteracy of Schramm that relied on the literacy of their contemporary, Karl Kraus.

Voegelin warned his audience that terms such as stupidity and illiteracy (along with ignorance, rabble, and several others) were not terms of abuse but of concrete description. He then turned to Musil's essay, "On Stupidity," which began with a commonsensical understanding of stupidity as an incapacity to perform a task that would, by normal expectations and conventions, be resolvable in a particular social and historical context. Thus, "what in one society and one historical situation has to be considered as stupid, in another situation may perhaps be described as clever" (CW, 31:98). Musil further distinguished between the simple, straightforward, or honorable stupidity of one who "has what one calls a 'dim wit'" and a higher or intelligent stupidity. Here the problem was "not so much lack of intelligence as failure of intelligence" for the reason that it "presumes to accomplishments to which is has no right."[37] With intelligent stupidity therefore one found a kind of "spiritual arrogance" or a "disturbance in the equilibrium of the spirit" of which the intelligently stupid one was never unaware (CW,

36 Voegelin discussed this problem extensively in a later essay on "The Eclipse of Reality," CW, 28:111ff.

37 Musil, "On Stupidity," 282–83.

31:101). That is, intelligent stupidity was a pneumopathological condition.[38] This was why Voegelin several times insisted: there is no right to be stupid.

We need not consider the details of Voegelin's delightful demolition of Schramm nor his account of how the German academics, church-personnel, and lawyers descended into a spiritual abyss by embracing the pneumopathological second reality embodied in Hitler.[39] Rather, let us consider Voegelin's remarks in Part II, "Toward a Restoration of Order." Here his focus was on the more "agreeable" sectors of society, those "very interesting Germans" who did not participate in crimes. The analytical tool for discussing this problem was the aforementioned distinction between first and second reality. In commonsense language, Voegelin distinguished between the "frame of human existence," as he described it in his letter to Heilman, and ideology. Second realities may have been differentiated and identified by contemporary German-speaking thinkers, but the reality so indicated was both older and more general (CW, 34:239).

Voegelin began his analysis not with Musil and Doderer but with an earlier example of an author responding to social disorder and disruption by evoking a fictional or at least a non-existent second reality. His first examples were from the early sixteenth to the seventeenth century, often referred to as the "waning of the middle ages," to use the title of Huizinga's great book. Voegelin identified Thomas More's *Utopia* as an instance that contrasted the existing evil social conditions of England with the "true moral order" sketched in More's book.[40] Rabelais' *Gargantua and Pantagruel* belongs to this same period of transition and loss of reality, but Voegelin's main discussion centered on Cervantes' *Don Quixote*.

The overarching problem Cervantes addressed in his satire was the decay or obsolescence of chivalry under the new conditions created by the nation-state. He structured his "novel" in terms of Don Quixote's three expeditions. In the first expedition the Don was a knight errant who in the spirit of chivalry sought, outside legal conventions, to help the humble and

38 Voegelin also discussed the "secondary virtues" such as "propriety" (*Anstand*), which was the subject matter of a book by Carl Amery, and "criminal stupidity," whereby a stupid person finds himself in a position to issue criminal orders. See Amery, *Capitulation: The Lesson of German Catholicism*, trans. Edward Quinn (New York: Herder and Herder, 1967) and CW, 31:102–6.

39 I can say, however, that having taught *Hitler and the Germans* several times to undergraduates, they were both amazed and indignant at the results, which showed they retained considerable common sense.

40 CW, 34:240; See also CW, 22:109–30 and 5:305–7.

humble the proud. He was alone and he retained more than a sense of justice: he wanted to rid the world of injustice. Moreover, he was indulged in his buffoonery as was illustrated by the tolerance of the innkeeper and his patrons. No one started a quarrel with the Don by challenging his fantasies of the basis of commonsense reality.[41] The Don's world, as Voegelin's friend Alfred Schütz said, contained "all the elements of Greek theology at the time of Homer: the envy of the gods, their intervention in favor of their protégés, their struggle for power, the subjection under inevitable fate."[42]

The second expedition, where the Don was joined by his squire, Sancho Panza, was more complicated because Sancho lived in first reality, commonsensical reality, or "paramount reality" as Schütz, following William James, called it. Accordingly, Sancho warned the Don that he was about to tilt at windmills, not giants, as the Don maintained. In order to communicate at all—because windmills were not in fact giants—Cervantes introduced a third party, the "enchanters" or "transformers" who could change windmills into giants for Don Quixote. And, of course, if they later turned out only to be windmills, this meant the magicians had been at work turning giants back into windmills. For Voegelin, the interesting aspect of this new situation explored by Cervantes was that commonsensical Sancho was willing to make concessions at least to the extent that, perhaps, magicians were involved after all. As the novel continued, Sancho lived increasingly in the second reality of the Don and thereby became increasingly imbecilic or stupid (*blöd*) as well as a "fellow-traveler and collaborator" in the Don's enterprise.

By the time of the third expedition, detailed in the second volume of the novel, Cervantes' audience had become familiar with his characters. Readers had come to expect a certain type of behavior from Sancho and the Don. This changed circumstance allowed Cervantes to introduce another ring of subscribers to the second reality. Sancho was persuaded to abandon his common sense because of the exalted social status of Don Quixote. On the third expedition, the two of them encountered a duke and a duchess who,

41 Cervantes, *Don Quixote*, trans. Edith Grossman (New York: Collins, 2003), ch. 3, 29ff.

42 Schütz, "Don Quixote and the Problem of Reality," in his *Collected Papers*, vol. II, *Studies in Social Theory*, ed. Arvid Brodersen (The Hague: Nijhoff, 1964), 141. Voegelin did not refer to Schütz's paper but it is clear that he used it in his own interpretation. See also the commentary of Miguel Unamuno, *Our Lord, Don Quixote: The Life of Don Quixote and Sancho with Related Essays*, trans. Anthony Kerrigan, Princeton Bollingen Series, LXXXV: 3 (Princeton: Princeton University Press, 1967).

as fictional readers of Cervantes' fiction, knew all about these two characters. The two presumptively real readers of Cervantes' real novel then entered into the second reality of the Don and made fun of him. By Voegelin's interpretation, Cervantes was indicating that the bored, unemployed and useless Spanish nobility made of his story a *divertissement* to entertain themselves. Voegelin used the Pascalian term to indicate how a real social class, the Spanish aristocracy, was prepared to enter the second reality because it was "fun" and was an alternative to the experiences of boredom and ennui that otherwise useless aristocrats would have to endure. Under later circumstances, Voegelin said, revolutionaries would likewise engage in intellectual stupidity because it constituted a *divertissement* from their otherwise boring lives.[43]

The implications were clear enough. First, second realities, whether that of the Don or of a contemporary ideologue (think of the importance of "environmentalism" today) can become socially dominant. Then, as did the Don in his conversation with the canon (Part I, Ch. 50), one might introduce the argument from authority. After all, if what the Don said was repeated in books published under the king's license, who would dare challenge that? Here Voegelin again referred to the Buttermelcher Syndrome. And then, in Part I, chapter 25 (p. 201), the Don declared: "I imagine that everything I say is true, no more and no less." Thus does the second reality displace the first, which is followed necessarily by friction between the imaginary and the paramount.

The great challenge in the treatment of second reality from Cervantes to Musil and Doderer is the change from satire to farce (*Burleske*). The difference, for Voegelin, was that satire is still connected to reality whereas there is no connection to reality with the "murderous imbecility" (*Mordsblödsinn*) of latter corruption exemplified by National Socialism. By Voegelin's interpretation, Karl Kraus certainly saw the problem of describing properly what social and spiritual corruption entailed, whereas "Doderer and Musil go deeper, insofar as they represent the problem as farce." Politically speaking there existed a formal community who sought to live within the second reality. "But such a society perpetuates the highest betrayal of humanity. And in this kind of society anyone who is not alienated from the first reality can only commit high treason" (CW, 31:256). Accordingly, the

43 CW, 31:242–43. Hannah Arendt discussed this later phenomenon in terms of the "temporary alliance between the mob and the elite" in *The Origins of Totalitarianism*, new ed. (New York: Harcourt Brace and World, 1996), 326–40.

literary form best suited to "imbecility," *Blödsinn*, which Voegelin later discussed in terms of a "loss of reality," was farce, not satire (CW, 6:360–61).

Two years after delivering the Hitler lectures, Voegelin was asked by the rector of LMU, Ludwig Kotter, to participate in a lecture series on the German university and the Third Reich (CW, 12:1–35). He was reluctant to revisit "this most disagreeable of topics" but agreed to do so on the grounds that it was an opportunity to attempt to dispel a certain "uneasiness" or "restlessness" among young persons when it came to discussing events associated with the Third Reich. The source of the uneasiness of the younger generation was obvious: they were entangled, by virtue of their membership in the historical community of Germans, in consequences of events for which they were in no way responsible.

Voegelin's criticism therefore was directed not at the uneasiness of students and other young persons (one is reminded perhaps of the appeal of Glaukon and Adeimantos to Socrates) but at the older generation and their "alibi" that younger persons must not judge because they did not experience National Socialism directly or at first hand (*miterleben*). He began by stating the obvious: just because one witnessed an event or suffered through it was no guarantee that one had the understanding, intellectual capability, character, and spiritual insight to grasp what had been going on.

More specifically still, Voegelin said that the history of a "spiritually forsaken" era can be written only from a perspective of spiritual integrity that permitted a spiritual judgment. In this context, by "spirit" Voegelin referred to the "openness of man to the Divine Ground of his existence: by estrangement from the spirit, the closure and the revolt against the Ground." Openness can be symbolized by the already familiar terms, *imago Dei* or Nous, and closure or estrangement by *stultus*, *idiotes*, and so on. So far as German intellectual life was concerned, it was certainly true that German literature was capable of conveying genuine spiritual insights (and here Voegelin again mentioned Musil, Doderer, and Gütersloh, but also Canetti and Mann) but this literature was also distinct for having had "no recognizable influence." And that too helped constitute the problem of the spiritually forsaken character of the German public scene, the evasiveness of the older generation, and the restlessness of the younger one.

Voegelin then reformulated the problem as a question. There was a substantive public as represented by German literature, but "why can't the substantive public, which clearly exists, be more effective in molding society in setting the pattern by which Germans act toward their fellow human beings?" Where did the transmission between private and public culture break down?

(CW, 12:18). Voegelin answered by pointing to the university and university culture, not simply during the period of the Third Reich, but starting in the eighteenth century with Wilhelm von Humboldt and his tenure, early in the nineteenth century, as Prussian education minister. Voegelin's pointing to Humboldt must have surprised his audience because Humboldt was widely admired for the educational reforms that created the still-existing dual high-school track of technical schools and "Gymnasien" and for establishing the University of Berlin (later Fredrick William University and later still Humboldt University).

Voegelin's criticism, however, was directed at the substance of Humboldt's achievement, not the extent of his success. Specifically, Humboldt's notions of *Bildung*, development or even cultivation, and his historicist assumption, that there existed substantive progress from antiquity to the present, were the foci of Voegelin's criticism. The consequence was that Humboldt's language was from the start the language of estrangement from, not openness to, reality. Such language, Voegelin argued, was evidence of Humboldt's existential closure against the Divine Ground, which Voegelin also characterized psychologically as being narcissistic.

Voegelin had already argued that existential tension toward the Divine Ground did not disappear when human beings refused to recognize it as the reality of experience. "Its problems continue to exist and in order to express them the language of philosophy must be replaced by a new idiom of estrangement" (CW, 12:21). For example, instead of the philosophical zetesis, one finds "moral perfection," instead of the Ground (*arche*) the "idea of perfection," in place of faith, "religious ideas," in place of God, an "ideal," and so on. In sum, in place of the genuine education expressed in Plato's art of "turning around," the *periagoge* of *Republic* 518d, one gets romantic and narcissistic *Bildung* (CW, 12:22; cf CW, 16:169f).

By the last third of the nineteenth century, the Humboldtian language of estrangement from reality had succeeded both in obscuring reality and destroying the sciences of human being. Accordingly, philosophy degenerated into epistemology, philology into linguistics, and historiography into historicism. This was "the phase of decline against which Nietzsche revolted," Voegelin said, and was followed by a "second estrangement idiom" that attempted to recover the sciences of human being. Here the great example was Max Weber.[44] The problem, however, was that, according to

44 For details of Voegelin's complex relationship to Weber. See Peter J. Opitz, "Max Weber und Eric Voegelin," in Volker Gerhardt, *et al.*, eds., *Politisches Denken: Jahrbuch, 1992* (Stuttgart: Mezler, 1992), 29–52.

Weber's science, there was no questioning possible of whether "values" actually referred to reality. So long as the national German state retained a degree of stability, the consequences were not politically catastrophic. From the end of the First World War, however, "the insight has grown that the Western ideological movements, as well as the non-Western political orders, require a specific analysis that cannot be dispensed with merely by declaring the various experiences of order to be 'value positions' and then not bothering further about their structure" (CW, 12:25).

After a century of education understood as *Bildung*, and notwithstanding the spiritual sensitivity of a person such as Weber, the consequences could not easily be managed, let alone reversed. The education transmitted through German universities, which was expressed in the language of estrangement and closure against the reality of the spirit, had the result of producing an "educated" elite incapable of having any public effect. They had become private persons, *idiotes*, incapable of understanding what happened around them, even if they experienced it "firsthand."

To the extent that Humboldtian education has remained effective it continued to seal off socially relevant numbers of persons from the life of the spirit. As a consequence, public authorities have been able to maintain public estrangement from reality, whereas the life of the spirit has been confined to public opposition. The great works of literature expressed this confrontation and suffering of estrangement even as "they work through the problem meditatively in order to penetrate to the freedom of the spirit. But they are not yet created out of freedom" (CW, 12:28). On the contrary, resistance to estrangement had simply emphasized the ambivalence of literature along with its ineffectiveness.

Summing up, Voegelin said that the problem of pneumopathology lay at the heart of the German university. It started with Humboldt's harmonization of the non-political subject with romantic and narcissistic individuality. A Humboldtian subject was not concerned with public affairs and so the university need not transmit knowledge of how to discuss public affairs rationally. Such a non-political narcissist was considered a virtuous person. This was possible only because of the initial non-recognition of reality and closure to the reality of the spirit. Henceforth "ideas" could provide psychological comfort to the spiritually weak. Rejection of the existential tension toward the Divine Ground entailed a destruction of the ordering center of a human being who then could no longer make a rational analysis of, or a rational appeal against, the phenomena of disorder. By denying the realities of the spirit because human beings must live within at least the appearance of reality, "there appears in place of the neglected reality the ersatz reality of the ideologies up to and including National Socialism" (CW, 12:32). And with the destruction of the reality of the spirit came the destruction of a public language relating to the reality of the tension towards the Ground and its replacement with various symbolizations of estrangement. As a result, when using one or another idiom of estrangement, there was nothing that could "really" be intended or wanted. It all took place within an imaginary second reality. This did not, however, make the language of estrangement or of second realty a "harmless illusion" because second realties could nevertheless form the basis for human action (CW, 12:33).

What, Voegelin asked, in conclusion, could be done about the current state of the German (or of any other) university? Because the heart of the malady resided in the pneumopathological consciousness inspiring university life, "the first step to recovery would involve making people aware of the evil and opening the situation up to public discussion." That was the intent of Voegelin's lecture. As for the individual, Voegelin pointed to God's words to Ezekiel (Ezek. 33:7–9):

> So thou, O son of man, I have set thee a watchman unto the house of Israel; therefore thou shalt hear the word at my mouth, and warn them from me.
>
> When I say to the wicked, O wicked man, thou shalt surely die; if thou dost not speak to warn the wicked from his way, that wicked man shall die in his iniquity; but his blood I require at thine hand.
>
> Nevertheless, if thou warn the wicked of his way to turn from it; if he do not turn from his way, he shall die in his iniquity; but thou has delivered thy soul.[45]

4. Loose Ends

Beginning in the 1960s, when Voegelin discussed Gnosis he tended to emphasize both the similarities between ancient Gnosticism and modern ideologies as well as their differences.[46] Indeed, in his New Year's Day 1953

45 Voegelin quoted this same passage in *Hitler and the Germans* in order to teach German clerics and theologians the "elements of Christianity" that they seemed to have forgotten. See CW, 31:200.

46 See Voegelin's 1962 lecture, "Ancient Gnosis and Modern Politics," HI, 71:11.

letter to Schütz, discussed in chapter two above, Voegelin made clear the distinction between ancient and modern Gnosticism (CW, 30:135–37). For many commentators, this approach was evidence only of a regrettable vagueness and inconsistency.[47] The reasons for this inconsistency, critics often argued, was that "the term 'gnosticism' seems to have originated in the eighteenth century," so that his usage was both anachronistic, and so violated his own Aristotelean hermeneutic principles, and it "inflated" the use of the term beyond where it contributed to the process to critical clarification, which is central to political science.[48] It seems to me these criticisms can be met by two observations. First, as noted, Voegelin was fully aware of the provisional nature of his use of the terms Gnosticism and Gnosis so that they might best be understood as elements in his "hermeneutic of suspicion."[49] Besides, as Hans Jonas has pointed out, very few of the ancient Gnostics referred to themselves that way, though the Christian critic, Irenaeus, certainly did refer to them that way.[50] Second, as Stephen A. McKnight argued, Voegelin's use of the term would be "complemented" by other spiritual movements such as hermeticism, magic, the tradition of *prisca theologica*, and so on.[51] This procedure, as we have indicated above, was followed by Voegelin in his own commentaries on his earlier work.

47 See, for example, Michael Franz, "The Concept of Gnosticism in the Analysis of Spiritual Disorder," *Political Science Reviewer* 34 (2005): 28–47; Eugene Webb, "Voegelin's 'Gnosticism' Reconsidered," *ibid.*, 48–49. Franz and Webb, however, revised their earlier positions. See Franz, *Eric Voegelin and the Politics of Spiritual Revolt: The Roots of Modern Ideology* (Baton Rouge: LSU Press, 1992), 18–19; Webb, *Eric Voegelin: Philosopher of History* (Seattle: University of Washington Press, 1981), 201.

48 Michael Allen Williams, *Rethinking "Gnosticism": An Argument for Dismantling a Dubious Category* (Princeton: Princeton University Press, 1996), 7; Stefan Rossbach, "'Gnosis' in Eric Voegelin's Philosophy," *Political Science Reviewer* 34 (2005): 102. For Voegelin's Aristotelean "critical clarification," see *The New Science of Politics*, ch 1; CW, 5:109ff.

49 I have discussed this problem at length in "Reduction, Reminiscence and the Search for Truth" in Peter J. Opitz and Gregor Sebba, eds., *The Philosophy of Order: Essays on History, Consciousness, and Politics for Eric Voegelin on his Eightieth Birthday, January 3, 1981* (Stuttgart: Klett-Cotta, 1981), 316–31.

50 Jonas, *The Gnostic Religion: The Message of the Alien God and the Beginnings of Christianity*, 2nd ed., revised (Boston: Beacon Press, 1958), 41–44.

51 McKnight, "Gnosticism and Modernity," *Political Science Reviewer* 34 (2005): 122–42. He developed this argument at length in *The Modern Age and the Recovery of Ancient Wisdom: A Reconsideration of Historical Consciousness, 1450–1650* (Columbia: University of Missouri Press, 1991).

For example, in April 1971, Notre Dame hosted a symposium, "New Departures in Western Political Thought: The School of Eric Voegelin," to commemorate the twentieth anniversary of Voegelin's Walgreen Lectures. The concluding talk was given by Voegelin (HI, 77:6). What seemed to Voegelin in retrospect to be new about *The New Science of Politics* was his conception of historicity. Aristotle's political science consisted of *Ethics* and *Politics* but as Voegelin mentioned several times, Aristotle never wrote a *Historics*, which was "a third dimension in political science in addition to ethics and politics. That is what I tried to introduce on this occasion." A second novelty was Voegelin's emphasis on the importance of consciousness "so that the central problem of every analysis of social order would be the analysis of the experiences that produced the symbols in which society expresses its order." Accordingly, *The New Science of Politics* indicated a *program* with "a lot to be added," and not a definitive account.

So far as the use of the term Gnosticism was concerned, first, no one at the time seemed to consider the distinction between Gnosis and Gnosticism to be fundamental. Voegelin several times remarked that the authorities on ancient Gnosis—Puech, Quispel, Bultmann, and Jonas, for example—seem to take the structural similarities between modern ideologies and ancient Gnosis to be obvious (CW, 30:387, 872). In addition, the great problem, as was indicated above in chapter two, was "dogmatization" and over-simplification. "So, Gnosis is not the panacea and the recipe for dealing with modernity" (HI, 77:6).

About a year later Voegelin delivered another lecture, "The Re-Emergence of Gnosticism in Modern Times" at the Hartford Seminary in Connecticut (HI, 77:7). In 1952, he said, he "hit upon the problem of Gnosis as an identifiable factor in a number of modern political theories," including those of Hegel, Marx and Comte. Here he encountered the familiar problem: it was not a question of whether Marxism was true. Marxism was not true; it was "an elaborate intellectual swindle" so that, as in his Munich lecture, the interesting problem was: "what kind of person would engage in that sort of swindle?" And Voegelin's initial difficulty was the absence of "intellectual instruments" to analyze cases such as Marx. Part of the instrumentation could be provided by the analysis of Gnosis.

As for ancient Gnosticism, Voegelin was now able to tie it to the problem of the "Ecumenic Age," which is discussed in detail in the following chapter. The argument was straightforward: ecumenic empires, starting with that of Persia and continuing through Alexander to Rome, compressed together under one political unit a vast array of ethnic groups, each with their own traditions, cultures, mores, and religions. When these empires eventually broke up, they did so on ethnic lines. But the post-imperial ethnic groups were not the same as those that were initially herded into the empire hundreds of years earlier. "And one of the most important tasks they carry out is that of resistance, not only the physical resistance; that was easily broken, but the spiritual resistance against the conquest has left its mark. And the ancient Gnostics are, in my opinion, resistance movements, particular experiences of resistance to the meaning of an Ecumenic Empire."

Voegelin then listed a number of examples of modern spiritual disorders, from Neo-Platonism to magic, that were similar to ancient Gnosticism but not identical. He then returned to Deutero-Isaiah, and the symbolism of Israel's exodus from itself, initially discussed in chapter three above. Here the emphasis was on the historical context of the ecumenic empire of Cyrus and of Jerusalem as its spiritual center.

> A second Exodus after the Exodus from Egypt, which constituted the ethnic people, under God, and now a second Exodus, which makes it the center of the Ecumenic mankind, which externally, on the political level, is the Empire of Cyrus, who on that occasion becomes the Messiah of the Lord, the anointed of the Lord.

The symbolism of Deutero-Isaiah was also the first example of a "third age" symbolism where now Israel was charged with an ecumenic liberation and transformation of humanity.

However, the parallel between the ecumenic messiah, Cyrus, and the ecumenic transfiguration of Israel led to nothing. The empire of Cyrus disappeared and Israel did not liberate humanity, which, as usual, led to a new problem: how to deal with the "disappointment?" The answer was to abolish the world of pragmatic politics by introducing the need for divine intervention, which constituted an imaginary vision of the apocalypse. And then, "after a couple of hundred years, you get disappointed [again], waiting for the divine intervention." As a third reaction, to this second disappointment, "the only thing you can do is get out of [the world]. And that is the Gnostic reaction." The premise, as was noted above, was not that the world was imperfect but that it was evil. And that conclusion was "unbalanced" because it had to ignore the fact that one lived in a world in which one also experienced a lot of good. Once again, therefore, Voegelin reminded his audience that, in order to create an imaginary second reality such as this "Gnostic reaction," one must ignore or eclipse primary commonsensical reality.

Let this suffice for the analysis of the critical or negative moment of this stage in Voegelin's work. What follows in this chapter and more extensively in chapter seven is the positive moment, the restoration of political reality as the subject matter of political science.

5. Political Reality

In September 1965 Voegelin was asked to give a talk to the German Political Science Association on the "fundamentals" (*Grundsätze*) of political science; he responded by proposing the title "What is Political Reality?" His initial point, which he had maintained for many years, was that the fundamental principles of political science were unlike those of mathematical or quasi-mathematical sciences insofar as "the core of political science is a noetic interpretation of man, society, and history that confronts the conception of order prevalent in its surrounding society with the criteria of critical knowledge of order" (CW, 6:342). He then explained, as he had done in *The New Science of Politics*, that the noetic interpretation of political reality was a relative late-comer, that societies already were there and already had what were to them perfectly acceptable non-noetic interpretations of man, society, and history and that therefore a noetic interpretation of political reality was bound to exist "in a critical argument" with non-noetic ones (CW, 6:343).

There was, then, inherently a "tension" within political reality that, historically, had resulted in the phenomenon of noetic interpretation. When one examined the genesis of this tension, it turned out to be found in the consciousness of specific concrete persons. Consciousness, thus, was the "locus" where order has been experienced, whether noetic or non-noetic. This was not a new discovery as was clear from Voegelin's studies of the prophets and philosophers. On this occasion, however, Voegelin emphasized an additional aspect of consciousness: the experience of human order by a specific concrete person "is itself a tension" rather than knowledge of an object (*Gegenstand*) because the specific concrete person experienced himself as being "ordered through the tension toward the divine ground of his existence." None of the elements that emerged from this exegesis of experience referred to "objects," and the result was not a "truth possessed." Rather, this nonobjective reality, which was "intangible" but "by no means ineffable," was precisely what made possible the conflicting interpretations and the "dynamics" of trying to find the right articulation of political order.

That is, behind the historical variation in interpretations and behind the conflict between noetic and non-noetic interpretations "lies the unity of the quest for the Ground" (CW, 6:346).

Noetic interpretations occurred whenever consciousness tried to become explicitly aware of itself and to understand its own activity. Voegelin called this phenomenon "noetic exegesis" and illustrated its early articulation by examining the classic formulations of Aristotle already discussed in volume three of *Order and History* and in earlier essays in *Anamnesis*. Human beings finding themselves ignorant of the Ground of the order of their existence, could not recognize such a condition if they were not already moved or drawn to move beyond ignorance. As we saw in chapter four, this directional factor in noetic consciousness was now called by Voegelin *ratio*, using the Latin term as a more focused version of Aristotle's Greek equivalent, *nous*, which in Aristotle held a wide range of meanings. Moreover, Voegelin equated this *ratio* to Bergson's "openness of the soul" to reality. By Voegelin's interpretation, the initial meaning of Aristotle's *nous* was the mutual participation of the divine in the human *nous* in such a way that humans experienced what Voegelin called "the knowing questioning and the questioning knowing" of participation in the Divine Ground of Being that was ordered by the directionality of the aforementioned *ratio*.

Voegelin stressed that the noetic act, this knowing participation in the Divine Ground of Being, existed only in contrast to a "preknowledge" of human being and order that stemmed from "the primary experience of the cosmos" or of a "comprehensive reality" that, as we have seen in the previous chapter, was initially expressed in myth. That is, noetic experience was more differentiated than mythic experience insofar as it made explicit its own logos and its *ratio*. Even though noetic consciousness could be differentiated from the mythic consciousness that directly expressed the primary experience of the cosmos, the former could never be a substitute for the latter. Rather, as we saw in chapter four, the primary experience of the cosmos remained as "background and foundation without which noetic knowledge or order would have no function" (CW, 6:349). Looking back to the formulations of the first three volumes of *Order and History*, these exegeses a decade later were, as with the different treatments of Gnosticism in *The New Science of Politics*, and *Science, Politics, and Gnosticism*, more precise.

Here Voegelin issued a warning against making these formulations overprecise—that is, construing them as objects of which noetic consciousness gained cognition. This would entail a "derailment" or, as Voegelin increasingly said, a *parekbasis*, a "departure" or a "digression" from noetic exegesis to dogmatism. It would amount to a "re-compactness" of an already differentiated experience.[52] In other words, noetic consciousness was as participatory as the mythical consciousness of participation in a consubstantial cosmos. Moreover, the symbolisms of noetic exegesis "arise in the meditative process" by which noetic consciousness interpreted itself with greater accuracy or "transparency" of self-understanding. Noetic consciousness, Voegelin said, achieved "the optimal luminous clarity" but could never attain an "Archimedean point from which participation itself could be seen as an object" (CW, 6:350–51).

At this point in his argument, Voegelin summarized his own analysis as having distinguished the following elements of noetic exegesis: (1) the *ratio* as the directionality of the tension of experience toward the Ground; (2) consciousness itself as the "luminosity of knowledge" concerning the *ratio*; and (3) consciousness as the retrospective discovery of itself as a process of questioning. This last element was indicated in chapter four with the example of Aristotle who understood himself both as a philosopher and also as a *philomythos*. In this last element, Voegelin discovered the problem of equivalence, which he treated explicitly in 1970 (CW, 12:115ff).

Voegelin then revisited a problem discussed in chapter one as the historicity of truth using the more precise language of reality and consciousness. The differentiation of philosophy from myth revealed a new structure of reality in contrast to the mythical image of the cosmos as a world "filled with gods," as Thales famously said. Instead, the philosophical conception of Being distinguished between the things of a de-divinized world and the world-transcendent Divine Ground of Being. Such a contrast, however, "obviously" did not imply "that it is reality that has changed, but only our conception of it." In this context, then, reality "becomes a kind of constant given, whose structure is discerned 'more clearly' by the philosopher than by the philomyther." However, these mythical and philosophical "images" were not representations of an existing datum independent of the experience of participation. That is, because conscious participation was also a reality, the differentiation between mythic and philosophic reality was part of the historical dimension of consciousness.

On the other hand, because consciousness was the reality of human participation and because this participation did, in reality, move from myth to philosophy, reality therefore was related to the differentiation of consciousness.

52 Voegelin's example was the creation of "metaphysics" as a subject-matter susceptible to dogmatic analysis. See CW, 6:358 n. 1; 381–84; 395–97.

This insight had the consequence that, even though under the aspect just discussed in the preceding paragraph, namely that reality did not change, it was also true that reality did change. "Hence reality is not constant. Thus, just as the changeability of reality, which we call history, can be forgotten because of the constancy of reality, so can the constancy of reality be forgotten because of its experienced changeability" (CW, 6:363–64). In the early volumes of *Order and History*, this insight was expressed in the image of a "leap in being." And just as Voegelin remarked regarding the image of a leap, that it was not a leap out of existence, so too in this later formulation "reality does remain constant, in spite of its changeability within the realm of participation" (CW, 6:364).

Voegelin has said that consciousness related itself to reality by expressive imagery. Here "reality" referred both to its own reality of participation and to the "termini" of participation, revealed by noetic exegesis, to be the de-divinized world and the Divine Ground. Accordingly, it was necessary to be careful to avoid the language of objectification or of intentional perception of worldly phenomena when discussing reality in the comprehensive sense just mentioned. This would also be a derailment, diversion, or *parekbasis*. There would be no problem of substituting the intentionality of perceptual consciousness towards objects or worldly phenomena "if man's participation were automatic, producing in consciousness correct images of reality and nothing beyond that" (CW, 6:366). Here one must distinguish the *form* of reality as participation and the *content* of the expressive images that more or less adequately intended the form. That is, consciousness had a degree of freedom such that it could design expressive images of reality that fell far short of the maximally adequate account of the form of participation, which returns us not so much to the problem of pre-noetic myth as to the problem of second reality.

Here Voegelin quoted Doderer's description of "happy-go-lucky people with no history, endowed with the well-being of born atheists, whose conduct is not necessarily that of the impious, and who are, in most cases, also churchgoers."[53] One way or another, Voegelin said, human consciousness expressed reality in the form of participation even when the existential tension was low or weak and the reality content of consciousness was limited.

The real distinction between the form of consciousness as participation and the more or less adequate content of expressive images, Voegelin said, "makes it possible to formulate more precisely the problem of the loss of

53 Doderer, *Die Merowinger*, 353; CW, 6:367.

reality" (CW, 6:368). When a person refused to live in existential tension toward the Divine Ground or in some other fashion attempts to refuse to participate in reality and thereby experience himself as a human being, the reality of the world and of the Divine Ground was not changed. What took place was that such a person both lost touch, more or less, with reality and remained a human being whose consciousness still intended a form of reality. In order to gain order and direction to his existence, such a person generated a second reality for this purpose. Typically, as indicated above, the source of the substitute images were found in the various *libidines* discussed by Pascal and Augustine. The consequence, as we have indicated several times, was a pneumopathological disturbance in the existential order of the person.[54]

Noetic exegesis, Voegelin said, was the interpretation of noetic experience. That is, as noetic, it provided a logos, a rational account, of participation in reality. By so doing, the logos of participation was brought into what he called luminosity of consciousness. As Voegelin wrote to Michael Murray, "I do not think philosophy exists somewhere in the abstract, but is a process of our becoming reflectively conscious of the reality in which we participate" (HI, 124:12). Noetic knowledge was not therefore, a collection of accounts of instances of participation characterized by several typical features. "Instead it is a concrete knowledge" that is, knowledge of a specific person, "of participation in which man's desire for knowledge is experienced as a being-moved-toward-the-Ground by the Ground" (CW, 6:381). And within the movement of consciousness toward the Divine Ground of Being, it "shines forth" or is luminous, and the consciousness of the person *knows* it. Voegelin's argument, at this point, shifted from a focus on reality to one of knowledge. That is, his emphasis had been on noetic exegesis as the reality of participation; now he sought to emphasize that the reality of participation was knowledge, or that noetic exegesis "brings a reality that is knowledge into the luminosity of consciousness" (CW, 6:381).

Understood now as the desire for knowledge, as in Aristotle's opening words of the *Metaphysics*, this reality of noetic exegesis engendered symbols that expressed the truth of the Divine, of the world, and of humanity and the relationships among these distinguishable elements of reality. This

54 A couple of years later Voegelin undertook a lengthy analysis of the deformed consciousness of the person who has deliberately lost touch with reality in "The Eclipse of Reality," in CW, 28:111ff.

desire, moreover, was experienced as the ratio of directional transcending towards the Divine Ground "even if the Ground is not consciously apprehended as the transcendent pole of this desire." Accordingly, noetic exegesis rendered intelligible the already existing logos of consciousness, which "belongs to the reality of participatory knowledge" (CW, 6:382).

The reality of knowledge (*Wissenrealität*) was not exhausted by the directionality of ratio. In chapter three we mentioned Heraclitus' discussion of the experiences of faith, hope, and love. Here Voegelin referred to those experiences as "sources of knowledge." He therefore concluded that it was "perfectly justified to speak not only of a *cognitio rationis* but also of *cognitiones fidei, amoris, et spei*" (CW, 6:382). Moreover, these modes of knowledge were woven together as a whole, even while noetic exegesis differentiated the *ratio* as a component of knowledge.

Understanding ratio in this way did not diminish its importance so far as the "fundamentals" of political science was concerned—which, to recall, was the subject-matter of Voegelin's talk. On the contrary; because ratio illuminated the structure of reality, it was the fundamental instrument of analysis, "which examines the truths of non-noetic experiences for their compatibility with the knowledge structure that is characteristic of noesis" (CW, 6:383). With the last observation we have returned to the original tension of conflict between noetic and non-noetic interpretations of order with which Voegelin opened this talk and many earlier ones.

*

In this chapter we have analyzed how, following his move to Munich, Voegelin returned to the problem of Gnosticism developed initially in *The New Science of Politics*. His focus had changed from a concentration on interpreting Gnostic texts to the kind of consciousness that a Gnostic speculation required to sustain itself as a meaningful enterprise. The first thing to be noted, therefore, was that Voegelin did not simply revisit a problem that he had dealt with already. Rather, he deepened his analysis and by so doing changed it into another kind of problem.

One can see this procedure in practice in the greater precision of Voegelin's language that was evident in the materials discussed in this chapter. For example, he no longer used the term "leap in being" to describe the difference between, for instance, pre-philosophic and philosophic insight. Instead of the term "derailment," he preferred *parekbasis*, originally used by Aristotle in the *Politics* (1160a30–b23) to describe the "deformed" or "perverted" forms of rule (cf. CW, 16:373; 399–400).

The most important conceptual insight discussed in the materials analyzed in this chapter was Voegelin's growing use of the term "second reality." What he had previously discussed in terms of an "ersatz religion," a Gnostic dream, or a dream reality henceforth would be discussed in terms of second reality. First reality, commonsense reality, or paramount reality remained the "frame of human existence" as he said in his 1957 letter to Heilman. In later essays he occasionally returned to the problems discussed in this chapter, but his treatment was much more matter-of-fact than it was on the occasion of his initial discoveries.[55] We will see, however, a similar kind of intellectual excitement that attended Voegelin's discovery of new problems in his reconsideration of the question of history, which we discuss in the following chapter.

55 Thus the relatively routine treatment of the German university during the Nazi period contrasted with the more lively treatment in the Hitler lectures. Or compare the later essay, noted above, "The Eclipse of Reality" (CW 28:111ff) with the initial elaboration of the problem of second reality (CW, 31:96ff; 239ff). By the 1970s Voegelin's treatment of so fashionable a fad in political and social science as "behaviorism" was one of mocking irony. See Voegelin's contribution to Henry Clark, ed., *The Ethics of Experience and Behavior Control* (Los Angles: USC Center for the Humanities, 1976); HI, 9:17.

CHAPTER SIX
History

1. The Problem of Equivalence

Beginning in the spring of 1959, the correspondence between Voegelin and Donald Ellegood, director of the LSU Press, and Ellegood's successors, indicated that Voegelin was changing the original program to be executed in the six projected volumes of *Order and History*. He did not provide a public and substantive account of the changes until 1974, with the publication of *The Ecumenic Age* as the fourth volume in the series. On March 9, 1959 Voegelin wrote Ellegood about his discovery of a "wealth of literature" that he had found in Munich and would incorporate into the volume on "the Ecumenic Empires and Christianity." He reported that the materials for the final three volumes had been organized and that he had been lecturing on the problems he had discovered regarding "modern Gnosis." He added that he had sent Ellegood under separate cover "a little booklet," presumably *Wissenschaft, Politik und Gnosis* (CW, 30:380). It looked as if the original plan was still intact: the first three volumes would be followed by three more dealing with developments after the Greeks. The "wealth of new materials" and his subsequent work on modern Gnosis might make the books a bit thicker, but apparently no major structural changes were contemplated. In the fall of 1959, Voegelin reiterated his plans (CW, 30:401–2).

By the following summer, matters had changed. In response to an inquiry from Ellegood on July 14, 1960 (HI, 23:28), Voegelin wrote a week later that he had been delayed owing to his having to work through "such outlandish materials as the Chinese and the Indian" and because of certain theoretical problems that had come to light and that he therefore had to deal with. Moreover, the "whole work . . . has gained a different complexion from the earlier volumes" because he no longer planned to proceed chronologically using the history of Western experience and symbolization to provide the subject-matter for analysis. The change was necessary because several distinct civilizations dealt with "identical problems." The consequence was that the unfolding of these problems as reflected in the Western materials was no longer to be understood as paradigmatic for all humanity. This insight, Voegelin said, came "as the consequence of an incredible stroke of luck: I have hit on something like a theory of relativity for the field of symbolic forms, and the discovery of the theoretical formula that will cover all the forms to whatever civilization they belong" (CW, 30:420–21). This discovery enabled him to recast the "enormous amount of materials" into an abbreviated text.

Voegelin's enthusiasm raised an obvious question: what did he mean by a "theory of relativity for the field of symbolic forms" that was somehow comparable to the theory of relativity in physics? In their editorial introduction to volume twenty-three of the *Collected Works*, Hollweck and Caringella said "there can be no doubt" that this new theory of relativity "is the direct consequence of Voegelin's discovery of the symbolism of 'historiogenesis,'" the earliest version of which dated from 1960.[1] The discovery of the symbolic form of historiogenesis was unquestionably important, as we discuss below; moreover, it is with great hesitation that one presumes to amend the judgment of such scholars as Hollweck and Caringella. Before considering in detail the problem of historiogenesis, it is important for the argument developed here to specify as clearly as possible what this "theory of relativity for the field of symbolic forms" meant.

To begin, recall that Voegelin was familiar with pre-Einsteinian relativity, which involved the very old problem of measuring speed relative to the velocities of the observers.[2] Second, he knew of Einstein's special and general theories of relativity. In his not always reliable *Autobiographical Reflections* he indicated that he studied Einstein's theory in high school (CW, 34:37–38). Third, one of the significant concepts developed by Einstein in connection with the physics of general relativity was the "principle of equivalence." Einstein explained, in simplified form, that while sitting in his office in Bern, in 1907 (and thus after what was later called the special theory had been developed) he suddenly realized that if he were in free fall in a gravitational field (as in an elevator after its cable broke) he would not be able to feel his own weight. As he put it in 1907: "we . . . assume the

1 "Historiogenesis," *Philosophisches Jahrbuch* 68 (1960): 419–46. A nearly identical version was published the same year in a Festschrift for Alois Dempf. A slightly changed version appeared in *Anamnesis* (1966), another in "Anxiety and Reason," around 1968 (CW, 28:52ff), and a further expansion, which presumably was definitive, appeared in *The Ecumenic Age*, and is discussed below.

2 See the discussion in "The Origins of Scientism" (1948) in CW, 10:171–73; 178–79; 184–85.

complete physical equivalence of a gravitational field and a corresponding acceleration of the reference system" such as an elevator in free fall.[3] It seems to me, therefore, that there are good anecdotal grounds to think, in the absence of any more detailed discussion by Voegelin of the parallels between the theory of relativity in physics and his own version, that his paper on "Equivalences of Experience and Symbolization in History" (1969) was the prime source of the "theoretical formula" mentioned in the 1960 letter to Ellegood. Among other things, as we argue below, the argument was developed from an earlier version of "relativity" that he presented in terms of the historicity of truth, which was discussed in chapter one.

That said, it is true that (so far as I have been able to determine) the problem of equivalence was first introduced in the 1960 version of "Historiogenesis." There Voegelin wrote:

> The equivalence of the aggregate of four mythospeculative types to philosophical speculation regarding the ground of being draws on our attention to the problem of equivalence of symbolizations in the various media of experience, as well as to the nature of the constant problems that find expression in symbolisms so widely differing in surface appearance as myth and philosophy. Especially from an exploration of equivalence—which we cannot undertake here—we may expect new light to fall on fundamental problems of philosophy. (CW, 6:103–4)

Working out a theory of equivalences of myth and philosophy, which is to say, of equivalences between more compact and more differentiated symbolisms, would indeed shed new light on fundamental problems of philosophy.

A few years later, in "What is Political Reality?" (1965), Voegelin had formulated a provisional definition:

> By *equivalence* I mean here that all experiences of the Ground are in like manner experiences of participation, even

3 Albert Einstein, "On the Relativity Principle and the Conclusions to be Drawn from It," in *The Collected Papers of Albert Einstein*, vol. 2, *The Swiss Years: Writings, 1900–1909*, trans. Anna Beck (Princeton: Princeton University Press, 1994), 388ff. See also Einstein, "On the Influence of Gravitation on the Propagation of Light," in *The Principle of Relativity* (New York: Dover, 1924), 99–108.

> though they may differ considerably on the truth scales of compactness and differentiation, of finding and missing the Ground. And from the equivalence of the symbols that emerge from the stream of participation there ensues, finally, the loving return to the symbols of the past, since they express phases of the very same consciousness in the presence of which the thinker finds himself. (CW, 6:357)

He repeated this summary account in the *Autobiographical Reflections* (CW, 34:133). The most extensive treatment however was in the "Equivalences" article cited above.

The search for the constants of human order in society and history was, Voegelin began, "at present, uncertain of its language." It was true that, in the comparative study of cults, ceremonies, myths or symbols, scholars readily enough have invoked the language of "equivalent" practices, myths, and so on. By so doing they were of course aware that the practices or symbols were different and that the sameness that justified the language of equivalence "does not lie in the symbols themselves but in the experiences that have engendered them." Also implied was the "theoretical insight that not the symbols themselves but the constants of engendering experience are the true subject-matter of our studies." What was constant in human history was not therefore the symbols "but man himself in search of his humanity and its order." Such a statement was clear enough, though the hermeneutic implications turned out to be complex. A search for the constants of the engendering experiences "can be conducted only by means of symbols which in their turn are engendered by the constants of which the comparative study is in search." This did not for Voegelin mean that the hermeneutic circle was vicious but that the study of symbols was a "reflective inquiry concerning the search for existential order" that eventually must become a philosophy of history. The search for a "theory of equivalences marks the point at which the comparative study of symbols attains to an understanding of itself as a search of the search" (CW, 12:115–16).

The question of constants could not be answered by examining a collection of propositions because "existence does not have the structure of order or, for that matter, of disorder, but the structure of a tension between truth and deformation of reality. Not the possession of his humanity but the concern about its full realization is the lot of man. Existence has the structure of the In-Between" and it was typically expressed in the language of tension between life and death, perfection and imperfection, order and disorder, and so forth.[4] The only thing constant in the history of humanity, "i.e., in the time dimension of existence, is the structure of existence itself (CW, 12:119–20). So what, then, is the structure of existence?

Voegelin again proceeded indirectly. It is one thing, he said, to argue that different symbols can be intelligibly engendered by the same type of experience. But if we stopped there, the result would be a collection of experiences as historical constants, which is to say the result would be articulated as a symbolism exempt from being "one more historically equivalent truth" and thus somehow external to "the time dimension of existence," which is impossible. Consequently "we must extend the differences of the symbols into the engendering experiences" and thus "speak of the equivalence not only of symbols, but of experiences as well." But then, what could possibly be construed as a "constant"? Historically the problem had been expressed by the term "depth." The meaning of the symbol "depth" however was far from self-evident. Moreover, the haziness of meaning was one of principle, not conceptual ambiguity. Depth "does not furnish a substantive content in addition to our experiences of God, man, the world, and society, of existential tension, and of participation" (CW, 12:123–24).

4 In chapter three above, we noted that Voegelin used the term "mediation" to refer to what was between the political order and the cosmic order, and that he later used the Greek preposition, *metaxy*, in-between, as a noun, which he often capitalized. In a 1964 letter to Manfred Henningsen, Voegelin explained the additional clarity his use of the term Metaxy had gained after he looked it up in the large Liddell-Scott lexicon. "It is a composite of *meta* and *xynon*. *Meta* means that the word has not only the meaning of a temporal and spatial interstice, but it also denotes something 'between' two things that is common to them, an adverb of substantiality that in fact can denote the consubstantiality of two things. *Xynon* has the meaning of commonality—the conjunction of the two, that is, an intensification of the consubstantial" (CW, 30:485). Voegelin had to clarify the meaning of Metaxy in several letters during the 1970s. See, for example, CW, 30:782. See also Dante Germino, "Eric Voegelin's Framework for Political Evaluation in his Recently Published Work," in E. Sandoz, ed., *Eric Voegelin's Thought: A Critical Appraisal* (Durham: Duke University Press, 1982), 120–23. William Desmond has also developed a "metaxic" philosophy independently of Voegelin. Indeed, he has not cited Voegelin so far as I know. See Desmond, *Being and the Between* (Albany: SUNY Press, 1955); *Ethics and the Between* (Albany: SUNY Press, 2001); *God and the Between* (Oxford: Blackwell, 2008). There is also a collection of excerpts from Desmond's work, *The William Desmond Reader*, ed. Christopher Ben Simpson (Albany: SUNY Press, 2012). As we argue below, Voegelin's concept of Metaxy was complemented by Metalepsis, the mutual penetration or participation of Divine and human, which he borrowed from Aristotle.

All the "depth" could convey by way of meaning was that "insight into the process of reality from which the equivalents emerge." Consequently, all one could say was that "there is depth below consciousness, but there is no depth below depth in infinite regress," which was what, in the last chapter, we took Voegelin to mean by his use of the term "unconscious." Indeed, the depth "renders no truth but the equivalent experience of the primordial field of reality" so that there was no substantive constant that was exempt from the status of an equivalent. "No phenomenon in the past or the future of the historical field is an ultimate truth of reality that would transform the search into a possession of truth." The symbolism of an ultimate truth was "engendered by the apocalyptic dream of abolishing the tension of existence" (CW, 12:129). But there was no apocalyptic truth of reality behind reality experienced so the consequence must be that the equivalence of symbols, which was extended to the equivalence of experiences, must be pushed farther into the depth that nourished experiences. In commonsensical language, all that could be said of the depth was that it was there.

In order to avoid any number of "derailments," such as would be afforded by opting for an imaginary, apocalyptic, and final truth, one must acknowledge the wholeness of the experience as being entirely present to itself from the appearance of equivalent symbols, to equivalent experiences, to the depth. "The wholeness of presence, of the experience, as a character in the experience itself can be suitably expressed by the symbol 'luminosity.'" That is, the experience was luminous to itself as a presence that was not an object for investigation, analysis, or reflection. Rather "the present analysis must be understood . . . as a meditative exegesis of the experience" (CW, 12:131). We examine in the following chapter the literary traces of Voegelin's meditations. In the present context, Voegelin's analysis indicated that meditative exegesis was engendered by experience expressing itself in symbols. Initially, therefore, the luminosity of consciousness was expressed by the articulation of symbols that differentiated the truth of reality "beyond the state achieved by previous equivalents." And finally, reflecting on the whole process, consciousness discovered itself "at the point of its presence where truth emerges from the depth" (CW, 12:131).

"The search for the constants of human order in society and history," which was the problem with which Voegelin began the analysis, had led to a revision or a subversion of the initial formulation. "For we have not found a constant in history but the constancy of a process that leaves a trail of equivalent symbols in time and space." As with the description of history as the "time dimension of existence," one could attach the term "history" to the trail of equivalent symbols that expressed "the moving presence of the process." And that was all. As for the process itself, that could be known only in the immediacy of its presence in the consciousness of concrete individuals. The "historical field" that resulted from the presence of the process in the consciousness of specific human beings and that deposited the laid-down trail of equivalent symbols "is not experienced by anybody concretely" (CW, 12:132).

This conclusion led Voegelin to one final insight. When Aristotle began the *Metaphysics* with the statement that "all men by nature desire to know," or as on this occasion Voegelin translated Aristotle's famous words as "all men reach out for knowledge [*tou eidenai oregontai*]," he was not making a generalization based on statistical data but was expressing an experience in his own psyche. This did not mean that we ignore the remark as subjective or fanciful "because we share with Aristotle the belief in the premise that a truth concerning the reality of man found by one man concretely does, indeed, apply to every man." And where did that belief come from? What was the origin of the "faith in this premise"? It was not engendered by "an additional experience of man's nature, but by the primordial experience of reality as endowed with the constancy and lastingness of structure that we symbolize as Cosmos" (CW, 12:132–33).

In other words, behind Aristotle's differentiated expression of human nature lay "the trust in the Cosmos and its depth" as "the source of the premises." Voegelin's equivalent expression of Aristotle's famous remark, namely "the reality of the process as a moving presence," also rested upon accepting "as the context of meaning for our concrete engagement in the search for truth" this same faith in the Cosmos. Indeed, the activity of searching for truth made sense only "under the assumption that the truth brought up from the depth of his psyche by man, though it is not the ultimate truth of reality, was representative of the truth of the divine depth of the Cosmos" that in turn may be apprehended in faith.

Voegelin's "theory of equivalence" could therefore be summarized analytically in two constituent elements. First, every equivalent symbol in the historical field was engendered by a concrete individual on a specific occasion, namely his or her search for truth. That search, second, may lead to the experience of an "equivalent truth" that ultimately rested on faith in the Cosmos but that "by engaging in it, man participates representatively in the divine drama of truth becoming luminous" (CW, 12:133). And truth becomes luminous in the consciousness of the truth-seeker with faith in the Cosmos.

Voegelin's theory of equivalence was a complex combination of analytic argument and meditative exegesis. For the most part he used the language of equivalence in a fairly commonsensical way that referred to the problem of compactness and differentiation of symbols and experience that has become familiar from previous chapters.[5] Whether the theory of equivalence was equivalent in the field of symbolic forms to the theory of relativity in the field of physics would probably require a more detailed exposition than Voegelin provided. However that may be, the term "theory of equivalence" or just "equivalence" appeared several times in *The Ecumenic Age*, a book that certainly compressed a great deal of historical material. It is probably true to say that Voegelin's reflections on equivalence did not delay the publication so much as provide him with a means of producing a digestible volume.

In contrast, it is also probably true to say that the discovery of historiogenesis did cause a delay. In January 1961 Voegelin again wrote Ellegood, this time from Notre Dame, giving additional reasons for the delay. The preceding November he had been mugged; he found the university library "useless for scientific work," which necessitated several trips to the Oriental Institute in Chicago, and he had to endure his own Festschrift celebration. Perhaps more significantly, he had discovered in Chicago materials dealing with the Sumerians about which he had known next to nothing. Even so, he expected the manuscript to be finished by the following summer (CW, 30:433–34). The summer came and went and nothing had appeared on Ellegood's desk. Ellegood made additional enquiries. In October and November 1961, Voegelin provided explanations for what he now called a "scandalous" delay. The first explanation again involved certain "theoretical problems" that entailed compressing the final three volumes into two. In particular, the final volume would deal with the question of what made contemporary politics and history an "epoch." Voegelin said he dealt with this problem in a 1961 lecture published as "World Empire and the Unity of Mankind" (CW, 11:134–55). We provide an analysis of this problem toward the end of this chapter.

The pressure of administrative duties had partially been relieved by an offer from the father of a former student, Stephen DuBrul, to provide

5 In chapter five we discussed the equivalence of Plato's image of the cave with the more differentiated Christian symbol of Grace. See also Voegelin's offhand 1967 question: "Now what is the difference between this force compelling you to turn around, in Plato, and the vision of Saint Paul on the road to Damascus? I don't know what the difference is" (CW, 33:294). See also CW, 12:113.

financial assistance for the Institute in the hopes that it would expedite the production of volume four. Again, however, unspecified "theoretical issues" intervened and caused additional delays.[6]

By February 1963 Voegelin had again reorganized the later volumes of *Order and History* from five to four, the final volume now to be called *In Search of Order*. Voegelin also reported that he had solved several pesky theoretical problems (CW, 30:458). In February 1965 he informed an audience in Montreal after delivering a lecture "In Search of the Ground" that *Order and History* was complete. Unfortunately, "it is a shelf [of books] in print, six more volumes—and that is preposterous. So I will have only one volume on systematic questions of the type of which I have given you an example tonight, and I'm using historical materials only as representative examples. That enormous manuscript is unpublishable."[7] By October 1966 the project had again grown into two concluding volumes, one now tentatively called *The Language of Consciousness* (CW, 30:517).

Three years later it still had not appeared.[8] Voegelin again explained to LSU Press, now directed by Richard Wentworth, that he had to digest and rework the arguments into "theoretical conclusions" that were adequate to the entire work. He again promised *In Search of Order*, now conceived *not* as a fourth volume of the *Order and History* series "but an independent work" (CW, 30:630). The "theoretical issues" would be published in yet another volume, *The Drama of Humanity*, which was the title of his 1967 Candler Lectures at Emory University discussed in the following chapter (CW, 33:174–242). *In Search of Order* was promised by mid-1970. By July 1970 the work was said to be going "quite well" though Voegelin hesitated "to give a definite date of delivery for the completed manuscript." And as for *The Drama of Humanity*, Voegelin did not wish "to make any commitments at the moment" because, as he said, "my work is always seriously hampered

6 CW, 30:445; 460–61; HI, 10:18; 30:1. Voegelin also reported that, with his assistants in Munich he had developed a synopsis for a book on *The World and the West* and had further elaborated his argument in "Historiogenesis," discussed below.

7 CW, 11:240. If my interpretation of the importance of the "Equivalences" article is correct, Voegelin was able to reduce the six volumes to two and to use the historical materials to provide representative examples because of it. What became of the manuscript of these six additional volumes is unknown. They do not seem to have been placed in the Voegelin papers at the Hoover Institution so far as I can tell.

8 Voegelin explained to M. Goscillo on April 21, 1969, that "the last volume of *Order and History* will not be out for quite a while, as it had proved necessary to rearrange the construction of the whole work" (HI, 15:13).

by deadlines, and for once in my life I want to write a book in peace" (CW, 30:661–62).

Nearly ten years after the initial proposal to downsize *Order and History* from five to four volumes, it was back up to five. Now the last two volumes were to be *Empire* and *In Search of Order* (CW, 30:749). A month later, on 22 February, 1973, they were to be "two sub-volumes" of a single title, *In Search of Order* (CW, 30:758). Two weeks later we were back to *Order and History*, with volume four still called *In Search of Order* and the last one called *The Height and the Depth.*[9] Additional correspondence between Voegelin and the Press ensued over the summer (HI, 24:1) and in September they agreed that volume four would be *The Ecumenic Age* and *In Search of Order* would be volume five (CW, 30:775).

This complex philological story unfolded over fifteen years. In that respect it was reminiscent of the lengthy gestation (though not the abortive end) of the *History of Political Ideas* discussed in chapter one. More skeptical readers may be reminded of Husserl's endless "archaeological" writings and the "continuously prolegomenous character," as Voegelin remarked, of Husserl's work (CW, 6:16). How this problem might have been avoided by a philosopher who understood his own work to be a zetetic enterprise is unclear.

It is true enough that these changes in the original program may be connected to various "liminal" personal and intellectual events as Szakolczai

9 "I would not support my wife's suggestion to call it something like *At Last!* or *Got It!"* (CW, 30, 760). At the end of March 1973, acting on the invitation of Geoffrey Barraclough, Voegelin made an application for a visiting fellowship at All Souls College, Oxford. He wrote to Denis Mack Smith, Dean of the college: "Volume V, entitled *The Height and the Depth*, deals with fundamental problems of Christianity and their vicissitudes in the modern period. Furthermore, the volume *From Reason to Revelation* has just been completed. . . . With the major special studies out of the way, I could turn to the long-planned philosophy of history under the title, *The Drama of Humanity*. This new work will include the new picture of prehistory that is emerging following the revision of the C-14 dates after 1966, as well as the entirely new picture of the origins of modernity in the Renaissance with special emphasis on Hermeticism, Neo-Platonism, Magic, Apocalypse, and Gnosticism as compound strands in the structure of the modern west" (HI, 6:9). Voegelin told Heilman, who wrote a letter on his behalf, that he was particularly interested in establishing contacts with British "Archaeologists and prehistorians" whose expertise promised to be helpful in finishing *The Drama of Humanity*. See *Robert B. Heilman and Eric Voegelin: A Friendship in Letters*, ed. Charles R. Embry (Columbia: University of Missouri Press, 2004), 267.

has suggested.[10] More simply, as Hollweck and Caringella said, it may be questionable "whether Voegelin was a book author in the commonly used sense. His method consisted rather in working out problems in the form of reflective and meditative essays; only when the problems could be organized in meaningful clusters would he organize them into a book" (CW, 28:xv). This certainly was the case for the later volumes of *Order and History*.

For anyone seeking to analyze Voegelin's later work, his refusal to be "a book author in the commonly used sense" posed a significant problem of interpretation. In this chapter and in the next one we make the following assumptions. First, Voegelin was a philosopher who followed the unforeseeable unfolding of problems. He began his academic life as a somewhat unconventional student of *Staatslehre*; deficiencies in this tradition of German scholarship along with his forced emigration led to Voegelin transforming himself into a political scientist in the North American sense.[11] The chief result of this phase of Voegelin's life was the *History of Political Ideas* and the first three volumes of *Order and History*. Both were "books" in the conventional sense of the term. But second, his removal to Munich, and despite the administrative responsibilities he had accepted, provided an opportunity unavailable at LSU to follow the problems wherever they led. His regular return engagements at Notre Dame, which provided him with relief from administration, and notwithstanding his occasional grumpy complaints about the library facilities there, provided additional opportunities for what might be termed unencumbered research.

Voegelin himself in his time as a "book author in the commonly used sense" had observed, regarding the work of Plato and Aristotle and regarding the work of Bodin, two attributes that described his own work beginning in the late 1950s. In an offhand criticism of "the history of philosophy on the doxographic level" that drew a sharp distinction between "Platonic transcendentalism and idealism" on the one side and Aristotelian "immanentism and realism" on the other, and then further simplified these two simplifications into contrasting "metaphysical systems," Voegelin observed: "In fact, neither Plato nor Aristotle have developed systems; they were much too engrossed with the discovery of new problems" (CW, 16:328). It seems to me that during this period, Voegelin was far more en-

10 Arpad Szakolczai, *Reflexive Historical Sociology* (Florence: Routledge, 1999), 66ff.

11 I have discussed these issues in detail in *Beginning the Quest: Law and Politics in the Early Work of Eric Voegelin* (Columbia: University of Missouri Press, 2009).

grossed with the discovery of new problems than coherently presenting the results of his analysis.

As a consequence, his literary production after the late 1950s was mixed and intermittent. And as he wrote of Bodin in the *History*, each of Bodin's literary works could be understood as expressing the same principles, though the successive productions were not simply repetitions. Rather, they "laid stress on different major complexes. The result is that each of his works, as it were, has an enormous bulge" while other aspects "dwindle out of proportion, and sometimes are reduced to a few summarizing sentences" (CW, 23:185). Something similar could be said of Voegelin's later work. There were "bulges" that continued for pages and even chapters that dealt in great detail with a newly discovered problem. In short, there were unquestionably problems of style and organization in Voegelin's later work. To cope with this difficulty, which was a reflection of his having become the author of a series of meditative and reflective analytical essays published between hard covers rather than a conventional book author, we begin with an analysis of the chapter on historiogenesis rather than with the "Introduction" or the several essays published prior to the appearance of volume four.[12]

2. Historiogenesis

Before undertaking the analysis, I would make two brief additional preliminary remarks to indicate the direction of the argument. First, the *History of Political Ideas*, the study of modern Gnosticism, and the early volumes of *Order and History* all made the assumption that history was properly conceived as "a process of increasingly differentiated insight into the order of being in which man participates by his existence" (CW, 17:45). Despite some hesitations expressed in the "Introduction" to the second volume of *Order and History* in the context of Jaspers' "axis time" (CW, 15:67ff), Voegelin largely subscribed to the notion that the process of increasing differentiation and regression from maximal differentiation could be discussed adequately in terms of historical succession. In the development and elaboration of his argument regarding order and history, Voegelin encountered two problems. First, the categorization initially envisaged five historically connected types of order; but as Voegelin increasingly mastered the empirical materials, as he said to his 1967 Montreal audience, the study grew so it could easily fill six more volumes. But more important, he discovered

12 See also Michael Franz's "Editor's Introduction," CW, 17:4–17.

that the empirical types, however many they were, could not be aligned in any time sequence or "course," a term he again borrowed from Vico.[13] Even in the earlier volumes of *Order and History*, it was clear that the differentiation of Hellas and Israel were not connected on a meaningful time-line, to say nothing of the contemporary but historically unconnected Chinese differentiations.

Voegelin realized that Jaspers, along with Toynbee and their predecessors, were focused on the "spiritual outbursts" of Moses or Plato or Lao-Tse as if they were phenomena that took place in time. Not only did this conception turn time into space with images of "place" and of being "in" time, it ignored what had been for Voegelin a major methodological verity: what mattered in human order and society, the subject-matter of philosophy of history and political science, was "the structure of experiencing consciousness," which included its self-interpretation (CW, 6:33; 17:49). And inasmuch as the actual experiencing consciousnesses knew nothing of one another, how could such experiences constitute an axis-time or any other kind of time, where "time" referred to a meaningful unit of some sort? But if these "hierophantic events" were unconnected, how could they constitute a coherent story? Even more puzzling, how could these unconnected spiritual outbursts result in "a universal consciousness of humanity" that had not previously existed? An initial analysis of these questions clarified the problem sufficiently so that Voegelin understood that the fact of spiritual outbursts and their connection to an axis-time was a way of coping with a "disturbing problem," namely that there could be no meaningful structures in history that reflected parallel spiritual movements, rather than a single "development" of humanity.

A second observation: in volume four, Voegelin resumed the analysis of cosmological symbolic forms discussed in volume one. But the intervening eighteen years made a difference not only in terms of additional specialized studies, but above all in the development of Voegelin's philosophy of consciousness. The analyses in volume four were, accordingly, both more complex and more precise. Above all, Voegelin's language was less likely to be misunderstood as indicating a story of gradual improvement in a search for, and an increasingly coherent apprehension of, truth and reality. Nor, for that matter, was history a story of decline into barbarism, compactness or

13 In Voegelin's study in the *History*, he noted that Vico ran into similar problems. See CW, 24:136–48. See also my *Eric Voegelin and the Foundations of Modern Political Science* (Columbia: University of Missouri Press, 1999), 363ff.

anything similar (CW, 17:51). Before considering the question "what is history?" we need to be clear about what history is not—and that is: it is not a time-line.

Sometime in the late 1950s, likely on one of his trips to the Chicago Oriental Institute, Voegelin discovered that unilinear conceptions of history could be found in such documents of cosmological empires as the Sumerian King List. Voegelin knew of such documents when writing volume one of *Order and History* but had not recognized their significance, namely that a unilinear conception of history did not originate in Biblical religion as was conventionally maintained.[14]

Voegelin opened the first volume of *Order and History* with the memorable (and already quoted) words: "God and man, world and society form a primordial community of being" (CW, 14:39). We know this "community" and its "quaternarian structure" because, as human beings, we participate "in the mystery of its being." In his later work, Voegelin used the more precise term "primary experience of the cosmos" to indicate the primordial community of being. The stories of the cause and origin of the gods or God, of human being and of the world have conventionally been indicated by such Greek-derived terms such as theogeny, anthropogeny, and cosmogony. The term Voegelin introduced for speculation of the cause and origin of social order was historiogenesis.[15] "The symbolists who develop the type let governance spring into existence at an absolute point of origin, as part of the cosmic order itself, and from that point down they let the history of their society descend to the present in which they live" (CW, 17:108–9). The story typically began with spectacular and legendary events and ended with pragmatic history or *res gestae*. The term historiogenesis, Voegelin said, was chosen "in consideration of the Israelite symbolism, in which pragmatic history is extrapolated back to Genesis in the biblical sense" (CW, 17:109).

Within the primary experience of the cosmos, cosmogony, theogeny, and so on were not sharply distinguished because they all express "the same mystery" with respect to this "primordial community." Historiogenesis expressed this overarching mystery in terms of the equally mysterious existence of

14 CW, 14:64. Voegelin provided an abbreviated account of the origins of the innovations in volume four in his 1976 conversations with members of the Thomas More Institute in Montreal. See CW, 33:307.

15 Voegelin wrote William Havard in 1970: "You speak of my habit of indulging in neologisms. That charge has frequently been made, but I am always baffled by it. The only neologism of any importance I am aware of is the term 'historiogenesis'" (HI, 17:1).

society. Voegelin then constructed an elaborate abstract formula to express the relations of these four symbolic forms to one another (CW, 17:110–12). The four of these forms together he called the "aggregate." The importance of the aggregate in the present context was Voegelin's discovery that the symbolism was "equivalent to a speculation on the Ground of Being in the language of noetic consciousness." This equivalence, obviously, was "recognizable in retrospect from the philosopher's position," which was one attained by the more differentiated consciousness. At the same time, however, the process of differentiation from the cosmological aggregate to the noetic speculation on the Ground of Being must be based on "structures of reality apprehended implicitly but not yet fully differentiated" (CW, 17:126).

The implications of Voegelin's discovery of the equivalence of the aggregate to the philosopher's noetic tension towards the Being that is One (to use Parmenides' formulation) were important. In fact, they amounted to an elaboration of an earlier Voegelinian formula: human nature does not change but is expressed in various degrees of compactness and differentiation. To begin with, each of the elements of the aggregate contained a noetic component that could be differentiated in retrospect from the perspective of the philosopher. Second, each of the elements of the aggregate was an autonomous rational construction insofar as its noetic component extended beyond the concrete area of reality that it expressed—namely the origin and cause of the gods, humans, cosmos and society. More specifically, historiogenesis was to be understood "as an autonomous symbolism emerging from the cooperation of pragmatic historiography with mythopoesis and noetic speculation'" (CW, 17:112). The mythical part of the historiogenetic speculation was not mere fantasy "but an attempt to present the reasons that will raise the *res gestae* of the pragmatic part to the rank of history" (CW, 17:113). That is, within the symbolism of the cosmological aggregate, historiogenesis was rational.

Several additional implications followed. First, the historiogenetic authors had criteria of relevance that led them to use what they quite well knew were mythical causes and origins of the *res gestae* of existing societies. Second, historiogenesis, within the aggregate of the cosmological myth, was equivalent to later kinds of historiography. Third, the pragmatic history that constituted the contents of historiogenesis was also subordinated to the cosmological myth, which was the reason why it only appeared explicitly to the more differentiated consciousness of the philosopher. Accordingly, "mythopoesis and noesis combine into a formative unit that holds an intermediate position between cosmological compactness and noetic differentiation. It will suitably be called mytho-speculation, i.e., a speculation within the medium of the myth" (CW, 17:113).

Voegelin used terms such as historiogenesis and mytho-speculation on the basis of his analysis of the primary experience of the cosmos, which in turn was expressed abstractly as the "aggregate." Voegelin's description of the cosmological myth in volume one of *Order and History* was reiterated in volume four, though the emphasis was different.

First, as in volume one, the cosmos was experienced neither as a world of objects of cognition nor the product created by the act of a world-transcendent God. It was what the Greeks called *to pan*, the whole, which included earth and heaven, stars and planets, the seasons and the rhythms of plant and animal life, life and death, and the plenitude of gods and spirits. The latter point, the intracosmic presence of the divine reality, cannot be overstressed inasmuch as it implied that the difference between polytheism and monotheism was secondary. Equally important, all the "things" of the cosmos formed mutual analogies for one another. It was as though everything mediated everything else as a cosmic "In-Between." Likewise the "consubstantiality" of the things of the cosmos emphasized the subordination of pragmatic history to the cosmological myth. Thus imperial rulers acted by virtue of their divine mandate and their success or failure was a result of divine dispensation.

Granted that the things of the cosmos were consubstantial, Voegelin drew attention to what had previously eluded his analysis: the cosmos was itself not a thing among other things but "the background of reality against which all existent things exist; it has reality in the mode of non-existence" (CW, 17:122). A couple of pages later Voegelin said this "background reality" was "a sort of matrix of existence" that could not, therefore, itself be an existent thing (CW, 17:124). In other words, within the form of the cosmological myth, the mutual analogies of beings could not point to, or be resolved by, a being (or Being) beyond the cosmos. Subject however to the noetic component of the aggregate, the complex of mutual analogies did evoke a sense of the mystery of existence of things somehow persisting above the abyss of nonexistence. This experience Voegelin identified as "the tension of existence out of nonexistence" (CW, 17:123). Perhaps more importantly, Voegelin now detected this tension *within* the cosmological myth, an insight that, even if he had been aware of it, he nevertheless had not previously emphasized.

Within the cosmological myth, therefore, the task of cosmogonic rituals expanded: they both expressed and overcame the sense that the cosmos was threatened by destruction. Thus the primary experience of the cosmos included the experience of the cosmos as existing on the edge of nonexistence. Experience of the mystery of being, and of the anxiety that accompanied the experience, seemed to Voegelin to be coeval with human existence. The source of this anxiety was the noetic element of consciousness that was always aware of instability within the compact mode of cosmological symbolization. The apprehension that existing forms of symbolization were not adequate to experiential reality became visible within the cosmological form by means of: (1) a search for mytho-speculative answers; and (2) the appearance of a variety of distinct kinds of time—rhythmic, linear, infinite and cyclical—as a way of dealing with, which is to say, both expressing and mitigating, anxieties connected to the problem of the nonexistent Ground. That is, even prior to the process of differentiation occurring in somebody's consciousness and discerned retrospectively from, for example, the perspective of the philosopher, the pressure of reality ensured that the compression of existence and nonexistence into intracosmic things by way of mutual analogies was sensed or apprehended as being vaguely unsatisfactory. This was a new insight.

As an example of the search for mytho-speculative answers and of the inadequacy of results, Voegelin used the familiar case of the kingship symbolized as a cosmological analogue mediated by, for example, the celestial universe and the intracosmic gods. But such a two-tiered arrangement also meant that, in order to assume the function of the nonexistent Ground, the celestial universe and the gods were somehow "more cosmic" than the king, human beings, and society. Thus reality required that the consubstantial intracosmic things be disrupted and formed into a hierarchy. But, Voegelin said, the astrophysical universe was still too much of an existent thing to serve as the nonexistent Ground, and the gods were too nonexistent to have any intracosmic presence. Thus, "there become visible the lines along which the cosmological style will crack until the cosmos dissociates into a dedivinized external world and a world-transcendent God" (CW, 17:127).

Even before the cosmological style cracked, instability or tensions were apparent both to those who lived within the cosmological myth and from the perspective of the philosopher. From within the cosmological style, reality was experienced either as a whole that expressed the nonexistent Divine Ground as a vague and inadequately symbolized presence or it was expressed as a manifold of existent things in tension from or toward the nonexistent Ground, which was invariably accompanied by a sense of anxiety. This was why mytho-speculations extrapolated areas of intracosmic things toward the Ground of their being by telling the story of their genesis from an absolute beginning, as in historiogenesis. However, the creators of, for example, the Sumerian King Lists, were very much aware that they had distorted the historical record to create a smooth integration of the present and of the present political order with the order of the cosmos. That is, they, no less than Hegel and Marx indulged in "metastatic magic" by "eclipsing the disturbing reality by projecting an imaginary second reality on a timeless line of time that comes to its end in the everlasting meaning of the authors' present" (CW, 17:113). Moreover, the creators of the King List were aware of their own distortions because the presence of the noetic element, as yet undifferentiated within the cosmological aggregate.

A similar instability to that created by mytho-speculation took the form of speculation on the variety of times. If one understood time to be the lasting of reality, then the modes of time would be as varied as the modes of reality experienced: the time of *to pan*, prior to the differentiation into existent things and the nonexistent Ground, was not that of its constituent elements, nor was that of biological evolution that of history, or the seasons that of political action—and so on. In other words, the time of a cycle was no more cyclical than the time of vegetative rhythms was rhythmical—or the time of unilinear history was linear. "By using the adjectives to denote modes of time, we do no more than acknowledge the diversification of reality as extending to the modes of lasting particular to each variant of reality." Even so, these diverse modes of lasting were not random, disordered, and arbitrary, but "partners in the reality of the cosmos" and their relations were governed by their participation in the reality of *to pan*. Moreover, we are able to understand the hierarchy of the order of the modes of lasting by means of a calendar that related them to the time of the celestial cycles, which "appear to be the very time of their own reality" and could be expressed in numbers (CW, 17:133–34).

In addition to what might be termed these spiritual challenges to the cosmological myth expressed in various anxieties and speculative attempts to deal with them, there were more straightforward political challenges. The assumption sustaining a stable cosmological civilization was that only in the form of an empire attuned to the cosmos could human beings live in the truth of their humanity under the gods. When, inevitably, the empire was attacked or suffered some other kind of calamity and disorder, the social and political breakdown "entails more than murderous unpleasantness." It was a "spiritual catastrophe" because the individual tension toward the nonexistent Ground as the source of order had not yet been sufficiently differentiated. As a consequence, pragmatic events, Voegelin's "murderous unpleasantness," were understood as the displeasure, indifference, anger, etc. of the gods. Put negatively, there was no room for a classic or Christian notion of human nature independent of the cosmological empire, "nor is there an opening yet for tension between the dimensions of man's existence as the *zoon noetikon* and *zoon politikon*" (CW, 17, 147). When nevertheless political catastrophe occurred, given that the existence of the empire was tied to cosmic rhythms, the possibility arose that, if empires could dissolve, perhaps even the cosmos was doomed. More positively, the anxiety induced by the consideration of cosmic political instability opened the possibility of a truth about God and history beyond the truth of imperial order as a cosmic analogue.

That such a possibility was actualized in philosophy and revelation may be taken as given in light of the arguments provided in above chapters three and four. In volume four of *Order and History*, however, Voegelin stressed the durability of historiogenesis as the cosmological style of truth, notwithstanding its basic instability and inherent bad faith. The two aspects of the break with the historiogenetic cosmological empires that Voegelin emphasized in volume four were not distinguished in volume one. On the one hand, it was possible to break with the imperial form as did the Israelites. However, notwithstanding the immediacy of God's revelation to Moses in the thornbush episode and Sinai, which ended the position of the ruler of the cosmological empire, "Pharaoh," as the mediator between divine and human order, those events were integrated as elements in the historiogenesis of the Israelites as a Chosen People. As we saw in chapter three, not even the later prophets broke with this historiogenetic and so cosmological, form.

On the other hand, the Greek differentiation appeared to proceed independently of the political order of empire. Even so, Hesiod's story of the ages of the world, Herodotus' extensive survey, and even Thucydides' "archaeology" could be understood as historiogenetic myths. The first, Hesiod's, was written in response to a personal threat but was representative of the Greek "dark ages." Herodotus wrote in response to the threat posed by imperial Persia to Hellenic society, and Thucydides dealt with the aftermath of the Persian wars, the great *kinesis* that threatened to destroy Hellas from within. That is, all three were written in response to the murderous unpleasantness of a general political-cosmic disorder—from the small town of Hesiod's Ascra to the entire world and then to the *acme* of humanity. The latter two, Herodotus and Thucydides, conventionally called historians, wrote their histories in response, specifically, to the actions and consequences of the expansive Persian empire, a fact of considerable significance for the argument of *The Ecumenic Age*.

Two final remarks concerning this new symbolism. First, once Voegelin recognized the autonomy of historiogenetic symbolism, it proved to be of great importance. Indeed, its 4000 years of existence turned it into a "millennial constant" (CW, 17:117). Second, historiogenetic symbolisms were tied to the societies in which they developed so that, when those societies were destroyed by the imperial power organizations that succeeded the specific societies, they then engaged in what Voegelin called "historiomachy" to see who was the oldest and so the "true" representative of humanity. On its own, historiomachy was "unprofitable," not to say comic. It did, however, compel the participants to familiarize themselves with one another's historiography—for polemic purposes, it was true. Even so, their historiomachic efforts established the basis for a history and chronography of the Ancient Near East and Mediterranean basin. "With the new chronographic genus of literature . . . we have reached the point at which the problems of historiogenesis change over into those of the genesis of world history" (CW, 17:166).

In this section we have often drawn attention to the implications of Voegelin's argument even while remaining fairly close to its development. We conclude this section with a synopsis, which Voegelin never made in so many words.

Historiogenesis connects the always precarious present political order to the mystery of existence out of nothing by postulating the fabulous origins of social and political order at the beginning of the cosmos. But there was always Marx's question: what happened before the origin of the cosmos? It will be recalled from the analysis in chapter two that Marx prohibited that question and by so doing also expressed a fundamental anxiety. Voegelin had shown that, within the cosmological form there was only the cosmos expressed by the aggregate of symbolic forms. There was no cosmic-transcendent origin but only a field of non-existence that was not (yet) a cosmic origin or a beyond—not that a cosmic origin or a beyond furnished an explanation so much as more adequate expression of a mystery, and mysteries are by nature inexplicable.

Another way of expressing the experience of reality as "cosmos" was to say, as Voegelin put it, that the experience was "tensionally closed." He meant by this term that the Ground of existing things was neither itself a thing nor a transcendent non-existent non-thing. And yet in reality it was evident from the more differentiated position of philosophy, tensional closure was fundamentally unstable "because the tension in reality between existence and nonexistence though experienced as real" within the cosmological style of symbolism, "does not become sufficiently articulate." Eventually what was "apprehended implicitly" became explicit and the tension toward the nonexistent Ground became differentiated in the human experience of reality (CW, 17:126–27).

At the center of the historiogenetic experience, whether Sumerian or Marxist, was anxiety. The authors of the symbolism wanted to show that what made the pragmatic historical materials worthy of transmission to posterity was their connection (through a fabulous act of mythopoesis) to the creation and unfolding of the order of the cosmos. "Anxiety," Voegelin wrote, and we reproduced as the epigraph to this study, "is the response to the mystery of existence out of nothing. The search for order is the response to anxiety" (CW, 28:71). Finally, cosmological order was plausible so long as it did not break down into "murderous unpleasantness." When it did, then to the anxiety about the origin of the cosmos and about the origin of social and political order was added the sense that the order of the cosmos itself was unstable. Such a spiritual and pragmatic social and political disintegration characterized the Ecumenic Age, to which we now turn.

3. The Ecumenic Age

Much of volume four of *Order and History* continued the chronological sequence that ended volume three. The "ecumenic age" referred to the period from the rise of the Persian around the eighth century BC to the fall of the Roman Empire around the eighth century AD (CW, 12:98). It constituted an "epoch" because these empires overwhelmed the two societies, the Israelite and the Hellenic, that had nourished the differentiated truth of existence achieved by philosophers and prophets—or as Voegelin said with increasing frequency, through the differentiation of pneumatic and noetic consciousness—beyond that gained in the cosmological empires. The fact that "the pragmatic order of history did not go the way of [the] spiritual order" of Israel and Hellas raised two new questions: (1) was the attempt at forming societies in accord with the truth of existence, as in Israel and Hellas, simply crushed by the new imperial powers or did the attempt fail for some other reason? And (2) did these new imperial powers belong to the same category as the earlier Near Eastern cosmological empires against which Israel and Hellas distinguished themselves and differentiated the truth of existence? In short, was there anything new about these imperial powers?

The short answer to these questions was: first, the "insight that concrete societies organized for action in pragmatic history were no proper vessels for the realization of transcendent order at all," was apparent both to Isaiah and to Plato. Accordingly, the new empires were not the agents that brought the realization that no finite society could properly represent the now differentiated truth of existence.[16] That insight had already been gained by the initial "leap in being" achieved by the prophets and philosophers. Moreover, the correlate, that universal humanity was distinct from the parochial humanity of specific concrete societies, seemed to imply that a plurality of societies had to be included if universal humanity were ever to achieve its adequate symbolic form. With that second insight, Voegelin said, appeared the "faint outlines" of "the fundamental division of spiritual and temporal order" (CW, 17:168–69). Not until St. Augustine wrote *The City of God*, however, "was a symbolism found that integrated the pragmatic and spiritual orders into a whole meaning, at least after a fashion, at least for Western civilization, at least for a time" (CW, 17:202). The weak point in Augustine's formulation, indicated by the qualifications quoted in the previous sentence could now be specified. It was not the "intermingling" of the two cities in history nor was it his extension of Plato's argument regarding eros, namely the two cities expressing two loves—of self to contempt of God or of God to contempt of self. Rather, Augustine's limitation was his subordination of "these great insights to a historiogenetic pattern whose unilinear history came to a meaningful end in the dual ecumenism of the Church and the Roman empire" (CW, 17:230). The historiogenetic form, that is, was incapable of accommodating the enlarged historical knowledge that inevitably accumulated over time. This was evident to Voegelin in the *History of Political Ideas*, as well as in *The New Science of Politics* (CW, 5:154ff, 176f; CW, 19:206ff), though he used less specific language there to indicate the limitation of Augustine's symbolism.

As to the second question, whether the new empires were of the same type as the older cosmological empires of the Ancient Near East, the answer was already clear: no, they were not. Conventionally historians discussed the Persian, Macedonian, and Roman empires as if they were akin to the Egyptian or Babylonian. However, in none of the latter conquests did the

16 For a solid commonsensical analysis of Voegelin's discussion of ecumenic empire, see, Geoffrey Barraclough, "Eric Voegelin and the Theory of Imperialism," in *The Philosophy of Order: Essays on History, Consciousness and Politics for Eric Voegelin on his Eightieth Birthday* (Stuttgart: Klett-Cotta, 1981), 173–89.

victors organize a Persian, Macedonian, or Roman society. They were all multi-society or multi-civilizational power organizations. Indeed, the Romans could not even produce a succession of Italian emperors. Accordingly, "the empire as an enterprise of institutional power . . . had separated from the organization of a concrete society and could be imposed as a form on the remnants of societies no longer capable of self-organization" (CW, 17:170, 271; cf. CW, 19:87–146).

Together, these two developments suggested a "curious convergence of trends" (CW, 17:170). On the one hand, the spiritual communities that maintained the experiences of revelation and philosophy tended to separate from the surrounding societies—as "schools" or "prophetic" organizations, for example—and the imperial organizations embarked on indefinite expansion without reference to existing societies. On the one side, the universality of spiritual order seemed to reach out towards the whole of humanity and on the other, the new empires seemed to seek to expand over the whole of humanity. In both cases the meaningfulness of specific concrete societies such as Israel or Hellas or many others was eclipsed by the importance of the new spiritual communities such as Christianity. In keeping with the principle that "the self-interpretation of a society is part of the reality or its order" (CW, 17:175), one could properly describe this convergence of trends as constituting the new epoch.[17]

Relying chiefly on Polybius, Voegelin argued that the *ecumene* was conceived not as a subject of order but as an object to be conquered. It was initially the inhabited world, then the known world—that is, an object of exploration, as it tended to become at the end of Alexander's anabasis—and finally it referred to the legal jurisdiction of Rome. It was never however a "self-organizing society" so that, while one can speak of an "Ecumenic Age," referring to the existence of imperial power organizations dominating several distinct societies, one cannot speak of an "Ecumenic Society." The

17 Voegelin's description of the expansion of ecumenic empires as limitless power organizations bore a remarkable resemblance to Hannah Arendt's discussion of nineteenth-century European imperialism, the meaning of which was summarized in Cecil Rhodes' remark, "I would annex the planets if I could." See Arendt, *The Origins of Totalitarianism*, new ed. (New York: Harcourt Brace and World, 1966), Part II, 121ff. Voegelin noted the resemblance as well in his 1961 Stevenson Memorial Lecture at the Royal Institute of International Affairs; see CW, 11:140. One of the implications, to be discussed at the end of this chapter, is that human beings still exist at least in some respects within the epoch constituted by Voegelin's "Ecumenic Age."

reason was obvious enough: conquest was exodus. In order to conquer one must leave home, both literally and figuratively. Voegelin, following Herodotus who first formulated the problem in terms of the envy of the gods, called such expansion a "concupiscential exodus from reality" undertaken behind the apparently realistic project of ecumenic conquest (CW, 17:188, 240). Such an enterprise could be conducted only if a concupiscential conqueror was willing to leave home literally. The ecumene therefore advanced or diminished according to the expansion or contraction of imperial power.

The search for spiritual order did not end with the annihilation of specific societies by the conquest nor was it to be found in the apparently meaningless acts of conquest.[18] Here Voegelin introduced the term "ecumenic religions" to describe the new spiritual communities established by the evangelism of Paul, Mani, and Mohammed. It was evidently not enough to observe, as did Polybius, the extraordinary large-scale nature of events—a sentiment that was strongly felt in Herodotus and Thucydides as well.[19] Those who underwent the events were compelled to reflect on their own position as participants in the process. By Voegelin's analysis, Paul, Mani, and Mohammed, no less than Anaximander, Plato, Aristotle and Augustine, were concerned with what Voegelin called a "spiritual exodus" (CW, 17:188ff).

The relation between concupiscential expansion and spiritual exodus constituted, he said, the great issue of the Ecumenical Age. From the side of conquest the problem was obvious: there were pragmatic limits to the limitless desire to conquer. The pretense of unlimited expansion was

18 Central here was the evidence of the report of Polybius that the victor over Carthage, Scipio Aemilianus, gripped Polybius' hand in fear and said, "A glorious moment Polybius; but I have a dread foreboding that someday the same doom will be pronounced on my own country" (*The Histories*, 37:20). Appian, *Punica*, 132, reported that Scipio wept and "was seen weeping for his enemies." He recollected the fate of Troy, the Assyrians, the Medes, Persians, and Macedonians. See Ernest Barker, *From Alexander to Constantine: Passages and Documents Illustrating the History of Social and Political Ideas, 336 B.C.–A.D. 337* (Oxford: Clarendon, 1956), 121ff. In a similar vein, after marching nearly 12,000 miles over eight years, Alexander's army had had enough upon reaching the river Beas in northern India. See Robin Lane Fox, *Alexander the Great* (London: Allen Lane, 1973), 368ff.

19 In "What is History?" an unpublished essay written around 1963, Voegelin argued that the beginning of a Herodotean inquiry (*historia*) that eventually turned into a Thucydidean write-up (*syngraphe*) of a historiographic text, as with Polybius, was the encounter of a concrete human being with a disturbance that the person involved considered worthy of remembrance. See CW, 28:10ff.

contradicted or "embarrassed" by actual limits—or what amounted to the same thing, by a refusal of an army far from home to keep going unto the ends of the earth. "The experience of this untenable result," Voegelin said, "prepares the situation in which the ecumenic rulers become ready to associate their empire with an ecumenic religion in order to channel the meaning of a spiritual exodus into a concupiscential expansion that has become flagrantly nonsensical" (CW, 17:258). The nonsensical element of the entire enterprise was obvious in commonsense terms as a futile quest to reach the ultimate horizon beyond which was supposed to be found the divine source of human universality.[20] In short, you can't get there from here.

The effort was not entirely a waste of time, however, because the failure of concupiscential expansion was followed by a retraction in alliance with a consciousness of universal humanity as found in the aforementioned universal religions. The actual ecumene was the habitat of human beings within the horizon of the cosmos. Or again, in commonsensical terms, if you succeeded in exploring the ecumene to its end, you end up where you began for the obvious reason that the shape of the actual ecumene is a sphere. As a result, the successful concupiscential explorer (or one reflecting on the achievements of the age of exploration) was compelled to acknowledge the mystery of the distinction between the ecumene and the cosmos.[21] Nothing could be changed by exploring space and annexing the planets (see also CW, 11:140).

Even when ecumenic rulers succeeded in associating their power organization with an ecumenic religious movement, there were problems with the complex synthesis. Granted, there was an "affinity of meaning" that connected empires claiming to organize humanity under one umbrella of administrative authority with spiritual outbursts that also claimed to represent humanity (CW, 11:136). Granted, in short, there was something to Jaspers'

20 A modern version was Khrushchev's remark that Yuri Gagarin went into space but didn't see God.

21 In this context, Thomas More's *Utopia* reflected an "intermediate situation" where his fictional wanderer, Raphael Hythlodaeus, whose name meant one "well-learned in nonsense," and who was said to have accompanied Amerigo Vespucci on his last three voyages to the New World, explained that he (like More himself) was at much at home in one place as in another since everywhere was equidistant from heaven. That is, the end of the journey lay beyond the world and wandering the world led not to any somewhere but to Utopia, which is to say, to Nowhere. See CW, 17:141; 22:109ff. See also St. Thomas More, *Utopia*, ed. Edward Surtz and J. H. Hexter (New Haven: Yale University Press, 1965), xviii, 301–3.

axial age inasmuch as the several world empires existed from Atlantic to Pacific at the same time as the spiritual outbursts.[22] Not that there was a causal connection between these phenomena (CW, 17:204), but that, taken together, they constituted a configuration of history (CW, 12:95ff; 28:37–42). Voegelin was quite clear about what was involved on the imperial side: "a power organization, informed by the pathos of representative humanity, and therefore representative of mankind—that would be the core, as it emerged from the historical phenomena, of a definition of world-empire" (CW, 11:136–37).

To achieve a similar precision from the side of the spiritual outbursts required a more detailed analysis. The problem centered on the meaning of the term "world," which "presents extraordinary difficulties to philosophical analysis" (CW, 11:142). In both ancient and modern usage "world" included the element of territory and persons living on it, but also the notion of an all-pervading order. In the classical sense the emphasis, as we have seen, was on the visible and external cosmic order. In Christian usage the accent lay more on the internal order of the person. The differences in meaning, Voegelin said, "apparently reflect the actual historical process in which the experience of human existence under a world-transcendent God has differentiated from the primary, more compact existence in a cosmos that includes both gods and men" (CW, 11:144). That is, the spiritual outbursts involve the differentiation of consciousness discussed above in chapter three.

The implication for a world-empire was that the element of a "world" implied more than the imperial dominion over territory and human beings. Here Voegelin closely paraphrased the opening words of the *History of Political Ideas*, written in 1940: "To establish an empire is an essay in world creation, reaching through all the levels of the hierarchy of being" (CW, 11:145; cf. 19:225). The essay in world creation was always related to the invisible order insofar as it was also an evocation of true existence within the world. "The character of an evocation attuned to the 'unseen measure' makes a human imperial creation analogically commensurate with the world, [and] endows it with the sense of a 'world'" (CW, 11:145).

Returning to the example of Polybius, while it was true that he wrote the history of a Rome that aimed at the rule of the ecumene, the story of

22 See Peter Wagner, "Palomar's Questions: The Axial Age, Hypothesis, European Modernity and Historical Contingency," in Johann P. Arnason, S. N. Eisenstadt, and Björn Wittrock, eds., *Axial Civilizations and World History* (Leiden: Brill, 2005), 87–106.

Scipio at Carthage indicated that even the telos of empire was senseless. Scipio's difficulty could therefore be specified more closely: on the one hand he recollected the cosmic rhythms of rise and fall, but on the other he rejected the cosmological rhythms in favor of a *telos* that, so to speak, cut across them (CW, 17:230). Such a position was necessarily inconclusive, not to say conflicted and even incoherent. In this context, the Gospel of Matthew (24:14) provided a solution: "And this gospel of the kingdom shall be preached in all the world [*ecumene*] for a witness to all nations; and then the end [*telos*] shall come." This new missionary order, Voegelin said, "sounds like a deliberate literary answer (although it hardly can be one) to Polybius" (CW, 11:151). That is, Saint Matthew declared that the telos of the ecumene was that it be filled with the Gospel, which is to say the telos of human action again lay beyond the world. In commonsensical language, one might say that the Ecumenic Age witnessed the dissociation of the primary experience of the cosmos into the opacity of concupiscential expansion and the luminosity of spiritual outbursts. However, there would always be those who would wonder if the dissociation was complete. Once the Gospel had filled the ecumene, what then?

With Matthew, the immediate reference to the apocalyptic expectations of Daniel (24:15ff) indicated that expectations of a new world were entirely in order. Voegelin said that Matthew's expectations amounted to "a metastasis, a new disposition in which there will be no problems of world-empires" (CW, 17:151). Like all metastatic expectations, it bought its own problems when the future ecumene did not show up on time—or, to date, not at all. In some of the passages of Saint Paul, for example, the penetration of the ecumene by the Gospel was quickly to be followed by the return of Christ and the elevation of ecumenical humanity to the Kingdom of God. As these expectations faded with time, the ecumene tended to become more purely spiritual and signify a humanity that received the Word. In other passages the ecumene tended to signify the institutionalized Church that continued its worldly existence under the protection of an empire (CW, 11:115). Such a compromise was inevitable inasmuch as metastatic faith invariably was eventually contradicted by the nonapocalyptic structure of history.

In "World Empire and the Unity of Mankind" (1962), Voegelin summarized his enquiry as follows: imperial organizations as attempts to represent humanity began with the cosmological imperial organizations of Mesopotamia and Egypt. As discussed above, the universal order was expressed by the myth of the cosmos. The second form, the ecumenic empire, gained a new truth of human existence but imperial order tended to become ecumenically expansive and only tentatively connected to an ecumenic religion that endowed the empire with the characteristics of a world insofar as the religion evoked the participation of human order in transcendent being. Ecumenic empires, furthermore, have been succeeded by "orthodox" empires where the association of imperial power and a religious world was "understood as a necessity" and became "stabilized over long periods" (CW, 11:154). In turn, the orthodox empires, by which were meant the Western European Latin Christian empire, the Eastern Greek Christian empire, the Islamic empire and the Far-Eastern Neo-Confucian empire, have been succeeded by the several national empires, starting in the eleventh century in the West, leading to such splendid power organizations as the Hapsburg Empire, a French, a Dutch, and a British Empire as well as such oddities as a post-imperial empire founded by Bokassa I in the Central African Republic. In turn these imperial entities, following the "global revolution of modernity" that also originated in the West and that has derailed on the one hand into the Gnostic *libido dominandi* and on the other into an "intramundane apocalypse," have resulted in ideological empires along the lines of liberal gradualist and revolutionary Marxist second realities (CW, 33:314).

The futility of the Gnostic enterprise has already been discussed. The futility of an intramundane apocalypse, which prohibited participation in the order of world-transcendent Being, was self-evident. Any intramundane apocalyptic efforts to transform the ecumene into a world were doomed before they commenced. "What can be achieved is only the apocalyptic concentration camp," which was obviously not a world either (CW, 11:154–55). About all that can be said of the "lethal stupidity" of such developments was that they may have a cathartic function insofar as they made abundantly clear to non-philosophers what philosophers already knew:

> That mankind is more than the global collective of human beings living at the same time. Mankind is the society of man in history, extending in time from its unknown origin toward its unknown future. Moreover, no crosscut at any time represents mankind by virtue of a common power organization. For the living can represent mankind universally only by their representative humanity; and their humanity is representative only when it is oriented toward the eschatological *telos*. Organization, to be sure, is necessary to the existence of man and society in this world, but no organization can organize mankind—even global ecumenicity of organization is not universality. The dream of

> representing universal order through the world of empire has come to its end when the meaning of universal order as the order of history under God has come into view. (CW, 11:155)

Voegelin's conclusion was that a five-thousand-year effort at trying to represent humanity by means of a finite organization in the present was over (see also CW, 17:272–73).

4. Exodus

The next two chapters in *The Ecumenic Age*, on "Conquest and Exodus" and "The Pauline Vision of the Resurrected," according to Caringella as reported by Franz in his editor's introduction, "originated as a single chapter that required division after it grew too long. This was a significant point. The two chapters should be read as a unit because a different light would fall on Voegelin's account of Paul if it were "regarded as an extension of the theme of conquest and exodus," rather than, presumably, some sort of Voegelinian "position" with respect to "Christianity."[23] We will have occasion to discuss some of the critical responses to Voegelin's alleged position with respect to Christianity in chapter eight. The consideration that the two chapters constitute a unit made sense so long as we recall Voegelin's interpretive principle: that analysis was concerned with experiences of convergent meaning as those experiences had become conscious during the Ecumenic Age and remained a constant in Western history ever since. "An analytically valid answer can be found only by referring the symbols of conquest and exodus back to the process of reality from which they emerge and to the experiences of the process which they try to articulate" (CW, 17:277). In particular an adequate interpretation would be sensitive to the problem of "convergent meaning."

The pragmatic conquest of the ecumene was connected to the spiritual exodus from the cosmological form insofar as the conquest proved to be both incomplete and pointless. Repeatedly, equivalent symbolisms manifested but did not resolve a convergence of conquest and exodus that was never final. Conquest and exodus, Voegelin said, "are movements *within* reality" even though the symbolism of movement pointed to a beyond of reality (CW, 17:278). Such a formulation may be paradoxical but it was not

23 CW, 17:23–24. The two chapters together fill 65 pages. The chapter on Historiogenesis is 58 pages and Voegelin's Introduction is 62 pages.

meaningless because, as noted above, "reality is not a field of homogeneous extension but is aetiologically and directionally structured" or "articulated," following Anaximander, whose symbolism featured prominently in Voegelin's analysis, into the nonexistent *Apeiron* (the Boundless) on the one hand and existent things on the other. The "things" necessarily "perish into that from which they were born; for they pay one another the penalty for their injustice according to the ordinance of Time" (Anax., A9, B1). Anaximander's insight, Voegelin said, symbolized "what may be called the tragic experience of history" (CW, 17:233). In Voegelin's own language, "things" did not exist on their own but from the Ground to which they returned. Thus to exist meant to participate in the *Apeiron*, which was timeless, and to participate in the succession of "things" as the appearance in time of the *Apeiron*. Reality, in short, was to be experienced as existent and as nonexistent, and the truth of the process was that it was in-between the two. This structure of reality was constant so that subsequent analyses, which attended to the several elements in detail, must presuppose the compact Anaximandrian linguistic formulation as the context of the later analyses. By the same token, even prior to Anaximander's linguistic formulation of the insight, human beings experienced reality as existent and nonexistent. In short: things always came into being and perished, which was what Voegelin meant by a "constant."

To avoid misunderstanding, Voegelin added: the nonexistence of the process was not an "absolute" truth of some sort, or a piece of sentimentality about the vanity of all things under the sun, but a discovery by a consciousness that reflected on the process of reality. For the philosophers, starting with Anaximander, the truth was and remained experienced as a search for the Ground of existence, because the *Apeiron* remained as mysterious after Anaximander's formulation as it was before. Voegelin connected Anaximander's formula to a remark of Augustine in his *Expositions on the Psalms*. There Augustine identified the love of God as the "existential exodus from the pragmatic world of power" as constituting the meaning of existence (CW, 17:230; cf. CW, 12:78ff). There is no reason not to expect to find equivalent pre-Anaximandrian formulas once we know what to look for. The truth of the process of reality, Voegelin said, revealed itself to consciousness (or is revealed to consciousness) where human beings were open to the mystery in which they participated by their existence; their openness to reality, moreover, permitted the reality of the process to inform their consciousness—or, in Voegelin's imagery, the reality of the process became "luminous in their consciousness" (CW, 17:243).

Again to forestall misunderstanding, Voegelin provided an exegesis of the report by Socrates in Plato's *Symposium* of his conversation with Diotima. The "truth" Socrates received on this (fictional) occasion many years before and retold third hand, was not information about reality but an event where the process of reality became aware of itself or "luminous" to itself in the soul, the psyche, or consciousness of the philosopher. Just as there was no information about reality lying around to be investigated, neither was there a cognitive relation between consciousness and the truth of reality that articulated itself (or was luminous) in the consciousness of the philosopher. Rather, there was a participation by consciousness in the truth of reality and that participation was understood by consciousness as a meaningful event in history. That is, the philosopher's insight, not the process of conquest, was historically meaningful.

Within the Anaximandrian symbolism human beings experienced themselves between the two modes of things and of the *Apeiron* in a "metaxic" or In-Between reality. Obviously, because the existing "things" appeared from, and returned to, the nonexistent *Apeiron*, the latter was ranked as "more real," because more durable than the generated and perishing things, a formulation Voegelin discussed as early as volume one. Consciousness of this metaxic reality, the *conditio humana*, to repeat, was not perceptual or cognitive but a participatory process in which reality became aware of itself or "luminous to itself" along with an awareness of its movement in the direction of the whole of reality and not in the direction of either of the two modes. In this context, "conquest and exodus symbolize enterprises of participation in the directional flux of reality" as a whole or of "eminent reality" as Voegelin on this occasion called it. That meant, as enterprises of participation "there is no question of a conquest of, or exodus from, reality" (CW, 17:279). What was manifest to consciousness was a tension within the process of reality that exhibited the structure just indicated.

In *Anamnesis*, Voegelin discussed this problem of In-Between reality in the context of Aristotle's *Metaphysics*, which added an "internal" dimension to this framework or structure. A human being, Aristotle said, began to philosophize in a state of wonder and perplexity (*aporon*). He was aware of his ignorance (*oietai agnoein*), from which arose a desire to know, starting with simple things but then to know about greater matters as well and finally to know about the Ground of Being (*arche*) (*Meta*., 982b18–23). Later in book lambda (*Meta*., 1972a26ff), Aristotle divided the search (*zetesis*) for the Ground of Being into two components, desiring the goal, the arche, and knowing it. That is, so far as the arche, the Ground of Being, was concerned, the desired and known were related. Accordingly, "the quest [i.e., zetesis] is not a blind desiring but contains the component of knowing [so that] we may characterize it as a knowing quest of a questioning knowledge," which is to say the desiring to know is already given direction and a kind of content insofar as it is attracted to the Ground (CW, 6:347).

To anyone familiar with conventional interpretations of Aristotle's "metaphysics," which was conventionally held to be the content to the *Metaphysics*, Voegelin's interpretation was remarkable.[24] But, as was mentioned above, Voegelin considered that Plato and Aristotle, "were far too engrossed with the discovery of new problems" to elaborate any "metaphysics" let alone a "metaphysical system," an observation that obviously applied as well to Veogelin (CW, 16:328). This is one reason why he restated his discoveries inasmuch as they appeared from different starting points. His purpose in so doing was to illuminate the "same" experiential reality that eventually could be expressed only by using paradoxical language. Repetition, overlap, and restatement appeared to be inevitable. As we shall see, for example, his discussion of *metalepsis* drew attention to his revisions of the earlier symbolism of the "leap in being." Likewise he formulated the differences between the noetic exegesis of Plato and Aristotle with the pneumatic symbolism of the Gospel in several different, but equivalent, ways.

To return to the exegesis of Aristotle, Voegelin next reversed his interpretation of these two passages from the *Metaphysics*, summarizing them by moving from the results to the motivation:

> Without the *kinesis* of being attracted by the Ground, there would be no desire for the Ground. Without desiring, in turn, there would be no questioning in confusion, and without questioning in confusion, there would be no awareness of ignorance. There could be no unknowing anxiety, from which rises the quest for the Ground, if the anxiety itself did not already manifest man's knowing that his existence is grounded in a Ground of Being that is not man himself. This directional factor of

24 Voegelin pointed out, however, that the term and the title of Aristotle's book were not Aristotle's. According to Plutarch (*Sulla*) the title was bestowed by Andronicus of Rhodes on the books organized in Sulla's library as the volume *meta ta physica*, the book "after the *Physics*" of Aristotle. To St. Thomas must be given the responsibility or blame of turning Aristotle's noetic exegesis into "metaphysics." See CW, 6:391–92.

> knowledge, which is present in the tension of consciousness towards the Ground, Aristotle calls *nous*. (CW, 6:347)

Aristotle then summarized the exegesis of the noetic desire for the Ground and of the being-attracted-by-the-Ground by the symbol of mutual participation, *metalepsis* (cf. CW, 30:557). The human noetic quest and the Ground that provided direction for it were tensionally connected insofar as they participated in one another.

> On the part of the human *nous* the knowing questioning and the questioning knowledge, that is, the noetic act (*noesis*), is a knowing participation in the Ground of Being; the noetic participation, however, is possible by virtue of the preceding genetic participation of the Divine in the human *nous*. (CW, 6:348)

In volume four of *Order and History* Voegelin resumed his discussion of metalepsis.[25] The word of the prophet, for example, "can be indiscriminately said to be spoken by the god or by the prophet," which attested to its "metaleptic status" (CW, 17:105). Indeed, the "word" need not even be auditory. In Isaiah 2:1 and Amos 1:1 it is "seen." Voegelin's point, it seems to me, was that metalepsis was more a paradoxical meditative than a univocal analytic symbol.[26]

To revert to Voegelin's analytical discussion of Anaximander, human beings experienced themselves in a metaleptic reality between the things and the *Apeiron*, which they could equally well articulate using the structured or "external" language of the Metaxy. Accordingly, when Voegelin wrote that "conquest and exodus . . . are movements *within* reality" he referred to the participation of human consciousness in the metaleptic metaxy (CW, 17:278).

Voegelin then reworked some of the problems analyzed in the earlier volumes of *Order and History* with an eye both to distinguishing noetic philosophical consciousness from "the certainty of historical uniqueness and ineluctability" of Israelite experience and symbolization as well as to indicate the equivalence of the two experiential complexes and their symbolisms insofar as they evoked a "convergent meaning." Philosophers, for

25 CW, 17:250f repeats or closely paraphrases the analysis in *Anamnesis*.

26 Consider in this context Augustine's discussion of this problem toward the end of his *Confessions*, XIII, xxv–xxviii.

example, were "concerned with the place of meaning in reality. There is meaningful luminosity of consciousness, emerging from a process that was deprived of it in the past and, quite possibly, will be deprived of it in the future" (CW, 17:282). At the same time, Voegelin gave particular emphasis to the passages in Plato's *Laws* (713ff) that emphasized the third age of Nous that followed the ages of Chronos and Zeus. With this third age, Voegelin said, "Plato has come as close to an apocalyptic symbolism as he could without losing the balance of consciousness that also comprehended the primary experience of the process in which things come and go," as was expressed in Anaximander's oft-mentioned formulation (CW, 17:291).

Finding an approximation or an equivalent to apocalyptic symbolism in Plato was but the first surprise Voegelin had in store. Consider the problem of the balance of consciousness and the unavoidability of paradox. The approach to apocalyptic symbolism held out the possibility of resolving Anaximander's formulation, but this possibility was also an impossibility. The "exodus from reality," we saw, "is a movement within reality." Thus "the philosopher has to cope with the paradox of a recognizable structured process that is recognizably moving beyond its structure." Such a formulation was itself paradoxical because it contained a pressure to resolve itself either into a lastingness that would become static or a transformation or transfiguration of reality, which was impossible in principle. Maintaining a paradoxical balance, which was "the very structure of existence itself," was now seen to be the task of the philosopher (CW, 17:291–92).

The difficulties of maintaining balance "arise from the constitution of reason through revelation," a formulation that also appeared unintelligible to the modern dogmatic opinion that distinguished so emphatically between reason and revelation. Such a distinction, however, was an error that Voegelin had criticized in the early volumes of *Order and History* on solid Platonic and Aristotelian grounds. "The life of reason," he said, "is firmly rooted in revelation. The issue of revelation as the source of reason in existence is conventionally anesthetized by carefully reporting the philosophers' 'ideas' without touching the experiences that have motivated them. In a philosophical study, however, the philosophers' theopahnies must be taken seriously" (CW, 17:292). Who, Voegelin asked, is this philosophical God, this philosopher's God? What does He reveal? And how is He related to the Biblical God?

Considered from the side of the experience of the recipient, there occurred considerable instability. Voegelin again insisted in this new context: "Revelation is not a piece of information, arbitrarily thrown out by some supernatural force, to be carried home as a possession, but the movement of response to an irruption of the divine in the psyche." Moreover, the movement of response was not limited before it began. Once the psyche moved "beyond the intracosmic gods toward the Divine Ground of all being, it will not cease moving before it has sensed the truly Tremendum, the ultimate, non-present Beyond of all divine presence" (CW, 17:296–97). The paradoxical structure of the exodus was that the Beyond both threatened to invalidate the theophanic events and the process of reality within which they occurred by seeming to hold out the possibility of transfiguring reality from a position achieved "in" the Beyond. This was, Voegelin said, the aspiration of the Gnostics that was explicitly precluded by the ambiguities, uncertainties, and paradoxes of Plato's formulations.

Voegelin related Plato's balance to the recollection of the death of Socrates for having been convicted of introducing new gods to the city. Central to Plato's understanding of revelation was "protection, as it were, against revelation itself" because, in a word, bearing witness to the new revelation could get you killed. Voegelin's point was not that, in the Platonic example, the philosopher (or Socrates, for that matter) was afraid of dying. Rather it was that the philosopher, like Jeremiah, would not countenance an attack on God's messenger. The response to God's appearance as the Nous constituted the psyche as the sensorium of the full amplitude of reality; it opened human consciousness to a whole of which the responsive participant was a part. "That is all," Voegelin said, but it is "considerably more than is conventionally realized." The structure of reality was not just "there" to be seen by anyone under any set of circumstances. It was a reality that revealed itself to the psyche when the psyche responded to the divine Nous. It was on these grounds that philosophy or science was possible. Again the reasoning was obvious enough: "No science as the systematic exploration of the structure of reality is possible, unless the world is intelligible; and the world is intelligible in relation to a psyche that has become luminous for the order of reality through the revelation of the one, divine ground of all being as the Nous" (CW, 17:301).

In other words, the life of reason in the world, whether in the emphatic sense of noetic luminosity of consciousness or the more subdued sense of analytical science, relied on the intelligibility of the world and of human participation in it. It also relied on a balance of consciousness that ensured that the movement within the structure of reality towards the Beyond did not turn into a short circuit whereby consciousness thought of itself as having taken up residence in the Beyond. Voegelin then restated the problem of Gnosticism as initially having attempted "to escape from the Metaxy by splitting its poles into the hypostases of this world and the Beyond," whereas "the modern apocalyptic-Gnostic movements attempt to abolish the Metaxy by transforming the Beyond into this world" (CW, 17:302). These imaginative constructions were the equivalent second realities discussed in the previous chapter.

"Plato kept the theophanic event in balance with the experience of the cosmos." In the *Laws*, for example, the real but gentle pull of the golden cord was in contention with the equally real but stronger pulls of the passions (644d–5c; cf. CW, 16:286ff). There was, within the Platonic myth no resolution of the theophanic event beyond the movement of reality toward a state undisturbed by disorder. As for the directional movement itself, it is

> a mystery indeed: Although we can experience the direction as real, we do not know why reality is in such a state that it has to move beyond itself or why the movement has not been consummated by an event of transfiguration in the past; neither can we predict the date for such an event in the future or know what form it will assume. The event, as it can happen any time, hangs as a threat or hope over every present. In fact, nothing happens; and yet, it might happen. (CW, 17:303)

This description of existential tension sounded a great deal like the description to the existential uncertainty characteristic of Christianity as described in *The New Science of Politics* (CW, 5:187ff). And yet Voegelin was writing of Plato and of Platonic balance.

The Platonic and Aristotelian balance was directly connected to the primary experience of the cosmos. It was true enough that Plato and Aristotle broke with the cosmological form of cosmogony, but "the noetic luminosity of existence does not impose the alternative of an absolutely creative Beginning" (CW, 17:57). Aristotle's cosmos apparently needed no beginning; the demiurge of Plato's *Timaeus* did not create the cosmos but was, indeed, limited by Necessity, *Ananke*. And yet, the very ambiguity of these experiences and their symbolizations, as discussed in chapter five, reflected the impact of the differentiating consciousness of the philosopher.

Some aspects of the problem of an "absolutely creative Beginning" were more elaborately articulated in the Judeo-Christian environment recorded in the New Testament than can be found in philosophy. The context of the Judeo-Christian experience, obviously, was provided by the "millennial Israelite background of differentiating consciousness." Specifically, the hold of the primary experience of the cosmos on human consciousness was decisively shaken "by Moses' experience and symbolization of divine reality as the 'I am' of the Thornbush Episode." This experience brought the deeper reality of an absolute Beginning directly into consciousness thereby eclipsing the concern of the philosophers with the apprehension of absolute Being as the source of (more or less visible) cosmic order. Moreover, the creative act continued into the present because the substance of the creative act was the "word."

> From the Beginning, reality is the divine word speaking in succession the evolution of being from matter through plant to animal life, until it speaks man who, in the persons of the patriarchs and prophets, responds by his word to the word spoken by god in history. The reality of the cosmos, thus, becomes the story to be told by the man who participates responsively in the story told by the god. (CW, 17:58)

This "assembly of symbols" did not constitute steps in a philosopher's analysis of reality but were "the potent precondition" for differentiations later articulated in the epiphany of Christ and the relation of Christ to the cosmogonic Beginning.

The "thinker" who connected the absolute Beginning with the presence of the divine Beyond in human consciousness was the author of John's Gospel. It opened with the words of Genesis 1:1, but the story was told reflectively as the story of the divine-creative substance: "In the beginning was the word; and the word was with God; and the word was God." That is, the word and God were paradoxically both identical and different. This "creative tension" then became "creative action" as God who had the word made all things by speaking the word (John 1:3). The created word, moreover, was "life" and its life was "the light of man" that shone in the darkness with such intensity that "darkness cannot overcome it" (or "the darkness comprehended it not"). The author of the Gospel then indicated that the Word of the Beginning was present in Christ as witnessed by John the Baptist (John 1:6ff; cf CW, 17:58–59).

John 8 resumed the reflection on the connection of the Word of the Beginning and the Word of the Beyond in the debate between Jesus and the Pharisees. The debate, Voegelin said, intended "to clarify the meaning of divine presence in a man." Accordingly, when the Pharisees ask, "Who are you?," Jesus replied, "Even the same that I said unto you from the beginning," which is to say, the Mosaic "I am" (John 8:25). Thus, "when the divine reality experienced as present in man's consciousness, the symbolic language sensibly appeals to the precedent of the word revealing itself in the consciousness of Moses rather than to the word of the Beginning" (CW, 17:59). It was sensible to appeal to precedent in order to be understood, but there still was novelty in Jesus' words. "For the God who spoke to Moses from the Thornbush, now speaks through the mouth of men to other men." And so the God of the Thornbush had become "the true Light, which lighteth every man that cometh into the world" (John 1:9).

That is, the "I am" of Jesus "reveals itself as the living presence of the Word in a man," whereas the "I am" of Moses was surrounded by such cosmological symbols as a Thornbush and the voice of an intracosmic God of the Fathers. Moreover, the "I am" of Jesus constituted the humanity of every person whereas the "I am" of Moses constituted him to lead Israel from the bondage of the cosmological empire of Egypt. The "I am" of Jesus did not establish a historical people but, for every person who responded to its appeal, dissolved "the darkness and absurdity of existence into the luminous consciousness of participating in the divine word" (CW, 17:59). The debate between Jesus and the Pharisees exemplified a conflict between the more compact revelations to Israel and the "luminous presence" of the word in Jesus. The Pharisees said to Jesus, how can this new teaching be reconciled with the teaching of Abraham? "Thou art not yet fifty years old, and hast thou seen Abraham? Jesus said unto them, Verily, verily, I say unto you, Before Abraham was, I am" (John 8:57–58). This was not acceptable to the Pharisees who "took up stones to cast at him" but Jesus escaped (John 8:59).

Voegelin then reiterated an observation he made of Jeremiah: "the great events of spiritual insight becoming articulate do not necessarily please everybody." As with Aristotle's discussion of metalepsis, the movement from the Beyond required a countermovement in the human person toward the Beyond, "out of history, toward eschatological fulfillment." Most people, however, "want to eat their cake of revelation and keep it in history," but it could not be done. The movement of the word from the Beyond into the existence of every person required the countermovement "toward the word that speaks through Christ" (CW, 17:61). In Jesus, Voegelin wrote, "the participation of his humanity in the divine word has reached the intensity of his absorption into the word" (CW, 17:62). And yet the cosmos was not abolished and continued to exist from the Mosaic Beginning, so that even Christ who was transfigured from the Beyond had to die a human death.

The Christian metaleptic reality did not abolish the cosmic even though, as Joseph McCaroll put it in a review essay of *The Ecumenic Age* preserved in the Voegelin archive:

> The accent has moved from the exploration of divine order in the cosmos to the proclamation of divine salvation from the disorder of the cosmos, from the experience of the directional movement of reality towards the Divine Ground to the consummation of this movement, from the human search to the divine gift, from man's ascent toward God through the tension of *Eros* to God's descent towards man through the tension of *Agape*. (HI, 79:10, 31)

But what then was the meaning of the transfiguration? This was what Jesus said to his disciples: "Behold, the hour cometh, yea, is now come, that ye shall be scattered, every men to his own, and shall leave me alone: and yet I am not alone, because the Father is with me. These things have I spoken to you that in me ye might have peace. In the world [*cosmos*] ye shall have tribulation: but be of good cheer; I have overcome the world [*cosmos*]" (John 16:32–33). Voegelin remarked: "That is all. But it is all that matters," as is evident from Jesus' subsequent prayers. For his disciples Jesus said: "I pray not that thou shouldest take them out of the world [*cosmos*] but that thou shouldest keep them from evil. They are not of the world [*cosmos*] even as I am not of the world [*cosmos*]. Sanctify them through thy truth: the word is truth" (John 17:16–17). For himself he prayed: "And now, O Father, glorify thou me with thine own self with glory which was there before the world [*cosmos*]" (John 17:5).

The divine reality, it seemed, could be experienced and symbolized both as Beyond and as Beginning.[27] The Beyond was present immediately in consciousness whereas the Beginning was mediated through the experience of intelligible things in the cosmos. Christ, who in death was victorious over the cosmos was not transfigured by the world that created and sustained the cosmos but returned to the word in the "creative tension" that existed "before there was a cosmos" (John 17:5). This was not a Gnostic attempt to escape the cosmos because Jesus sent his disciples into the cosmos, as he had been sent by God, so that they could convert others to the truth of the word so that God's love becomes manifest in them (John 17:18–

27 See also Voegelin's notes on "Types of Beyond," HI, 84:9.

24). Voegelin summarized these passages from the Gospel according to John: "When the formerly unknown god of the Beyond reveals himself as the goal of the eschatological movement in the soul, the experience of the cosmos becomes an ever more disturbing mystery." Why should there be a cosmos at all if the best a person could do is to live in it as if he were not of it? This question, Voegelin said, "brings the mystery of reality into full view." The elements of this mystery had already been enumerated by the philosophers though now with a new intensity in the Gospel: (1) there was a cosmos wherein the person participated by his existence; (2) the person was conscious of the reality of which and within which he was a partner; (3) consciousness was differentiated in the process of history; (4) in the process of history the person discovered that reality was engaged in "a movement toward a Beyond of its present structure. A cosmos that moves from its divine Beginning towards a divine Beyond of itself is mysterious indeed; and there is nothing wrong with the question as such" for the obvious reason that the questions expressed but did not abolish the mystery (CW, 17:64–65).

The Ecumenic Age discussed the Pauline theophany as well as passages from the Gospel of John. In Voegelin's discussion of Paul the accent of the analysis shifted from maintaining balance to the potential for derailment of a consciousness of mystery into metastatic expectations of a solution to it. "The aura of possibility surrounding the mystery can be condensed into an expectation, with certainty, of a transfiguring event in a not too distant future" (CW, 17:304). Historically, of course, this was simply a fact, though it could hardly be said to be central to Pauline theophany.

The potential of distortion by way of metastatic imagination, as in *The New Science of Politics*, "is inherent to the mystery of meaning. If the mystery were not real, the distortions would have no appeal." Voegelin then illustrated his point with an exegesis of Romans 8:18–25. The resolution of the tensions of existence that rested on hope amounted to Anaximander's coming-to-be (*genesis*) without perishing (*phthora*). Hope for, not the direct experience of, the resolution is an expectation that, because it rested on grace, never gave way or led to disappointment even though reality was never transfigured.

Voegelin argued that, given the emphasis on metalepsis, there were close parallels between Paul and Plato and Aristotle, although the "accent" had shifted "from the divine noetic order incarnate in the world to the divine pneumatic salvation from its disorder." McCaroll summarized the differences as follows:

1. The freedom and *Agape* of the transcosmic God revealed Him to be the creator of the cosmos whereas Plato's Demiurge is limited by *Ananke*; St. Paul's creator God emerges victorious over the forces of resistance in the cosmos, including death.
2. The telos of St. Paul's vision is a state of *aphtharsia* (imperishing) whereas for Plato and Anaximander things perish back into the *Apeiron* according to the ordinance of time. For St. Paul the process of creation, fall, and redemption, leads to the imperishing eschatological end.
3. In St. Paul, human being is the site where the movement of reality becomes luminous in its actual occurrence. The vision is of the Resurrected Christ in whom the fullness of the divine dwells bodily, which Voegelin took to mean "the full differentiation of man as the area of reality in which the movement of the whole of reality towards the goal of *aphtharsia* becomes luminous for this movement." (HI, 79:10, 33; cf. CW 17:305–6)

In short, Plato did not elaborate on the unbalancing directionality of the movement within reality. Instead, his consciousness of the paradox of reality remained within the balance of Anaximander's genesis and phthora, of *Apeiron* and Time. Paul focused more directly on the implications of the movement—of genesis without phthora, as Voegelin put it. In consequence, "the metastatic expectation of the Second Coming has begun its long history of disappointment" (CW, 17:305–6).

The "accents" may be different, but this merely reflected the fact that "Paul was not a philosopher; he was the missionary for the Christ who appeared to him on the road to Damascus." Moreover, the difference in "accents" needed to be understood within their agreement that "meaning in history is inseparable from the directional movement in reality." History was to be understood as that part of reality where its directional movement achieved luminosity, or self-understanding, in consciousness; history "happened" in the metaleptic In-Between where human being responded to divine presence and divine presence evoked the human response. Paul's vision of the Resurrected in Romans 8 convinced him that all humans could gain redemption if they were as open to the divine presence as Jesus was. "Faith in Christ," Voegelin said, "means responsive participation in the same divine *pneuma* that was active in the Jesus who appeared as the vision of the Resurrected" (CW, 17:307).

Voegelin's point was not intended to discuss Christological dogma but to consider the meaning of a vision and to provide exegesis of it by the person who experienced it, namely Paul. Paul's vision was not a dogma to be accepted or refused "but an event in metaleptic reality that a philosopher can do no more than try to understand to the best of his ability." Because the vision occurred in the Metaxy, the question of subject and object did not arise. There was only the vision as received and the response of a human being to divine presence. In any event, Voegelin attempted to do just that, which did not entirely endear him to those who preferred dogmatic formulations. Indeed, as he said, events of spiritual insight do not please everybody.

The different "accent" expressed through Paul's "mythopoetic genius" did not mean that his vision was disconnected from reason or "irrational" and somehow beyond critical analysis. Instead, and making allowances for Paul as a missionary rather than a philosopher, and one whose mythical language was less precise than that of Plato and Aristotle, the symbolism, Voegelin argued, was equivalent, though "the dynamics of existential truth has shifted from the human search to the divine gift" (CW, 17:310). Instead of an exegesis of human participation in divine reality, Paul's myth evoked an anticipation of perfection.

Here Voegelin reformulated his analysis of myth. "Myth is a symbolism engendered by the experience of divine presence in reality. In its cosmologically compact form, it is an intracosmic story about the gods and the divine origin of things." It retained its status as an intracosmic story so long as the noetic field was not differentiated as the awareness of a theophanic event within metaleptic reality.[28] Thus, for example, the Platonic myth of the cosmos was not itself a cosmological myth but a "true story" of the divine presence in reality and of the philosopher's consciousness in tension towards the Divine Ground (cf. CW, 6:70). The noetic theophany dissolved the compactness of the myth in much the same way as the Pauline myth did but with the difference that the Pauline myth achieved an additional differentiation as compared to the Platonic, symbolized by grace unbounded by necessity. Or, as Voegelin put it in his 1971 talk at Notre Dame: in the *Timaeus* Plato formulated his experience of divinity by saying that

28 In the 1967 "Drama of Humanity" lectures, Voegelin said myth was a "body of symbols that had in fact been found adequate by the members of such civilizations for expressing their experience of the cosmos in which they lived" (CW, 33:189; cf. 190–92). Or in 1965 he indicated that myth could be defined "fairly exactly and there can be no exceptions to it, as imputation to other intracosmic things of a Ground. It is myth when you tell a story of an intracosmic Ground" (CW, 11:233).

> the cosmos is the Son of God the Father. But if you compare this formulation of Plato, "the Cosmos is the Son of God," say, with the Gospel where you can find "Christ is the Son of God," you'll see the difference. In the Christian complex the symbolism of the Son of God has shifted to the consciousness in the existence of man. He is a differentiation of the problem of truth as being an accessible and immediate experience in the existence of man. (HI, 44:6; cf. CW, 12:391)

Specifically, Paul's vision carried him beyond creation to its source, namely "the freedom and love of divine creativity," discussed above in terms of the Beginning in John's Gospel. Paul experienced the revelation that the human orientation to the Divine Ground was moved by the transcosmic God and His love. Accordingly, a new and more differentiated myth than that of Plato was required to express Paul's new experiential insight. "In the perspective of the goal, the myth must become the story of the fall from and return to the imperishable state of creation intended by divine creativity. It must become the drama of creation and fall, of fall and redemption, of death and resurrection, and of the ultimate return of creation to its imperishable glory" (CW, 17:315). Paul's myth pursued the drama of the movement to its conclusion in the eschatological events of transfiguration of reality. In Paul's myth, God is victorious.[29]

Voegelin next revised his account of the experience that he had earlier described as a "leap in being." The truth of existence, he said, "emerges from the theophanic events in history. Initially, in classical philosophy, the discovery of noetic consciousness "is inseparable from the consciousness of the discovery as an event that constituted meaning in history." The discovery constituted an "advance" over the compact experiences and symbolizations of preceding existential order—as in Aristotle's remarks regarding the philosophos and the philomythos. This same "advance" implied three other things: (1) the equivalence of myth and philosophy along with the "advance;" (2) the site of this "advance" was the consciousness that made the discovery so that this

29 It is also worth pointing out that Voegelin's exegesis of Paul's vision and its mythopoetic expression was unusually personal. For example (pp.312–13): "When reading the First Letter to the Corinthians, *I have always the feeling. . .*" Or: "this sentence is the key to understanding Paul's experience of reality *or so at least it appears to me*." Or: "What I have called the 'homogeneous medium of reality' *in which I felt Paul moving* from *phthora* [perishing] to *aphtharsia* [imperishing]." Voegelin seldom used the first person singular in this way.

theophanic event—the "advance"—did not take place *in* history rather it *constituted* history and its meaning; and (3) the noetic theophany revealed consciousness to have the structure of metaleptic divine-human reality. Thus "history," as noted above, was the area of reality where these advances in insight took place and also was the history of theophany (CW, 17:316–17).

The difference between what was previously described as distinct "leaps in being" was also revised. In philosophy the "accent" fell on "the cognition of structure" or of human nature, as the philosophers said, whereas with Paul the "accent" fell "on the exodus from structure." The difference, as argued above, was not contradictory, however, and did not "compel a choice between alternatives. On the contrary, the two conceptions together act out, in the luminosity of consciousness, the paradox of a reality that moves beyond its structure." Now Voegelin, whose "personal" language was noted above, had become aware of the problem of equivalence and of a further paradox. "When the paradox of reality becomes luminous to itself in consciousness," specifically in Voegelin's consciousness,

> it creates a paradox of history in suspense between the Ananke [Necessity] of the cosmos and the freedom of eschatological movement. That the two branches of the paradox are distributed, in the Ecumenic Age, over the noetic theophanies of the Hellenic philosophers and the pneumatic theophanies of the Israelite-Jewish prophets cannot be explained. The process of history is a mystery as much as the reality that becomes luminous in it. (CW, 17:324–25)

The symbol "history" therefore must be expanded to accommodate both noetic and pneumatic theophanic events.[30]

5. Universal Humanity

The historical process analyzed in terms of the "Ecumenic Age" was paralleled in China by "an equivalent process." Chapter six of *The Ecumenic Age*

30 The balance of this chapter of *The Ecumenic Age* was concerned chiefly with the rejection of theophany, for which Voegelin coined the term "egophany" to designate alienation and self-alienation from reality as maximally differentiated. It consisted in recasting the intellectual, spiritual, and political pathologies and deformations previously discussed in terms of Gnosticism, Second Reality, metastasis, and so on.

provided an analysis of the Chinese ecumene and the concluding chapter, "Universal Humanity," dealt with "the philosophical problems that arise from this growth of a second ecumene."[31] The Chinese and Western historical processes were equivalent in the following respect: when the mythical horizon of the cosmological order that expressed the mystery of divine presence was abolished, that is, when consciousness of reality differentiated from the truth of the cosmos the truth of existence, the first pragmatic consequence was that the cosmos became understood as a territory to be conquered. Both China and the West suffered the same diminution of meaning insofar as the transformation of a cosmological order into an ecumenic territory abolished temporarily the habitat meaningful for human beings, namely to exist in a social order surrounded by mystery.[32] Once conquered, the ecumene required a new horizon of mystery in order that it serve as a meaningful human habitat.

By Voegelin's analysis, the early Chinese cosmological compactness of a clan society headed by a kind of king (*wang*) styled the "son of heaven" (*t'ien-tzu*) who ruled "all under heaven" (*t'ien-hsia*) as well as a territorial state (*kuo*), had by the second century B.C. dissociated into power and spirit. On the one hand were powerful politicians and generals with their legal advisors and on the other the Confucian and Taoist sages. "The foundation of the [Han] empire can be defined, therefore, in Chinese terms, as the victory of the *kuo* over the *t'ien-hsia*: the empire was an inflated *kuo* without spiritual legitimacy" (CW, 17:370). Eventually a synthesis of spirit and power was achieved and stabilized "in the neo-Confucian orthodoxy" but this order was not the cosmological order "of the early kingdom before it had dissociated into *t'ien-hsia* and *kuo*" (CW, 17:370). Voegelin concluded, therefore, that there were indeed two ecumenes existing at the same time.

Hence the new questions to be analyzed in the concluding chapter: (1) are there two "mankinds," each having its own history and each developing its own ecumenic age? And (2) if not, if there was only one mankind, then in what sense were the Western and Far Eastern historical processes part of one Ecumenic Age? (CW, 17:371; cf. 17:50). Voegelin began the analysis by restating the ecumenic problem in its Western form. He introduced other

31 CW, 17:342. See also Manfred Henningsen, "The Death of Civilizations: Huntington, Toynbee and Voegelin –Three Variations on a Theme," *European Journal of Social History* 17 (2014): 161f, and Henningsen, "A New Politics of History," in Opitz and Sebba, eds., *Essays on History, Consciousness and Politics*, 416–28.

32 See David Walsh, *Guarded by Mystery: Meaning in a Postmodern Age* (Washington: Catholic University of America Press, 1999).

materials from time to time, allowing his train of thought on occasion to follow more a meditative than an analytical course.

In the Western Ecumenic Age, the truth of existence was expressed in noetic and pneumatic experience and symbolization that was differentiated from the truth of the cosmos expressed in cosmological myth. The analysis of the philosophers reached the divine *Aiton* (cause) as the source of order in reality; it differentiated the structure of existence in the metaleptic reality of divine-and-human, but it did not embrace the structure of divine reality in the spiritual depth of creation and salvation. "Only through Paul's response to his vision did the philosophers' *athanatizein* [immortalizing] expand to the pneumatic *aphtharasia* [imperishing]; the paradigmatic polis [of Plato's *Republic*], into the organization of man's spiritual as distinguished from his temporal order; and the Third Age of the Nous [in Plato's *Laws*], into the eschatological structure of history under the one God of all ages" (CW, 17:375).

Voegelin first provided a somewhat opaque summary account of the anthropological implications of his new understanding of history and then spelled out some of the implications. First, the summary: the noetic and pneumatic differentiations of consciousness contained the insight that history was the process wherein the differentiations occurred. Because these differentiations provided greater understanding of one's humanity, history became visible as a dimension of existence beyond individuality. Because these events were experienced as human responses to divine presence, history was a divine-human process. Because the events were experienced as "immortalizing movements," history was discovered to be a divine-human process wherein reality moved beyond its own structure, which is to say, history was discovered to be eschatological. The historical dimension of humanity was characterized as much by calendar dates as by divine out-of-time lasting so that the historical dimension of humanity was neither the time-of-the-world nor eternity but the reality of divine presence in the Metaxy; what ensured that humanity was universal was the divine element present in the Metaxy.

The new anthropological insight concerned the eschatological dimension to history and thus to the humanity of persons. The analysis began from the already secured noetic insight that the structure of existence was metaleptic. The most fundamental aspect of human existence was our biophysical existence in society on earth conducted in the time of the external world. Reflecting on the course of societies in pragmatic existence led Voegelin to construct "the type concept of the 'Ecumenic Age'" to describe the limited worldly process. Human existence became historical when it participated in the metaleptic movement of divine presence and thereby humans became aware of universal humanity. By itself the type concept delimited a specific historical unit of meaning; but the type concept did not exist by itself but as part of the experiential complex that included a consciousness of universal humanity. Hence the conflict between the distinctive Western Ecumenic Age and the Chinese, to say nothing of large numbers of societies existing elsewhere in the world that would also have to be included in universal humanity.

This problem, Voegelin said, could now be succinctly resolved:

> The divine-human flux of presence is a given only as far as it is founded in man's biophysical existence on earth; the divine presence itself, though experienced by man who exists in time and space, is not a spatio-temporal given. The historical dimension of humanity, thus, is no more a given than the reality of man's personal existence in the Metaxy. Universal mankind is not a society existing in the world, but a symbol that indicated man's consciousness of participating in his earthly existence, in the mystery of a reality that moves towards its transfiguration. Universal mankind is an eschatological index. (CW, 17:376)

Less succinctly, Voegelin explained, that universality was required if there was to be a humanity in any sense other than that of a collection of members of a biological species. If *homo sapiens* had a history and *equus ferus caballus* did not, if there was a difference between humankind and horsekind, this was because humans could respond to "the movement of divine presence in their souls" whereas horses could not. The implication therefore was that the humanity who had a history "is constituted by the God to whom man responds." What complicated matters, however, was not God but humans who may or may not respond to the movement of divine presence.

We have already noted in several contexts that the process of differentiation of consciousness from compactness to different degrees of differentiation was a historical reality. So was the attempt to retreat into a "re-compacted" reality, which turned out to be an imaginary second reality. The process of differentiation, moreover, did not take place everywhere or at the same time: "the great noetic and pneumatic differentiations occur, not among Paleolithic hunters and fishers, but in ages of cities and empires." Accordingly, "the structure of man's earthly existence in society . . . is somehow involved in the process of differentiating consciousness" (CW, 17:377). Such an observation had nothing to do with fantasies of historical progress or decline but merely reflected the commonsensical observation that when the theophanic events occurred and made history visible as the "transfiguring process," the events occurred to human beings with specific and particular spatio-temporal existence. Moreover, this process was of interest to human beings because of the sacredness experienced as the divine presence to which humans responded—or did not.

The significance of the differentiation achieved during the Ecumenic Age could now be specified more exactly. The limit of the cosmos, to use the Greek symbol, was the *okeanos*, just as the known world was called the *oikoumene* (see CW, 17:262–68; 340–42). Once the mythical-cosmological oikoumene-okeanos experience had disintegrated, it could not be restored. The habitat of human beings, as we have seen, could be conquered, but the surrounding mystery could be restored only by the self-understanding or luminosity of an outburst of spiritual consciousness. The process of transfiguration in which all human beings at all times could participate then replaced the okeanos as the horizon of divine mystery for humanity that was, in turn, expressed historiographically. Voegelin concluded that the "triad" of ecumenic conquest, spiritual outburst, and historiography were equivalent to the oikoumene-okeanos symbolism of the myth. "The triad is a unit of experience in process of differentiation and symbolization. This process, in its personal, social, and historical dimensions, is the period that I have called the Ecumenic Age" (CW, 17:385).

In other words, the three elements of the triad formed a unit. History, as the horizon of divine mystery that surrounded the spatial extent of the ecumene could only appear to a spiritually sensitive consciousness under the impact of concupiscential expansion. And the expansion itself was senseless without the historiographic account that related the otherwise senseless events to the truth of existence in terms of divine mystery. "There is," Voegelin said, "no consciousness of epoch unless something that can be experienced as epochal is happening indeed in the process of reality" (CW, 17:385). Voegelin then made explicit the implications of that statement.

He began his explication by clarifying what the experience of an epochal event, in this context, meant. It was not, he said, a complex of events, the creation of empires accompanied by spiritual outbursts that happened "in" history in such a manner that the historiographer was in the business of recording their appearance. That would be the approach of perceptual or subject/object consciousness not that of a participant in the process of reality who had become aware of his participation—the experience symbolized by the metaphor of "luminosity" that we have so often encountered. Just as with the noetic participatory consciousness of the philosopher in the theophanic event has been described as a tension toward the Divine Ground of existence, a similar characterization could be made with historical consciousness. That is, the actual process of historical differentiation of consciousness that understood itself as "epochal" was the same as the source of our understanding of the process. That meant that real, concrete participants in the process of history could not assume the position of an outside observer.

In one sense, Voegelin's point was simple: just as with noetic consciousness so too historical consciousness provided an insight, a real differentiation of our consciousness of reality. Reality was there as it was before and after the experience of differentiation. All that has changed was our understanding of it, which had become more adequate than it had been prior to the experience of differentiation. This was the simple hermeneutic that originated in the early volumes of *Order and History*.

Because the reality in question was historical, however, matters were more complex. Why? "Because the structure [of reality] in question happens to be the [historical] movement of reality beyond its structure." That is, historical consciousness or historical insight was a part of reality that became aware of itself as having an eschatological direction towards transfiguration. "The insight gained is not merely a man's knowledge about a structural oddity in which he may be interested or not, for the gaining of the insight is itself an eschatological event that illuminates the transfigurative structure in man's humanity" (CW, 17:386–87). This was why Voegelin several times remarked that he was not discussing questions of "theology" (CW, 17:96ff; 373; 386).

Instead of derivative questions of textual exegesis, Voegelin was concerned with the concrete problems of the historical differentiation of consciousness that human beings had of their humanity, starting with the human being named Eric Voegelin. The personal sense of epoch grew increasingly apparent in the closing pages of *The Ecumenic Age*. This could hardly be surprising insofar as history was there described as being revealed to human consciousness as the horizon of divine mystery. If historical consciousness was discovered to be a process of transfiguration, such an event could occur only when individual human beings were actually aware of the movement towards eschatological fulfillment—or, to use Voegelin's preferred locution, when consciousness became "luminous" for its own movement in the direction of eschatological fulfillment. As we shall argue in the next chapter, Voegelin's use of meditative essays was a natural and intelligible development from his analytic and anamnetic recoveries of experiences of reality that had been lost or forgotten.

To return to Voegelin's argument: his discovery of human awareness of this transfiguration, namely the experience of reality moving beyond its structure, constituted an epochal event, a genuine new discovery. It did not, however, abolish the old symbolizations of the order of reality so much as integrate them into the process of transfiguration that constituted universal history. "This result of the analysis," Voegelin said, "can be expressed in the following proposition: In the Ecumenic Age, the process of reality is discovered as a spatially and temporally open field, with man's existence in eschatological tension as its center of consciousness" (CW, 17:387). Moreover, the awareness of this structure that consisted of the movement of reality beyond its structure—the eschatological direction of history—was precisely what made this discovery of historical consciousness universal. For historical consciousness, in this context, all human beings, past, present, and future, participated in the process of history, with varying degrees of socially concrete diversity—from the more compact primary experience of the cosmos to different degrees of disengagement and differentiation.

This discovery of the "epochal structure" of a transition from the truth of the cosmos to the truth of existence raised for Voegelin several additional questions: (1) Why were there epochs anyway? Why was the structure of reality not known from the start? (2) Why was the discovery confined to a few philosophers and prophets? Why not everyone? (3) Why, once gained, were the insights not generally accepted? Why did the epochal truth undergo its own history of imperfect articulation, skepticism, dogmatization, decline, recovery, etc.? Or as students (and not just students) sometimes say: why is it all so difficult?

Such questions were not meant to be answered but rather themselves symbolized the mystery of the structure of history as, Voegelin said, the Question. The actual form of the Question varied in terms of the experience of reality of the questioner. "The meaning of the Question can be ascertained, therefore, only by tracing the modes from the setting of the primary experience of the cosmos, through transitional forms, to their setting in the context of noetic and pneumatic differentiations" (CW, 17:389). Since the latter differentiations could be dated chronologically, by a simple process of inference, the earliest experiences of reality would take the form of the primary experience of the cosmos. The question to be raised next, but hardly answered on this occasion is: how early?[33]

Traditionally scholars have been concerned with the answers to the Question. Voegelin, however, was more concerned with the Question "as a constant structure in the experience of reality and, since the experience is part of reality, in the structure of reality itself" (CW, 17:399). Even in the cosmological style of truth, the Question was complete. The cosmos was experienced as precariously stabilized in a present that may be disordered by the process from which order emerged. What maintained order was the participation of humans in the divine-cosmic process through rituals of cosmogonic renewal. The subsequent differentiations of noetic and pneumatic experience and symbolization, including the experience of the eschatological movement of and in reality, shifted the accents strongly from stability to precariousness. Not that the cosmos was ever simply stable—as earthquakes, the end of the ice age, or the precession of the equinoxes all attest—but that precariousness was even more strongly evident in historical human activities than in cosmic changes. But as human society was understood as part of cosmic order, disturbances in the former were understood as cosmic disorders. Hence the completeness of the Question even in the form of the cosmological myths.

In other words, the Question remained the same but the ways of asking it changed. One of the commonsensical reasons for the change(s) was that empirical knowledge of the process of history has accumulated over time and, once human consciousness became aware of the historical dimension to existence, this knowledge had to be incorporated into the human historical response. But more than a commonsensical need to integrate "more" history in 1500 AD than in 1500 BC was involved. Voegelin discovered in *The Ecumenic Age* that history was not a finite collection of accounts of events but a process that continued so long as human beings participated in it. Moreover, history also remained the horizon of the divine Mystery so that no amount of empirical knowledge of an ever-lengthening series of events could possibly dissolve the Mystery, precisely because it had no end in time.

The structure of historical reality has not, however, stopped some thinkers most notably, as we saw in chapter five, Hegel, from arguing that

33 Henningsen observed that the discussion of the Chinese ecumene and Universal humanity "indicated that [Voegelin] was stepping outside the Western boundaries of his perspective and into the scientific field of scholarship regarding the symbolism of the Upper Paleolithic and the origins of human consciousness" (Henningsen, "The Death of Civilization," 161–63).

an answer to the Question can at last be formulated in the System of Science because enough, or perhaps all, history has taken place so that there was no further need to raise the Question in any form. Indeed, on occasion, as we saw with Marx, further questions have been prohibited. But even Hegel had to allow that considerable time had to pass before, to use his language, the *Geist* became sufficiently self-conscious in the *Geist* of Hegel for him to write the System of Science. Or rather, again to use his language, the universal self-conscious *Geist* used the particular *Geist* of the individual G. W. F. Hegel to write the System of Science and in that way became fully and concretely self-conscious. One way or another, the Question was answered. In reality, however, as was argued in the previous chapter, the construction of the System as a second reality "is meant to assuage the anxiety of a man who cannot face the Mystery of Reality" (CW, 17:403).

Voegelin then raised a final analytic question: what was the relationship between the process of differentiation that evoked a consciousness of the Question and the lapse of immanent time that produced the ever-lengthening series of events and accounts of them?

He began his answer with the not-too-helpful remark: "To formulate the problem means practically to resolve it" (CW, 17:407). How? First, Voegelin reiterated that "the divine-human In-Between of historically differentiating experience is founded in the consciousness of concrete human beings in concrete bodies on the concrete earth in the concrete universe." That is to say, a specific individual, in this case Eric Voegelin, was required to "found" the experience. Second, there was no "length" of time within which things take place; rather the reality of things had a time dimension. Third, these things were hierarchically related from the inorganic to the vegetative and animal, to the existence of human being in metaleptic tension toward the Divine Ground of Being. Fourth, there was a process of the Whole, *to pan*, of which the In-Between reality of the historical process was a part. Fifth, this "part" was where the Whole became aware of itself as having an eschatological movement beyond itself and its own structure. Sixth, within the process of the Whole, some things lasted longer than others—for instance, the earth lasted longer than the humans who lived there—and what we call "time" without additional qualification denoting, say, the lifetime of a tree, of a cat, or of a human being, was the lastingness of the universe that could be measured by movements in space, such as a year or a second. But, finally, even the lastingness of the astrophysical universe is not a "time" within which things happen but a time dimension to the Whole that comprised the Divine reality whose mode of lastingness was expressed by such privative symbols as timelessness and eternity. Thus, the resolution of the problem: "Things do not happen in the astrophysical universe; the universe, together with all things founded in it, happens in God."[34]

The hierarchic structure of human being from the inorganic to conscious existence in metaleptic tension toward the Divine Ground carried with it two implications for Voegelin's understanding of philosophical anthropology. First, "only because the strata of reality participate in one another, through the relations of foundation and organization, in the order of the cosmos, can and must the true dimensions of the strata be related to one another, with the time dimension of the universe furnishing the ultimately founding measure." On the one hand, the lower strata conditioned but did not cause the higher; and on the other, the several strata participated in one another mutually, which was yet another meaning of metalepsis. This was the "primary relation" among the several strata and it was "of fundamental importance in the present context because it reveals the process of history to extend structurally, through participation, into the other strata of reality, including the physical universe" (CW, 17:409). Very simply, there could be no experience of metaleptic reality, of the divine-human In-Between without human bodies that were physically at home in the universe. Second, "the physical universe as the ultimate foundation of the higher strata in the hierarchy of being cannot be identified as the ultimate reality of the Whole, because in the stratum of consciousness we experience the presence of divine reality as the constituent of humanity." Accordingly, third, in human consciousness we were aware of both the foundation from the physical depth as well as the creative constitution of reality from the height of the Divine Ground. Finally, therefore, so far as modes of lasting were concerned, the order of the foundation of the universe "comprehends the time dimensions of the other strata in the hierarchy of being." However, in the order of creation from the Divine Ground of Being, the time dimension—or rather, the "divine mode of lasting that we symbolize as eternity"—comprehended "the time dimension of the other strata of reality, including the universe" (CW, 17:409).

34 CW, 17:408. See also CW, 17:264. There Voegelin directed his readers to his paper, "The Moving Soul" that was originally to be published in *In Search of Order*, but now published in CW, 28:163–72. Voegelin sent Henry Margeneau, whose *Nature of Physical Reality* (1950) prompted his reflections, a copy of the paper in 1969; Margeneau replied rather inconclusively (see HI, 24:15; CW, 30:624–25). It was also circulated to several other physicists, including Gern Hartmann and Mike Jones (HI, 24:15). See also Voegelin's 1980 "Outline of Reflections: Experience and Time," HI, 84:9.

Such a formulation was contradictory only if we made the assumption that the metaphors of "strata" and "hierarchy" implied a static set of layers akin to a geological formation. For Voegelin the contrary was true: the hierarchy was not static but was a movement, *kinesis*, of reality from the depth, the *Apeiron*, to human being, to as many levels of the hierarchy as could be discerned empirically; *and* it was the countermovement from the divine height through human consciousness as the site where the movement of the Whole was aware of itself as having eschatological direction. This was what was meant by the summary statement that reality was metaleptic. The Mystery of the historical process was therefore connected to the Mystery of reality that erupted as the universe, the earth, the things that dwell upon the earth, including human being who was conscious of the Mystery of the divine-cosmic order that had motivated the oldest cosmogonic symbolism. How could it be otherwise if universal humanity, if history, were the reality of participation in the whole?

6. Transition

We have come to the end of the analysis of a volume the editor judged unrivalled "in terms of philosophical depth, theoretical range or explanatory power" (CW, 17:1). Voegelin twice reflected on the significance of the book. At the end of his "Introduction" he remarked that he had just presented "the form that the philosophy of history has to assume in the present historical situation," which, to repeat, was *not* to arrange events on a historiogenetic time-line. The "new form" of analysis moved (in historiogenetic terms) "backward and forward and sideways" following experiential patterns of meaning that "revealed themselves in the self-interpretation of persons and societies in history." This was why Voegelin could argue that, for example, the authors of the Sumerian King Lists, no less than Hegel or Comte, were fully aware that they were mutilating the historical record in order to construct second realities.

The analysis revealed, he said, a "web of meaning" with distinct "nodal points" that revealed "dominant lines of meaning." He mentioned five: (1) the advance from compact to differentiated consciousness distributed over a plurality of ethnic cultures; (2) the specific noetic and pneumatic differentiations distributed over Hellas and Israel; (3) the ecumenic-imperial outburst that forced the ethnic cultures into a new ecumenic society; (4) the reactions of the ethnic cultures to imperial conquest; (5) the imperial conquest as introducing the meaning of humanity beyond tribal and ethnic societies. He then concluded: "From the Ecumenic Age, there emerges a new type of ecumenic humanity, which, with all its complications of meaning, reaches as a millennial constant in the modern Western civilization." In other words, we are still living in some respect in the Ecumenic Age.

Voegelin's own consciousness of epoch carried specific implications for his own work.

> In our time, the inherited symbolisms of ecumenic humanity are disaggregating because the deforming doctrinalization has become socially stronger than the experiential insights it was originally meant to protect. The return from symbols that have lost their meaning to the experiences that constitute meaning is so generally recognizable as the problem of the present that specific references are unnecessary. The great obstacle to this return is the massive block of accumulated symbols, secondary and tertiary, that eclipses the reality of man's existence in the Metaxy. To raise this obstacle and its structure into consciousness, and by its removal to help in the return to the truth of reality as it reveals itself in history, has become the purpose of *Order and History*. (CW, 17:107)

That purpose determined the organization of the last two volumes of the series as Voegelin conceived it in 1974. Volume four presented "the genesis of the ecumenic problem and its complications." The final volume was to contain "the contemporary problems that have motivated the search for order in history" in the consciousness of Eric Voegelin.

Voegelin again reflected on the significance of *The Ecumenic Age* in his concluding words to the volume. The analyses he had presented, he said, "are the mode of questioning engendered in the contemporary situation by a philosopher's resistance to the distortions and destruction of humanity committed by the 'stop-history' Systems. They are an act of open participation in the process of both history and the Whole" (CW, 17:410). In the event, Voegelin's publications after volume four, including the posthumously published *In Search of Order*, consisted of two different kinds of documents. There were those that expressed the philosopher's resistance to the abovementioned distortions and destructions of humanity. Like so many of his other works, these were critical analyses. In addition, however, Voegelin also produced several meditative essays wherein he reflected on the full amplitude of metaleptic reality.

CHAPTER SEVEN
MEDITATION

1. "The Drama of Humanity"

In the late essays and lectures, Voegelin worked out much of the argument that was published in the final volumes of *Order and History*, *The Ecumenic Age*, volume four, and *In Search of Order*, volume five. In addition however, in these essays and lectures as well as in volume five, he presented the results of his argument in the literary form of a meditation. However, we introduce this chapter with a discussion of Voegelin's Walter Turner Candler lectures, which Voegelin delivered at what was then Emory College in April 1967, under the title "The Drama of Humanity."[1] The discussion of "The Drama of Humanity" is followed by thematic analyses of several of Voegelin's late essays and lectures and a discussion of *In Search of Order*, which brought so many of these problems into sharp focus. We proceed in this deliberate fashion for two reasons: (1) it follows the development of Voegelin's own discussion, and (2) proceeding directly to *In Search of Order* without discussing how Voegelin got there is more apt to induce perplexity than understanding. But even if perplexity were the outcome, that too may be the first step to understanding.

1 CW, 33:174–242. Voegelin was invited to Emory in the spring of 1966 (CW, 30:502). At the time I was a graduate student at Duke and my supervisor, John Hallowell, was a friend of Voegelin. He once asked me to pick Voegelin up at Raleigh-Durham Airport. I drove well below the speed limit from RDU to the (no longer standing) Jack Tar Hotel in downtown Durham and enjoyed for my trouble an hour-long *Privatseminar*. When Professor Hallowell informed us that Voegelin would be speaking at Emory, Tom Flanagan (who, as an undergraduate, had attended Voegelin's lectures at Notre Dame) and I made plans to drive from Durham to Atlanta. We listened to Voegelin's lectures but (speaking only for myself) hardly understood what he said. The notes I took at the time prove it. A few years later, when I was an associate professor at York University in Toronto I heard his 1978 lecture on "Structures of Consciousness." Voegelin's words were transcribed from a video by my friend and former student, Zdravko Planinc, who was also in the audience. We were all very impressed by what we heard but still relatively clueless as to what Voegelin meant.

"The Drama of Humanity" was delivered seven years before the appearance of *The Ecumenic Age*. During the intervening years Voegelin left Munich for the Hoover Institution at Stanford.[2] He entertained the possibility of developing a network of institutes centered on the Hoover, and of scholars, including his own students in Munich, from around the world to conduct scientific studies of human affairs.[3] In addition, he began his studies on the Neolithic and Upper Paleolithic symbolism that likely would have made its way into the volume *The Drama of Humanity*, had it ever been written (CW, 30:13). One consequence was that his 1967 lecture constituted a kind of bridge between the initial empirical and historical work that led to

2 The negotiations with the Hoover can be followed reasonably accurately in Voegelin's correspondence, CW, 30, starting in the spring of 1967. The official letters and the correspondence with Richard Allen, who effectively brokered Voegelin's move to the Hoover, in HI, 6:10 and 18:28, provide a more complete picture. The aftermath of his departure from Munich is discussed in CW, 30:715 and in Hans Maier, "Eine Münchener Schule: Die Politische Wissenschaft in Deutschland und das Geswister-Scholl Institut," in Peter Cornelius Mayer-Tasch, ed., *Münchener Beitrage zur Politikwissenschaft* (Freiburg: Verlag Rombach, 1980), 15–29. See also Klause von Beyme, "Die deutsche Politikwissenschaft im internationalen Vergleich," in von Beyme, ed., *Politikwissenschaft in der Bundesrepublik Deutschland: Entwicklungsproblem einer Disziplin* (Oplanden: Westdeutscherr Verlag, 1986), 20; Leonard Reinisch, ed., *Politische Wissenschaft heute* (München: Verlag Beck, 1971), vii–x; "Politischen Wissenschaften in München," *Suddeutsche Zeitung*, 29 June 1963; "Der Gründer blieb schmollend fern," *Suddeutsche Zeitung*, 18–19 November 1978; "25 Jahre politische Bildung in München," *Suddeutsche Zeitung*, 28 December 1983; see also Voegelin's "exit interview": "Die Dummköpfe von links und rechts," (Munich) *Abendzeitung*, 15–16 February 1969 (HI, 75:6). See also Hans Maier, "Eric Voegelin und die Deutsche Politikwissenschaft," in Peter J. Opitz and Deitmar Herz, eds., *Eric Voegelin: Wanderer zwischen den Kontinenten* (Munich: Eric-Voegelin-Archiv, LMU, 2000) Occasional Papers, No. 14, and Voegelin's discussion of the "succession" at the Munich Institute (CW, 30:715).

3 Voegelin corresponded with scholars associated with organizations such as the Center for the Comparative Study of Civilizations, the International Society for the Study of Time, the Institute for Intercultural Research, the Eranos Foundation and the Academic Institute of Rome. Nothing permanent came of this activity, though Voegelin did attend several conferences. The proposal for a Hoover-centered network with the purpose of resisting the obsolete ideological climate of so many university departments and still reach students who, in Voegelin's opinion, were engaged in resistance to ideological irrationality by conducting the contemporaneous student revolt, was outlined in a 1970 memo (HI, 18:28). See, for example, Voegelin's extended correspondence with Professor Hans A. Fischer-Barnicol (HI, 19:4).

The Ecumenic Age and the summary of the "theoretical" arguments initially outlined in *Anamnesis* and the problems he developed in several subsequent essays and lectures dealing with the structure, formation, and deformation of consciousness. The problem of meditation scarcely appeared in "The Drama of Humanity."

Following some polite introductory remarks, Voegelin indicated his initial subject-matter was to link the drama of humanity to the contemporary situation. He divided the three lectures into four sections and explained that he had "to bring a few things which properly would belong in the third of these lectures" into the first one so that the series "will have a slight red shift from the first to the second, [and] from the second to the third. I cannot finish all the materials concerning the cosmic problems in the first, and not all the consciousness problems in the second; but then I have to shorten the third because I have to bring that [consciousness] in here, in order to start properly."[4]

It was, he said, "unusual" to speak of the drama of humanity and not the drama of man, but the difference was important. The contemporary self-understanding of man—of human being—used such terms as modern man, secular man, post-Christian man, and so on.[5] Using "a critical empirical and philosophical vocabulary" rather than contemporary clichés, one would speak of "modern man" first as a fundamentalist, second as philosophically illiterate, and third as "burning with apocalyptic fire" and thus divided by fear of the world as it is and filled with expectations of a better tomorrow.

By a fundamentalist Voegelin simply meant a dogmatist. Historically, the first dogmas were religious, which were followed by metaphysical dogmas and then by ideological ones. These dogmas were not to be understood as expressions of an orthodoxy but as a literalism devoid to any engendering experience for which any given orthodoxy was designed as a kind of protective shield. Reflecting that historical development, the most obvious expression of dogma, namely war or "dogmatomachy," over the past four centuries had changed from wars between adherents of religious dogmas to the twentieth-century wars between adherents of ideological dogmas. So far in the twenty-first century wars seem to be between adherents of religious and ideological dogmas.

4 HI, 74:1. Most of the lecture is reproduced in CW 33:174–242, though not the first paragraph from which the previous quotations were drawn.

5 Later versions, of course, would include other "post-" attributes such as post-industrial and post-modern.

The obvious inadequacies of fundamentalism have provoked sensitive thinkers, starting with Descartes, to resist and attempt to recapture the underlying realities and "reconstitute the understanding of man's relation to his surrounding reality, including divine reality" (CW, 33:176). From Descartes to William James, Henri Bergson, and Alfred North Whitehead, the results have been "peculiar" insofar as a high degree of literacy with respect to dogma has been combined with poor analyses of the experiences upon which the dogmas rested. Thus one found considerable illiteracy regarding the essential problems of human existence with enormous literacy regarding the peripheral ones.

The combination of dogmatism and illiteracy, finally, has had "particularly disastrous" consequences for Western civilization inasmuch as Western civilization "has grown through acculturation. That is, it had not developed on the basis of a prior cosmological civilization the self-understanding of which would have been grounded on a cosmological myth. By Voegelin's reading, Western civilization began with the conquest of the Roman Empire or of "Mediterranean civilization" by the "comparatively primitive" Germanic tribes. As a result, Western civilization had no "archaic period" akin to the Egyptian, for example, where coherence could be sought during a period of upheaval, disorder, and alienation by consulting practices, scriptures, and art, along with the original mythical order that might be thousands of years old. In contrast, "we have nothing we can fall back on." Thus, during periods of disorder and alienation in Egypt, evidenced in one of Voegelin's oft-consulted texts, the "Dispute of a Man, Who Contemplates Suicide, With His Soul," the author of the "Dispute" could consult an archaic myth to debate his Soul because both the Man of the "Dispute" and the Soul accepted that the myth articulated the experience of reality.[6] But in contemporary Western civilization, once cultural concepts had been destroyed or lost, one encountered a "radical alienation" and a correspondingly desperate attempt to recapture experiences of reality.

One way to do so in a once accultured and now decultured civilization would be to search for experiences of reality outside Western civilization. "That is why people all of a sudden become Zen Buddhists." Even so, the search for experiences of reality outside an exhausted Western dogmatism was also, starting in the nineteenth century, part of a pattern of historical

6 "The Dispute" is translated by John A. Wilson, in *Ancient Near Eastern Texts Relating to the Old Testament*, ed. James B. Pritchard (Princeton: Princeton University Press, 1950), 405–7. Cf. CW, 12:60ff; 33:192–96.

activity "in which all previous history is thrown out" so that all that remained was the modern "point" of time in which we have to live. "Living on a point, throwing out all past history, that is perhaps the characteristic of the modern apocalyptic mood" (CW, 33:178–79). One further distinction, between the great apocalyptics of the nineteenth century, namely Comte, Hegel, and Marx, and those of the twentieth and twenty-first centuries was that the earlier thinkers were, in fact, accomplished historians whereas their epigones are not. More recent apocalyptics simply expressed the dogma that because the present was felt to be intolerable, something meaningful must be coming along. What that might be was left up to the individual imagination.[7] With or without any actual historical knowledge, all such expectations were simply arbitrary historiogenetic constructions.

In contrast, Voegelin argued that history needs to be understood—and here he used the formulation of T. S. Eliot—as the intersection of time with the timeless (cf. CW, 33:33ff.), which he called the flow of "presence," in fact, "of a divine presence." Without such an understanding of history as presence there would be no reason to be concerned with such matters as the text of the "Dispute" or, indeed, of anything else in the past. Voegelin's reasoning was clear: the reality expressed in the "Dispute," or in Plato's *Republic*, or the Gospel of Mark had a presence in our present because it expressed the permanent tension of immanent and transcendent poles of human experience. What else could the experience of divine presence be?

Voegelin then explained his title. "Man" referred to the classical philosophy of human nature, which as Voegelin had several times explained, cannot change despite the expectations of the apocalyptics. As we saw in chapter one, Voegelin also spoke of the historicity of truth to refer, among other things, to the way that human beings understood themselves. Moreover, the discovery of human nature, the nature of man, or the idea of man, whether modelled on an artifact or an organism, was also a historical event. That was why Voegelin argued, as we saw in chapter five, that although Aristotle reported the stable features of human being in the *Ethics* and *Politics*, he never wrote a *Historics* to account for the event of the discovery of these stable attributes of individual and political life. This "reflective element" would address the problem that human nature also contained a specific self-understanding by which human being was related or related itself to other sectors of the "quaternarian structure" of reality introduced in volume one

7 For example, Charles A. Reich's *The Greening of America* (New York: Random House, 1970) was at the time a very popular example of this genre of literature.

of *Order and History*. The changing element of "envisaging" unchanging human being in the context of other kinds of being was what Voegelin meant by "humanity." In short, "*humanity* means man in a mode of understanding himself in his relation to God, world, and society, and these modes change. *History* would be the drama (if a meaning in it [history] can be discovered) of humanity, of the self-understanding of man" (CW, 33:186).

Voegelin then discussed once again the cosmological style of truth, including the "Dispute" as an expression of alienation that did not quite achieve an understanding of human existence as immediately under God. Rather, as was noted above, "Man" in the "Dispute" decided that the best way to restore order was to join Re in the barque of the sun, which is to say, to commit suicide, and in death add his ordering power to that of the god who then might be powerful enough to restore order on earth. The differentiated experience of immediacy under God, Voegelin called "the epiphany of man," by which he meant as well that human beings became aware of themselves as distinct from the consubstantial cosmos. The two types of experience of this epiphany, we have seen, Voegelin called noetic and pneumatic, the one tending toward analysis of the structure of experience, the other as a response less to structure than to the divine presence.

In this context, as in his previous work, Voegelin was concerned chiefly with noetic differentiation in human consciousness, where consciousness meant "the experience of a tension in existence toward the Ground of one's own existence" (CW, 33:199–200). Voegelin reiterated his distinction between consciousness as the *site* where participation in the Ground was experienced, which was always present in human being, and as the *sensorium* of participation, which was the historically differentiated means by which one became aware of one's participation in tension toward the Ground and made such participation the subject-matter for conceptual analysis. Awareness of participation was the historical achievement of those human beings whom Voegelin referred to as philosophers because that was how they referred to themselves. Philosophically speaking, therefore, consciousness was always both site and sensorium. Accordingly, when consciousness became conscious it also became "the center of all order." Order was no longer simply a cosmic datum and already there; of course there was still a cosmos, but personal and political order was henceforth an achievement of "attunement," as he said in earlier volumes the *Order and History*.

The consequence for the previously discussed cosmological experience, now referred to as the primary experience of the cosmos, Voegelin said, was "disastrous." No longer were gods, humans, society, kings, people, heaven, earth, animals, plants, and so on, constituents of the cosmos. Henceforth, the experience of immediacy under God divided reality into God and everything else, which Voegelin called "world." The world, in that sense, was "the remnant of the cosmos" left over when the gods had been expelled and God was experienced and symbolized as a world-transcendent reality (CW, 33:201). Correspondingly, as we have seen, the world became immanent in relation to the world-transcendent Ground of Being, God. All these terms, as Voegelin argued in *Anamnesis*, were "linguistic indices" that expressed the content of the experience of a now differentiated consciousness. That is, consciousness as the site of participation engendered the linguistic indices of immanence and transcendence. The three terms—consciousness, immanence and transcendence—constituted, Voegelin said, a "triangle" that "must never be broken terminologically" (CW, 33:203).

So much for consciousness as site of participation; what then was consciousness as the sensorium of such participation? That is, what happened within the drama of humanity when humans recognized their own specifically human attributes as creatures that were conscious of their own participation in reality, were self-reflective, and produced language symbols that explicated this experience of consciousness to consciousness? The first consequence, Voegelin said, was that the philosopher produced an "idea" or a "universal idea" of man, of human being, or of humanity. Prior to the differentiation in self-reflective consciousness of the immediacy of all human beings under God as the source or the Ground of common humanity, there could be no universal idea of man. And when the experience of immediacy was forgotten or eclipsed there followed a "partial" or "fragmented" idea that claimed to be universal. But in fact one could not have such fragmentary ideas in the absence of an already present universal idea that then could be denied. "Before the structure of universality developed, nobody claimed to be universally man. But once it was developed, every idiot could claim that idiocy is the universal characteristic of man" (CW, 33:204).

A second "universal idea," developed after the destruction of the primary experience of the cosmos, was that all the divinities that used to be cosmic were now concentrated in the one world-transcendent God to be found nowhere in the world. "Thus, you have an idea of universal divinity corresponding to the universality of man," the origins of which could be traced to Egypt during the third millennium. The Christian approximation, which received an appropriate formulation in the remark of St. Thomas, that Christ was the head of humanity and not only of the Christian community, was "not very effective," because, as Voegelin put it, one would have to explain "how Christ is the head of the Mystical Body in, say, the Mesopotamian Empire."[8]

> A real philosophy of history based in the problem of universal divinity, as I'm trying here, for example, has, as far as I know, never been done. It's an idea very slow in developing. We have a prehistory of two thousand years before Christ and a post-history of two thousand years following Christ, but it is still not, you might say, generally accepted. One still makes exceptions to that universal divinity as the one divine Ground of all being. (CW, 33:204)

The third universal was that of a world common to all human beings that exhibited an autonomous structure that was neither cosmic, nor divine, nor human. These, Voegelin concluded, were the three principal universal ideas: universal humanity, universal divinity, and universal world. As with the previous triad or "triangle" of consciousness (as site), immanence and transcendence, so too with consciousness (as sensorium) the three universals went together as a unit (CW, 33:206).

Voegelin then discussed some "special problems" taken initially from the *Upanishads* (cf. CW, 30:276) and the *Apocalypse of Abraham* (cf. CW 28:96–99; 395–98; 17:398) to illustrate the general points he had just made. Although it was true that, as a technical term, the Ground of Being appeared only in philosophy, it was also true that "the search for the Ground always goes on in the cosmological sphere" as well. In ancient Egypt, for example, speculation on the name of the god responsible for the creation of the world was equivalent to the Ionian speculation on the kind of element that was the origin, the *arche*, of things. But once the speculative process began, a problem arose: if a single polytheistic god could not be used as the origin of all beings, what *was* their origin? "On that occasion—again one has to be aware of these things—the term *being* is introduced." That is, the speculation that began by naming concrete gods and their creative activities now used universal terms. Specifically, "the term *being* is introduced for all these realities" so that, instead of speculating on what god or what element was responsible for this or that thing, the new question was: "What is the Ground of all Being, the arche, the origin of it all?" These speculative problems

8 CW, 33:203–4; 301; see also Thomas, *Summa Theologica*, III.8.2–3. This is a problem to which Voegelin returned in subsequent work.

returned us to the experiences of transcendence discussed in chapters three and four in connection with Parmenides (CW, 33:211).

With the experience of transcendence came the possibility of derailment and the option of ignoring one or another parts of the first "triangle," along with the possibility of understanding the existent and non-existent modes of the being of reality by analogy with one another. That is, once consciousness was differentiated, the problem of understanding the relation of consciousness to the cosmos came into focus because the cosmos was still there. Hence the development of the terms discussed in the previous chapter—Plato's argument that the things of the world "participate" in the eternal, non-existent, world-transcendent ideas, for example, or Aristotle's argument regarding mutual participation, *metalepsis*, to which we return below.

In a letter to Gregor Sebba, who was instrumental in bringing Voegelin to Emory (indeed, who tried to induce Voegelin to choose Emory over the Hoover Institution), Voegelin thanked him for his "kind labors" and noted that "the most important part" of the lectures in his opinion, was the Theory of Universals.[9] He considered this theory, and the supporting argument regarding the "triangle" of consciousness-immanence-transcendence to be

> the decisive advance over the classic and medieval philosophy of universals, as well as over the "clear" or "innate" ideas that still plague Descartes. The Universals of consciousness do not abstract essences from the world-immanent things, but indicate the structure of reality (concretely) in the perspective of a differentiated consciousness. I am working on that problem now. (CW, 30:523)

To understand what Voegelin meant by saying that the "Universals of consciousness . . . indicate the structure of reality (concretely) in the perspective of differentiated consciousness" we first consider his remarks on the structure of consciousness and its formation and deformation. Here the emphasis, as ought to be obvious at this point in the argument, was on noetic analysis. The "concrete" discussion of consciousness in the last section of this chapter, on meditation, emphasized equally the noetic and the pneumatic modes of participation in reality.

9 CW, 30:522–23; cf. 528, 569–70. The University of Maryland also attempted to recruit Voegelin (HI, 38:22).

2. The Structure of Consciousness

In November 1978 Voegelin gave a talk on "Structures of Consciousness" at York University, Toronto, that summarized several themes we have already introduced (CW, 33:353ff.). "Consciousness," he began, "is the something that is conscious of something," and what it is conscious of is reality. "And this relation between consciousness and reality to which it refers, that I shall call following Husserl's terminology, *intentionality* of consciousness." This intentional consciousness was "something that man has and man concretely, man in bodily existence." Consciousness was not, however, only intentional but "is also at the same time an 'event' in reality, an event more correctly in the 'process' of reality." The process of reality included biological as well as physical evolution "behind" what may approximately or summarily be called "historical evolution." This was a grand process "in which man with his consciousness is appearing lately," which is to say, recently. In current language Voegelin was referring to "deep" history or "big" history.[10]

That same year Voegelin looked back to his discussions with Schütz during the 1940s regarding Husserl. As discussed in chapter one, Voegelin reiterated that Husserl's "magnificent work" was confined to the intentionality of consciousness but ignored a pre-intentional consciousness of participation, which Voegelin on this occasion called "reality-consciousness" and described it with the familiar adjective, "luminous" (CW, 12:311–12). A few years later, at a talk he gave at a weekend seminar in Tutzing, south of Munich, Voegelin further clarified the implications of the imagery or metaphor of luminosity. When we were conscious of something, even if the object of consciousness was imaginary, Voegelin said he would speak of "reality in the mode of thing-reality." Moreover, he "suspected" this was because the something about which one spoke "is the result of the fact that human consciousness is located in a body and that, in relationship to our bodily localization, all that of which one has consciousness—this 'something'—is co-experienced as being 'outside' this bodily existence" (CW, 33:391).

10 See, for example: Cynthia Stokes Brown, *From the Big Bang to the Present* (New York: New Press, 2007); David Christian, *Maps of Time: An Introduction to Big History* (Berkeley and Los Angeles: University of California Press, 2004); Robin Dunbar, *The Human Story: A New History of Mankind's Evolution* (London: Faber and Faber, 2004); Brendan Purcell, *From Big Bang to Big Mystery* (Dublin: Veritas, 2011); Andrew Shyrock and Fred Smail, *Deep History: The Architecture of the Present* (Berkeley and Los Angeles: University of California Press, 2011); Fred Speir, *The Structure of Big History* (Amsterdam: Amsterdam University Press, 1996).

By the late 1970s Voegelin had found an elegant, if somewhat formular, language to indicate the distinction he sought to convey in his previous discussions of consciousness as site and as sensorium (cf. CW, 12:90). Consciousness was not simply intentional because the subject belonged to the same reality that it knew as an object so that this subject-object relation was itself "an event in another reality" that encompassed both subject and object. "For this encompassing reality, as far as I know, we have no generally accepted philosophical term. Nietzsche dealt with it often and called it 'It,' and I will stick to that" and speak of "It-reality." In a later discussion Voegelin said he "became aware of it [i.e., It-reality] for the first time in the studies of Karl Kraus on the [usage of] 'it' in language."[11]

This It-reality was an "It" because within this reality such a thing as consciousness occurred in the same sense as physical or biological realities occurred. "That is to say that this It-reality, when it was brought into relationship with consciousness becomes luminous," presumably because consciousness "illumines" It-reality from within as an internal awareness. "Corresponding to intentionality," Voegelin continued, "I speak of luminosity. The subject of this luminosity, in which the event 'consciousness,' occurs as a predicate, is not the human ego, but the It-reality. This [i.e., the It-reality] becomes luminous." Accordingly, there were to be found two structures of consciousness, the one where human being was the subject, namely intentionality, and the other, namely luminosity, "of which we must say that 'It' is the subject and that consciousness is the predicative event in the 'It.'" So far as the reality of consciousness per se was concerned, the two must not be separated insofar as "human consciousness always contains both structures" (CW, 33:392).

Voegelin had, therefore, discovered (or rediscovered) a reality in which consciousness occurred; reality, "the object of intentional consciousness, is now becoming the subject, of which consciousness, as one of its events, has to be predicated." This meant, therefore, that reality was a subject. "Can we say that that reality is conscious? or that reality knows? or is the subject of knowledge?

11 CW, 33:398. Here Voegelin gave as an example the phrase, "it rains," which referred to "an event surrounded by a reality to which the rain is then a predicate" (CW, 33:398). The same linguistic structure exists in German (*es gibt*), and in French (*il pleut)*. Indeed, Paul Caringella pointed out that Emmanuel Levinas used exactly that phrase to exemplify his own version of "It-reality," the "*il y a*" of French. See Caringella, "Eric Voegelin and Emmanuel Levinas," a paper presented at the American Political Science Association meeting, San Francisco, 31 August 1996. Apparently Greek peasants say "God rains," not "it rains." See Patrick Leigh Fermor, *Mani: Travels in the Southern Peloponnese* (London: Murray, 1958), 72.

I don't think so."[12] A different term than saying reality was conscious was therefore required. Voegelin thus used "the term that is most clearly related to the similar treatment of such problems by medieval thinkers; I'm using the term *luminosity*. Reality becomes luminous in consciousness and consciousness then intends the reality for which the reality has become luminous in consciousness." Obviously this was a complex structure "because the reality of which man is constituted as an event in its process becomes an object for that consciousness that has arisen in it" (CW, 33:355–56). To use a formulation of chapter six, reality becomes self-conscious in human consciousness.

There was, therefore, a "double structure" of consciousness as intentionality and then as "an event of luminosity in reality." None of this would be known, however, if consciousness did not also have the gift of "expressing itself in language." So language was an additional "structural element" in this "complex," namely the method by which the communication between human beings and their intentional and as well as luminous consciousness is conducted.

Language, Voegelin said, "breaks forth" in the process of consciousness as the luminosity of reality. That is, when reality became luminous in human consciousness, it did so by letting a human being find the language terms needed to express his or her experience. And once language had broken forth, language, now understood in terms of intentionality, signified the reality intended. Under the aspect of luminosity, language arose in a historical process; under the aspect of intentionality it signified reality as an object. "Both breaking forth and intentionality . . . belong to language" (CW, 33:537).

Language, by this argument, was not simply given, either as a luminous "breaking forth" or as a reflective intentional object. One could, of course, speak conceptually in the context of intentionality and so of thing-reality. However, "when discussing the reflection of consciousness on luminosity, I prefer to speak of symbols" rather than concepts. "The expression 'symbol' is always determined by the dominant component of consciousness, the luminosity of the 'It.' Everything that emerges in symbols of consciousness and in language symbols is the luminosity of the 'It'" (CW, 33:393). But more than these two

12 Robert McMahon observed that "though calling reality 'conscious' in this way may seem odd, the oddness emerges from our intentionalist prejudices." On the other hand, "because human beings are real and conscious, reality is conscious. Reality proves consciousness of itself through the human consciousness of reality." See "Eric Voegelin's Paradoxes of Consciousness and Participation," *Review of Politics* 61 (1999): 120. We return to this problem below.

components—intentionality and luminosity—was involved in the "complex" of consciousness. There was also the possibility of "reflecting on the complex of consciousness" including both components. This was neither analysis by means of concepts nor symbolic in-dwelling, to borrow a term of Michael Polanyi. Rather, Voegelin said, "I would like to speak of a further component in the structure of consciousness, which I call *reflective distance*." Here the problem of intentionality-and-luminosity was "transposed into a language of reflection in which this problem is spoken of as though it were a reality independent of reflection." But, of course, it was not independent of reflection because reflection was already present as a component of consciousness.

Thus we now had three components in consciousness that were co-present in various degrees of articulation but that could not be identified with one another. This is a very complex structure of consciousness indeed (CW, 33:393–94). It led, moreover, to a new problem, which Voegelin here called the problem of truth. Truth was first understood as reality becoming luminous for its structure in consciousness through a process in which human beings participate. And then this reality, insofar as it became luminous in the consciousness of a human being, became "knowledge" in relation to the intentionality of consciousness. Accordingly, "truth does not refer only to a reality outside of man and confronting man, but also to the process of reality in which man himself becomes an event, the event of the carrier of consciousness" (CW, 33:357).

This insight allowed Voegelin to clear up one persistent and fallacious left-over from the era of doctrinal formulas expressed in the proposition: "the experience is an illusion," which was typically applied to expressions of the world-transcendent Ground, the word of God, the place of the gods in the cosmos, and so on.

> First, the intellectual structure of the objection: the proposition is a piece of loose thinking, quite common in everyday speech. Speaking carefully, one would have to say that an experience is never an illusion but always a reality; the predicate *illusion* should be used with reference, not to the experience, but to its content, in case it has illusionary character. Taken by itself, the incorrect wording is worth not more attention than is necessary to avoid a misunderstanding. In the context of ideological polemic, however, the transfer of the predicate is subtly used for the very purpose of creating a misunderstanding, *viz.*, that the incorrectly worded proposition in the foreground carries, in its

> own right, the possible sense of the background proposition. The transfer diverts attention from the inarticulate premise. The result is a nonsense proposition designed to forestall the question whether the possible sense in the background makes really sense in the concrete case. Let us, therefore, break the taboo and ask the question we are supposed not to ask: What does it mean when the content of the experience is to be characterized as an illusion? It can mean one of two things: either radically, that the object experienced by a subject does not exist at all; or, gradationally, that the object exists but on closer inspection reveals characteristics different from those apparent in the object as experienced. In either case, the judgment of illusion rests on control experiences of the potentially or actually existent object outside the experience. With this observation, however, the reason—or at least one of the reasons—why the possible sense in the background must be kept in the dark becomes visible. For a judgment of illusion can pertain only to experiences of existent objects, not to experiences of participation in nonexistent reality. Thus, the veiled sense in the background, if made articulate, proves to be just as much nonsense as the proposition in the foreground. (CW, 12:67–68)

That is, the proposition, "the experience is an illusion" rests on two insupportable assumptions: (1) the fallacy of misplaced concreteness that accorded priority to the dogmatic and conceptual formula rather than to the experience and its symbolization; and (2) the hiding of this fallacy by obscuring the premise, namely that consciousness was only world-immanent and that humans were unable to apprehend realities beyond the world. It was, therefore, a strategy based on dismembering the first "triangle" that Voegelin mentioned in "The Drama of Humanity."

In a more positive vein, Voegelin concluded that human beings employed a plurality of languages that expressed and corresponded to the state of luminosity and state of intentionality, which Voegelin previously discussed in terms of compactness and differentiation of consciousness.[13] Thus, to use Voegelin's formulation, "there is a series of such states of consciousness of

13 See also Tilo Schabert, "Les langes d'Eric Voegelin: Aurour de la Conscience et de la Réalité," in Thierry Gontier, ed., *Politique, Religion et Histoire chez Eric Voegelin* (Paris: Cerf, 2011), 16–30.

increasing luminosity and increasing knowledge of reality as an object." Such "languages" included imperial cosmological myths, preceded by tribal myths and even pre-mythical imagery and ritual, and later the myth of the polis, the philosopher's myth, revelation, doctrinal formulations, "theology," apocalyptic, Gnosticism, Neoplatonic systems, mysticism and so on (CW, 33:357).

This entire array of problems Voegelin called the "meditative complex," which existed as a whole prior to being analyzed in terms of intentionality and luminosity—of consciousness, of language, and so on. "One must not fragmentize the complex and pretend that a structural element in that complex can be isolated and made an object of independent study, because then this complicated structure of intentionality and luminosity is gone" (CW, 33:361). Henceforth when Voegelin used the term "complex" he intended a concatenation of symbols that must not be isolated from one another (CW, 30:865).

The increased precision that Voegelin was seeking in the language of his argument during the 1970s permits us to make a kind of retrospective clarification of several terms that he had introduced earlier. For example, Plato's prepositional noun, Metaxy, discussed in chapter six, which Voegelin first used as a technical term in 1964 (CW, 6:324ff), was described in more detail a few years later as

> a reality that partakes of both time and eternity and, therefore, does not wholly belong to the one or the other. There appears to be a flow of existence that is not existence in time. Since modern philosophy has not developed a vocabulary for describing the Metaxy, I shall use the term *presence* to denote the point of intersection in man's existence that is, and is not, time. (CW, 12:77)

Later in his 1971 article on Hegel, Voegelin wrote that "the In-Between of existence is not an empty space between two static entities, but the meeting ground of the human and the divine in a consciousness of their distinction and interpenetration. This consciousness of the Metaxy is in historical flux" (CW, 12:233). In the element of historical flux one recognized precisely the drama of humanity. Again, a few years later, Voegelin was even more precise: not only was the Metaxy not an "empty space between the poles of the tension," it was "the 'reality of the spiritual'; it is the reality of man's converse with the gods [*Symp.*, 202–3], the mutual participation (*methexis*, *metalepsis*) of human in divine and divine in human reality." Of course, it was always possible to reduce the metaleptic tension to a causal explanation of bodily functions or to some sort of psychology. However, "to move within the Metaxy, exploring it in all directions and orienting himself in the perspective granted to man by his position in reality, is the proper task of the philosopher" (CW, 12:283).

Voegelin restated the "proper task" of the philosopher first discussed in detail in volume three of *Order and History*. Philosophy understood as the unfolding of noetic consciousness in history, was an event, the symbolic articulation of which intelligibly expressed "the experience of existential unrest in the process of becoming cognitively luminous." Obviously philosophy was not "the first nor the last symbolization of Man's humanity in quest of its relation to the Divine Ground," though it was "the first in articulating the structure of the quest itself" as Voegelin was, in fact, recapitulating in the lectures and articles that we have been citing in this chapter (CW, 12:287–88). When existence in the Metaxy became conscious of itself, or "luminous to itself," namely in philosophy, the order of existence was not changed. On the contrary, the "differentiation of Reason," as Voegelin put it here, changed only "the level of critical consciousness concerning the order of existence" (CW, 12:288). This formulation was a more precise version of Voegelin's imagery in the early volumes of *Order and History* that the "leap upward in being is not a leap out of existence" (CW, 14:49; 17:56–58, 291–302).

Specifically, philosophy as zetesis, as a quest for the Ground, became aware both of its own intentionality and of the surrounding reality of which it was a part and within which the quest took place. "The mystery is the horizon that draws us to advance toward it but withdraws as we advance; it can give direction to the quest of truth but it cannot be reached; and the beyond of the horizon can fascinate as the 'extreme' of truth but it cannot be possessed as truth face to face within this life" (CW, 12:326). Intentionality and mystery, Voegelin said, were additional "structures" of consciousness not in the sense of a fixture but of "moving forces in the process of reality becoming luminous." The "balance of consciousness" thus was a "third structure" where the desire to know reality as the object intended by consciousness did not however turn into "an intentionalist desire to know the mystery of the horizon and its beyond as if it were an object this side of the horizon." Nor did the consciousness of mystery limit "the desire to know by assuming objects this side of the horizon to belong to the sphere of mystery."[14] Corresponding to the aforementioned understanding of truth as dealing both with reality outside human existence as well as of the process of reality within which human being was an event, was truth as "a perspective of reality, arising from man's participation, with his conscious existence, in the reality of which he is a part" (CW, 12:326). Truth, that is, was both a balance of consciousness and an awareness of a balance of consciousness. Once this insight had been grasped, deformations of consciousness were understood as equivalent to a loss of balance and thus, as well, to a loss of reality.

In a final consideration of the structures of consciousness, in 1982 Voegelin gave a lecture on "The Beyond and Its Parousia" (CW, 33:396ff). The "Beyond" referred to Plato's *epekeina*, which he used in the image of the sun in the *Republic* (509b14). According to Voegelin, it was a "general symbolism of the divine reality, that is, the one beyond all the reality of the gods of the cosmos." And yet divine reality was also present and "formative in the direction of order and justice. So *parousia* is the general term for the presence of the divine reality in all reality." But this formulation introduced "complications" with the term reality "because on the one hand there is a divine reality, [and] on the other hand, the divine reality is the reality that is present in all reality." This conception of a beyond and of its presence in reality

> implies that there is something that has to be formed. There seems to be a counter-pole to the *epekeina* that resists formation or requires formation and, if formed, can still resist the formation and deform the formation into some deformed type of entity. So we have in the process of reality a very complicated series of events filled with the tension of formation, resistance to the formation, resistance to deformation of formation, and so on.

As with the earlier discussion of thing-reality and It-reality, there was an "obviously inconsistent terminology" that "on the linguistic level cannot be dissolved." The reason, as was clear from the earlier analysis, was because in reality both thing-reality and It-reality existed "together in one structure of consciousness, which structure I call the *paradox of consciousness*" and

14 CW, 12:237. See also Kenneth Keulman, *The Balance of Consciousness: Eric Voegelin's Political Theory* (University Park: Pennsylvania State University Press, 1990), and Glen Hughes, "Balanced and Unbalanced Consciousness," in Hughes, ed., *The Politics of the Soul* (Lanham: Rowman and Littlefield, 1999), 163–83.

it reached from consciousness and reality into language and could not be avoided, reduced, or explained away. All one can do, Voegelin said, was think about these things, which in turn re-introduced the human ability of "reflectively distancing" ourselves "from the paradox in which we are involved and talk about it—and such talk is called *philosophy*." Indeed, "all philosophy is conducted in reflective distance within consciousness about consciousness" (CW, 33:399). It may be, as Robert McMahon observed, that although we are actors in the drama of being we see ourselves as spectators in the audience. This was not the end of the paradox, however, because we can become aware of the paradox, which made it intelligible even if it did not dissolve it.[15]

3. Deformations

Voegelin began his 1981 Tutzing lecture by raising a familiar theme: scientific investigation must begin from the actual situation wherein one lived and within which searching for truth first appeared as a real problem.

> How does one know that what one has at hand is not the truth; and how does one reach this insight if one does not know what the truth is for which one must first search? Thus, from the very beginning, we find ourselves in a state of existential tension that consists in the act that we observe phenomena of untruth, the problems of disorder in our surroundings, and that, because of such observations, we set out to find an order from which we know, from the outset, that such a thing exists, but that it must first be found. (CW, 33:384)

Already, therefore, the philosopher has found himself or herself within the by now familiar tensional field of being moved and seeking, of active and passive, accompanied by an awareness in the psyche that this movement was occurring.

This starting point bore a family resemblance to the approach first roughly articulated in *On the Form of the American Mind*, that political science began with analysis of the self-interpretation of societies. It was

15 McMahon, "Eric Voegelin's Paradoxes of Consciousness and Participation," 126.

expanded in Voegelin's discussions of race ideas, in the *History of Political Ideas*, and in *The New Science of Politics* where he made the sharp distinction between symbols of self-interpretation that occurred in political reality and concepts of political science that analyzed them. As he described the starting-point in his 1973 *Autobiographical Reflections*: "The motivations of my work, which culminates in a philosophy of history, are simple. They arise from the political situation," by which he meant not only the "murderous unpleasantness" of pragmatic politics during the twentieth century but the ideological climate of opinion that made scientific or rational analysis of political reality so difficult and occasionally dangerous as well (CW, 30:118).

Not the crude external deformations of political mass movements but the deformations of consciousness concern us here. The two were connected insofar as both constituted "restrictions" on consciousness. As Voegelin observed in his 1977 contribution to the first English edition of *Anamnesis*, if both ideological political movements and the climate of opinion expressed in "school philosophies" were produced by such restrictions, it was also true that "I had observed the restriction, and recognized it as such, with the criteria of the observation coming from a consciousness with a larger horizon, which in this case happened to be my own." The conclusion Voegelin drew, which in fact had guided all his analyses of political as well as interpretive phenomena, was clear:

> any analysis of consciousness, I had to conclude, has no instrument other than the concrete consciousness of the analyst. The quality of this instrument, then, and consequently the quality of the results, will depend on what I have called the horizon of consciousness; and the quality of the horizon will depend on the analyst's willingness to reach out to all the dimensions of the reality in which his conscious existence is an event; it will depends on his desire to know. A consciousness of this kind is not an a priori structure, nor does it just happen, nor is its horizon a given. It rather is a ceaseless action of expanding, ordering, articulating, and correcting itself; it is an event at responsive openness to the appeal of reality, at bewaring the premature satisfaction, and above all at avoiding the self-destructive phantasy of believing the reality of which it is a part to be an object external to itself that can be mastered by bringing it into the form of a system. (CW, 33:305)

The most obvious of these deformations we have examined in chapter two on Gnosticism and in chapter five in the discussion of second reality, "stupidity," the eclipse of reality, and so on.[16] Here we consider a couple of related problems. In the quotation just given, Voegelin referred to the "phantasy" of treating the reality of participation, namely It-reality, as if it were thing-reality. We have already encountered this problem in terms of dogma or doctrine. In the "Immortality" article Voegelin provided a succinct account of the origins and limitations of dogma, which on other occasions he was content simply to analyze.

The problem of dogma was connected to the fact that language symbols such as immortality "are not concepts referring to objects existing in time and space but carriers of a truth about nonexistent reality." Moreover, the experience of truth expressed in such symbols was itself experienced as nonexistent "inasmuch as it [i.e., the experience of truth] is nothing but a consciousness of participation in nonexistent reality." And this same mode of nonexistence was attached to the symbols because "they convey no other truth than that of the engendering consciousness. . . . As a consequence, when the experience engendering the symbols ceases to be a presence located in the man who has it, the reality from which the symbols derive their meaning has disappeared." This by now familiar problem of experience and symbolization was connected to the problem of dogma because the symbols did exist in the world and so may be perceived, "but their truth belongs to the nonexistent experience which by their means articulates itself."

The intangibility of the experience of truth meant that, however careful the exegesis, the symbols and the experience that engendered them might dissociate into "a piece of information and its subject-matter. There is no guarantee whatsoever that the reader of the account will be moved to a meditative reconstitution of the engendering reality; one may even say the chances are slim, as meditation requires more energy and discipline than most people are able to invest." Hence the tendency towards dogmatic simplicity in order to preserve at least something of the insight by way of propositions such as "the soul is immortal."

Such propositions, however, might engender their own experiences:

> there is the seminarian, as a Catholic friend once bitterly remarked, who rather believes in Denzinger's *Enchiridion* than in God; or, to avoid any suspicion of confessional partisanship,

16 See also CW, 12:316–17; 28, 111ff.

> there is the Protestant fundamentalist; or to avoid any suspicion of professional partisanship, there is the professor of philosophy who informs you about Plato's "doctrine" of the soul, or of the idea, or of truth, though to conceive of Plato as a promoter of doctrine is preposterous. (CW, 12:53–54)

In turn, dogma could be met with skepticism or with counter-dogma and the whole complex could disintegrate into "a heap of broken images," as T.S. Eliot said. The replacement of "broken images" expressed what Voegelin called "the revolt of man" in "The Drama of Humanity" or an egophanic revolt, to use the formulation of *The Ecumenic Age* (CW, 33:218ff; 17:326ff). In short, the existential truth that was to have been preserved by the dogma was in fact deformed by it; such truth therefore could not be preserved dogmatically. Only "a return to the reality of experience which has originally engendered the symbols" could do that (CW, 12:73). Accordingly, dogma was to be avoided by political science, though its formation as a protective measure was at least intelligible.[17]

There were two other subtle modes of deformation to be mentioned in this context. The first was discussed in Voegelin's 1974 essay, "Reason: The Classic Experience." Human being, Voegelin began, was not "a disembodied psyche ordered by Reason" but embodied in such a manner that Reason participated in animal, vegetative, and physical being. The psyche, moreover, experienced not only the noetic attraction and movement towards the Ground of Being and its order, but also the pull of the passions away from the Ground. In this context Aristotle spoke of the "synthetic" nature of human being and Voegelin spoke of the "integral" nature of man (CW, 12:268).

Humans and animals shared some kinds of experiences, such as pain or fear, at least with respect to pain-inducing or fear-inducing situations. Humans alone, apparently, understood their existence in a state of precariousness and were aware that they were not self-created, autonomous beings that carried the origin and meaning of existence within themselves. This precariousness existed within the limits of birth and death, which to be sure were biological realities. For human beings, however, they were also mysteries. Humans alone raised questions about the meaning of it all, including birth and death; to use the classical formula, they *wondered* about the ultimate Ground or cause or foundation of all reality, including themselves.

17 Other accounts can be found in CW, 6:372–79; 12:292–95; 33:175–77, 296–97.

That is, human beings were not just living beings, animals, but animals who raised questions about the questionable status of being human.

Reason, Nous, Voegelin said once again, was differentiated "as a structure in reality" by Plato and Aristotle, as was argued in detail in chapter six, from "trust (*pistis*) in the divinely ordered cosmos and love (*philia*, *eros*) for the divine source of order" (CW, 12:283). Voegelin then remarked that the classical sense of Reason "has the definite existential content of openness toward reality in the sense in which Bergson speaks of *l'âme ouverte*." Without that experiential or empirical content, the symbol "Reason" would become an empty abstraction and so able to be filled "with various nonrational contents." More particularly in the present context of deformation, if the content of Reason was ignored, "if Reason is existential philia, if it is the openness of existence raised to consciousness, then the closure of existence, or any obstruction to openness, will affect the rational structure of the soul adversely" (CW, 12:283–84).

When Heraclitus wrote of "sleepwalkers" (B 89), or Sophocles spoke of Prometheus' revolt against the Divine Ground as a "disease," or Plato spoke of injustice as a "sickness," they were referring precisely to Bergsonian closure of the psyche to the Ground as states of "existential disorder."[18] It was not, however, until the "shattering experiences of ecumenic imperialism" and the widespread existential disorientation that accompanied it that "the bond between Reason and existential order" achieved conceptual clarity and precision with the pair of terms, conciliation and alienation. Here Voegelin referred to Cicero's *Tusculan Disputations*:

> As there are diseases of the body, so there are diseases of the mind (*morbi animorum*); the diseases are generally caused through a confusion of the mind by twisted opinions (*parvarum opinionum conturbatio*), resulting in a state of corruption (*corruptio opinionum*); the diseases of this type can arise only through a rejection of Reason (*ex apernatione rationis*); hence, as distinguished from diseases of the body, mental diseases can never occur without guilt (*sine culpa*); and since this guilt is possible only for man who has Reason, the diseases do not occur in animals.[19]

18 *Prometheus Bound*, 978; *Gorgias*, 480b1.

19 Voegelin summarized *Tusc. Disp.* IV, 23–32. Quoted in CW, 12:275. See also CW, 33:329–30 and *Cicero on the Emotions, Tusculan Disputations, 3 and 4*, trans. with commentary by Margaret Graven (Chicago: University of Chicago Press, 2002).

The symptoms of the uniquely human diseases of the mind include: "restless moneymaking, status seeking, womanizing, overeating, addiction to delicacies and snacks, wine tippling, irascibility, anxiety, desire for fame, stubbornness, rigidity of attitude, and such fears of contact with other human beings as misogyny and misanthropy" (CW, 12:276). To this commonsensical symptomatology Cicero added the observation that such practices were evidence of psychopathology when they become habitual and chronic to such as degree that they unbalanced the rational order of an individual's life. Such a person was "impenetrable to argument because he considers his indulgence to be the rational thing to do" (CW, 12:276–77). The result of enacting one's life in the mode of alienation as described in Cicero's symptomatology sounds entirely modern, particularly if one added drugs and social media into the mix.

The conclusion Voegelin drew from his discussion of Cicero and of the Stoics of Cicero's time, was that although the disease affected both Reason and the passions, it originated in the same "questioning unrest" as philosophy, "in man's freedom to actualize the meaning of humanity potentially contained in the unrest or to botch the meaning" (CW, 12:277). The difference in outcomes lay chiefly in the response of a particular human being and whether that person was open to the divine presence that gave direction to the unrest or not. Moreover, the rejection of Reason in the name of Reason, which concerned some of the Stoic philosophers, notably Chrysippus, also sounded very modern. Voegelin concluded that the "mysterious force" that disturbed the rational order of existence arose from isolating Reason from its context in reality, namely the tension of existence between life and death. The reality symbolized by "life" may be offered by the God but can be gained only with human cooperation.

A second equally subtle deformation Voegelin discussed in his 1971 essay on Henry James' novella, *The Turn of the Screw*.[20] Voegelin explained his "misgivings" regarding his original epistolary essay interpreting James' text and indicated that scientific advances during the preceding quarter century enabled him to account to the "fuzziness" of James' symbols "as well as the general fogginess of meaning pervading his work." Specifically, Voegelin said, it was a consequence of "a certain deformation of personal and social reality that was experienced by such artists at the turn of the century and expressed

20 This essay is a "postscript" to a letter of 1947 to Robert Heilman. See CW, 12:134ff, esp. 149–71. See also the correspondence between Voegelin and Quentin Anderson (HI, 6:21).

by means of symbolistic art. The indistinctness and ambiguity are inherent to the symbols which express deformed reality" (CW, 12:151).

The deformation to which Voegelin referred was the shift from openness toward reality to "closure against, and denial of, its reality." As the historical process unfolded, the symbols that expressed the experiences of openness, "God, man, the divine origin of the cosmos, and the divine Logos permeating its order," became increasingly unintelligible and were replaced or eclipsed "by the imagery of a self-creative, self-realizing, self-expressing, self-ordering, and self-saving ego that is thrown into, and confronted with, an immanently closed world" (CW, 12:151). The artists, including James, who placed themselves in a position of deformation also developed symbols from within the deformation that expressed their experience. The tension between reality and its deformation in artistic consciousness never was entirely obliterated—for otherwise the symbolism of any specific artist would not be recognizable as expressing even a deformed version of human existence. However, this conflict between reality and its symbolization could be sufficiently repressed that it did not become "explicitly thematic" in any given work of art.

Artistic works that were the product of deformed consciousness, Voegelin said, "are not always easy to understand. The reader, in order to extract the full meaning, must supply the critical consciousness of reality, as well as the range of its possible deformation, which in the work itself does not become sufficiently thematic." Such a situation induced a peculiar hermeneutic problem. Even if a reader could apply his or her own critical consciousness to a work of art, there may arise a doubt as to whether a symbolism was obscure because the critical consciousness of the reader was insufficiently comprehensive to grasp the real significance of a text or other work of art or whether the artist's consciousness was insufficient properly to make the point he sought to make.

> Hence, the interpreter is faced with a critical task indeed. He cannot simply follow the symbolism wherever it leads and expect to come out with something that makes sense in terms of reality. He must rather ascertain, first, what kind of reality has become the victim of deformation and, second, what kind of deformation it has suffered. The task is especially difficult in our time, because the interpreter in his turn may have succumbed to one or the other of the dominant deformations of existence which characterize the age. He may be inclined to use as his

> instrument of interpretation one of the so-called theories, as for instance psychoanalysis, which themselves are symbolizations of deformed existence. If the author of the work happened to symbolize a psychoanalytic deformation of existence, a psychoanalytic interpretation will perhaps make matters no worse than they are. But that is not the case of James. Psychoanalysis superimposed on the deformation he wanted to symbolize could result in an impressive mess.[21]

The problem Voegelin addressed here was essentially the same one he discussed in the context of changes in the intellectual climate of opinion between St. Thomas' time and his own. In the *Summa contra Gentiles*, Aquinas could still assume "that a rational debate with an opponent was still possible" or at least that it seemed to be possible. Seven hundred years later, the speculations of classical scholastic metaphysics, which were created by Reason "on the experiential basis of existence in truth," had become "useless in a meeting with edifices of reason erected on a different experiential basis." Under contemporary conditions, therefore, the analyst must both account for the noetic structure of existence and for the deformed second realities "with regard to both their constructs and the motivating structure of existence in untruth" (CW, 12:38, 50–51).

Voegelin then proceeded to analyze James' symbol of the garden as a paradise lost and concluded that "there is something dusty about this Jamesian garden and its deformed humanity." It reminded Voegelin of his experience of the Gustave Moreau museum in Paris "where the accumulation of the master's work overpowers the viewer with the pedantic richness of its ornamental sterility," to which Voegelin added a similar judgment regarding the Franz von Stuck Villa in Munich. Such an appraisal, Voegelin said, was "not a stricture on the artists as masters of their craft; on the contrary, only because they are masters can they bestow on a defect, which otherwise would be a private matter, a stature that commands public attention. The judgment pertains not to the aesthetic, but to the existential, quality of the work" (CW, 12:162).

21 CW, 12:152. See also Voegelin's memo to the editor of the *Southern Review* where this essay first appeared (HI, 44:1), and his letter to Donald E. Stanford on a similar problem in the poetry of Wallace Stevens (CW, 30:665–66). The mention of Freudian psychoanalysis in this context referred to Heilman's critical discussion of the interpretations of Edna Kenton and Edmund Wilson. See Heilman, "The Freudian Reading of 'The Turn of the Screw,'" *Modern Language Notes* LXII (1947): 433–45.

In some instances the existential deformation in the hands of an aesthetic master produced what might be termed exquisite boredom. The defect in the work of art simply reflected the artist's defective consciousness of reality.

> The author partakes of the deformity he explores so strongly himself that he cannot place his figures in the open horizon of a fully developed tragic, or comic, or ironic consciousness. As a consequence, he cannot characterize his figures by the shadow their deformity would cast if they were exposed to the light of open reality, but rather will become a "realist" who describes a real deformation of reality without being quite clear about the reality deformed. (CW, 12:163)

Voegelin reiterated the point made above, that even with extreme examples the artist cannot abolish the critical distance between reality and its deformation in the work of art. True, the deformity may be unable to find expression in terms of open existence but only in terms of privation and suffering; but even so, such deformed symbolisms still expressed the loss of the experience of openness to the cosmos precisely by expressing the experience "of being closed up within oneself, and of the moods of anxiety and alienation which accompany such contraction." That is, the person who was afflicted with "contraction" was perfectly well aware of it and of its source. Here Voegelin again mentioned Nietzsche who in his "dialogue with Pascal" failed quite deliberately to participate in the divinely ordered cosmos by refusing to open his soul to Grace.

"Enter the critical reader" who may be unable to escape the presence of the deformed consciousnesses who predominate in articulating the meaning of the "age," but who nevertheless was not obliged to pretend that their deformed affliction "from which they suffer so gorgeously is not a presence that keeps their suffering going," but that in no way was necessary. As Voegelin put it in his Hitler lectures, there was no right to be stupid. The "critical reader," who self-evidently cannot be afflicted with the contraction of existence and loss of reality, proclaimed as a necessity by the artist, then "becomes aware that he is afflicted with the author, whatever the author's affliction may be." Hence the sense of "dustiness" arose when the opacity of the artist's consciousness did not dissolve into luminosity and insight.[22]

22 CW, 12:164. In terms of the aforementioned problem of first and second reality, the activist dreamer who sought to transfigure first reality was obviously aware of

We may draw a few conclusions from this consideration of deformations of consciousness. First and most obviously, human beings had an "inclination to think in thingly propositions about experiences which are not experiences of things." Accordingly, the "primary structure" of the divine-human encounter "must be distinguished from the reflective symbolization of the poles of the tensional encounter as thingly entities" (CW, 12:381–82). Such a distinction, like all distinctions, occurred as an event in reflective consciousness and was not an element of the "primary structure." There was, therefore, something inevitable in this "inclination" that could not be extinguished but about which human beings must be reflectively aware. As noted above, a paradox can be made reflectively intelligible though it cannot be dissolved.

Second, the differentiation of the Platonic Beyond, the *epekeina*, also brought into focus a "counter-pole" that resisted formation from or by the Beyond. And even if it were properly formed by the Beyond, as we quoted Voegelin above, this counter-pole "can still resist the formation and deform the formation into some deformed type of entity" (CW, 33:396). Once again, that is, the process of formation and deformation were indissolubly connected and cannot be resolved, which, of course, was another way to express the reality of the tension of existence.

Third, the deformations of consciousness were tied to consciousness of reality in the same way as second realities were tied to the first realities the imagination sought to destroy. Here Voegelin spoke of a "suspension of consciousness" of reality, using this "cautions" formulation

> because it frequently is difficult, if not impossible, to determine in the case of an individual activist whether the suspension is an act of intellectual fraud or pervasive self-deception, whether it is a case of plain illiteracy or of the more sophisticated illiteracy imposed by an educational system, whether it is caused by a

it as unsatisfactory. "He is well aware of the difference between first and second reality. . . . When he acts, he expects such action to form the first reality into conformity with the second reality of his dream. The activist dreamer must know the trick action, as distinguished from ordinary action, that will have the extraordinary result of transfiguring the nature of things. He must imagine himself to be a magician." Unfortunately for the activist magician, "the magic, of course, does not work. . . . Neither the expense of spirit and intellect in the elaboration of the dreams, nor the expense of blood and money in the attempts to realize them, have transfigured reality" (CW, 12:323–26).

> degree of spiritual and intellectual insensitivity that comes under the head of stupidity, or whether it is due to various combinations of these and other factors such as the desire to attract public attention and make a career.

Whatever the modality of "suspension," the imaginative project must comply

> with the logic of a revolt against reality. The dream world is not the real world, nor does the dream story told by the activist ever really happen. As a project of action within the reality it intends to transform, however, the dream story must intelligibly and persuasively refer to the real world as the medium of its action. The dream of revolt against reality is structurally bound to the structure it wants to destroy. (CW 12:316–17)

From these several deformations of consciousness, one turns with a sense of relief back to the problem of consciousness of reality. And for that question we first must understand what Voegelin meant by meditation.

4. Meditation

Klaus Vondung remarked, with respect to volume five of *Order and History*, that it was not yet another "break" with the approach taken in volume four as volume four had broken with its predecessors. "In terms of 'genre,' it definitely was no longer an analytical story of the 'order of history' concerning the topics Voegelin had been struggling with all the time."[23] Before considering the contents of the final volume of the series, let us consider the preparatory work, not only in the late essays and talks, that eventuated in the "philosophical meditation" of *In Search of Order*, but as an issue that "Voegelin had been struggling with all the time," including in his early work. The term "meditation," by the time Voegelin wrote *Anamnesis* and *The Ecumenic Age*, was already highly significant. What did Voegelin mean by it?

23 Vondung, "Rereading Eric Voegelin's *Order and History*," *International Journal of the Classical Tradition* 11 (2004): 92. See also Arpad Szakolczai, *Reflexive Historical Sociology* (Florence: Routledge, 1999), 69 and Gregor Sebba, "Eric Voegelin: From Enlightenment to Universal Humanity," *Southern Review* 11 (1975): 924–25.

We can get a first commonsense approximation from a remark he made in passing in "Anxiety and Reason" (CW, 28:92). Occasionally one encountered a phrase such as "from myth to reason," he said. Indeed, there were books with such titles. But, Voegelin argued, "reason is not a style of truth," unlike philosophy. So what was the difference? Truth, the truth of human order or existential truth, "corresponds to a man's actualization of his relation to the Ground through ritual, meditation, faith and prayer, but does not correspond to the degree of differentiation." That is, living in truth could be understood first of all as a practice, an "actualization" of a person's lived relation to the divine Ground. And the modes of actualization listed here were ritual, meditation, faith and prayer. By actually undertaking or taking part in ritual, meditation, faith, and prayer, one could order one's actual, concrete existence in relation to the Ground of Being. But these practices did not correspond to the degree of differentiation of consciousness because: (1) as was discussed in chapters three and six, "reason may be highly effective in the order of cosmological societies even when it has not yet articulated the field of non-existence;" (2) because, as was argued above in this chapter, reason "may seriously impair the order of existence when it has [been] differentiated but is not actualized through meditation;" and (3) reason "may become a source of disorder rather than of order when it is bandied about as a topic of the time, as in the Age that derives its name from Reason."

In short, when one took into account not simply the analytical differentiation of reason but its existential actualization through meditation, then "the superiority of philosophy appears less convincing." The commonsensical reason was obvious: there were political orders based on ritual, faith and prayer, such as the ancient Egyptian cosmological order, the Christian, Muslim, Buddhist, Confucian, Hindu, etc., orders, but there has never been a philosophical political order—though there have been counterfeit versions, namely ideological political orders.[24] About all one could say concerning philosophy as a way of life was already said by Aristotle. Despite the analytical superiority of philosophy and even its spiritual superiority, societies are governed by politicians, not philosophers. Moreover, when philosophy has been cultivated in societies ordered by other styles of truth, such as Christianity or Islam, there invariably have arisen such vexing and perplexing matters as "two truths" or the question of philosophy as an ancillary to theology. "Such oddities,"

24 See also Voegelin's remarks in "The Spiritual and Political Future of the Western World," in CW, 33:67–88.

Voegelin wrote, "point to limitations in the truth of philosophy." Moreover, it might be an exaggeration, but it would not be misleading to say, as was noted above, that the limited appeal of philosophy was likely connected to the limited capabilities of most human beings to actualize the life of reason by means of meditation. In a word, meditation is difficult (CW, 28:92f).

Gabriel Marcel distinguished a problem from a mystery by noting that problems had solutions whereas mysteries were lived, contemplated, or meditated upon. Voegelin had an equivalent distinction in mind when he noted that philosophy became doctrinal because "the practice of meditation has disappeared as a cultural factor" (CW, 33:303). We noted above that philosophical consciousness in search of the Ground was both aware of its own intentionality and of the mystery that surrounded it and constituted a horizon that drew philosophical consciousness toward the Ground even as it withdrew as consciousness advanced. As Voegelin put it above, the mystery of the Ground "can give direction to the quest of truth but it cannot be reached" (CW, 12:326).

The opening pages of the "Foreword" to *Anamnesis* contained another commonsensical account of what meditation meant for Voegelin. He began by recalling that, as early as *On the Form of the American Mind* (1928), he was aware of the centrality of philosophy of consciousness for political science. Lacking both philosophical and historical knowledge, all he could do was make and record his criticism of existing accounts. Studies over the ensuing decades, he said, led to the important insight "that a 'theory' of consciousness on the sense of generically valid propositions concerning a pre-given structure was impossible" (CW, 6:33). The reason was that consciousness was not a given to be deduced or described from the outside but, as has been shown several times, was "an experience of participation in the Ground of Being whose logos was to be brought to clarity through the meditative exegesis of itself." Instead of a "theory" of consciousness as the result of sustained investigation, Voegelin concluded that in its place one found "the reality of the meditative process; and this process had to go through its phases of increasing experience and insight." That discovery—namely that consciousness was a process of increasing insight into its own logos, its own account of itself—shaped the structure of the three parts to *Anamnesis* illustrating "the principal phases of the meditative process."

To recapitulate a point made above: Part One on "Remembrance" referred to the anamnetic breakthrough of 1943 discovered in the course of his correspondence with Schütz. The memorial notice of Schütz, the 1943 letter on Husserl, the paper on the theory of consciousness and the anamnetic experiments constituted, we noted, a "meditative unity" (CW, 6:41). The insights developed in Part One sustained the analyses of the *New Science of Politics* and the early volumes of *Order and History*. Part Three, "The Order of Consciousness," was "the provisionally last phase" of a meditation begun in 1943 and was discussed in chapter five above in the analysis of Voegelin's 1965 paper, "What is Political Reality?" Between these two parts of the book Voegelin placed several studies undertaken over the years on "concrete cases of order" and "analyses of consciousness that make the human order in society and history intelligible." These were also discussed in chapter five.

Consciousness, Voegelin had said several times, "is the luminous center radiating the concrete order of human existence into society and history," which was what made political science "empirical" in the precise sense of being an enquiry into experience.[25] As was discussed in chapter one, the historicity of truth required that such an empirical political science required in turn an ongoing, constant, and dialectical exchange between concrete examples of order and analyses of consciousness that "show how the analyses of consciousness arise from the work on the historical materials" (CW, 6:34).

One can detect an awareness of the importance of philosophy of consciousness in *On the Form of the American Mind*; in the *Herrschaftslehre* of the early 1930s one finds explicit evidence that Voegelin was aware of the importance of meditation for the philosophical analysis of human being or for philosophical anthropology.[26] The first chapter of the latter study, "To Determine the Concept of the Person," noted: "The determination of that which a person essentially is, takes place when the attempt is made with adequate means in a fundamental form of philosophical thinking that, following the name given it by Descartes, we will call meditation." The illustration of what meditation entails, however, was taken from Augustine's *Confessions*, particularly books ten and eleven where Augustine investigated memory and time.

"Every meditation requires a beginning that also gives it direction." For Augustine the initial question was: where does the soul find God when

25 See Cooper, "Eric Voegelin, Empirical Political Scientist," in *The Restoration of Political Science and the Crisis of Modernity* (Toronto: Mellen, 1989), 271–82.

26 For details, see William Petropoulos, "The Person as *Imago Dei*: *Herrschaftslehre* and *Political Religions*," in Glen Hughes, ed., *The Politics of the Soul* (Lanham: Rowman and Littlefield, 1999), 87–114, and William Thompson, "Philosophy and Meditation: Notes on Eric Voegelin's View," in Hughes, ed., *The Politics of the Soul*, 115–35.

it seeks Him in order to find peace in Him? The goal was not knowledge but "a point in the movement of his soul at which his soul finds peace" or "when no driving impulse remains in the meditative course." Toward the end of chapter 40 of Book Ten, Augustine spoke of finding a "safe place" where the soul was no longer restless. What this "place" actually was, Voegelin said, could be seen "only by the one who follows the whole movement of the confession, who has himself enacted the confession to God" (CW, 32:227). In the concrete experience of Augustine, when Augustine reflected on what he loved when he loved God, and when the philosopher followed his meditative *via negativa*, the procedure eliminated all the things of the world in search of God. In chapter six Augustine eliminated corporal beauty, pleasures of the eyes, melodies, the smells of flowers and so on. "And yet" for the soul God was in these things too. "God is all that has been negated, and again, at the same time, He is not that either." All the propositions about God had simultaneously been asserted and negated but the love of Augustine for God gave the soul direction that was "strictly determined by the structure of being," from the body to the soul to "the spacious chambers of memory (X:8), which included the memory that remembers itself (X:13). But even the core of the person as the reiteration of memory was still "world-immanent" and so must also be transcended. "This course reaches it unequivocal end . . . when, after exhausting all that is predicable, it reaches the place that is no longer a place in any palpable sense of the term."[27]

In addition to a meditative course oriented by spatial images, of levels, for example, there was another "oriented to the image of the flow of time, to the coming into being and the perishing of things," which Augustine followed in Book XI. Instead of seeking a secure place that was not a place, now the soul sought peace in a time that was not a time, but "a Sabbath of eternal life and a peace in God."

The two principal schemata were oriented first to being and second to becoming; the first used images of space, the second of time. From the first came the "leap" to God; from the second, an awareness of what endured through the flow of events. "When I look toward what is permanent, in the *intentio* that is to carry me to God, I experience my distance from God and realize that I am not with Him, but immersed in becoming, in moral decay

27 CW, 32:228–31. In Voegelin's copy of Augustine's *Confessions* in his library at the University of Erlangen, he placed numerous slips of paper to mark several passages in Books 9 and 10 and occasionally underlined words and phrases (in pencil).

in time." Both ways led to the same goal, that of the meditating person loving God

> and therewith the understanding person to insight into the essence of the human person, who can be characterized by his openness to a transcendent being, by his being a frontier between the world, with its being and becoming, and a super world. The person is, as we have said, the point of intersection between divine eternity and human temporality; in the person finitude is revealed as the essence of the world. The person is the experience of the limits demarcating world-immanent finiteness from the transcendent infinite. (CW, 32:235–36)

This procedure was "dialectical" in the sense that Augustine's terminology changed as the meditation proceeded and the terms were both posited and negated. For Augustine, however, the person was not the focus of his meditation but rather the relation of God and the world or the Creator and creation for which the person was the locus where that relationship was experienced. For modern philosophy, starting with Descartes, the focus was on the relation of the person, or rather the subject of cognition, and the world, as Voegelin pointed out in his 1943 letter to Schütz discussed in chapter one (CW, 6:57–59).

Voegelin's essays contained several examples of meditative texts. Moreover, the term appeared with increased regularity in his later works.[28] In his 1967 conversation with members of the Thomas More Institute in Montreal, for example, Voegelin noted that "I can quite definitely see that I got in the practice of meditation by reading the *Upanishads*, by reading the *Symposium* of Plato, by reading the *Confessions* of St Augustine. These are the classics of meditation to which one has to return."[29] T. S. Eliot, whose citations by Voegelin have been quoted already in this chapter, might also have been included.

28 Three major pieces included the term in their titles: "The Beginning and the Beyond: A Meditation on Truth," (1977), CW, 28:173ff; "Wisdom and the Magic of the Extreme: A Meditation," (1977), CW, 12:315ff; "The Meditative Origins of the Philosophical Concept of Order," (1981), CW, 33:384ff.

29 CW, 33:303. In 1936–37 Voegelin offered a private course at his apartment in Vienna to study the *Upanishads*, Plato, Plotinus, Augustine, Maimonides, and Descartes to introduce the notion of philosophical meditation as the *Grundform* of philosophizing, by which he meant the activity that arises from the experience of meditation. See CW, 28:xxvii–xxviii n. 19, and HI, 86:3.

Around 1944 Voegelin wrote a short essay, "Notes on T. S. Eliot's *Four Quartets*."[30] The poems, Voegelin said, were "the spiritual autobiography of a Christian poet. As the history of a Christian soul, they are a meditation; as a work of a poet they are an incantation." The two qualities were as inseparable as content and form in a work of art. Indeed, the interpenetration of form and substance "enabled Eliot to write a metaphysical poem without writing a metaphysical disquisition." As a meditation, "the poem deals with the life of man and his death, with time and eternity, with the world unredeemed and redemption, with ecstasy and contemplation, with action and stillness," a subject-matter familiar from Augustine's *Confessions*. For a full understanding of the poem, Voegelin argued, the reader "has to go beyond the text of the poem" and to reconstruct for himself or herself the lyrical and musical symbolizations of "theological, cosmological, metaphysical, and biographic categories."

Voegelin then proceeded to analyze systematically Eliot's meditations in each of the four poems—from the present in "Burnt Norton," to the ancestral in "East Coker," to the new world of America in "The Dry Salvages," which turned out to be not such a new world after all so much as a Beyond of Europe and its history, as was the last quartet, "Little Gidding," a saintly place from which "the metaphysical poets drew their inspirations" and that signified "the last stage in the history of the soul, where it comes closest to 'the intersection of the timeless with time'" but nevertheless did not reach, so much as return us, the readers, to the beginning in Burnt Norton: "History is now and England" (IV.5.24). The image of human being as explorer or voyager concluded at the beginning of the last stanza:

> We shall not cease from exploration
> And the end of all our exploring
> Will be to arrive where we started
> And know the place for the first time. (IV.5.26ff)

Voegelin's analytical exegesis depended for its persuasiveness on his having recreated imaginatively in meditation Eliot's experiential intentions.

A second example was Voegelin's exegesis of Shakespeare's Sonnet 129, which, as did Eliot, discussed human being "joined spirit and body,"

30 CW, 33:33ff. See also Glen Hughes, "'A Pattern of Timeless Moments': T.S. Eliot's *Four Quartets* as a Poetic Expression of Eric Voegelin's Philosophy of Existence and History," *Voegeliniana*, No. 70 (Munich: Geschwister-Scholl-Institut für Politikwissenschaft, 2008).

in this instance "on the exuberant use and misuse of symbols in the praise bestowed on the beloved object of desire."[31] For Voegelin, however, Sonnet 129 was not, as is conventionally maintained, simply about sex.

> Th'expense of Spirit is a waste of shame
> Is lust in action,

which opens the poem, also referred to political activists who waste their efforts on dreams whose lust in action included the *libido dominandi*. Such lust, moreover,

> Is perjured, murderous, bloody full of blame,
> Savage extreme, rude, cruel, not to trust.

The extremeness indicated by the adjectives, Voegelin argued, was to Shakespeare evidence of an existential disorder:

> Enjoyed no sooner but despised straight,
> Past reason hunted. . .

and close to madness. For Shakespeare, as for Voegelin, the consciousness in pursuit of the *libido dominandi* was never unaware of its own futility: the dreamer knew he was dreaming "past reason." Madness and reason, Voegelin observed,

> are not simply alternative types of existence, nor will they of necessity succeed each other in the course of a man's life; they both are always present in the structure of consciousness. The temptation of the "extreme" will always endanger the balance, and the imbalance will never be quite unconscious of its madness. The joy proposed will turn into a woe, when the dreamer realizes the dynamics of his joy to have depended on reaching the extreme. The tensions are alive and threaten the balance with deformation. In the concluding couplet Shakespeare summarizes his self-analysis:
>
> All this the world well knows yet none knows well,
> To shun the heaven that leads men to this hell.

31 CW, 12:328ff. The Eliot quote is from CW, 33:34.

> The heaven of the extreme continues to fascinate; the balance remains in danger, however much we know about the heaven's hell. (CW, 12:329)

A third example was Voegelin's exegesis of Socrates' words at the end of the *Republic* when he discussed the tale told by Er, a "tale of immortality, of human choice and divine judgment." It was, Socrates said, "the tale that was saved and will save us if we are persuaded by it" (*Rep.*, 621c), regarding which, Voegelin observed, "it is the tale that Socrates makes his own word of persuasion; the tale which, if accepted, will make us beloved (*philoi*) to ourselves and to the gods."[32] The "tale that saves" expressed an existential truth, but one that was apparently not available to everyone. And even if saved,

> the truth now living in the Word is still surrounded by the forces of death. The man who returns from the light to the cave will speak the Word to those who cannot hear what they hear; he will be mocked, persecuted, and like Socrates be put to death. When the living are dead, the dead who are living have no audience. So it was in the time of Socrates; so it was true in the time of Christ; and so it is today.

There was almost a "constant discord" between "the saving Word saved from death and its nonacceptance by man in society and history" because it depended on "man's openness to the order of love," which was hardly universal (CW, 12:335).

Far from a recipe for salvation, the "saving tale" revealed worldly existence sharply and clearly as In-Between and "as engaged in a transfiguring movement from imperfection to perfection. Reality is experienced as moving beyond its own structure, and on man is put the burden of his freedom to participate in the movement or to resist it." Accordingly, when Voegelin revisited the myth of the cords in the *Laws* (644e–645c), he argued that the truth conveyed by the myth was limited by the mystery that surrounded it. "The discord between truth and untruth in existence does not disappear when it becomes conscious as the truth of existence." If we ask: why were we placed in "this not altogether pleasant movement from imperfection to

32 CW, 12:334; cf. CW, 16:113. See also James Babin, "Eric Voegelin's Recovery of the Remembering Story," *Southern Review* 34 (1998): 341ff.

perfection," we become conscious of the mystery. After all, as we saw, the stronger pulls of the steely cords also come from the gods, and not just the gentle pull of the golden cord (CW, 12:335–37; cf 16:285ff).

"Behind the truth of the discord" expressed in the image of the stronger and gentler cords, "there lies the mystery of the reality in which the discord becomes luminous as its truth. The 'true story' is true because it raises the question to which no further answer in truth is possible." In the context of the myth, both sets of cords were real so that neither could be ignored. There was no way to follow only the steely cords as the truth of reality or simply to follow the golden cord. Even less could one pretend to a dream "of a tensionless, harmonious state of vegetative existence. The answer to the questions raised by the process of reality is not to be found by imaginative dreaming; it is to be found through participation in the process, following the pull of the golden cord as far as the counterpull of the steely cords will allow." As to *why* reality had the structure that the philosopher's noetic insight discovered, unfortunately that could not be answered by noetic insight. The structure of reality remained mysterious (CW, 12:337–38).

Understanding Aristotle, no less than understanding Plato or Hesiod, required a meditative reenactment of the experiences they conveyed. Indeed, all the Greek thinkers after Hesiod, who may be taken as constituting at the origin of the Greek literary record, were aware that what they had to say "came not from . . . natural reason but from divine revelation." Moreover, they were all aware of living within "the tension of seeking and receiving, that is to say, in the dual movement of the godly and human type, in which the human *responsio* takes place in answer to a movement that originates in God." The common opinion, then, that the Greeks, and especially Aristotle, were concerned with "natural reason" was simply "a crude inadmissible falsification of the historical documents."[33]

33 CW, 33:386. In a contemporary letter to John Guegen Voegelin was again explicit and uncompromising in his rejection of the "probably Thomistic" view that philosophy was a work of "natural reason" whereas Christianity was "revealed." Voegelin referred Guegen to *The Ecumenic Age* where he "carefully elaborated the superiority of the Johannine and Pauline visions over the Platonic vision." Though "Plato is clear and outspoken about the revelatory component of his noetic enterprise, about the 'vision' (*opsis*) as he calls it" (HI, 82:10). Similarly in his *Autobiographical Reflections* Voegelin noted that the "theophanic core of classical philosophy" and "the presence of the pneumatic stratum in its compact form" was denied because of Christian doctrine (CW, 34:134ff).

The difference between "reason" and "revelation" now appeared to Voegelin as a consequence of the distinct ethnic and linguistic cultures of the Greeks as compared to that of the Israelites and Christians. As we have seen, the accent with the Greeks fell upon the search, the zetesis, for truth, *aletheia*. Once differentiated, the old truth became a lie, a *pseudos*. Among the Israelites and their successors, their predecessors were not liars but persons who had heard or otherwise received the truth and whose reception and articulation of it therefore had to be reinterpreted. Voegelin attributed this hermeneutic difference to differences in social structure and, in particular, to the absence of a national or imperial priesthood among the Greeks.

For example, Aristotle's *Metaphysics*, book delta, provided a list of word definitions. Proceeding on the basis of "a type of scientific-philological premise," Aristotle only "slowly brings out, in a meditative sense, what such words as *origin* or *reason*, and similar terms could possibly mean in the spiritual movement of the search for wisdom." In contrast, "in a revelatory context such as the one expressed by the Israelite-Christian culture, recourse is always made to the godly spirit, the *ruach*, from which the Greek translation, *pneuma*, was made. The spirit—I therefore call this accent on revelation 'pneumatic'—is the ethnic determinant on the problem field of Christianity, which grew out of the Jewish-Israelite context." We have already noted in chapter six the novelty of Voegelin's argument of equivalence between noetic and pneumatic symbolism and his insistence that differences were matters of contingency, emphasis, or accent.

The reason for this otherwise unusual argument was Voegelin's longstanding and fundamental concern with the context of the engendering experiences of variegated but equivalent symbolizations. In the present context, Voegelin argued that both noetic and pneumatic positions "are present in the problem of meditation. The tension exists between being moved from the godly side and the search from the human side. Thus the godly and the human sides are assumed in a process of seeking and being moved [to seek]. Such symbols as I have used here—a godly reality that moves, a concrete human being who seeks, a process of seeking and being moved—I call a complex," which in this context referred to an experiential process that must not be dismembered into separate pieces (CW, 33:388–89). Instead of looking at analytically distinct elements, therefore, "one must concern oneself with the process that actually takes place, that is, with the meditative events." Meditative analysis of meditative events was not fragmentary (CW, 33:390). On the contrary, the meditative reenactment of a meditative complex was, so to speak, holistic.

The implications of Voegelin's explicit emphasis on meditation held implications for many of his previous formulations. The truth of existence, he several times argued, was not a matter of information being correctly conveyed but of "meditative articulation," which thereby turned it into "the ordering force in existence" (CW, 28:91). Similarly, when Voegelin asked, "what does *participation* mean?" he replied: "What it actually means you can experience, of course, only in meditative experience." That is, participation now appeared to Voegelin as yet another paradoxical complex:

> In *participation* there is first a relation of identity because they [= the participants] must have something in common, a sort of area of overlapping; the same relation also does *not* hold true because they are *not* identical; when you get these relations and nonrelations of identity you can call the whole thing together: *participation*. (CW, 33:252)

Such a focus on meditation also applied to Voegelin's own words, which was one reason why the term appeared as often as it did in his later writing. Toward the end of "Wisdom and the Magic of the Extreme," for example, Voegelin said: "What has come to its end" in this article, "is a *meditation*, a philosopher's effort to explore the structures of existential consciousness."[34] Such meditations have a historical dimension, which was why Voegelin could move so effortlessly from T. S. Eliot to Plato and Aristotle to the Egyptian "Dispute of a Man with his Soul." Accordingly, a brief reflection on the historical structure of meditations makes for a suitable conclusion to this section.

"A noetic movement through the Metaxy of existential consciousness wants to find the balance of truth between the intentionalist desire to know reality as an object, and the mystery of reality in which such a desire to know the truth occurs," Voegelin wrote. This noetic movement also had to deal with the forces of imagination and of language that mysteriously emerged in the human response to reality of which the human being was a part and in that response produced images and symbols to

34 CW, 12:371. By "existential consciousness" Voegelin meant the "movement in which man's consciousness of existence emerges from the primary experience of the cosmos. Consciousness becomes luminous to itself as the site of the revelatory process, of the seeking and being drawn" ("The Gospel and Culture," CW, 12:207; see also CW, 12:208–9).

express itself. Such images and symbols were subject to correction and ever more comprehensive insight but also to deformation, untruth and the creation of second realities. "Even more, the differentiating advances of truth can become the source of new types of untruth, when visions are misused to obscure areas of reality outside their more immediate field, or when visionary symbols are subjected to the deformative processes of doctrinization and literalization."

Finally, "it will not escape the reader that the summary of historical characteristics has emerged from a meditation to which it is supposed to apply." That is, Voegelin's summary statement summarized the meditation he had just completed and had written up in the article "Wisdom and the Magic of the Extreme." The point was obvious: "There is no Archimedic point outside history from which an exploration of existential consciousness could be undertaken; there is no truth of existence other than the truth emerging in the flux of presence. History is indeed more than an object of intentionalist consciousness; the mystery of its process is a dimension of consciousness itself." And that consciousness was always somebody's. In this instance it belonged to the specific person, Eric Voegelin (CW, 12:371–72).

The position of the philosopher today was not that of Plato so that he or she could not simply rely on Plato's language to express or articulate his own meditation. And yet there are recognizable equivalents between, for example, the strong pull of the steely cord and the strong influence of what Voegelin called the public unconscious: "To be aware of this situation, and to make no concessions to the *anoia* [folly] of unbalanced, fragmented consciousness, is the philosopher's obligation today." As was true with Plato, Augustine, Bodin, Bergson, etc., the philosopher was

> obliged to recognize the *mache athantos* [undying struggle] as the movement towards the experienced *eschaton* of immortality and yet not indulge in the dreamer's phantasy of an eschatological transfiguration to be pleromatically [fully or completely] accomplished by his own dreams and actions. The fulfillment of this obligation I have tried to recover, through an anamnetic meditation, certain structures of consciousness whose repression by the public unconscious is one of the causes of the contemporary disorder. (CW, 12:373–74)

After the foregoing analysis of the meaning and significance of meditation, the actual operations of meditative consciousness turned out to be comparatively straightforward. As noted above, it amounted to a permanent and ceaseless action of expanding, ordering, articulating, and correcting itself through a "responsive openness to the appeal of reality" (CW, 12:305). Insofar as such a consciousness was aware of itself as an action and an effort—and how could it not be?—it was reflective. Such reflection was meditative.

5. The Unfinished Story

As with so many of Voegelin's books after the *History of Political Ideas* was abandoned, there was a significant philological drama surrounding the publication of *In Search of Order*. The initial concern centered on the unfinished or fragmentary nature of the text. As early as the 1981 Tutzing conference, Thomas Hollweck, Peter von Sivers, Jürgen Gebhardt, and Peter Weber-Schafer, all of whom had been Voegelin's students in Munich, considered that the publication of the manuscript was "most problematic," not least of all because the "preliminary studies," later published in the *Collected Works*, had not been reworked by Voegelin to be part of the final manuscript.[35] In early November, Gebhardt wrote to Ellis Sandoz: "we have to keep in mind that this text is only a fragment. Being chapter one and chapter two of part one to be entitled 'The Paradox of Consciousness'" (HI, 129:424). The implication seemed to be that the book would be too short. Later that month Lissy Voegelin wrote to Beverly Jarrett of LSU Press indicating what she thought the "preliminary studies" were, and suggested the subtitle, "The Unfinished Story."[36]

In the spring of 1987 Gebhardt wrote to Beverly Jarrett:

35 Von Sivers to Paul Caringella, 17 October 1985, HI, 129:424. The preliminary studies were not identified in this letter. Voegelin's German students were also concerned that LSU Press, still Voegelin's publisher, were more interested in publishing quickly than ensuring that the resulting book was scientifically acceptable.

36 HI, 123:2, 3. Lissy Voegelin suggested that the preliminary studies included "The Beginning and the Beyond" along with the "Equivalences" article and "Wisdom and the Magic of the Extreme." It was also possible that "The Beyond and its Parousia" and "The Meditative Origin" might have been included. In the event all were published in CW 28 and 33. Lissy Voegelin was also not entirely pleased with the objections to publishing a short text as volume five of *Order and History*. As she noted in her Foreword, "In his last months I saw him, almost every day, reading and rereading the manuscript, making slight corrections occasionally, as always pointing out to me: This will be volume 5" (CW, 18:13).

> To my surprise the volume is again entitled *In Search of Order* now; why did you give up the *Unfinished Story*? I agree with this change but I wish somebody had told me about it. Now you changed it back to *In Search of Order*. I'd like to raise the question whether "the Meditative Story—An Unfinished Story" isn't even more fitting in order to bring out the quintessence of the volume. What are your reasons for cutting out this caption? (HI, 123:2)

No answer was left in the archival record.

An undated note by Paul Caringella reported on the eulogy by Gregor Sebba at Voegelin's funeral. Volume five, Sebba said, "remains unfinished" and the Introduction to *The Ecumenic Age* remained "the apex" of Voegelin's philosophy. "And the very title he chose for the last, fifth volume, 'In Search of Order,' told those who can read that this work could never be finished and that its author would die over it." After reading the final thirty pages on Plato's *Timaeus*, Caringella reported, Sebba changed his mind (HI, 129:424). In his editorial introduction Sandoz provided a kind of final observation: the "fragmentary character" of volume five was "most fitting" because the theoretical presentation evoked an unfinished story. Accordingly, *In Search of Order* "can be said to symbolize Voegelin's philosophical vision of history as an unfinished tale, one told by God in the reflective language of spiritually gifted men and women open to the mystery of truth emergent by divine-human encounter in the In-Between of participatory existence, human reality par excellence. Form and content thereby interpenetrate" (CW, 18:15).

Two additional remarks: first, as Klaus Vondung noted, "In Search of Order" could easily be the "superordinate title" for the entire five-volume series because of Voegelin's "continuous intellectual development" that the several volumes document.[37] Vondung's remark took on greater significance in the context of Gebhardt's epilogue to volume five where he noted that the book acquired its telos "at the very moment of being read by other men and women" (CW, 18:125). Second, volume five was called *In Search of Order* not *A Search for Order* or something similar because, as Charles Embry noted, Voegelin had discovered that his experience of order, in the raw form of "awe" or "wonder" preceded the conscious search *for* order, as if one knew what one was looking for—in which case, one would no longer have to keep searching.[38]

37 Vondung, "Rereading Eric Voegelin's *Order and History*," 93.

38 Embry, *The Philosopher and the Story-Teller: Eric Voegelin and Twentieth-Century Literature* (Columbia: University of Missouri Press, 2008), 73.

Turning now to Voegelin's text, he began with some playful remarks on what constitutes the beginning of a chapter on the Beginning. However, "the chapter is not a piece of information about familiar objects in the external world; rather it seeks to communicate an act of participation in the quest for truth." Communicating such an act must be done in a specific language, such as English, but if successful it would be evidence of a "philosopher's language" that was part of a much longer historical process, not all of the participants in which communicated in English. Yet they too spoke a "philosopher's language," which raised a significant question: "What is the structure of reality that will induce, when experienced, this equivocal use of the term 'language'?" Voegelin immediately answered: the equivocation "is induced by the paradoxical structure of consciousness and its relation to reality" (CW, 18:28–29).

We have encountered this paradoxical structure before: consciousness is both (1) perceptual, structured by intentionality corresponding to the structure of reality as thingness, and (2) capable of apprehending reality not as a thing but as that in which consciousness "occurs as an event of participation between partners in a community of being." The second meaning was the subject-matter of Voegelin's discussion, which followed the argument already presented in "Structure of Consciousness," and adumbrated in the opening words of the Introduction to *Order and History* (CW, 14:39). Reality and consciousness of it moved back and forth as a "complex experience" from the position of an intended object to a predicative event that, Voegelin said, "becomes luminous for its truth." That is, consciousness experienced itself or was aware of itself as "an event of participatory illumination in the reality that comprehends the partners to the event." Consciousness was self-conscious, to be sure, but in such a way that it was aware of itself (as it were) as a junior partner. The metaphor of luminosity, as we have argued, was meant to indicate both passivity (consciousness was illuminated) and activity (consciousness was "illuminating" insofar as it was self-conscious). Because consciousness experienced itself as both, Voegelin spoke of a paradox and of a complex that could become consistent and intelligible only by steps. "If the spatial metaphor be still permitted," he wrote, "the luminosity of consciousness is located somewhere 'between' human consciousness in bodily existence and reality intended in its mode of thingness." Voegelin then reintroduced the distinction between thing-reality and It-reality and noted that the equivocation of language was replicated in the equivocations of structures of consciousness and of a reality that was the object of consciousness and the subject of which consciousness was predicated. So, to recall the original playful question: where was the beginning?

It may come as no surprise that there was no beginning to this complex of equivocations because the language to express it was necessarily paradoxical. "Words and their meanings are just as much a part of the reality to which they refer as the being things are partners in the comprehending reality; language participated in the paradox of a quest that lets reality become luminous for its truth by pursuing truth as a thing intended." This was paradoxical because truth was not a thing intended though it was pursued as if it were, and the status of reality that became aware of itself in consciousness (or became luminous for its truth) was far from evident (CW, 18:30).

Voegelin then illustrated the sense of his use of the term "complex" by discussing, first, whether language was natural or conventional and second, the familiar distinction between the concepts of science and the luminosity of mythic and revelatory symbols. But what has any of this to do with the Beginning? To answer, Voegelin proposed a concrete textual analysis, and what could be more appropriate than Genesis 1? God's creative word looks like a Beginning, except that it raises other questions: to whom is God addressing his word? What kind of reality is evoked when God speaks? How, in short, did the human authors of Genesis evoke a reality where the spoken word created the structures of which it speaks? In Voegelin's conceptual language, how did the authors of Genesis find the language to express It-reality?

> The answer is given by Genesis 1:2: "The earth was waste and void, darkness was on the face of the deep; and the spirit [breath] of God was moving over the face of the water." Over an emptiness, over a formless waste of something there moves, perhaps like a storm, the breath or spirit, the *ruach*, of God, or rather the plural divinity, *Elohim*. The It-reality, thus, is symbolized as the strong movement of a spiritual consciousness, imposing form on a formless and nonforming countermovement, as the tension between a pneumatic, formative force (*ruach*; in later Greek translation, *pneuma*) and an at least passively resistant counterforce. Moreover, the tension in the It is definitely not the tension of a human consciousness in its struggle with reality for its truth; it is recognized as a nonhuman process, to be symbolized as divine; and yet it has to convey an aura of analogy with the human process because man experiences his own acts, such as the quest

> for truth, as acts of participation in the process of the It. When the authors of Genesis 1 put down the first words of their text they were conscious of beginning an act of participation in the mysterious Beginning of the It. (CW, 18:33–34)

After disposing of a series of doctrinal misconceptions, Voegelin concluded that we are all conscious, upon reading the words of Genesis, of taking part in a process that did not begin with the participants, including God, but "with the mysterious It that encompasses them all" (CW, 18:35).

The story told in Genesis about the beginning of humanity through the history of the Patriarchs, the Exodus, settlement kingdoms, exile, and so on was meant to be true as an account of events, "but what do the story and its truth mean in terms of experience and symbolization?" How does it look from the "perspective" of It-reality? Obviously it is not a quasi-thing-reality story of *res gestae*, a "possession for all time" akin to Thucydides' account of the war between the Spartans and the Athenians. Voegelin's answer was, first, that the story of Genesis was a "quest for truth," but also that "the event of the quest is part of the story told by the It" as well as a story told by the human questioner who seeks "to articulate the consciousness of his quest as an act of participation in the comprehending story." The quest for truth therefore did not result in acquiring information that was always available, but was the creative telling of a story. How else could a human being give an account of his quest as a response to a divine movement, except by telling a story? In that way the truth of reality appeared through the story from a reality filled with yet unrevealed truth (CW, 18:38–40).

Very well, the story aimed to tell the truth and to evoke order against the already-present disorder by the force of its truth, but how did the listener recognize that the story was true? Why should anyone believe it? The answer, Voegelin said, lay in the "paradoxic structure" of the story as "both a narrative and an event." The narrative conveyed various insights about thing-reality in the mode of intentionality; as an event, the story articulated an experience of It-reality, of the divine-human encounter. In this second sense the language of the story did not refer to anything external. It constituted an event "in which It-reality becomes luminous for its truth." It was "luminously symbolic" so that participation in the meaning of the story precluded any doubt about its accuracy. Genesis was not, therefore, either a narrative expounded by a revelatory God or a story of an imaginative human being: it was both, which was precisely what conveyed its paradoxical character as both narrative and event. The same paradoxical character attached to other true stories besides that of Genesis. As a generalization, the story of the quest, under other concrete circumstances than that experienced by the fifth or sixth century by the authors of Genesis, was also "the reality of an It-story that tells itself through the events of the participatory quests for truth." That would include the story Voegelin was telling in the course of this book, *In Search of Order*, which began with a beginning that was and was not the Beginning (CW, 18:41, 44).

When any questioner attempted to account for his participatory quest, the question of a Beginning prior to or beyond the actual beginning arose. This "Beyond," which we have discussed above, was not a spatial preposition but a "symbol expressing the participation of the temporal story in the dimension of the It-reality out-of-time." Thus, the presence of the Beyond, which was experienced in the present of the quest for truth, imposed on the external dimension of past-present-future the dimension of divine presence. We are again introduced to the "flux of presence" as the experience of the questioner's participatory meditation on a "mode of time in which the It tells its tale," including its beginning. The questioner, then, became aware of his own experience between the thing-reality of his own embodied consciousness and the Beyond-reality (CW, 18:45).

Voegelin then reiterated a point made above, that the story of the quest for truth was accompanied by a story of resistance to truth. In addition, he raised a new question: since the resisters did not disagree with the reality of the truth against which they raised their resistance, "Why do they resist a truth they neither deny nor can change? And what are the experiential sources that endow resistance with such strength of meaning that it becomes a constant force in history?" The surface motivations were obvious: people were often convinced that something was wrong with reality. Or, as Voegelin said, "the story of their existence is not the story that the It-reality wants to tell" (CW, 18:50). The miseries of the Ecumenical Age provided sufficient historical evidence of widespread "murderous unpleasantness," as we saw (CW, 17:142).

Now, the superficial or surface motives did not tell the whole story, because, as we also saw, truth is not information but a real event expressed in symbols that arose from the human response to the appeal of reality. The same human imaginative power that enabled a response to the appeal of reality allowed humans to imagine themselves to be the sole creators of truth. Then one imagined oneself as gaining power over reality rather than as a creative partner within a reality of which one was a participant. Under such circumstances, "the image of the world becomes the world itself. By his imagination, we may say, man can out-imagine himself and out-comprehend the comprehending reality." This imaginative perversion from participating consciousness to autonomous creative power had been present in human beings from the start, not as an error or mistake but as a constant potential or as a temptation. It occurred when resistance to existing symbols became carried away into imagining that the resister was not just rejecting the particular symbolism as inadequate, which it may well have been, but was rejecting the entire process of reality within which he was a participant. But no one can escape reality. There was, therefore, a difference between the assertive resistance to untruth and the self-assertive resistance to truth (CW, 18:53).

Voegelin then reformulated the problem of reflective distance. As we noted above the thinker engaged in the quest for truth could become or remain aware of the structure of the quest through an act of remembrance—of the beginning of the quest, of the attraction of reality and the movements and countermovements in the Metaxy—and then express this remembrance by way of reflective symbols—the tension of the Metaxy, thing-reality, It-reality, intentionality, luminosity, and so on. Such symbols, therefore, were "manifestations of a consciousness that is structured not only by the paradox of intentionality and luminosity, but also by an awareness of the paradox, by a dimension to be characterized as a reflectively distancing remembrance," which Voegelin identified with Plato's noetic anamnesis. Once again, however, the act of reflectively distancing remembrance did not just happen: imaginative remembrance was coeval with the potentiality of imaginative oblivion, and so was deliberately undertaken or chosen.

To summarize Voegelin's argument to this point: the structure of consciousness may be symbolized by the complex consciousness-reality-language and the paradoxes of intentionality-and-luminosity, of thing-reality-and-It-reality. This structure was not simply "there" but was reflectively present in consciousness in a plurality of different ways, all of which were accompanied by reflection on the phenomena of this plurality. Voegelin began *Order and History* with the words "the order of history emerges from the history of order." In *In Search of Order*, he remarked "whatever the order of history may ultimately be, there is a history of order because the truth of consciousness is documenting itself as a historical process through the reflectiveness of symbolizing consciousness. The history of consciousness . . . is internally cognitive" (CW, 18:59).

The opening of the second chapter of *In Search of Order* returned to the problem of deformation, only this time not artists such as Henry James but philosophers provided the subject-matter. More precisely, Voegelin revisited the "German idealistic philosophers" not simply to provide a critical analysis as he had done in the "Hegel" article but to understand their speculation as formative, not deformative, as efforts at dissolving doctrinal and propositional "encrustations accumulated through centuries of thinking in the intentionalist subject-object mode."[39] Unlike Voegelin's discovery of reflective distance as a structure of consciousness, the German idealists speculated upon the "reflective identity" of the act of their imagination with reality. This "philosophy of identity," Voegelin said, expressed a real resistance to deformation but did so in the same linguistic style as the deformation it resisted.

In the example of Hegel Voegelin focused "on the peculiar structure of a deformed formative purpose that serves as the principle" of the construction of the speculative system (CW, 18:69). To understand this particular structure, Voegelin postulated "two Hegels," but wrote only an exposition of "Hegel I." A second example, which included Hegel but extended beyond him was the "God-is-dead movement." There was a serious speculative element to it but also a "comic touch: The God who is declared dead is alive enough to have kept his undertakers nervously busy by now for three centuries." Voegelin summarized the comic element of such "deadly serious" speculation: "the only one permitted to laugh in the situation appears to be God" (CW, 18:83). A third example was provided by Leibniz. As with his remarks on Hegel and the death-of-God movement, Voegelin's analysis "should be understood, not as a criticism . . . but as an attempt to clarify the mode of the public unconscious prevalent in his time, a mode that the great thinker could not escape while resisting it" (CW, 18:97). Voegelin's present discussion of Leibniz's famous question: "why is there something rather than nothing?" was undertaken chiefly in terms of the deformation of the symbol God. The God of Leibniz, he said,

> appears to be a personality who can either cause the universe to exist, an activity which seems to require some effort, or take the easier way of doing nothing at all, a formulation of choice that moves one to wonder why God who "carries the reason of his existence *avec soi*" should not have chosen the even simpler way

39 CW, 18:63. David Walsh undertook essentially the same project in *The Modern Philosophical Revolution: The Luminosity of Existence* (Cambridge: Cambridge University Press, 2008).

> out of such decisions by not being the *causa sui* in the first place. The extraordinary experiential argument provokes some distancing reflection: As distinguished from Leibniz's God, I for my part find it easier to do something rather than to sit around and do nothing; this finding is complicated, however, by the experience that sometimes when I am doing something I feel I am doing nothing, as when I am engaged in *divertissements* in the Pascalian sense; but furthermore, even when I feel that I am not doing nothing when I am doing something, as for instance just now when I am writing this sentence, my mind will still not be paralyzed into peace by the certainty of doing something rather than nothing, because my action is disturbed by doubts about whether the meditative story I am producing is, within the limits of my human existence, truly the substory of the comprehending story it endeavours to be. (CW, 18:98–99)

In short, Leibniz's "experiential argument" is evidence only of "imaginative oblivion" present in the mode of the public unconsciousness of his time.

Hegel, Leibniz, and the God-is-dead speculation, Voegelin argued, needed to be understood as efforts of formative experience in opposition to even more deformed structures in their contemporary "public unconsciousness." As with the "critical reader" who was obliged not to pretend that the deformations of the "age" were necessary, the same obligation existed for the philosopher. Accordingly, the language of the gods symbolized "the experienced Parousia [presence] of the Beyond." That is, the God who was experienced as present was also the God who was beyond this concrete presence, and the language used to render intelligible this experience was always problematic. The imaginative symbols used were not intentionalist concepts although

> they have linguistically the appearance of language in the mode of thing-reality. As a consequence, if the language of the gods is misconstrued as a conceptual language referring to a divine entity "beyond" the experience of the Beyond and its Parousia, the gods must die when their language is superseded in the differentiating process of the quest for truth by a more adequate language. The historical scene becomes littered with dead gods. (CW, 18:84)

The death-of-God movement, no less than the deformations of Hegel and Leibniz, presupposed the rediscovery of fundamental experiences, however defectively they may have been symbolized.

When Voegelin looked for an undeformed expression of reality, it comes as no surprise that he returned to the Greeks, first to Hesiod and then to Plato. With Hesiod the Muses both remembered and mediated the divine Beyond to the gods whose "existence" expressed the moving presence in the experience of a "not-experientiable ordering force." Within Hesiod's myth, for example, Zeus had a beyond, but he was still a god and an immortal because, for Hesiod, the presence of the divine was not differentiated sufficiently from the Beyond. The structures of Hesiod's consciousness were "compactly divine," so that Voegelin restated Hesiod's insight "in a language more differentiated than Hesiod's but less deformed than Hegel's," which Voegelin had himself developed:

> One would have to say that the gods are immortal because they are born from the participating presence [Parousia] of the Beyond in the divine-human tension of the Metaxy, but that the immortals partake of temporality because they are also born from the participatory presence of the responsively imaginative, human consciousness in the limitation of its bodily located temporal mortality.[40]

Or again:

> The questing struggle for the truth of reality is the struggle of reality for its truth; it occurs within reality and involves the whole of the hierarchy of being, from the basic material structures to the formative experience of the non-experientiable Beyond. Immortality is experienced by mortals; what has been born in time will die in time; its immortality is gained from its participation in the story of the It-reality. (CW, 18:89)

The paradoxical language that Voegelin had discovered and employed illustrated the reality that "the linguistic means are not quite sufficient to meet

40 CW, 18:89. One recalls again the remark Voegelin made to the University of Virginia student newspaper, *The Daily Cavalier* (29 September 1977): "It is impossible to die unless you are immortal" (HI, 82:3).

the analytical demands" (CW, 18:105). All the philosopher could do, under the circumstances, was endeavour to understand this paradoxical reality and the "tensional complexes" by which it was expressed.

By Voegelin's reading, that was Plato's great achievement in the *Timaeus*. That some kinds of beings appeared to be more than others or some kinds of eternity appear to be more eternal than others, were reflections of the paradox governing the complex consciousness-reality-language. Plato was aware, Voegelin argued, in reflective distance of the paradox of consciousness and of the structures of thing-reality and It-reality that governed the language of reality. One could not escape the use of paradoxical language, even in reflective distance and by being fully aware that it was paradoxical "short of creating a language beyond reality and its paradox." Accordingly, there was a fundamental philosophical problem of speaking unambiguously of a paradox governing reality while using a language that was itself part of the reality governed by paradox. Plato tried to evoke a "super-constant" beyond the paradoxical language that expressed the various tensions of reality, but the result was that the tensions became "acutely conscious," not that they were resolved (CW, 18:110–11). In the event, Plato used the symbol *monogenes* to express the oneness of the cosmos, not in a numeric sense "but the experienced oneness of existential tension of a *periechon* [comprehending] that is all of the 'things' while comprehending them in the intelligible whole of the process." Corresponding to the genetic *monogenes* Plato coined the term *monosis* (*Tim*., 31b) which was also a "oneness," this time a revealed tensional oneness in reality.

As Voegelin explained Plato's remark: "The Cosmos has been generated *monogenes* in order to make it image most perfectly the *monosis* of the divine *paradigm*. *Monogenesis* as the image of *Monosis* thus parallels the symbolization of Time as the image of Eternity." Unfortunately, *monosis* disappeared from the vocabulary of philosophy under the impact of the disorder of the Ecumenic Age. All that remained was the "genetic *eikon*" of *monosis*, namely the symbol *monogenes*. "The Gospel of John made it the attribute of the Son of God (1:14, 18; 3:16, 18)." This movement of the symbol *monogenes* from the Cosmos to Christ, "reveals the movement of experiential emphasis from the God who creates the order of the Cosmos to the God who saves from its disorder" (CW, 18:112–13).

Moreover, in some respects, Plato's formulation of the "movement" was more analytically adequate than the later efforts by Christian theologians at finding an understanding for their faith. Specifically, Plato's account of the Beyond and its Parousia, discussed above, was more adequate than the preference of dogmatists for compact personal gods unencumbered by the mystery of divine revelation and human response.

> But the mystery resists and persists. The noetic thinker, who is conscious of this persistence, knows that even the *fides* [faith] of the One God does not put an end to his quest for the truly One in a reality that has to tell a story of tension and movement. For a Plato, therefore, the experienced reality of the continuing quest moves all symbols of divinity into a reflective distance in which the awe inspired by the mystery of divine revelation blends with a skeptical detachment aroused by its all-too-human symbolization. (CW, 18:115)

Thus, the Beyond could not be symbolized as the One God because it would turn this One God into just another god, which the differentiation of the Beyond was intended to overcome. Accordingly, all the gods, including the One God "have to live under the pressure of a divine Beyond that endows them with divine life while threatening to let them die from their compactness." This was true in Christianity as well as with Thomas' tetragrammatic God beyond the personal God.[41]

The gods and God did not disappear, but the Beyond did not "let them live in peace" either. The implication Voegelin then drew with respect to the insight regarding compactness and differentiation was remarkable but, if one has been able to follow the argument, not altogether surprising. The terminology and reality to which it referred "would not be simply historical stages of consciousness, the one succeeding the other in time, but poles of a tensional process in which the revelation of the Beyond has to overcome progressively a hard core of compact resistance without ever dissolving it completely" (CW, 18:116).

The multivalent paradox of order-disorder, mortality-immortality, perfection-imperfection, and so on was both known and lived inasmuch as human being was embodied and the embodied psyche or human consciousness was one of the "things" of the cosmic order of things. We live in an order of things that is also flawed by disorder and the Cosmos is therefore a disordered order "in movement toward order." Thus, as we saw, humans participate in the disorder of things as much as in their order. Likewise, we know that truth is a meditative quest within the paradox of

41 See Thomas, *Summa Theologica*, I.13.11 and CW, 6:396.

reality, thought, and language, not a doctrine even though we find it difficult to think other than in the mode of thingness. In the absence of true doctrine, which we already know amounts to the fragmentation and deformation of the process of reality becoming luminous for its truth, there was only the "mutual illumination of symbols" that occurs only in human consciousness (CW, 18:117).

The human quest for truth was an event in cosmic reality that was also the "place" or "site" at which reality revealed itself. The event, therefore, was experienced both as moving within the tensions of thingly existence and those of "visionary existence," namely "as a movement towards an unflawed order beyond the order that is flawed by the disorder of thingness." At the same time, this "place," namely human consciousness, was moving beyond itself and thus revealed itself in reflective distance to be penultimate, not final. What, Voegelin asked, did that mean?

> It means that the quest for truth is ultimately penultimate. In the quest, reality is experienced as the mysterious movement of an It-reality through thing-reality toward a Beyond of things. Neither the things nor the non-things involved in this process are objects external to it; they are structured in the process, discerned through the quest for truth. Moreover, as the things and non-things are not external to the quest, the quest and its language are not external to them; in reflective distance, the quest itself is discerned as a "placed" event in the mysterious movement. For the questioner has to tell his story of his struggle for the unflawed order from his position in the flawed order of thingly existence; and he can tell it, therefore, only in the flawed language that speaks of non-things in the mode of things. (CW, 18:119)

Included in the flawed things and flawed language were the gods and the language of gods. This meant that the story of the quest enhanced rather than dissolved the Mystery of "paradoxic penultimacy." So even though the movement of the quest beyond its penultimate place and its thingly language led to beyonds beyond being, "when the paradoxic experience of not-experientiable reality becomes conscious in reflective distance, the questioner's language reveals itself as the paradoxic event in the ineffable becoming effable" (CW, 18:119–20). The tension or paradox of speaking what could not be spoken could not be dissolved by some hyper-speculation because, in reflective distance, the questioner experienced his own speech "as the divine silence breaking creatively forth in the imaginative word that will illuminate the quest as the questioner's movement of return to the ineffable silence." Accordingly, there was no objective or object to the quest. There was only "reality itself becoming luminous for its movement from the ineffable, through the Cosmos, to the ineffable" (CW, 18:120).

In other words, there could be no simple exploration of the divine, the ineffable, It-reality, except by way of things and the (effable) language of things in which the divine, It-reality, the ineffable, etc., was formatively present. The questioner, in short, had to tell his story of a quest for the unflawed order of being from his own flawed order with its flawed language that spoke of non-things as if they were things, which is what Voegelin meant by saying, "the quest for truth is ultimately penultimate." This penultimate mystery was of a "Cosmos that exists in the tension of Taxis-Ataxia [Order-Disorder], in the tension of thing-reality and It-reality, [that] becomes luminous for the ultimate mystery of a Creator God who, when he creates, has to create a tensional Cosmos." Here "luminosity" meant awareness by means of "the meditative wandering" through the various tensions of existence to become aware of the mystery of the Beginning (CW, 18:120).

This presentation of Voegelin's "meditative process," which was itself an analysis of Voegelin's literary account, also had no "object" but was simply an event that raised the experienced tensions of Voegelin's meditative process into the consciousness of the analyst and of the consciousness of the reader of the analysis, which of course Voegelin had already done.

Finally we come to Voegelin's summary of the linguistic results of his meditation:

> The comprehending It-reality moves formatively through the thing-reality from a Beginning that does not begin in things. The Beginning and the End of the story are experienced as a Beyond of the formative, tensional process of reality. There is no epiphany of structure in reality without a structuring force beyond the manifest structure; there is no revelation of divine ordering force in the quest for truth without a divine reality beyond the manifestation of its order in the event. The meditative wandering through the constants in the tensional process thus becomes luminous for a reality beyond the tensions that cannot be attained within tensional existence. (CW, 18:123–24)

Here "luminous" referred to a meaning that "shines through" the reality that existed in the foreground. Beyond the constants of the tensions of existence and their paradoxic expression was not a principle that would replace the tension of order-disorder with Cosmic order. On the contrary, there was only the divine reality formatively present as the ordering pole of the existential tension and the divine reality experienced as a Beyond of the tensional process. This was one more in-between, this time "between the God who reveals himself in the presence in time and the God who remains the experienced but unknown reality beyond time." This in-between was, moreover, ultimate in the sense that it could not intelligibly "be out-experienced or out-symbolized by further experiences of reality. This experienced ultimacy of the tension becomes luminous in the symbol 'divine'" (CW, 18:124). This experienced ultimacy, in short, "shines through" the symbol "divine," which explained why the experience and the story it told were necessarily unfinished.

CHAPTER EIGHT
TIDYING UP

1. Voegelin and "Christianity"

In his New Year's Day 1953 letter to Alfred Schütz answering some of his friend's comments on Christianity, Gnosticism, and *The New Science of Politics*, Voegelin wrote of some "critical tidying up" achieved by what he called "essential Christianity," as distinct from the various religious doctrines and liturgical practices of Christians. "Essentially," he wrote, "my concern with Christianity has no religious grounds at all." He was simply interested in the fifteen hundred years between "antiquity and modernity" in light of the history of political ideas. For example, he wrote Schütz, Plato's parable of the Cave raised the questions of who forced the prisoner to turn around and who dragged him to the light. "Here you have the problem of grace on the Platonic level cast in the language of parables or myths. It is this 'forcing' that in essence is differentiated in Christian 'revelation' or grace as the experienced intrusion of transcendence into human life, which can break in from the outside so overwhelmingly that it may call human freedom into question, as it did with Paul or Augustine."[1]

Voegelin's concern in 1953 was with the experiential rather than the doctrinal differences between philosophy and what he still for simplicity called revelation.[2] We have seen in the last two chapters how the "crisp distinction" between philosophy and revelation or between noetic and

1 CW, 30:122ff. A slightly different translation is found in *A Friendship that Lasted a Lifetime: The Correspondence between Alfred Schultz and Eric Voegelin*, trans. William Petropulos, ed. Gerhard Wagner and Gilbert Weiss (Columbia: University of Missouri Press, 2011), 171ff.

2 As early as 1942, Voegelin was explicit that his "method" in connection to his treatment of Christianity in the *History of Political Ideas* was not one of critical exegesis. As he wrote to Waldemar Gurian, "I have tried to introduce a method of interpretation which sees the Gospel reports as reflections of religious experiences disposing thus of the main arguments of historical skeptical critique" (24 January 1942; HI, 15:27).

pneumatic experiences and symbolizations "became less marked" (CW, 18:23). One might summarize the argument of *In Search of Order* with the observation that a noetic exploration, within the Metaxy, of existential consciousness aimed at a balance between the intentionalist desire to know reality as object or as thing-reality and the mystery of It-reality within which this desire to know its truth took place. The noetic movement had to deal with the variegated imaginative symbolism and expressive language that emerged mysteriously as constitutive of the human response to the reality within which human beings participated. That is, intentionalist imagery was subject, historically, to correction as the structure of reality and of human consciousness became clearer, even while the comprehensive mystery remained. Thus the truth of reality did not appear all at once so much as part of a process of becoming luminous to itself but also of becoming deformed and lost.

In 1953 one could see how easily Schütz might have misunderstood Voegelin's argument that the differentiation achieved by "revelation" was somehow an improvement over "philosophy." After the elaboration of the concept of historiogenesis in *The Ecumenic Age*, however, the straight-line treatment that moved from (say) myth to philosophy to revelation clearly made no sense. And, in fact, a great deal of the criticism directed Voegelin's way following the publication of *The Ecumenic Age* concerned his treatment of "Christianity" in the chapter on "The Pauline Vision of the Resurrected," which turned out not quite to be the same thing as "Christianity" (CW, 17:303ff). As Federici noted, "the break with the original program and the new emphasis in *The Ecumenic Age* infuriated many of Voegelin's Christian readers."[3] Voegelin's alleged turn away from "Christianity" is the first thing that needs to be tidied up.

In a 1959 review, Frederick D. Wilhelmsen praised Voegelin's argument in *Israel and Revelation*.[4] In 1970, Wilhelmsen sent Voegelin a copy of an article he had written on St. Thomas.[5] Voegelin thanked him for the reprint and congratulated him for "a truly excellent study of the metaphysical problem. I agree heartily with you." Because they had a "common interest in the same problem," Voegelin explained that he approached things from a

3 Michael P. Federici, "Voegelin's Christian Critics," *Modern Age* 36:3 (Summer 1994): 332.

4 Wilhelmsen, "Israel and Revelation," *Modern Age* 1 (Spring 1959): 182–92.

5 Wilhelmsen, "The Triplex Via and the Transcendence of Esse," *The New Scholasticism* 44:2 (1970): 223–35.

different starting-point, "not from the metaphysical symbols themselves, as you do, but from the wealth of symbols concerning the movement of existence" as developed by Plato and Aristotle and that led to "the formation of the so-called metaphysical concepts." He proceeded in that fashion, he explained, because "it makes clear that metaphysical concepts are symbols which only make sense as the terminal points of the existential movement of participation in the divine" (CW, 30:672).

In 1975 Wilhelmsen reviewed *The Ecumenic Age*. "Voegelin," he said, "is essentially an apostle with a mission." He did not explain of whom Voegelin was an apostle nor what his mission was. Instead, he described Voegelin as "a Platonist and for Platonists there is no ultimate distinction between being and meaning." As a result, "Dr. Voegelin is very cranky about the Resurrection, but unless it happened his entire speculation about history is worthless; but then everything else is equally worthless." Wilhelmsen added that "I am setting aside mystical experience," which is to say, he would not consider "privileged experiences of the divine," in favor of "a very wise Church" that "has seen to it that men acting thanks to propositional creeds judge men presuming to have privileged experiences of the divine."[6]

To take the last problem first: it is true that Voegelin did discuss in *The Ecumenic Age* the distinction between dogmatic and mystical theology (CW, 17:96, 327). Indeed, the problem was discussed at greater length in the *History of Political Ideas* (CW, 21:177ff). Perhaps the clearest exposition of Voegelin's "mysticism" was contained in a letter to Gregor Sebba written a couple of years prior to Wilhelmsen's review. Voegelin was responding to Sebba's remarks on "Reason: The Classic Experience" (HI, 35:6). For Voegelin, "mysticism" was a field of differentiation of consciousness expressing an

> awareness that the symbols concerning the gods, and the relations of gods and man, whether Myth or Revelation, are secondary or derivative to the primary experiences of divine presence as that of reality beyond any world-contents and beyond adequate symbolization by an analogical language that must take its meanings from the world-content. In that sense, Thomas is a mystic, for he knows that behind the God of dogmatic theology there is the tetragrammatic abyss that lies even behind the *analogia entis*.

6 Wilhelmsen, "The New Voegelin," *Triumph* 10:1 (January 1975): 32–35.

> But in that sense also Plato is a mystic, for he knows that behind the gods of the Myth, and even behind the Demiurge of his philosophy, there is the real God about whom one can say nothing. It may horrify you: But when somebody says that I am a mystic, I am afraid I cannot deny it. (CW, 30:751)

Indeed, Voegelin went on to explain, he could not undertake what Sebba had called "de-reification," or undo what Wilhelmsen had called "conceptualization" and Voegelin called "dedoctrinalization" unless he were a mystic (CW, 30:672, 752). In later letters, Sebba explained that he was neither horrified nor shocked by Voegelin's self-understanding (HI, 35:6). In short, Wilhelmsen preferred the "propositional creeds" of "a very wise Church" to "experiences of the divine" that, from such a propositional standpoint, did indeed presume to be "privileged." That a mystic philosopher might have had a different experience did not seem to have occurred to Wilhelmsen.

Gerhart Niemeyer was a long-time friend of Voegelin and colleague at Notre Dame who had written extensively in praise of Voegelin's work prior to *The Ecumenic Age* (HI, 27:13). Though not as dogmatic or aggressive as Wilhelmsen, Niemeyer professed himself, as one "who considers himself a Christian," to be deeply disappointed with Voegelin's discussion of Paul. The reason, he said, was because Voegelin's "treatment is dominated by the notion of equivalences" so that Paul was "put in the same category as Plato." He concluded that "this once Voegelin has approached a great spiritual reality from a standpoint extraneous to it."[7]

A couple of years later Harold L. Weatherby discussed Voegelin and Christianity also in the pages of *Modern Age*. Weatherby began by expressing his agreement with Niemeyer and argued that the Incarnation amounted to an "abrogation" of the Metaxy that abolished the "incompleteness" of all other religious experience.[8] Weatherby send Voegelin a copy of his article

7 Niemeyer, "Eric Voegelin's Philosophy and the Drama of Mankind," *Modern Age* 20 (1976): 228–39. See also Niemeyer's review of *The Voegelinian Revolution*, in *The Review of Politics* 45 (1983): 133–35.

8 Weatherby, "Myth, Fact, and History: Voegelin and Christianity," *Modern Age* 22 (Spring 1978): 144–50. This article was preserved in the Voegelin library at the University of Erlangen along with three letters, the first from Weatherby to Voegelin (20 November 1978), Voegelin's response (6 December), and Weatehrby's reply to Voegelin (15 December). As early as 1961 Voegelin had expressed a very frank appraisal of *Modern Age*. As he wrote to Heilman that year, "Then I got to know a bit more about 'conservatives,' with the resulting insight that if anything is more of a

and Voegelin responded. He began his reply: "In the first place, I have never written about 'Christianity.' 'Christianity' is an abstract, vaguely covering two thousand years of history. . . . In my chapter on the 'Pauline Vision' I have dealt precisely with this subject-matter, on the basis of the Pauline letters, the only source that we have for the problems of the vision."[9] Voegelin pointed out the obvious: Weatherby did not criticize Voegelin's use of the Pauline sources but argued "only that the picture emerging is not that of the 'Christ' of scholasticism. On that point I agree with you heartily: to bring the difference to attention was one of the purposes of my study."[10]

Voegelin then took issue with Weatherby's interpretation of a passage in Aristotle (*Meta*., 1072b), and turned finally to his own use of the term Metaxy. Weatherby had written (p. 145) that Voegelin meant "the temporal and historical (as opposed to a hypothetically eternal) condition of our being," to which Voegelin replied:

> Well, that is precisely what I don't mean by it. The development of the term "Metaxy" intends to make it clear that there is no purely "temporal" history, that history is the flux of divine presence in time, what Plato calls the "parousia" of the Beyond and what in the Christian context is called Incarnation. The epiphany of the "Christ" (not to be separated from its recognition as such by the Apostles) has brought the divine presence in history to its ultimate clarity. The recognition of this presence, however, entails the understanding of "incarnating" presence in other epiphanies than that of the Christ, i.e., of the historical Jesus. If

drip than a liberal it's a conservative. The matter was clinched in the last days when I got a good look at the crowd in *Modern Age*, the conservative periodical. One thing they have in common with liberals: a profound respect for the sacred right not to know too much and not to work too much. I have a feeling, perhaps wrongly induced by environmental accidents [Voegelin had been mugged and had to spend time in the hospital—"from the hands of the robbers I fell into the hands of the doctors"], of an intellectual flabbiness that cannot end well" (CW, 30:428–29).

9 Voegelin was not being ironic or merely shocking by saying he did not write about "Christianity." In his 1973 *New Orleans Review* interview he said: "I have my doubts as to whether Christianity exists at all." See Peter Cangelosi and John William Corrington, "Philosophies of History: An Interview," *New Orleans Review* 3:2 (1973): 137.

10 A few years later David Walsh made a similar point: "it is virtually impossible to fault Voegelin's handling of the New Testament texts," in "Voegelin's Response to the Disorders of the Age," *Review of Politics* 46 (1984): 266–87.

you read the *Ecclesiastical History* of Eusebius you will find, in Book I, previous such "incarnations," as for instance the Thornbush Episode, interpreted as presences of "Christ" in a less "perfect" revelatory form. If, in opposition to such understanding of the "presence" you assume, as indeed you do, that "history has come to its end with the appearance of Christ," you will get into the Augustinian difficulty of understanding all history after the epiphany of "Christ" as a waiting for the end (in the Second Coming)—the understanding that has caused, in the face of continuing history, the medieval intellectual revolt from Anselm to Thomas. This splendid revolt, a response to divine "presence," however, is again not the end of divine presence. Modern metaphysics is, in its turn, a revolt against the intellectual insufficiencies of scholastic metaphysics in expressing the experience of divine presence adequately. And what occurs in the twentieth century is the new revolt against modern metaphysics as an adequate instrument of expressing the truth of divine presence. . . . In this revolt I am participating to my modest part.

Weatherby replied that he may not have understood Voegelin's use of Metaxy either, but even so,

it does seem obvious to me that we are approaching certain fundamental questions from radically different points of view. For instance, I make the assumption from the outset that the body of Catholic teaching as it has developed since New Testament times is true and that the development has been the work of the Holy Spirit leading the Church into a progressively fuller comprehension of what was given in the original Epiphany—in the Incarnation. Consequently I see no great difficulty in what you refer to as the Augustinian "understanding [of] all history after the epiphany of 'Christ' as a waiting for the end (in the Second Coming)." Such a view is certainly a New Testament one; it is common to the Fathers whom I have read, and, I should say, simply a part of the Christian "given." If history is, in fact, still continuing—which in one sense, of course, is undeniable—it is not, from a Christian point of view, a history which has any purpose beyond the fulfillment of what has already been revealed in

> Christ. That, of course—that for Christianity history is complete and the "Metaxy" abolished—is the burden of my argument in the article, and your letter confirms my impression that on this matter we differ widely.[11]

Also in 1978 Eugene Webb provided an analysis of "Eric Voegelin's Theory of Revelation."[12] Webb began by discussing the anxieties regarding participation in the "quaternarian structure" of reality introduced in the Introduction to *Israel and Revelation* (CW, 14:39), and of the differentiations of consciousness that Voegelin described with the metaphor of the "leap in being." He pointed out the changes in terminology from reason and revelation to noetic and pneumatic consciousness and argued that, in noetic differentiation, the final awareness remained with the questioning consciousness whereas the pneumatic center remained relatively obscure in the depths of the psyche. Revelation or theophanic events, Webb explained, "whether it is noetic or pneumatic in its emphasis, never provides information about the world; rather, it renders explicit what was always implicit in the substratum of experience." Webb's chief point was that revelation could not be considered "subjective" or arbitrary. Granted that an informational understanding was derived primarily from the scientific analysis of thing-reality or from "rational inquiry" as Webb put it, nevertheless, because the pneumatic tradition of revelation focused on the center of experience rather than on the noetic periphery, the tradition deriving from pneumatic differentiation has always been susceptible to deviations in the direction of "information" coming straight from God, which is to say, Gnosis, not mysticism.

Turning to *The Ecumenic Age* and the chapter on Paul's vision, Webb noted, as Voegelin did in his letter to Weatherby, that Voegelin focused on

11 In chapter two and chapter six we discussed the consequences of Augustine's *saeculum senescens*, that all subsequent history was a waiting for the End, a senseless appendage to the Roman Empire. Obviously Voegelin "differed widely" with Weatherby insofar as he also considered the empirical consequences of Augustine's historiogenetic argument, namely that it was rejected by the "splendid revolt" against symbolizations that eventually were no longer persuasive. See CW, 19:206ff; 24:56–57.

12 *The Thomist* 42 (1978): 95–122. In part this article replied to Niemeyer's criticism in *Modern Age* but also to Thomas Altizer's remarks, "A New History and a New but Ancient God? A Review Essay [of *The Ecumenic Age*]," *Journal of the American Academy of Religion* 43 (1975): 757–72. See also CW, 12:292ff.

Paul's text because it recorded the disciple's experiences; Jesus' experience was always mediated by texts and interpretations of others. Moreover, Paul's vision of the resurrected was to be understood "as a symbolic expression of the actual event of pneumatic differentiation with Paul himself," and not "any sort of external miraculous manifestation," which in Voegelin's understanding could not possibly be a revelation because revelation—pneumatic experience—was never information about the external world or thing-reality but was an internal experience of the luminosity of It-reality. "If Paul's revelation," Webb wrote, "were limited to the viewing of an external physical body and the hearing of physical sounds, he would have no spiritual authority." In fact, Webb argued, Paul's spiritual authority was based on the experience of the God who entered his consciousness through the vision that thereby transfigured him, as Voegelin had said (CW, 12:321f.). The "vision" therefore had nothing to do with doctrine or the propositional creeds of a very wise Church, which were not, in any event, erected until the Council of Nicaea in 325.

What, then, did Voegelin make of the resurrection? It was not, obviously, information about unusual biological events nor was it a fideistic dogma that believers could accept or not. Webb suggested the symbolism of the resurrection (as distinct from Paul's vision of the resurrected) expressed "an act of trust in the divine generosity. This act of trust is itself rooted in concrete experiences of the soul—both the experience of the profound longing of the individual for continuing life and the experience of God who draws the soul to himself and discloses himself to it in the theophanic event."[13] Webb, as Voegelin, never lost sight

13 Webb, "Eric Voegelin's Theory," 117. John J. Ranieri, who earlier had criticized Voegelin for having "noeticized" the Israelite experience in volume one of *Order and History*, (Ranieri, "Taming Israel: Voegelin and the Problem of Israelite Order," in William M. Thompson and David L. Morse, eds., *Voegelin's Israel and Revelation: An Interdisciplinary Debate and Anthology* [Milwaukee: Marquette University Press, 2000], 211), but without explaining how one might otherwise proceed if the objective were to account for Israelite experience, raised a similar objection regarding Voegelin's treatment of Paul. "The apostle," Ranieri wrote, "has come to realize that God has nothing at all to do with death. The raising of Jesus from the dead testifies to this. From a Pauline perspective, Anaximander and Plato (and Voegelin) are mistaken in having the divine involved in any way with perishing" (Ranieri, *Disturbing Revelation: Leo Strauss, Eric Voegelin and the Bible* [Columbia: University of Missouri Press, 2009], 89). If one were to avoid a dogmatic rendering of the resurrection as an "event" occupying thing-reality, Ranieri has simply echoed Webb's point regarding the experience of divine generosity.

of the experiential reality that sustained both symbolic and dogmatic expressions.[14]

One final discussion of Voegelin and Christianity deserves mention. In 1983 James M. Rhodes wrote an analysis of "Voegelin and Christian Faith."[15] Rhodes began from a remark Voegelin made in *Anamnesis* (CW, 6:74–77), that in "process theology" one found a symbolism that sought to express the relationship between human consciousness, consciousness-transcending innerworldly realities (thing-reality) and "the world-transcending Ground of Being" in the language of an immanent (and necessarily analogical) process. "I am inclined to believe," Voegelin wrote, "that the process theological attempt and its expansion, a metaphysics that interprets the transcendence system of the world" (that is, in Voegelin's later language, the movement from consciousness to consciousness-transcending thing-reality to world-transcending It-reality) "as the immanent process of a divine substance, is the only meaningful systematic philosophy" (CW, 6:74). The reason why Voegelin said what he did in *Anamnesis* was because process theology and its metaphysical "expansion" alone made it possible to understand the divine substance analogically with human consciousness, which was what Voegelin had set as his philosophical purpose.

As we have seen in the preceding chapters, the world-transcendent God, the Ground of Being, could be experienced only in participatory human consciousness because that was where the process of the It-reality occurred, and not in the thing-reality of the external world perceived by intentional consciousness. Second, "the human mind had access only to its own experiences of the divine, and could not penetrate that reality in such a manner as to grasp it from within."[16] Such an account of "revelation," which maintained the transcendence of the Divine Ground of Being as well as the

14 Voegelin's own remarks on the response of Wilhelmsen and Niemeyer were briefer. In a letter to Michael Berheide, who had asked him about the relation of his work to political and economic conservatism, Voegelin replied that conservatives did find some support in his work because noetic and pneumatic consciousness lay at the heart of the Western tradition, but that the support of traditionalists was nevertheless limited: "recently conservatives like Niemeyer and Wilhelmsen have become quite critical of my work because they do not like my analysis of the New Testament writings or of Thomas. That is quite understandable because certain deformations in the ideological sphere result from fundamentalist deformations in the theological sphere—and the deformations in the theological sphere are cherished as part of the 'tradition'" (CW, 30:863).

15 *Center Journal* 2:3 (Summer 1983): 55–105.

16 Rhodes, "Voegelin and Christian Faith," 66.

metaleptic "contact" between human consciousness and God, "greatly distressed" Voegelin's Christian critics, Rhodes said. "They objected to his notion of equivalences, to his idea of the strictly metaleptic, partially mythical and noninformational content of pneumatic vision, and to his concept of the Kantian parameters of faith." Both Wilhelmsen and Niemeyer were "bothered" by Voegelin's way of discussing meaning by confining "its realization in human existence to one mode of being, that of the Metaxy, and seemingly mythologizes, or refuses to acknowledge, its simultaneous unfolding in the external world, in the birth, life, death and resurrection of Jesus."[17]

Unless I quite misunderstand Rhodes' point (which is certainly possible), he was critical of the distinction between Paul's vision of the resurrected as attested in the letters of the apostle and the resurrection as a pragmatic historical event. "The issue here," Rhodes wrote, "is profound: Can there be history other than the history constituted in the Metaxy of differentiating consciousness?" Not for Voegelin, at any rate, because of the obvious question: what would such a history be? For Rhodes, Voegelin's "theory of incarnation" was "stunning," namely "that the process through which his god achieved illumination in human minds, and which had produced myth, noesis and pneumatism as equivalents *is* incarnation" in the sense that all movements in tension toward the Ground of Being in the Metaxy were necessarily "theophanic incarnations" because they were experienced by specific individuals. Accordingly, "before New Testament times, God's Word had already become flesh in Egyptian pharaohs, Hellenic poets, Chinese mystics, Greek philosophers and Israelite patriarchs. Jesus was a member of this series, a special one to be sure, but a member nonetheless, and he was followed directly by Paul, and then by other favored individuals in subsequent ages." So far as I can tell, Voegelin would agree with Rhodes not only in light of the texts from *The Ecumenic Age*, which Rhodes quite correctly cited, but from his correspondence with Weatherby discussed above, which was unknown to Rhodes, and from his later reflections as well. It remains to be seen whether this "stunning" theory of incarnation needs to be a distressing and bothersome as it appeared to be to Wilhelmsen, Niemeyer, and possibly Rhodes.[18]

17 Rhodes, "Voegelin and Christian Faith," 81, 83.

18 Other less penetrating (or more polite) criticisms of Voegelin's discussion of "Christianity" include: Bruce Douglass, "The Gospel and Political Order: Eric Voegelin on the Political Role of Christianity," *The Journal of Politics* 38 (1976): 25–45;

2. Philosophy and the Gospel

From the foregoing chapters, one obvious conclusion is that the relation between noetic and pneumatic experience and symbolization is complicated. To begin with the most evident distinction: "the philosopher is a man in search of truth; he is not God revealing truth" (CW, 12:79). That said, there were, in Voegelin's later work, no hard differences between, say, a philosopher and a prophet. As he put it in 1984, "there is no such thing as an absolutely prophetic event" because prophetic means "a certain insight into reality that is both luminous and intentional" but that "is given a very compact form by the prophets of Israel." By the same token, "there is no simple noetic form" either because "the noetic form is the searching part of a tension in which we search for something to which we are moved to search from the other side—it would be the prophetic or pneumatic part." Accordingly, "we can also say that Plato was a prophet," much as was done by medieval Islamic philosophers (CW, 33:417–18). And yet, "the practice of philosophy in the Socratic-Platonic sense is the equivalent of the Christian sanctification of man; it is the growth in the image of God in man" (CW, 12:223).

The language of equivalence, which seemed to be rejected by Wilhelmsen and Niemeyer, was deliberately used by Voegelin to indicate both sameness and difference. It was, therefore, paradoxical. In "Wisdom and the Magic of the Extreme," Voegelin explained what he had in mind. He began with Plato because the philosopher's account of his vision (*opsis*) was so thoroughly articulated "that its reality not only is luminous to itself but illuminated the structure and modality of visionary truth in general" including that experienced in "the noetically less differentiated Christian visions."[19] A comparison of Platonic with Christian symbols would also bring out "the pneumatic limitations in the Platonic vision."

The Hellenic and Judaic-Christian visions agreed in several respects: the importance of truth in existence, of the exodus from the "undying struggle"

Douglass, "A Diminished Gospel: A Critique of Voegelin's Interpretation of Christianity," in Stephen A. McKnight, ed., *Eric Voegelin's Search for Order in History* (Baton Rouge: LSU Press, 1978), 139–54; William Thompson, "Jesus' Unsurpassable Uniqueness," *Horizons* 16 (1989): 101–15; Michael P. Morrissey, *Consciousness and Transcendence: The Theology of Eric Voegelin* (Notre Dame: University of Notre Dame Press, 1994), 227ff; James Rhodes, "Christian Faith, Jesus the Christ, and History," *The Political Science Reviewer* 27 (1998): 44–67.

19 CW, 12:365ff. The elaboration of what Plato meant by "vision" is in CW, 12:348ff.

for truth by way of immortalizing action or the revelation of the saving tale, of the problem of the Beyond and of intermediaries between the world and the Beyond. And finally, the experiential complex of both philosophy and the Gospel was one of revelation-struggle-salvation.

The chief difference within this visionary structure was clearly expressed in the central questions of these visions. Plato asked "who is the God" that drew human consciousness from the Beyond of a cosmos full of gods and did so as a presence, even though the God that was that presence was not one of the traditional gods? The Christian visionaries, in contrast, did not have to ask that question because the God was the God of the fathers, of Moses, of Israel, and the prophets. Instead they asked, "Who is this Messiah, this Christ, this vessel of divinely immortal presence, this living Word of the truth?" And by asking that question they received, if not an answer, at least a vision, "the presence of god in the man whose word spoke the truth of suffering and salvation in the man Jesus" along with further questions "concerning the criteria of its truth," which in turn were elaborated with "noetic astuteness."

This did not mean, Voegelin stressed, that the "spirit of God" was a synonym for Nous. Rather it symbolized "a stratum in the appeal-response on the divine-human encounter that had not been sufficiently differentiated in the noetic visions, i.e., the full meaning of the divine saving presence in existence." On the pneumatic side, this was also why Voegelin discussed Paul's *vision*. It was not just, as he explained to Weatherby, that "Christianity" was too abstract to be analyzed properly, but also because Paul did not know Jesus personally but only through the other apostles who did—and through the divine Spirit who reached from the depths of God to the hearts of human beings. To use the language earlier introduced to describe the common experiential complex, the difference between the two was that the stress of revelation in the pneumatic symbolism fell upon salvation rather than on struggle.

Voegelin wrote two other papers dealing with philosophy and the Gospel. The one, "The Gospel and Culture" (1971) could be read as a response to criticism of the treatment in *The Ecumenic Age* of "Christianity." The other, "Quod Deus Dicitur," (1985) was a kind of postscript to *In Search of Order*. Many of the themes discussed in these two essays recapitulated the arguments discussed in the previous chapter.

Voegelin began the first essay by introducing a question: how was it that the Gospel could become a "state religion" in the Roman Empire and yet could hardly be understood today? The issue, Voegelin said, was one of relating the Gospel to philosophy. To illustrate the matter, he proposed first to discuss an ancient and a modern example. The ancient example was the *Dialogue with Trypho* of Justin Martyr (d. ca. 165) for whom "Christianity is not an alternative to philosophy, it is philosophy itself in its state of perfection; the history of the logos comes to its fulfillment through the incarnation of the Word in Christ" (CW, 12:173). The modern example was the *Dutch Catechism* (1966), the opening chapter of which was called "Man the Questioner," and the gist of which was the reverse of Justin's problem. Justin started as an enquiring mind and after searching through the philosophical schools "came to rest in the truth of the Gospel." The authors of the *Catechism* "are at rest in an unenquiring state of faith" and want to enquire how their faith was an answer to the mysteries and enigmas of existence. What was at issue in the raising of the modern question was a conflict, "not between the Gospel and philosophy, but rather between the Gospel and its unenquiring possession as doctrine" (CW, 12:174).

Once the issue had been properly framed, it could be subject to noetic analysis, namely that "this luminous search in which the finding of the true answer depends on asking the true question, and the asking of the true question on the spiritual apprehension of the true answer, is the life of reason." This insight then could be applied to the Gospel. "The Gospel, to be heard, requires ears that can hear; philosophy is not the life of reason if the questioner's reason is depraved (Rom. 1:28). . . . It will be necessary, therefore, to recover the question to which, in Hellenic Roman culture the Gospel is the answer" (CW, 12:175). Because the question involved the "humanity of man," it was the same question today as it was during the time of Jesus or of Plato. The problem, therefore, was to disentangle the expressive symbols from the deformations of doctrine, including modern ideological doctrine. The way to do so was to return to the experiences and symbolizations of philosophy and the Gospel.

Voegelin began with a discussion of the metaxic pair, life and death, and the saving tale. He started with Euripides[20] and moved by way of the *Gorgias* (492e) to the *Republic* (621b–c) to chapter 12 of the Gospel of John. Both philosophy and the Gospel articulated the experience of

20 "Who knows if life be what men call death/and what men call death, life." The lines are from Euripides' *Phrixus*, fr. 833, are quoted in E. R. Dodds, ed., *Plato: Gorgias* (Oxford: Clarendon, 1959), 300. See also the comments of Bernard Lonergan in *A Third Collection: Papers by Bernard Lonergan, S.J.*, ed. Frederick E. Crowe, S.J. (New York: Paulist Press, 1985), 188–92. See also 195–96, 219–21.

"direction in existence; and as we follow it or not, life can be death, and death can be life eternal." In philosophy, the reality that the question of life or death expressed was told in the saving tale originally told by Er, the man of all tribes or "Everyman," and retold by Socrates at the end of the *Republic*. And behind Er's tale "there stands the authority of the representative death suffered by Socrates for its truth" as told in the *Apology*. Four centuries later, what Socrates expressed ironically in the last words of the *Apology* "had become the self-understanding of man in the culture of the Hellenistic-Roman *oikoumene*." Once again the universal truth of existence required the authority of a representative to suffer death:

> The dramatic episode of John 12 is the Christian equivalent to the philosopher's *Apology*. . . . Even the *daimonion* that sustained Socrates in his course by not raising its warning voice has its equivalent in the reflection of Jesus:
>
> Now my soul is troubled. What shall you say?
> Father, save me from this hour?
> No, for this purpose I have come to this hour.
> Father, glorify your name. (CW, 12:180–81)

Voegelin's exegesis of the symbols of life and death in the avoidable executions of Socrates and Jesus did not so much alter the structure of existence as authenticate the truth of reality (CW, 12:181–88). Even so, there remained a difference between the Platonic God "who plays with man as a puppet" and the God of the Gospel "who becomes man to gain his life by suffering his death." Voegelin then spelled out these differences:

> The movement that engendered the saving tale of divine incarnation, death, and resurrection as the answer to the question of life and death is considerably more complex than classic philosophy; it is richer by the missionary fervor of its spiritual universalism, poorer by its neglect of noetic control; broader by its appeal to the inarticulate humanity of the common man; more restricted by its bias against the articulate wisdom of the wise; more imposing through its imperial tone of divine authority; more unbalanced through its apocalyptic ferocity, which leads to conflicts with the conditions of man's existence in society; more compact through its generous absorption of earlier strata

> of mythical imagination, especially through the reception of Israelite historiogenesis and the exuberance of miracle working; more differentiated through the intensely articulate experience of loving-divine action in the illumination of existence with truth. (CW, 12:189)

Voegelin again cautioned against using simplified dichotomies such as reason and revelation because, as indicated in previous chapters, they shared a common noetic core, on the one hand, and the philosophers were fully aware of the "revelatory" presence of the gods in the divine Beyond of their own civilization.

As we have seen in previous chapters, the noetic symbols seeking or searching, zetein, and drawing, helkein "do not denote two different moments but symbolize the dynamics in the tension of existence between its human and divine poles. In the one movement there is experienced a seeking from the human, a being drawn from the divine pole" (CW, 12:183). Likewise, to be drawn after or to follow Christ "means to continue the event of divine presence in society and history" because, as John 17:25–26 made clear, there was no "message" of Christ but "the event of the divine Logos becoming present in the world through the representative life and death of a man." Almost as an aside, Voegelin reflected: "One can imagine how a young student of philosophy, who wanted to work himself out of the various doctrinal impasses into which the school philosophers of the time had maneuvered themselves, could be fascinated by the brilliance of these succinct statements that must have appeared to him as the perfection of the Socratic-Platonic movement in the In-Between of existence."[21]

Such a philosopher would have good reason to come to such a conclusion. Not only was the noetic core of the Gospel expressed in the philosophical language of pull and counterpull, there was the same consciousness of existence in a metaleptic human-divine participatory encounter "and the same experience of divine reality as the center of action in the movement from question to answer" (CW, 12:192). Finally, there was the same

21 CW, 12:190–91. William M. Thompson called Voegelin's image of the "young philosopher" an "autobiographical comment." See Thompson, "'The Gospel Movement': Pulls and Counterpulls in Voegelin's Interpretation of Christ and Christianity," in Glen Hughes, Stephen A. McKnight, Geoffrey L. Price, eds., *Politics, Order and History: Essays on the Work of Eric Voegelin* (Sheffield: Sheffield Academic Press, 2001), 440.

awareness of a newly differentiated insight that Voegelin earlier described as a "consciousness of epoch."

What had changed were the "spiritual dynamics" that were experienced in "an extraordinary divine irruption in the existence of Jesus" symbolized in Colossians (2:9) as "the whole fullness of divine reality (*theotes*)" that "dwells bodily" in Jesus. The differentiation in the Gospel was not that of a moving beyond the "natural reason" of the pagan philosophers. Such limitations of philosophy rather reflected the limitation of the cosmological mode of experience and symbolization found in Greek culture. The "Gospel movement," Voegelin argued, was also part of the revelatory process that began with the Amon Hymns of Dynasty XIX in Egypt. That is, the process of separation of the *theotes* that came to "its climactic revelation in Christ" began with the separation of the Unknown God from the known gods of the cosmos whose "divine presence," as was argued above, was still experienced in and by way of those gods. The "good news" was, in this context, the revelation of the Unknown God through Christ. This was why, for example, Paul praised the Athenians for having raised an altar to the *Agnostos Theos*, the very God whom he had come to proclaim (Acts 17:16–34). Voegelin added: "More could be added, as the *Nunc dimittis* of Luke 2:29–32, but the passage quoted [from Acts] will be sufficient to establish the Unknown God as the god who is revealed through Christ" (CW, 12:199).

Voegelin concluded with the observation that "in the historical drama of revelation, the Unknown God ultimately becomes the God known through his presence in Christ." However, the separation of dogmatic and mystical theology after Origen made this drama almost unknown to the Christian Church.

> At a time when the reality of the Gospel threatens to fall apart into the constructions of an historical Jesus and a doctrinal Christ, one cannot stress strongly enough the status of the Gospel as a symbolism engendered in the Metaxy of existence by a disciple's response to the drama of the Son of God. The drama of the Unknown God who reveals his kingdom through his presence in a man, and of the man who reveals what has been delivered to him by delivering it to his fellowmen, is continued by the existentially responsive discipline in the Gospel drama by which he carries on the work of delivering these things from God to man. The Gospel itself is an event in the drama of revelation. The historical drama in the Metaxy, then, is a unit through

> the common presence of the Unknown God in the men who respond to his "drawing" and to one another. Through God and men as the dramatis personae, it is true, the presence of the drama partakes of both human time and divine timelessness, but tearing the drama of participation asunder into the biography of a Jesus in the spatiotemporal world and the eternal verities showered from Beyond would make nonsense of the existential reality that was experienced and symbolized as the drama of the Son of God. (CW, 12:199–201)

A Gospel, Voegelin concluded, was "the symbolization of a divine movement that went through the person of Jesus into society and history." Thus the revelatory movement ran its course in the person of Jesus, in the social drama of his contemporaries, both positive and negative (Matt. 16:21–23; 27:46), and in the historical consequences and antecedents.

> The mystery of divine presence in existence had grown in the consciousness of the [Gospel] Movement long before the drama of the Gospel started; and the symbols which the evangelist uses for its expression—the Son of God, the Messiah, the Son of man, the kingdom of God—were historically at hand through the Egyptian Pharaonic, the Davidic royal, the prophetic and apocalyptic symbolisms, through Iranian traditions and the Hellenistic mysteries. (CW, 12:204)

What was new in the Gospel, to repeat, was "the event [of divine presence] of its full comprehension and enactment through the life and death of Jesus." The various ambiguities and even contradictions, and the different degrees of comprehension were reflected in the different meanings attributed to the several symbols—Son of God, Messiah, and so on—"until the Christ is revealed, not in a fullness of doctrine, but in the fullness of Passion and resurrection" (CW, 12:204).

Voegelin then explained what he meant by the "fullness" represented by Jesus' life and death by reference to Matthew's account of John the Baptist in Chapter 11, and to Jesus' changing the Old Testament text from Malachi 3:1 to indicate that John the Baptist was not "the forerunner of Israel's Yahweh" but "the forerunner of the Unknown God who is present in his Son Jesus" (Matt. 11:7–10). In Chapter 16, Jesus "resumes the differentiation of his own status" from that of his predecessors. Specifically, Jesus sought to transfigure the Israelite Messiah from "the field marshal of the Pantocrator" of Revelation 19:11–16 into the Son of God "who calls to him the poor in spirit, the gentle, the pure in heart, the peacemakers, those who hunger and thirst after righteousness and are persecuted for righteousness' sake" of Matthew 5. In short, "whatever meanings the symbolism of the Anointed of Israel may have carried hitherto, they are now relegated to the past by the presence of the Unknown God in the Son."[22]

There followed an account of what Voegelin took to be Jesus' consciousness of what it meant to be the Son of God, namely that he must go to Jerusalem and suffer a representative death (Matt. 16:21). In the noetic language Voegelin favored: "In the In-Between of existence, man is faced with the choice of denying his self and the devil or denying Jesus and the Unknown God" (CW, 12:207). Voegelin's imaginative experiential analysis began with his reflection on the declaration (*logion*) of Matthew 11:27:

> All these things are delivered to me by the Father,
> And no one knows the Son except the Father,
> And no one knows the Father except the Son
> And anyone to whom the Son chooses to reveal him.

The dangers Voegelin wanted to discuss when this passage was initially introduced were: (1) turning it into a doctrine that one could believe or not; and (2) deforming an orthodox doctrine into a Gnostic one (CW, 12:200).

22 CW, 12:206. This was Voegelin's position in the early volumes of *Order and History* as well. In *The World of the Polis*, for example, he discussed the differentiation expressed in Paul's letter to the Romans (7–8) on the life of the spirit and existence in faith and noted that the apostle was oblivious to the persistence of Judaism "because it does not take into account the problems of compactness and differentiation." Thus for people who live in the unbroken Jewish tradition the problems of faith in Christ, the "new law" and so on, did not exist. "The chosenness of Israel does not rest on the observation of the law [by the Jews], but on the act of divine grace, which Saint Paul apparently did not perceive." These "sons of God," the Jews, had no need for the Son of God for their salvation. Judaism had its own theology expressed in more compact or particular symbols than the more differentiated and universal symbols of Christianity. "Nevertheless, every order has its own present under God, as we formulated the principle; and this present is not abolished when it becomes a past in retrospect from a differentiated experience of order," in this instance, Christianity. The coexistence of compact and differentiated experiences and symbolizations of order was part of the mystery of human being in history and could not be dissolved (CW, 15:78–79).

Having discussed the experiential context of the declaration, the noetic problems that led to doctrinal hypostases, imbalance in the understanding of reality, and the ever-present temptation of indifference, Voegelin concluded with an enumeration of the principal problems that followed from the differentiation achieved by the Gospel:

1. As was true with philosophy, the differentiation achieved by the Gospel distinguished it from the primary experience of the cosmos. This "preemption" was nevertheless historical, so that "the cosmological past of experience and symbolization must be intelligibly related to the differentiated consciousness to which it has given birth."
2. The cosmos was still real but could not be symbolized by intracosmic gods. Yet they had to be "symbolized as symbols of earlier stages in the process of revelation." Accordingly, how to symbolize the experiential tension toward the Unknown God without making him "known" remained a problem.
3. The existential tension toward the Unknown God was not the whole of reality, which raised the problem of turning the cosmos into the "alien earth" of the Gnostics from which one must attempt either to escape or to transfigure into something more congenial.
4. In summary, because the foregoing problems were not sufficiently clarified, the danger of a Gnostic derailment continued historically up to the present.

Voegelin concluded by reiterating a point already made in *The New Science of Politics* (CW, 5:187–88):

> The strength of the Gospel is its concentration on the one point that is all-important: that the truth of reality has its center not in the cosmos at large, not in the nature of society or imperial rulership, but in the presence of the Unknown God in a man's existence to his death and life. This very strength, however, can cause a breakdown, if the emphasis on the center of truth becomes too intense that its relations to the reality of which it is the center are neglected or interrupted. (CW, 12:210)

Specifically, "the full differentiation of the truth of existence under the Unknown God through his Son" created a cultural field open to the possibility of new, self-declared Christs showing up, as indeed we have seen often enough over the past two centuries (CW, 12:112, 201; 33:240–41, 423).

3. What God is Called

A final and an unfinished work of Voegelin was dictated in January 1985 to Paul Caringella as the author was dying at his home in Palo Alto. The question raised by the title referred specifically to the discussion by St. Thomas of "The Existence of God" in the *Summa Theologica* (I.2.3). As is obvious by this point, we are not dealing with perceptual consciousness. "We are not facing God as a thing but as a partner in a questing search that moves within a reality that nevertheless we speak about using the intentional language of thing-reality." Moreover, and with equal obviousness, at every point, because the noetic search for the structure of reality was itself a questioning, "we are faced with the problem of an inquiry into something experienced as real before the inquiry into the structure of its reality has begun" (CW, 12:376–77).

The problem was linguistically complex because the paradoxical structure of the process had never been sufficiently analyzed. As a consequence there was insufficient clarity about the difference between "the paradoxic structure of the divine-human encounter in the search, on the one side, and the symbols arising in reflection on the culturally concrete expression of the search on the other." The first, the paradoxic structure, was apparent only to meditative consciousness; the second, dealing with symbols that have arisen "in reflection" was much more common as the several familiar dichotomies of faith and reason, philosophy and theology, and so on. And the latter have by convention come to be the language in which the discussion has been conducted. As a result, the discussion has been superficial because it did not penetrate "to the fundamentally paradoxic structure of thought that is peculiar to the participatory relation between the process of thought and the reality in which it proceeds" (CW, 12:378).

Voegelin then offered an analysis of Thomas' "proofs" regarding the "question of God" and concluded that "there is no divinity other than the necessity in tension with the contingency experienced in the noetic question." However, Thomas was hampered insofar as he had to provide an exegesis of the truth of revelation within the context of Judaic-Christian faith using the philosophical symbols derived from Hellenic civilization but without taking into account the distinct cultural contexts (which Voegelin had several times noted) of the two. Specifically, Thomas was handicapped by his attempt to undertake "a meditative analysis as a syllogistic proof" (CW, 12:379–80). Voegelin then traced the subsequent formulations and criticisms of them through Leibniz, Descartes, Kant and Hegel, all of which suffered from inadequate analyses of the consciousness of reality owing to an "inadequate distinction between the process of noetic analysis and the reflective symbols describing the historic process of analysis," which was precisely what Voegelin had been working on for most of his life.

Voegelin reiterated a point made earlier, that we have an "inclination to think in thingly propositions about experiences which are not experiences of things. The primary structure of the divine-human encounter must be distinguished from the reflective symbolization of the poles of the tensional encounter as thingly entities" (CW, 12:381–82). In this respect, Thomas was not as clear as his predecessors, Plato in the *Phaedrus* and *Timaeus*, or Anselm of Canterbury, in the *Proslogion*. Nor was Thomas as clear as Voegelin.

"In the *Proslogion*, Anslem's analysis is explicit about the limits of the noetic quest." In Chapter XIV, Anslem acknowledged that the God found by reason was not (yet) the God that was present in the seeker already in terms of the formation of his existence prior to the quest. Chapter XV formulated the issue precisely as the limitation of noetic analysis: God was not just a greater than which cannot be noetically conceived but a greater than which can be conceived.[23] Moving to the second part of the *Proslogion*, Anslem was no longer concerned with the limits of noetic analysis but with the "analogical exploration of the divine light beyond human reason," formulated by him as a prayer for understanding, that is, a prayer to God that he might understand his faith. Prayer expressed the "true source" of Anslem's effort, namely "the living desire of the soul to move toward the divine light. The divine reality lets the light of its perfection fall into the soul; the illumination of the soul arouses the awareness of man's existence as a state of imperfection; and this awareness provokes the human movement in response to the divine appeal." Obviously Anslem, no more than Thomas, was not providing a "proof" in any normal or syllogistic sense of the term. Rather, in prayer, he was exploring the rational structure of his faith (CW, 12:385).

Granted that the topical matter of the "the existence of God" could hardly be in question during the conduct of prayer, then where did Anslem's so-called ontological proof come from? The philological answer was clear:

23 CW, 12:383. See also the longer analysis in CW, 28:191ff.

it arose in the context of a debate between Anslem and Gaunilo of Marmoutiers who adopted the position of the *insipiens*, the "fool" of Psalm 14:1, who "said in his heart there is no God." The philosophical significance of the language of the proof, therefore, came from the context of a debate with a fool. "The symbolism of the noetic quest threatened to derail into a quarrel about the proof or nonproof of a proposition when a fool enters the discussion. The existence of God can become doubtful because, without a doubt, the fool exists."[24] Voegelin concluded: "If the fool's part in the positive propositions is forgotten," that is, the fact that the positive propositions are advanced only to counter the negations of the fool, "there is always the danger of derailing into the foolishness of believing the truth of these propositions to be ultimate."[25] It is scarcely necessary to add that the same kind of "trick" is employed by contemporary so-called atheists who, as did Gaunilo for purposes of the debate with Anselm, contracted their souls to that of a fool and thereby they lost contact with reality.

4. Summing Up

What is one to make of these late meditative essays?

First, it seems to me, that if "The Gospel and Culture" and "Quod Deus Dicitur" are not the work of a Christian philosopher, what is? It is clear that they are not the work of a dogmatist, whether Christian or not, and it is clear why. As Voegelin explained more than once, for Christians, revelation had to be something entirely new, constituting an epoch in history. Accordingly, "the presence of the pneumatic stratum in its compact form in earlier human thought was neglected and even denied." Hence the doctrine, which we have noted previously, of pagan natural reason to which might be added supernatural revelation. "That the Greek thinkers were highly conscious of having received a revelation when they discovered the *Nous* as the Ground of Being was simply ignored" along with the theophanic core of classical philosophy (CW, 34:134).

At the same time, as was discussed in the previous two chapters, instead of the End of everything, a second coming, a Messianic event, and so on,

24 CW, 12:385. For an extended discussion of the character of a fool, see CW, 28:198ff as well as CW, 12:385ff.

25 CW, 12:389–90. This was not the final word Voegelin intended to write. As Caringella noted, five texts were appended to the last words Voegelin dictated and upon which he intended to comment to bring the essay/meditation to a conclusion.

"the symbols that expressed the experiences of the psyche, of its consciousness, of its noetic and pneumatic structure, were recognized as symbolizations of truth emergent in the process of history, which in one part is a process in this world, while in another part it is a theophanic process." When that happens, the pneumatic and noetic symbols became secondary because no worldly symbolization was adequate to express the truth of human understanding in tension towards the Divine Ground. "This further articulation of a stratum of experience beyond the symbolization of noetic and pneumatic divine presence is what, after Pseudo-Dionysius, came to be called mysticism" (CW, 34:137–38). Moreover, mysticism so understood could be discerned as far back as literary records exist—and perhaps into the oral and pictorial record as well.

A second observation: in the *History of Political Ideas* Voegelin discussed the declining authority of the Church when it came under attack from the rationalism of the Enlightenment, which had very little, beyond the use of the term "reason," in common with the noetic analysis of philosophy. The problem Voegelin was concerned with centred on the historicity of truth or the drama of humanity, namely the atrophy of symbolic expressions of reality under changing and novel circumstances. In his later language, the necessity of using the language of thing-reality to evoke the experiences of It-reality led to an increased opacity and a decline of analogical symbolization into fundamentalist doctrine. Although it was difficult to regain the original meaning of philosophy or of the Gospel, it was quite easy to get a grasp of the problem.

> Anybody who has ever tried to explain to a convinced Marxist that the idea of a communist stateless society is a derivative eschatology, and that Marxism is not a "scientific" socialism—or who has tried to explain to a fanatic of world organization that terms such as *world peace*, *peace-loving nations*, or *aggressors* are not concepts of empirical politics but symbols of an intramundane eschatology—can gauge by the reaction of his victim how senseless it must have appeared to an early Christian if somebody had argued against Incarnation by offering biological reasons. (CW, 24:55)

In this situation, he explained, the Church had historically shown "admirable wisdom" by not attempting to modernize its symbolism and thereby destroy whatever remained of the experience of the mystery of transcendence.

Less admirable, however, was the inability or the refusal of the Church to deal with the problem of dogmatism and the rationalist counter-dogmatic critique. "It is not for us to offer a solution," Voegelin wrote in the *History*, but part of the solution would entail making intelligible the dimensions of meaning that attach to Christianity. A second part of the solution would be to "make intelligible the categories of myth as an objective language for the expression of a transcendental irruption." It would show myth to be a more adequate and exact instrument of expression than any rational system of symbols. As Voegelin put it in "The Gospel and Culture":

> Myth is not a primitive symbolic form but the language in which the experiences of human-divine participation in the In-Between become articulate. The symbolization of participating existence, it is true, evolves historically from the more compact form of the cosmological myth to the more differentiated forms of philosophy, prophecy, and the Gospel, but the differentiating insight, far from abolishing the Metaxy of existence, brings it to fully articulate knowledge. (CW, 12:188)

To explain how myth might be made intelligible, Voegelin wrote in the 1940s, "would require a new Thomas rather than a neo-Thomist" (CW, 24:56). Voegelin may not have been a new Thomas, but a generation after writing those words he had indeed produced a solution for which a new Thomas was then sought.

Index